UNIX®
Weekend Crash Course™

Arthur Griffith

D1418360

Hungry Minds™

Best-Selling Books • Digital Downloads • e-Books • Answer Networks • e-Newsletters • Branded Web Sites • e-Learning

Cleveland, OH • Indianapolis, IN • New York, NY

UNIX® Weekend Crash Course™

Published by
Hungry Minds, Inc.
909 Third Avenue
New York, NY 10022
www.hungryminds.com

Library of Congress Catalog Card Number: 200202443

ISBN: 0-7645-4927-8

Printed in the United States of America

10 9 8 7 6 5 4 3 2 1

1B/SU/QU/QS/IN

Distributed in the United States by Hungry Minds, Inc.

Distributed by CDG Books Canada Inc. for Canada; by Transworld Publishers Limited in the United Kingdom; by IDG Norge Books for Norway; by IDG Sweden Books for Sweden; by IDG Books Australia Publishing Corporation Pty. Ltd. for Australia and New Zealand; by TransQuest Publishers Pte Ltd. for Singapore, Malaysia, Thailand, Indonesia, and Hong Kong; by Gotop Information Inc. for Taiwan; by ICG Muse, Inc. for Japan; by Intersoft for South Africa; by Eyrolles for France; by International Thomson Publishing for Germany, Austria, and Switzerland; by Distribuidora Cuspide for Argentina; by LR International for Brazil; by Galileo Libros for Chile; by Ediciones ZETA S.C.R. Ltda. for Peru; by WS Computer Publishing Corporation, Inc., for the Philippines; by Contemporanea de Ediciones for Venezuela; by Express Computer Distributors for the Caribbean and West Indies; by Micronesia Media Distributor, Inc. for Micronesia; by Chips Computadoras S.A. de C.V. for Mexico; by Editorial Norma de Panama S.A. for Panama; by American Bookshops for Finland.

For general information on Hungry Minds' products and services please contact our Customer Care department within the U.S. at 800-762-2974, outside the U.S. at 317-572-3993 or fax 317-572-4002.

For sales inquiries and reseller information, including discounts, premium and bulk quantity sales, and foreign-language translations, please contact our Customer Care department at 800-434-3422, fax 317-572-4002 or write to Hungry Minds, Inc., Attn: Customer Care Department, 10475 Crosspoint Boulevard, Indianapolis, IN 46256.

For information on licensing foreign or domestic rights, please contact our Sub-Rights Customer Care department at 212-884-5000.

For information on using Hungry Minds' products and services in the classroom or for ordering examination copies, please contact our Educational Sales department at 800-434-2086 or fax 317-572-4005.

For press review copies, author interviews, or other publicity information, please contact our Public Relations department at 317-572-3168 or fax 317-572-4168.

For authorization to photocopy items for corporate, personal, or educational use, please contact Copyright Clearance Center, 222 Rosewood Drive, Danvers, MA 01923, or fax 978-750-4470.

Hungry Minds is a trademark of Hungry Minds, Inc.

About the Author

Arthur Griffith worked as a computer consultant and a systems level programmer from 1977 to 1997. In 1997, he turned to writing as a full-time occupation.

Mr. Griffith was first introduced to UNIX in 1985, when he installed a BSD system on a DEC 750. This was followed by the development of a specialized network communications protocol to transmit encrypted data over a UNIX wide area network. He also developed HP-UX software that gathers, stores, displays, and plots downhole data from drilling operations. He developed a national network of UNIX machines that communicated with one another using special tones designed to test the quality and fidelity of long-distance telephone lines. Using Sun's Solaris and Motif, he wrote the animated graphics portion of a real-time system, monitoring offshore drilling activities.

Mr. Griffith spent several years as a compiler writer. He has developed or maintained compilers for such languages as C, COBOL, SATS, and PL/exus. He implemented a special language (along with its GUI IDE) that is used to control the configuration of communications satellites and their ground stations. He also implemented several small scripting language interpreters for both procedural and nonprocedural languages.

Mr. Griffith's most recent books include *Java XML and JAXP*, the *KDE/Qt Programming Bible*, the *GNOME/GTK+ Programming Bible*, and *Peter Norton's Complete Guide to Linux* (with Peter Norton).

Credits

Acquisitions Editor
Terri Varveris

Project Editor
Kala Schrager

Technical Editor
Terence Collings

Copy Editor
Gabrielle Chosney

Editorial Managers
Kyle Looper
Ami Frank Sullivan

Senior Vice President, Technical Publishing
Richard Swadley

Vice President and Publisher
Mary Bednarek

Project Coordinator
Dale White

Graphics and Production Specialists
Sean Decker
Laurie Petrone

Quality Control Technicians
Andy Hollandbeck
Carl Pierce
Linda Quigley

Permissions Editor
Laura Moss

Media Development Specialist
Travis Silvers

Proofreading and Indexing
TECHBOOKS Production Services

Cover Design
Clark Creative Services

To the people of Homer, Anchor Point, and the North Fork that runs between them. My Alaska home.

Preface

This book is a fast romp through the fundamentals of UNIX. You will discover how to use the commands and facilities of UNIX to get things done, and, at the same time, you will get a pretty good notion of how it all works behind the scenes. At its heart, UNIX is a very simple operating system. Sure, it can seem a little cryptic from time to time, and parts of it seem to work like magic, but there is a consistency that runs throughout UNIX — once you learn a few pieces of it, the rest of it is easier to understand because it seems familiar.

So clear out a weekend and get ready to cram. I have gone to a great deal of effort to lay out the information in a reasonable order. My primary goal is to present the information in such a way that any questions you might have are answered immediately. When I read a technical book, I like the feeling of satisfaction I get when I finish a chapter and know that I understand the subject.

It is a good idea for you to have access to a UNIX terminal as you go through the sessions so you can enter commands and see exactly what is being described. If you try things yourself, your understanding will be more complete.

Today, many different versions of UNIX are available. Among the companies that produce their own versions (in no particular order) are Sun Microsystem (Solaris and SunOS), IBM (AIX), Hewlett-Packard (HP-UX), Apple (OS X), Compaq (Tru64UNIX), SCO (Xenix and UnixWare), and SGI (Irix). FreeBSD and Linux are the most popular free versions of UNIX, and they are both packaged and supported by a number of companies.

UNIX has always been the server of choice. The Internet started with UNIX, and it is still mostly based on UNIX systems. Super computers, real-time systems, embedded systems, and databases are based on some form of UNIX. The capabilities of UNIX make it ideal for robotics and the production of animation for films. And lately, UNIX has started to make a move toward desktop computing with the X11 graphical user interfaces and Apple's OS X.

UNIX began as a game and wound up as a computer revolution. It has been quite a while since the revolution occurred, so most of us consider the way UNIX does things as the way computers normally work. Many of the most fundamental computing concepts originated with UNIX, such as the hierarchical file system with directories that contain files and subdirectories. The first versions of UNIX employed interactive terminals with dial-up connections (after all, UNIX was invented by the telephone company).

A certain philosophy underlies the design of UNIX that enables you to construct a utility of your own design in a single command line. The UNIX commands are composed of small utilities that each do a single job. On a single command line (or in a command script), you can pipe the output of one command into the input of another, and pipe that output into another, and so on, until you have a chain of simple little programs performing a complex task. This philosophy of using very simple programs in combinations makes UNIX relatively easy to use. I have made every effort to present these commands in a context that makes their purpose and usage clear.

Welcome to the world of UNIX. Most people like working in UNIX once they get a feel for it. A lot of work still needs to be done, and we need all the help we can get.

Layout

UNIX Weekend Crash Course is organized into 30 sessions, which are grouped into six parts. Each session is designed to be completed in 30 minutes and is followed by a quiz that will help reinforce your understanding of the most important concepts from that portion of the book. Of course, no law dictates that you have to complete this tutorial in one weekend. You can set up your own schedule according to the amount of time you have available. Each session stands on its own, which means that as long you go through the sessions in order, you can choose your own pace.

Part I: Friday Evening introduces you to UNIX, helps you get logged in, and shows you how to look around at the files and the programs that are running.

Part II: Saturday Morning contains tutorials on the two main UNIX text editors, followed by an introduction to the workings of the interactive shell programs.

Part III: Saturday Afternoon goes into more detail on the file system and describes some of the more useful UNIX utilities.

Part IV: Saturday Evening presents a sequence of tutorials on writing shell scripts.

Part V: Sunday Morning explains some of the more advanced programming techniques provided for you by UNIX.

Part VI: Sunday Afternoon introduces you to UNIX security and networking and builds on previous information to describe a few UNIX internals.

Appendix A: Answers to Part Reviews provides answers to the part review questions that appear after each of the six parts.

Appendix B: What's on the CD-ROM? describes the contents of the CD-ROM that accompanies this book.

Conventions Used in this Book

When you start a session, be prepared to spend at least a half hour of continuous study. As you move through each session, you will see the following four icons in the margins of the page. These icons act as milestones, helping you track your progress:

**30 Min.
To Go**

**20 Min.
To Go**

**10 Min.
To Go**

Done!

Three additional icons are used to help you easily identify important information:

This icon provides additional information that is pertinent to the subject being discussed.

This icon provides a trick or a special technique that can be used to make things go a little easier.

This icon tells you where you can find related material in other sessions.

This book provides many examples of text commands that are entered from the command line. The command prompt can look like anything, but the text of the book assumes that the command prompt is a dollar sign ($), which is the default. Thus, commands appear in the text as follows:

```
$ ls -l *.png
```

In cases where commands are entered by the superuser (for whom the default prompt is a percent sign), the commands appear as follows:

```
% ls -l *.png
```

All other computer text, whether it is output from a program or the source code of a program, is presented in the same font as commands:

```
$ cat index.html
<html>
<head><title>An empty page</title></head>
<body>A minimum body</body>
</html>
```

Some of the UNIX commands are the same as English words, or very much like English words, so it is necessary to differentiate them in the text. For example, the UNIX command named echo is formatted differently than the word echo in the text. Also, if a word has a special meaning to UNIX, it is shown in italics where it is defined. For example, the term *pipe* refers to the UNIX connection made from the output of one command to the input of another.

The convention in this book is to represent key combinations that include the Ctrl key in the form Ctrl+D, which means that you would press the Ctrl key and the D key together. In UNIX documentation, however, this key combination is represented in various ways, including Ctrl-d, crtl-d, or C-d. The use of each version is specific to the context and the topic being covered, but you should be aware that all of these key sequences mean the same thing.

Acknowledgments

I want to thank Margot Maley Hutchinson at Waterside for making everything happen. I also want to thank the very friendly (and occasionally patient) Terri Varveris for believing that I would be able to write this book. Gabrielle Chosney helped immensely by being very picky about the way I abused the English language. Terry Collings kept me from making a fool of myself by being very picky about technical accuracy. Kala Schrager helped by being picky about everything else, and by keeping all parts of the book in motion and headed in the right direction. And I want to thank my wife, Mary, who listens patiently to my complaints and then inspires me to get back to work by saying something like, "Well, that's okay. Just write another couple of pages while I go shopping."

Contents at a Glance

Preface vii
Acknowledgments x

FRIDAY...2
Part I—Friday Evening 4
Session 1–The Many Flavors of UNIX 5
Session 2–Logging In and Out 13
Session 3–The File System 23
Session 4–The Running Processes 35

SATURDAY..48
Part II—Saturday Morning 50
Session 5–Introduction to the vi Editor 51
Session 6–Introduction to the emacs Editor 63
Session 7–Fundamentals of the Bourne Shell 73
Session 8–Using the Bourne Shell 85
Session 9–Using Other Shells 95
Session 10–Regular Expressions 105

Part III—Saturday Afternoon 118
Session 11–Files and the File System 119
Session 12–File System Operations 131
Session 13–The World's Handiest Utilities 143
Session 14–The man Pages 155
Session 15–E-mail 165
Session 16–Writing Shell Scripts 175

Part IV—Saturday Evening 188
Session 17–Shell Scripts with Conditionals 189
Session 18–Shell Scripts with Loops 201
Session 19–Users and the passwd File 211
Session 20–Batch Editing 221

SUNDAY..234
Part V—Sunday Morning 236
Session 21–Batch Editing with awk 237
Session 22–The Perl Programming Language 247
Session 23–Writing and Compiling a C Program 257
Session 24–More Handy Utilities 271
Session 25–A Few Daemons 281
Session 26–The X Window System 293

Part VI—Sunday Afternoon **304**
Session 27–Archiving and Compressing Files 305
Session 28–Security 315
Session 29–Network Security and the Apache Server 325
Session 30–When UNIX Boots 335

Appendix A–Answers to Part Reviews **349**
Appendix B–What's on the CD-ROM? **363**
Index **369**
Hungry Minds, Inc. End-User License Agreement **385**

Contents

Preface vii
Acknowledgments x

FRIDAY...**2**
Part I—Friday Evening **4**
Session 1—The Many Flavors of UNIX **5**
    The Origins of UNIX **5**
    The Structure of UNIX **6**
        Starting processes 8
        Keeping processes running 8
        Process isolation 8
        Types of processes 9
        Dynamic allocation 10
    The UNIX Shell **10**
    Getting Connected **11**
Session 2—Logging In and Out **13**
    Entering the User Name and Password **13**
        The command line login procedure 14
        The graphic login procedure 14
        The command line prompt 15
    How the Shell Locates a Command **16**
    A Few Simple Commands **18**
        Echo 18
        Who 19
        Date 20
        Man 20
    Logging Out **21**
Session 3—The File System **23**
    The Basic File Structure **23**
        Some standard names 24
        Absolute and relative path addressing 25
        Navigating with dot, dotdot, and tilde 26
    Using ls to Get Information About a File **27**
    Locating Files and Determining File Types **29**
        Find 30
        File 31
        Which 32

Session 4—The Running Processes 35

  Listing the Running Processes 35

  Starting and Stopping Processes 39

    Background processes 39

    Priority setting with nice 39

    Signals 40

    Signaling a process 42

  Orphans and Zombies 43

  Fork and Exec 43

SATURDAY 48

Part II—Saturday Morning 50

Session 5—Introduction to the vi Editor 51

  From Line Editor to Screen Editor 52

  Creating a New File 53

  Editing Text 55

    Line operations 55

    Word operations 56

    Character operations 57

  Searching Through the Text 57

  Setting Options 58

  A Summary of vi Commands 59

Session 6—Introduction to the emacs Editor 63

  The emacs Editor Takes Many Forms 63

  Creating, Editing, and Saving Files 64

  Screen Description and Some Term Definitions 66

  Keys and Commands 67

  Searching the Text 68

  Summary of Basic emacs Commands 69

Session 7—Fundamentals of the Bourne Shell 73

  The Command Line 73

  The Environment of the Shell 74

    Defining your own environment variables 75

    The standard set of environment variables 76

  Command Line Expansion 78

  The Ins and Outs of Commands 79

  Quoting and Escaping 82

Session 8—Using the Bourne Shell 85

  Running Shells Within Shells 85

    Running a different kind of shell 85

    Taking the environment variables with you 86

    Starting a shell to execute commands from a file 87

    Logging in as another user 88

  Using Built-in Shell Commands 89

    The . (dot) command 89

    The unset command 89

The type command 90
The hash command 90
The readonly command 90
The set command 91
The ulimit command 92
Setting Your Prompt 92
Session 9—Using Other Shells 95
How to Select a Shell 95
Introduction to csh and tcsh, the C Shell 97
Startup and shutdown 97
Environment variables 97
C Shell command history 98
Aliases 99
Introduction to ksh, the Korn Shell 100
Korn Shell command history 100
Functions 101
Introduction to bash, the Bourne-Again Shell 102
Other Shells 103
Session 10—Regular Expressions 105
Expression Construction 105
Grepping 106
Advanced Grepping 108
Regular expression operators 109
Other versions of grep 112
The Flags of grep 113

Part III—Saturday Afternoon 118
Session 11—Files and the File System 119
Setting File Permissions 119
Understanding the octal form of file permissions 120
Setting initial file permissions 121
Adjusting File Timestamps 123
Working with Files and Directories 123
Changing file names 123
Duplicating files 124
Deleting files 125
Creating directories 125
Changing File Ownership 126
Linking Files 126
Session 12—File System Operations 131
Device Nodes 131
The terminal device node 132
Hard disk drive device nodes 133
Pseudo terminal device nodes 134
Some special device node names 134
Creating a device node 135

Hard Disk File Systems **135**

Other File Systems **137**

Floppy drives 138

CD-ROM drives 138

Internal File System Structure **138**

Organization by inodes 139

Synchronizing 140

Session 13—The World's Handiest Utilities **143**

Viewing Text Files **143**

Looking with more 143

Looking with less 144

File peeking with head and tail 145

The things cat can do 146

Dumping a file byte by byte 146

Sorting and Selecting **147**

Date and Time **148**

Accessing the system clock 149

Watching the clock 151

Session 14—The man Pages **155**

Viewing UNIX Documentation with man **155**

An example man page 157

The structure of a man page 159

The Options of man **160**

Viewing UNIX Documentation with xman **161**

Getting Help from Other Sources **162**

The Internet 163

The info utility 163

Session 15—E-mail **165**

E-mail and the Internet **165**

Using mail 166

Using elm 168

Using pine 170

Communicating with Other Users **171**

Granting and denying message permissions 171

Sending a message 172

Receiving and responding to a message 173

Sending a message with wall 173

Session 16—Writing Shell Scripts **175**

Simple Scripts **175**

Command Line Arguments **177**

Using the arguments 178

Using all the arguments 179

Using Environment Variables **182**

Using the existing variables 182

Setting environment variables 183

Part IV—Saturday Evening **188**
Session 17–Shell Scripts with Conditionals **189**
  Testing for True or False **189**
    A summary of the if command 191
    A summary of the test command 192
  Testing for a Pattern Match **194**
  Completing the Script **196**
  A Script to Adjust Your Environment **197**
Session 18–Shell Scripts with Loops **201**
  Loop while True **201**
    Keeping a loop running 203
    Prompting and looping 203
  Loop until True **204**
  Looping for a Count **205**
  Processing Command Line Options **208**
Session 19–Users and the passwd File **211**
  The Keys to the System **211**
    /etc/passwd 211
    /etc/group 213
    /etc/shadow 214
  Passwords **216**
    Setting your password 216
    Cracking passwords 216
    Selecting a good password 217
Sesson 20–Batch Editing **221**
  Making Text Substitutions with tr **221**
  Editing Files with sed **223**
    Internals and addressing 224
    Storing commands in a file 225
    The sed editing functions 226
    A few one liners 229

SUNDAY **234**

Part V—Sunday Morning **236**
Session 21–Batch Editing with awk **237**
  Introduction to awk **237**
  The Pattern and the Action **238**
  Storing an awk Program in a File **239**
  Formatting with the print Statement **240**
  Formatting with the printf Statement **241**
  The Beginning and the End **242**
  Conditions and Loops **243**
  One Liners **244**

Session 22–The Perl Programming Language **247**
  Introduction to Perl **247**
    A simple Perl program 248
    Creating a simple Web page 248
  Variables **249**
  Subroutines **250**
  Conditional Execution **251**
  Looping **254**
Session 23–Writing and Compiling a C Program **257**
  Hello, World **257**
    A more complete version of hello world 258
    Handling command line arguments 259
  A Hexadecimal Dumping Program **260**
  A Complete C Program **263**
    Multiple source files 263
    Compiling separate source files 265
    A better way to compile 266
  Core Files **267**
Session 24–More Handy Utilities **271**
  Comparing Two Files **271**
  Comparing Two Text Files **272**
  Comparing Three Text Files **273**
  Merging File Differences **274**
    Merging two files with diff 274
    Merging three files into one 275
    Interactively comparing and merging two files 276
  The Calendar **277**
  A View from the Top **278**
Session 25–A Few Daemons **281**
  The Internet Services Daemon **281**
  The Network File System Daemon **282**
  The Scheduling Daemon **284**
  The Printer Daemon **286**
    The problem with printing 287
    Using lp and lpr 287
    Formatting print jobs with pr 289
Session 26–The X Window System **293**
  The X Connection **293**
    Addressing the server 294
    The X messages 295
    The window manager 296
  An X Application **297**
  Widgets **300**

Part VI—Sunday Afternoon 304
Session 27–Archiving and Compressing Files 305
Introduction to Archiving 305
Packing and Unpacking 306
Compressing and Uncompressing 307
Gzipping and Gunzipping 307
Bzipping and Bunzipping 308
Zipping and Unzipping 308
Using cp 309
Using tar 310
Special-Purpose Archivers 312
Using dd 312
Using ar 313
Using cpio 313
Session 28–Security 315
Introduction to UNIX Security 315
Types of Attacks 317
Trojan horses 317
Worms 318
Denial of service 318
Buffer overflow 318
Security Checklist 319
Passwords 319
Updates and patches 319
Firewalls and services 320
NFS 321
Mail 321
FTP 321
Additional considerations 322
Session 29–Network Security and the Apache Server 325
Internet Configuration Files 325
The /etc/protocols file 326
The /etc/services file 326
The /etc/hosts file 327
The /etc/hosts.allow and /etc/hosts.deny files 328
Internet Configuration Utilities 329
The ifconfig utility 329
The arp utility 330
The route utility 331
The netstat utility 331
The Apache Server 332
Installation 332
Security 333

Session 30–When UNIX Boots **335**

   In the Beginning **336**

   The UNIX Kernel **336**

      The scheduler task 337

      The paging task 338

      The init task 338

   System Initialization **338**

   Running fsck **341**

   Mounting Devices **341**

   The rc Scripts **342**

   Getty **343**

   Shutdown **343**

Appendix A–Answers to Part Reviews **349**

Appendix B–What's on the CD-ROM? **363**

Index **369**

Hungry Minds, Inc. End-User License Agreement **385**

UNIX®
Weekend Crash Course™

☑ **Friday**

☐ Saturday

☐ Sunday

Part I — Friday Evening

Session 1
The Many Flavors of UNIX

Session 2
Logging In and Out

Session 3
The File System

Session 4
The Running Processes

PART

I

Friday Evening

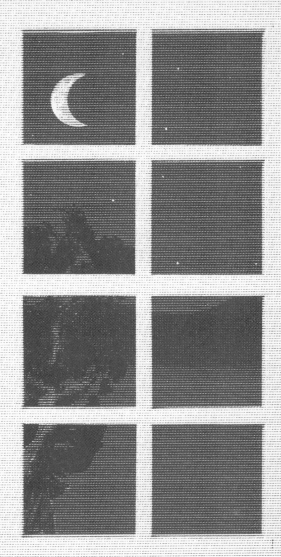

Session 1
The Many Flavors of UNIX

Session 2
Logging In and Out

Session 3
The File System

Session 4
The Running Processes

The Many Flavors of UNIX

Session Checklist

✔ The origins of UNIX

✔ The structure of UNIX

✔ The UNIX shell

✔ Getting connected

30 Min. To Go

O riginally only one operating system could be called UNIX, but several systems that have been derived from the original are in use today. These systems, which share the same basic design philosophy, are commonly referred to as members of the UNIX family. Hewlett-Packard, Sun Microsystems, and IBM are among the companies that support their own versions of UNIX. Although some systems that trace their origins to UNIX have added their own special flavor to the system, they are similar enough in philosophy and design to be immediately familiar. All members of the UNIX family share a fundamental set of characteristics, utility programs, and procedures.

This book is concerned with fundamental UNIX — the areas that are common to each version. The concepts you learn in this book should be applicable to every version of UNIX.

The Origins of UNIX

"UNIX" was originally a trademark name belonging to Bell Labs. The UNIX system name, along with rights to the source code of the software, has changed hands a couple of times and is currently the property of Caldera International. Caldera sells and maintains the latest version of UNIX under the name UnixWare, which means that no operating system on today's market carries the name "UNIX." In fact, the UNIX name is increasingly being used in a generic sense to refer to the entire (and very large) family of operating systems.

UNIX is not an acronym. The developers of UNIX, Ken Thompson and Dennis Ritchie, had been doing work using a full-blown mainframe system from Honeywell and GE called MULTICS, from which they derived the name for their tiny system. Originally the name was written down as "UNICS," but it soon became UNIX. Some of the fundamental forms (such as command line options) found in UNIX are very much like the ones in MULTICS.

The original UNIX was written in machine language by using a simple mnemonic translator known as an *assembler*. After Dennis Ritchie devised the C programming language in 1973, he and Thompson used C to rewrite the central program, or *kernel*, that runs UNIX. This proved that it was possible to write low-level operating system software in something other than assembly code. Additionally, the C language was designed to be portable. As soon as a version of the C compiler was devised to generate object code that was executable on a specific computer, it became possible to compile a UNIX kernel that would run on that machine. Suddenly, a portable operating system became possible. A relatively small amount of customization, along with a little assembly language, was necessary to actually port the system.

It was possible for a company to acquire a copy of the UNIX source code, which was written in a high-level language, and adapt it to accommodate special hardware requirements. Companies saved time and money by modifying the existing UNIX system to fit new or modified computers. Although porting the system to new hardware required some work, it was significantly simpler than writing a system from scratch.

The fact that UNIX was a portable operating system was not the primary reason for its success. UNIX is also an excellent design. The first versions of UNIX were full of innovations that are still used today. Some of these innovations have become so fundamental that we simply assume things work that way. For example, UNIX introduced the idea of a hierarchical file system of directories with each directory holding a number of other directories and files. UNIX was the first system to be based on a small and simple kernel controlling a set of device drivers to handle all of the input and output. Previously, the code controlling the devices was part of the operating system itself.

One of the most outstanding innovations is dynamic allocation of resources. UNIX made it simple for a user, or program, to dynamically create and destroy directories and files. In a similar fashion, by using some special C language function calls, a program can easily dynamically allocate and free almost any amount of memory that it needs. If a program requests more memory than is available, the system swaps portions of memory to disk to create make room. The memory swapping is invisible to a running program.

Possibly the most important UNIX innovation is the concept of small programs, each performing simple tasks, being connected to form a single command that performs a complex task. As you explore future sessions and become familiar with these little utilities, you can create large sophisticated commands from a collection of small commands without doing any programming whatsoever. This particular innovation is known as the *UNIX philosophy*. This philosophy is difficult to explain and nobody has written a manifesto, but each utility is written with this idea in mind: Every UNIX program uses a standard method for input and output, which makes it a trivial matter to connect two or more commands.

The Structure of UNIX

At the center of a running UNIX system is a single program called the kernel. The purpose of booting a UNIX system is to get the kernel running. From the moment it starts, the kernel is in charge of everything that happens in the computer.

The Development of UNIX

Several people were involved in writing (or maybe what they did should be called inventing) the original UNIX. Ken Thompson and Dennis Ritchie are the most well known, but significant contributions were made by Brian Kernighan, Rob Pike, Rudd Canaday, Doug McIlroy, and Joe Ossanna.

Development began in 1969, but it took a couple of years to get a viable UNIX system up and running. A Digital Equipment PDP-7 was used for the first implementation. In 1970, UNIX was moved to a larger machine, named PDP-11, where UNIX began to really take shape. A 1972 document titled *UNIX Programmer's Manual* stated, "The number of UNIX installations has grown to 10, with more expected."

Early work on UNIX was performed at AT&T's Bell Labs. However, because AT&T was a tightly regulated monopoly, the government prohibited the sale of UNIX until the breakup of AT&T years later. UNIX became available to students nationwide when it was licensed to universities in 1974. During this period, the University of California at Berkeley developed its own version of UNIX, known as BSD, which quickly made its way around university campuses. The AT&T version became known as System 3, and later — after revisions and updates were made — as System V (pronounced *"system five"*).

System V and BSD were both UNIX, but minor differences between the two existed. Although both systems were based on the same fundamental philosophy of small single-purpose utilities running under a simple kernel, the exact names and nature of these utilities varied. Eventually, they each copied the capabilities of the other. By the time System V 4 and BSD 4.3 were released, they were still two distinct systems, but with equivalent capabilities.

By the early 1980s, most university students could access UNIX. As these students graduated and entered the workforce, a new demand for a commercial UNIX emerged. Only a few years later — due to the breakup of the AT&T monopoly — the first commercial versions of UNIX began to appear. The use and popularity of UNIX caused computer companies to specialize in UNIX support and UNIX software development.

During the period when System V and BSD were becoming more similar, other flavors of UNIX began to emerge from other companies. One major version is the Solaris operating system from Sun Microsystems. IBM has a version of UNIX named AIX, and the Hewlett-Packard version is named HP-UX. And that is just the tip of the iceberg — there are literally hundreds of proprietary versions.

Recently, the free versions of UNIX, such as Linux and FreeBSD, have caused UNIX to spread even further. FreeBSD has been around longer than Linux, but the Linux operating system has caught on and is being run on more and more computers every day. Linux is a child of the Internet and runs on everything from IBM mainframes to wristwatches.

Millions of UNIX systems are in operation today. However, because the UNIX operating system can be obtained from so many sources, some of which distribute it for free, no records state exactly how many systems are currently in use. When the question is asked, "How many UNIX systems are there?" the only correct answer is, "Lots."

The list of tasks performed by the kernel is amazingly short because it delegates most of the work to other programs. Some UNIX kernels perform more tasks than others, but at a very minimum, the kernel — or its immediate lieutenant processes — is responsible for starting processes, stopping processes, managing the running of processes, managing memory allocation, and communicating with running processes. Responding to a request from one process may require communication with another process, so some form of interprocess communications is also a requirement.

Starting processes

When the kernel first starts running, it performs several tasks to initialize the system, including starting a process called `init`.

The `init` process starts all the other process running. When the kernel and `init` first start running, they read a set of configuration files that lists all the programs that need to be started immediately. Among these programs are device drivers, which perform the fundamental task of communicating with the computer's hardware and peripheral devices. For example, one device driver handles each disk drive, one handles each printer, one handles the keyboard, one reads the computer system clock, and so on.

A number of different things can cause a program to start running. When no login exists on a specific terminal, that fact is detected and a program is started to display the login prompt on the screen. This program responds to your login name and password and sends a message to `init` requesting that it start another program that will become responsible for receiving and acting on the commands entered at that terminal. Depending on which program is started, you may be prompted for a simple command line entry from the keyboard or for a mouse click. After you log in, if you enter a program name from the command line, a message is sent to `init` to start the program running.

Keeping processes running

The kernel maintains a list of all running processes and allocates time slots to each so that each is assured of getting CPU time. Important programs can either be allotted larger time slots or can be given time slots more often than less important programs. In addition, more important programs can interrupt less important programs whenever something must be done. The kernel acts like a traffic cop, controlling which process runs and which one freezes and waits.

The kernel assigns a priority number to each process to keep track of which processes are more important than others. You have the ability to set the priority number for your own programs, but you cannot set the priority above a certain level. Certain processes are critical to the operation of the computer and must retain a higher priority than others. You can use certain UNIX commands to take a peek at the current, and ever changing, table of running processes. One of these commands is discussed in Session 2.

Process isolation

Each process is allocated its own block of memory and cannot read from or write to the block of memory allocated to another task. Additionally, a process cannot read from or write to the memory space of the kernel. Every process is completely isolated in everything that it does, which means that a process cannot cause another process to crash, nor can it crash the system by fouling up the data in the kernel area. Of course, errors do occur, but it is extremely rare for a process to misbehave and cause operating system problems. Because of process isolation, many UNIX systems run for years without being rebooted. Most reboots take place when the system is upgraded to a new version of UNIX, when changes or repairs are made to the hardware, or when a power failure occurs.

This isolation of processes means that a process cannot directly communicate with the outside world, but the process can communicate with the kernel, so the kernel must supply communications. The kernel provides a *system call* that can be used by a process to make a request and receive a response. The kernel answers some of these requests itself — such as the system call that returns the list of processes currently running. However, processes designed to perform a specific task answer most of the requests. For example, if a program makes a system call requesting that a character be written on the display, the kernel passes the chore to the program responsible for the console.

Types of processes

You can visualize the system as a kernel that is in charge of running a collection of processes, and these processes are using the kernel as a communications path to talk to one another. Most programs specialize in performing one particular task. Every program running on a UNIX system falls into one of four categories:

- **Kernel.** There is only one kernel. As the core of the operating system, the kernel is in charge of everything.

- **Device driver.** A device driver is a special process responsible for sending data to and retrieving data from a single hardware device such as a disk drive or printer. Device drivers can either be included as part of the kernel or are dynamically loaded as separate modules when needed. Typically, the kernel starts device drivers when the computer first boots. After they are loaded, the device drivers sit and wait until there is a request to access the device that they control.

- **Daemon.** A daemon is similar to a device driver because it sits and waits to receive a request; however, a daemon is not connected to a hardware device. One of the most common examples of a daemon is a print spooler, which receives all print requests, organizes the requests by collecting the data that needs to be printed, and passes the print jobs to the printer device driver one at a time. The device driver simply prints what it receives, so the daemon prevents multiple print jobs from getting all mixed together. Many types of daemons perform many types of jobs, but mostly they just sit and wait.

- **Application.** An application is any program that does not fall into one of the other categories. Applications run in isolation and communicate with the rest of the world through kernel system calls.

No real physical difference exists between an application and a daemon — they differ in their purpose and in the way they communicate with the outside world. On the other hand, a device driver is very special; it must be constructed in such a way that it can communicate directly with hardware and can be managed by the kernel as part of the system configuration.

Dynamic allocation

Dynamic allocation is another important task performed by the kernel. Whenever a new process is started, the kernel allocates memory to the process so that it has a place to run. If a running program needs more memory, the program uses a system call to request memory from the kernel. The kernel does what is necessary to make sure the program has sufficient space to run.

As a group, the running programs normally require more memory than actually exists in the hardware; thus, the kernel assumes the responsibility of storing all or part of the running programs to dynamically allocated space on disk. Certain sophisticated algorithms are responsible for this swapping, because great care is necessary to prevent swapping from taking up all the CPU time and grinding the entire system to a halt.

The UNIX Shell

10 Min.
To Go

By now, you should understand the fundamental workings of a UNIX box. A single program, called the kernel, is the core of the operating system. The kernel provides little snippets of time to each process, and each process periodically requests something of the kernel.

Imagine an application program that displays a simple string of characters (*a prompt*) on the screen and then waits for keyboard input. This is what happens when you log in — an application program issues a prompt that appears on the screen, and the program then sits and waits for you to type something. This application program, with all its knowledge of the system, is simply sitting and waiting for your commands. This program knows most of the system calls, including the call that makes a request for the kernel to run another program.

You can think of this program as your own personal wrapper around the kernel that translates the otherwise cryptic ways of communicating with the kernel. Any program that does this sort of thing is called a *shell*. A shell acts as a translator between you and the kernel and thus becomes as your interface to the entire system.

With windowing and a mouse, you can establish a different kind of interface to the system. As this interface becomes more mature, you are increasingly able to handle system configuration settings and various other UNIX tasks within windowing applications. However, most of the work done with the UNIX system is through the command line of a shell program. You can work in both environments simultaneously by opening a shell window. This combination of approaches turns out to be a very good way to work because it allows you to use windowing applications while maintaining access to the shell's command line.

A few commands are built into the shell, some of which are discussed in Session 16. Most commands, however, are simply the names of programs. If you enter a command that the shell program does not recognize, it looks around for a program by that name. If the shell finds a program, it issues an order to the kernel to run the program. The shell then relinquishes control of the screen and keyboard to the new program until it stops running. When the program stops, the shell resumes control.

Entering one command at a time may seem limiting, but it really isn't. As you become more familiar with how the command line works, you will find yourself entering more than one command at a time and hooking them together to perform several tasks in tandem. A command can also be run in the background as its own process, which allows the shell to maintain control of the keyboard and screen and prompt you to enter another command. You can even enter a command on the command line and have it execute at a specified time in the future. You can change the manner in which a command is executed by using options and flags on the command line. When you get one of the more complicated commands working the way you want, you can store the command sequence in a file. Saving complex commands in files allows you to make an elaborate command or sequence of commands into a single command of your own design. Sessions 5 and 6 explain the process of entering commands, and later sessions show you how to create your own commands.

Getting Connected

UNIX is a multiuser system so you must enter a user name and password to get access to the system. This allows UNIX to identify each user and prevent users from viewing each other's files. Using separate access paths, many people can be connected to the system simultaneously. A connection to a UNIX system can be made in a variety of ways:

- **Dumb terminal.** The original method of connecting to UNIX was through a dumb terminal, which is nothing more than a keyboard with a screen to display characters. A dumb terminal connection is either made by being directly connected to the computer or through a modem. In any case, tapping the keyboard a couple of times gets the computer's attention, and the daemon process waiting for input from the hardware port attached to your terminal prompts you for a login.

- **Console.** The UNIX name for the main display and keyboard that are usually wired directly into the computer is the *console*. This is the most common way to access personal UNIX systems such as Linux and FreeBSD that run on a PC. On a PC, the console is usually a graphics terminal and can be used as a simple terminal that runs a shell, a graphics system using the X Window System, or both at the same time.

- **X terminal.** This type of terminal falls into the smart terminal category, but its intelligence is limited to being a graphics display. An X terminal has a keyboard, a mouse, and has the complete X windowing protocol built in. From a remote location, the user is provided with a windowing interface that is exactly like the interface at the console. Several of these X terminals can be connected and running simultaneously — the only real limitation is the computer's ability to keep up with everyone.

- **Terminal emulator.** Because desktop computers are now so common, using a terminal emulator has become a common way to connect to a UNIX system from a remote location. Your PC runs a program that causes the UNIX host to see the PC as either a dumb terminal or an X terminal.

- **Telnet.** A computer can be used as a terminal by running a telnet client program that emulates a terminal and provides the capability of logging in to a remote computer. Telnet is a standard internet protocol designed to perform this task.

When any one of these connections is made, a daemon process in the UNIX computer displays a login prompt. Responding to this prompt is the subject of the next session.

Done!

REVIEW

This session briefly discusses the heritage of the UNIX family of operating systems. Although many flavors of UNIX exist, the underlying philosophy of operation is the same. This session also includes a brief overview of how the UNIX system works.

- Although UNIX began as a single operating system on a single computer, it is now a large family of operating systems running on many kinds of computers.
- One reason for the growth of UNIX is that it was the first operating system written in a higher-level language, which made it relatively easy to port to other systems.
- An underlying philosophy of UNIX is that a standard method of linking together simple utilities can allow you to perform more complex tasks.
- The kernel is the program at the heart of the operating system that controls everything. The kernel starts, runs, and stops all other processes.
- A shell process manages a login session by prompting for input and by passing messages to the kernel to perform various tasks.
- You can log in to a UNIX computer in a number of different ways, such as a dumb terminal, the console, or an X terminal.

The next session is about logging in and looking around. As a user, you can customize your environment to suit your preferences and the kind of work you plan to do.

QUIZ YOURSELF

1. The UNIX kernel is written mostly in what language? (See "The Origins of UNIX.")
2. What caused UNIX to be ported to so many different types of computers? (See "The Origins of UNIX.")
3. How do separate processes talk to one another? (see "The Structure of UNIX.")
4. What is a device driver? (See "Types of processes.")
5. Why is the UNIX application controlling a login session called a shell? (See "The UNIX Shell.")

Logging In and Out

Session Checklist

✔ Entering the user name and password

✔ How the shell locates a command

✔ A few simple commands

✔ Logging out

30 Min. To Go

This session describes the login and logout procedures for UNIX systems. No matter how you choose to access a UNIX system, the login procedure requires you to enter both a user name and password to gain access, and then the system prompts you for a command. After the login is accomplished, you can use some simple utilities to determine the contents of the home directory. Your login session consists of you entering commands and the shell program obeying the commands that it understands. You can enter many different commands. The shell may have to search for some of the commands that you enter, but you can tell the shell where to look. Most of the UNIX commands are simple, and a few are described in this session.

Entering the User Name and Password

You can log in to a UNIX system from the command line or through the X Window System. These login procedures are both actually the same thing, but they look a little different. The traditional method is by responding to prompts on a text-based terminal to enter a user name and password. On a graphics terminal connected to a system running the X Window System, the login is often achieved by entering the user name and password in a dialog box.

The command line login procedure

Every user, even the system administrator, accesses a UNIX system in exactly the same way. The first thing you see on a UNIX terminal is a prompt that looks something like this:

```
login:
```

There may be a line or two of text immediately above the login prompt that advertises the type of system and possibly the system name. At this point, you enter your *user name* — the name assigned to you by the system administrator when your account was created. The computer must know the name that you enter, or you will not be able to log in. After you enter your user name, press Return.

 Some keyboards have a key labeled Return, and others have a key labeled Enter. They are the same — either one of them produces the standard ASCII carriage return character and sends it to the program.

You will find that just about everything in UNIX is case-sensitive, including login names. As far as UNIX is concerned, there are 52 letters in the alphabet — 26 little ones and 26 big ones. UNIX considers the names "Aaron," "aaron," "AARON," and "aaroN" to be completely different

After you enter the user name, the next thing you see is a prompt that looks like the following:

```
password:
```

At this point, you must enter the password and press the Return key. As you enter the password you may notice an important security measure — the password does not appear on the screen. Your keystrokes are either not echoed at all or appear as a string of asterisks, which prevents someone from looking over your shoulder and reading your password.

If you enter a valid user name and password, you are rewarded with a prompt that enables you to input your first command. In other words, the process that prompted you to log in has quit running and turned control of the keyboard and screen over to the shell program, which is now responsible for responding to your commands as long as you are logged in.

The graphic login procedure

If the login is through the X Window System, a login dialog is displayed on the screen, either with a text entry window labeled login or two text entry windows labeled login and password. In either case, the graphic login procedure is the same as the text-based procedure, except that graphics are involved. Simply enter a valid user name and password to log in.

The login window display is almost always customized, so I will not attempt to describe the appearance of the login dialog. Its design may include pictures that relate to the company, the project the computer is being used for, or just some graphic design that the system administrator likes. The login dialog may also include options to select the desktop environment or the window manager. The desktop environment determines the appearance and operation of the entire windowing system and could be named Motif, Gnome, OpenLook, KDE, or one of several others. The window manager is a background process that assumes responsibility for such tasks as displaying windows and detecting mouse clicks. If you don't know what these options mean you can just ignore them and accept the default settings.

More information on the X Window System is provided in Session 26.

After you log in, you may see a window with a command line prompt. This is a default window running a shell program, which is displaying a prompt and waiting for your input. If you do not see a window containing a prompt, you need to determine how to open such a window. You may be able to start it from an icon located on the root window (the main background window covering the entire display, sometimes referred to as the desktop window). Alternately, a button or an icon on a bar across the top or bottom of the screen may open such a window. If not, try clicking each of the mouse buttons on the root window to get a menu to pop up. Using one of these icons or menu buttons, you should be able to find a selection named "terminal," "xterm," "console," or something similar. Remember, the kernel and the other processes are protected, so the worst that can happen from your experimentation is that you need to log in again.

The command line prompt

After you have a shell program running, it prompts you for input. The exact appearance of the prompt, like everything else in UNIX, is configurable, so it can be set to look like just about anything. The traditional default prompt is a simple dollar sign followed by a space so the most common default prompt, with the cursor, looks like this:

```
$ _
```

It is quite common to customize the prompt to display the name of the current directory, the name of the computer, the name of the user logged in, the current time, or any combination of these and other things. To keep things simple, this book uses the simple dollar sign prompt.

Instructions for customizing your prompt can be found in Session 6.

At this point, nothing else is going to happen until you make a request. A reasonable first action is to look around. To determine the name of the current directory, enter the command pwd (print working directory). Enter the three letters of the command, press Return, and the shell responds with the directory name followed by a prompt for another command. The resulting display looks something like this:

```
$ pwd
/home/arthur
$
```

As you can see, my directory is named /home/arthur. The UNIX file system is made up of dozens of directories, all of which are filled with files and other directories. One of these directories belongs to you and is known as your *home directory*. When you log in, your session always begins in your home directory. Unless some special effort has been made to name it something else, your home directory bears your login name. The exact location of your home directory in the UNIX file system depends on how your user account is set up. A standard System V UNIX, for example, often defaults to placing the home directories inside a directory named /usr, as opposed to a Linux system, which normally places them inside a directory named /home. Other variations exist, but other than organization, the location of a home directory has no particular meaning. However, it is normal to place all home directories in the same directory so that they are easy to find.

More information on the general directory structure is given in Session 3.

Now that you know who and where you are, the next thing to do is find out what is in your home directory. Some files, even some directories, may have been put in your home directory when your user account was created. To see what they are, use the ls (list) command to get a list of the files and directory names:

```
$ ls
Desktop     iliamna.tiff  mbox   redoubt.tiff  spool          x.log
Nautilus    mail          radio  sig           statement.pdf
$ _
```

Your list will certainly be different from this one. The first time you log in, your home directory may show no names at all. There may be files and directories in your home directory that you don't see listed because any name that starts with a period is ignored by ls unless you specify that they are to be included in the list. Files with names that begin with a period are called *hidden files*, although they are not meant to be hidden very well. For example, some configuration settings for your shell program are contained in one or more hidden files in your home directory. If you want to see a list of all the files and directory names, simply add the -a option to the ls command:

```
$ ls -a
```

The output from this command probably includes one or more hidden files with names like .profile, .bash_profile, .cshrc, and .tcshrc. The shell programs that have been configured to run from this login determine the file names that appear. By making changes to these hidden files, your account can be configured for more than one shell and, because a shell is nothing more than an application program, you can easily switch from shell to another.

Sessions 6 and 7 provide information on configuring and running shells.

How the Shell Locates a Command

*20 Min.
To Go*

When you enter a command, the shell looks for the specified command on the disk drive and, if it is found, the shell executes the command. Commands can be located in different places scattered around the disk. You can instruct the shell to look for commands in certain standard locations, such as /bin and /usr/bin, as well as some special places that you may have used to store some programs of your own. The search process is achieved by providing the shell with a list of directories in what is known as an *environment variable*. An environment variable is a special name that the shell program memorizes and then uses when it needs the information. The environment variable that instructs the shell where to look for programs to run is named PATH.

Normally, quite a few environment variables are already set when you log in. The system configuration sets some of them, and it is normal for your login procedure to set some by having them stored in hidden files located in your home directory. PATH is the most fundamental of the environment variables because it determines where the shell looks for a command, and thus which command is actually executed.

Setting and using environment variables is discussed further in Sessions 5 and 6.

If you want to look at all the environment variables that are currently set in your shell, use the env command with no options. The result will resemble the following:

```
$ env
WINDOWID=41943166
HOSTNAME=arlin
HISTFILESIZE=1000
USER=arthur
MAIL=/var/spool/mail/arthur
JAVA_HOME=/usr/java/java
DISPLAY=:0
SHLVL=1
SHELL=/bin/sh
HOME=/home/arthur
PATH=/bin:/usr/bin:/usr/local/bin:/home/arthur/bin:.
$ _
```

This list of environment variables is probably shorter than the one that your system displays. Many different programs require that environment variables are set, so you will probably find definitions used by software installed on your computer. The following list briefly describes the environment variables in the example:

- WINDOWID is the unique identifier for the window where the shell program is being run.
- HOSTNAME specifies the name of the computer.
- USER specifies the name of the current user.
- MAIL specifies the name of the directory that contains incoming mail for this user.
- JAVA HOME specifies the location of the Java installation.
- DISPLAY specifies the unique identity of the screen displaying the windows. This is necessary because there could be several terminals connected to one UNIX system.
- SHELL specifies the name and location of the shell program.
- HOME is used by several different programs to locate the home directory of the user.
- PATH contains a list of directory names separated by colons.

The order of the directories listed in PATH is important because the shell program searches the directories in the order that they appear. In this example, when you enter a command the shell looks for it in the following directories:

```
/bin
/usr/bin
/usr/local/bin
/home/arthur/bin
.
```

The last directory in the list (the dot) instructs the shell to look in the current directory. Including the dot means that you can switch to some directory not included in the PATH and still run programs stored in that directory as long as another program by the same name is not found at some other location earlier in the PATH.

If you enter a command that the shell can't find on the path, it responds with a not found message. An attempt to run a nonexistent program named frammis looks like this:

```
$ frammis
frammis: not found
$ _
```

There is no real disadvantage to adding as many directory names as you like in the path. The shell knows that when you run a command, you are quite likely to run it again, so the first time you enter a command the shell memorizes its location. This means that the shell doesn't have to look through a list of directories the next time the command name is entered. When you log off, the list disappears and has to be built from scratch the next time you log in.

A Few Simple Commands

The UNIX philosophy of keeping each program as simple as possible has resulted in a large number of relatively simple commands. That is, each UNIX command does just one thing, but most of them have options that can be used to modify exactly how they do it. Some commands are more complicated than others and have lots of options because the job that they do can be done several different ways.

Echo

The echo command is so simple that, at first, it doesn't seem to serve any purpose. The only thing that echo does is output whatever string of characters it finds on its command line, as in the following example:

```
$ echo This line is to be echoed.
This line is to be echoed.
$ _
```

That's all echo does. In fact, if you leave the line blank, echo responds by displaying a blank line:

```
$ echo

$ _
```

In spite of its simplicity, the echo command can be very useful. For example, you can use echo in conjunction with the capability of the shell to display the value stored in an environment variable. If you put a dollar sign ($) in front of an environment variable name, the shell replaces the name with the value stored for that name. The following example demonstrates how you can determine the contents of the PATH by using echo:

```
$ echo $PATH
/bin:/usr/bin:/usr/local/bin:/home/arthur/bin:.
$ _
```

You can also include environment variables within a string of text. The result consists entirely of text because echo displays everything on the line:

```
$ echo The directory $HOME is my home directory.
The directory /home/arthur is my home directory.
$ _
```

Inside shell scripts, the echo command works nicely as a utility to format output messages, as is demonstrated in Session 16. As simple as it is, echo is probably one of the most frequently used commands in UNIX.

Who

10 Min. To Go

The who command can be used to list every user logged in to the system. To see the list, simply enter the command with no options, as follows:

```
$ who
root      tty1      Oct  4 14:42
jimbo     pts/0     Oct 18 16:03
jimbo     pts/1     Oct 18 16:22
dave      tty12     Oct 14 06:29
jessica   ttyL      Oct 18 12:43
$ _
```

This example lists five active login sessions, each tagged with the date and time that the person logged in. You can see a root login that has been active since October 4, and it is now at least October 18, because three logins occurred on that date. The root session is logged in through the port labeled tty1, dave through tty12, and jessica through ttyL. Depending on the system and how it's configured, the tty ports are normally either the console or a dumb terminal connected to a serial port. It is likely that the two ports named pts are *pseudo ports*, which means that they are not physical ports but are probably shell sessions logged in through some kind of windowing environment. Nothing guarantees that the name of the port matches the port type, but that's what the names indicate if they follow the standard naming convention.

Users can also determine their own identity with the who command. If you log in and out of different accounts, or find yourself logged into several systems at once (which can happen with windowing and a network), you can easily lose track of your current login. To identify yourself, enter the following:

```
$ who am i
arlin!herbert    pts/2    Oct 14 10:29
$ _
```

The output tells you that you are logged in to a computer named `arlin` as a user named `herbert`. You have been logged in since 10:29 a.m. on October 14.

Date

The `date` command can be used to display the current date and time in just about any format you can imagine. If you are the superuser, `date` can also be used to set the system clock. The simplest way to use `date` is to enter it without any options and let it display the information in the default format:

```
$ date
Mon Oct 22 15:49:42 AKDT 2001
$ _
```

A number of formatting options can be used when displaying the date. For example, the date can be displayed as the name of a day of the week followed by the date in a compressed form, like this:

```
$ date +"%A %D"
Monday 10/22/01
$ _
```

%A specifies that the day of the week be displayed, and %D specifies that the date be displayed in mm/dd/yy format. Enough of these formatting code options are available to make it possible to display the date just about any way you want. The next section tells you how to determine the formatting options and much more.

Man

Session 12 goes into detail about online UNIX documentation, but it may come in handy before you get that far, so this is a brief introduction. The man utility can be used find all the information you need about a particular command. Simply specify the command that you want to know about as the argument to the man command. For example, if you want to know all the options for date, enter the following:

```
$ man date
```

If you can't wait for Session 12, you can find out everything there is to know about man by typing:

```
$ man man
```

You can navigate around a man page in various ways, which are discussed further in Session 12, but you can get to all the information by using the up and down arrow keys.

Logging Out

Just as there are two ways to log in to a UNIX system (command line and graphics), there are two ways to log out. If you are working from the command line, to log out you can simply stop the shell from running. The kernel detects the loss of the shell program and restarts the process that prompts for a login. This simple command closes the shell and logs you out:

```
$ exit
```

The exit command is not a program like the other commands described in this session. It is a command that is built into the shell itself. When you enter the exit command, the shell quits running immediately, so control of the terminal gets turned back over to the system.

Every process in UNIX uses ASCII characters. Many processes, especially the older ones, recognize some of the standard control characters, such as STX (Start of Text), ETX (End of Text), and an important one named EOT (End of Transmission). These control characters can all be entered from the keyboard by using the Ctrl key (Ctrl+B is STX, Ctrl+C is ETX, and Ctrl+D is EOT). To tell the shell that you are finished and will not be typing any more, simply enter Ctrl+D. The result is exactly the same as if you had entered the exit command.

If you logged in through a graphic window, you need to log off by using the mouse to make a menu selection. If you use the exit command (or press Ctrl+D) at the command line prompt, the shell quits running and the window containing it closes, but you are still logged in. Although every desktop environment is different, there is a logout selection on a menu somewhere. All you have to do is find it and you're out.

Done!

REVIEW

This chapter teaches you how to log in and out of UNIX. It also describes some of the basic commands you can use to locate files and directories and determine other system information. The shell, acting as the interface to the system, becomes the face of UNIX from the viewpoint of the user.

- The first line of UNIX security involves a user name and password that every user must enter in order to access the system.

- Whether logging in from a command line prompt or from a windowing interface, the process is basically the same.

- The shell can remember useful information by storing it in environment variables, and the shell is capable of using the information when called upon to do so.

- Among the commands that can be used to immediately display information are pwd, ls, env, who, date, and man.

Session 3 continues our exploration of files. There are different kinds of files, and a good deal of information exists for each file.

QUIZ YOURSELF

1. What are the differences between logging in through a dumb terminal and through a windowing interface? (See "Entering the User Name and Password.")

2. What directory are you in when you first log in? (See "The command line prompt.")

3. What command would you use to list all of the files, including the hidden files? (See "The command line prompt.")

4. When you enter a command, how does the shell know where to look for it? (See "How the Shell Locates a Command.")

5. What two things can you enter to stop a shell program from executing? (See "Logging Out.")

SESSION

3

The File System

Session Checklist

✔ The basic file structure

✔ Using 1s to get information about a file

✔ Locating files and determining file types

**30 Min.
To Go**

This is the first of three sessions about the UNIX file system. It describes how the file system appears to a user and discusses a set of commands that you can use to obtain information about files, such as who owns the file, how large it is, and what it contains. This session also provides an explanation of file access permissions and how you can determine who has been denied or granted access. You can move about the file system by making any directory on the system into your current working directory, as long as you have the proper access permissions. A set of semistandard names is used on directories to give you an idea of where to look for things. You can also use various utilities to tell you where files are and exactly what is inside them.

The Basic File Structure

The file system on a UNIX computer takes the form of a single hierarchical tree of directories. The tree begins with a directory named /, known as the *root directory*. All other files and directories (including floppy drives, multiple hard disk drives, and networked computers) appear as names at some level within this one directory.

Note

In just the first three sessions we have come across three different things that go by the name of "root." The *root login* is the default user name of the super user, which has the power to override all permissions. The *root window* of the X Window System is the main window covering the entire display. And the *root directory* contains all other directories and files. This isn't as confusing as it seems because the context always makes the meaning clear.

The cd (change directory) command makes it possible to switch to a location other than your home directory. The new location becomes your current working directory. For example, to change to the root directory, enter the following command:

```
$ cd /
```

After you have entered this command, you are no longer in your home directory. Instead, you are in the root directory, which you can verify by using the pwd command. We use expressions like "switch to" and "change to" because it somehow feels like we have moved from one place to another. The truth is, nothing has changed except the default directory name stored inside the shell.

You can use the cd command to change to any directory you want. For example, if your home directory is named /home/clifford, you can change to it from any other directory with the following command:

```
$ cd /home/clifford
```

Actually, there is an easier way to get to your home directory. If you enter the cd command with no arguments, the cd command assumes that you want to go home and takes you there.

Some standard names

If you use the ls command while in the root directory, you get a list that contains several directory names. The names of these lower-level directories are fairly standard, but you will find variations from one system to the next. The following list contains the names and contents of typical directories found on many systems:

- /usr — This directory contains programs and data that are not directly involved with the workings of the operating system, such as directories containing documentation and utilities for software development. Some applications, such as databases, store their files here. Many systems store the users' home directories here as well.

- /usr/bin — The name bin is short for "binary," which is another way of referring to a compiled executable program file. This directory contains a collection of utilities that are part of the UNIX distribution, but are not directly involved with the fundamentals of the operating system. This directory includes utilities for software development, playing audio, e-mail, graphics programs, and just about anything else that has nothing to do with the operation of UNIX itself.

- /usr/sbin — The executable commands in this directory pertain to configuring various parts of the system and setting up the environment. This includes utilities to configure networking, add and remove user logins, and monitor system activity, as well as other programs that deal with the operating system.

- /usr/lib — This directory is used by software development. It contains libraries of program modules that are linked with executable programs.

- /bin — This directory contains a collection of executable commands that process information provided by the operating system. There are things such as the various shell programs, ls, pwd, and other utilities to work with files and directories. Most of these are fundamental programs that have been a part of UNIX for a long time.

- /lib — This directory contains a collection of shared libraries that contain executable modules used by programs as they are running.
- /home — Some systems use this directory (or one that is similarly named) to contain the home directories of the users. Originally, all the login directories were kept in the /usr directory, but today it is more common to put them in a directory of their own.
- /etc — This directory contains the system configuration scripts and files. The configuration files for almost every installed utility, daemon, device driver, networking, and even for the kernel are included. These files contain configuration settings and utility scripts for things as varied as login passwords and the default e-mail program.
- /dev — This directory contains the special files that are used as links for connecting UNIX software to hardware devices such as serial ports and disk drives.
- /mnt — Devices are often mounted as directories inside this directory. You may find directories with names such as /mnt/cdrom and /mnt/floppy. It is also common, in a network of UNIX computers, to mount the disk drives of other computers by using directory names that are the same as the name of the remote computer.
- /tmp — This is a working directory. Many different processes use /tmp as workspace to store temporary files. Most programs that use this directory clean up after themselves, but if they don't, you may have to remove the old files in some other way. Procedures can be set up to make the directory self-cleaning.
- /var — Many applications use this directory to store data that may vary from time to time. These items may include temporary work files that need to remain in place until the program runs again, database tables, and configuration files for utilities that allow you to dynamically change the settings as they run.
- /boot — This directory, or one with a similar name, contains the UNIX kernel, as well as programs and information that the kernel uses. Frequently, however, the kernel is simply placed in the root directory as an executable file.

Be aware that the actual directory names on your system are almost certainly different from the names listed here. Also, exactly which programs are stored in which bin directory is not as clearly defined as the descriptions in the list may imply.

You will pick up several other naming conventions as you work with UNIX. For example, a directory named include is full of C and/or C++ programming header files, a directory named src contains programming source code, and a man directory contains documentation in the format that the man utility uses. These names are only guidelines, but it is useful to be familiar with them in case you want to find something.

Absolute and relative path addressing

The directory system is in the form of a huge tree. Within the root directory are other directories, which in turn contain other directories, and so on. The most straightforward way to address a file (or a directory) is to use its full path name, like this:

```
$ cat /usr/lib/bcc/include/asm/limits.h
```

The cat command reads the file or files named on its command line and displays the content to standard output. This command is named cat, which is short for concatenate, because it can be used to combine files. The address of the file, composed of the full path name beginning with the root directory, is known as an _absolute address_. The address is called "absolute" because it can be used from anywhere in the file system without any doubt about the name and location of the file being referenced.

The other type of file addressing depends on the current directory. You can list the contents of the `limits.h` file with the following two commands:

```
$ cd /usr/lib/bcc/include/asm
$ cat limits.h
```

The `cd` command uses an absolute address to change to the directory containing the `limits.h` file. The `cat` command uses a _relative address_ to name the file to be listed. (The address is known as "relative" because the location of the target file is relative to the current directory.) The file name does not begin with / (a slash character), so the shell assumes that the current directory name is to be used as the first part of the file name, which specifies the location of the file as in or beneath the current directory. The following is another way to list the contents of `limits.h`:

```
$ cd /usr/lib/bcc
$ cat include/asm/limits.h
```

In this example, the `cd` command uses an absolute address to move to the /bcc directory. The `cat` command addresses the file with a path name that does not begin with a slash, so the shell assumes that it is a relative address and inserts the absolute address of the current directory in front of the file name to come up with a full absolute address.

You can also use the same addressing scheme for commands. For example, if you want to execute the du (disk usage) command to find out how much disk space is being used in your home directory, you can enter the command in the usual way and have the shell look for the du command in the PATH directories:

```
$ du
```

However, if your path, as defined by the PATH environment variable, does not include the directory named /usr/bin, the program will not be found when you enter it on the command line. To overcome this, you can specify the full path to the command as follows:

```
$ /usr/bin/du
```

This means that you can run any program, from anywhere, even if it is not in your PATH definition, by simply using its full name.

20 Min.
To Go

Navigating with dot, dotdot, and tilde

The directory name referred to as "dot" is actually just a period and is an alias for the current directory. You may remember from the previous session that you can use a period as a directory name when defining the PATH environment variable. The period is an instruction to the shell to look in the current directory when searching for a command. Suppose you don't have a period in your PATH definition, and you want to execute a program named du, which is in the current directory. You can do that by entering the following command:

```
$ ./du
```

The directory name referred to as "dotdot" is two periods and is an alias for the parent directory of the current directory. For example, if the current directory is named /user/pete/ forms, you can list the names of the files in the /usr/pete directory this way:

```
$ ls ..
```

If there is a directory named /usr/pete/notes, and your current directory is /usr/pete/forms, you can list the names of the files in /usr/pete/notes like this:

```
$ ls ../notes
```

You can combine more than one "dotdot" to address files and directories higher up in the directory tree. If /usr/pete/forms is the current directory, you can list the file and directory names in /usr like this:

```
$ ls ../..
```

The tilde character (~) is another shorthand for a directory name. A tilde can be substituted for the absolute address of your home directory. For example, you can get a listing of the files and directories in your home directory this way:

```
$ ls ~
```

Using ls to Get Information About a File

The ls utility has many options. One of these options is the -l (ell) option that instructs ls to display one file or directory name per line and include other information on the same line. The following is an example of the "long" format displayed by the ls command:

```
$ ls -l
drwxrwxrwx    5 sidney    users           4096 Jan 30  2000 Desktop
drwxr-xr--    3 sidney    users           4096 Jun 10 17:54 Nautilus
-rw-rw-rw-    1 sidney    users         115549 Jul 26  2000 iliamna.tiff
drwxrwxrwx    2 sidney    users           4096 Jun  3 12:51 mail
-rw-rw-rw-    1 sidney    users          27390 Jun  4 07:55 mbox
drwxrwxrwx    2 sidney    users           4096 Aug 14  2000 radio
prw-rw----    1 sidney    users              0 Sep 29 07:59 drvmaxl
-rw-rw-rw-    1 sidney    users             95 Mar 22  2000 sig
brw-rw----    1 root      root         2, 120 Jun 25  2000 fd0hd1440
-rw-r--r--    1 sidney    users          74128 Jul 29 07:59 statement.pdf
-rw-rw-rw-    1 sidney    users           6693 Feb  2  2000 x.log
```

The name of the file or directory is listed at the far right. To the left of the name is the date the file was either created or last modified, whichever is more recent. The time of day is included if the date is in the same year as the system clock.

Immediately in front of the date is the file size. The actual information displayed depends on the type of file. In this example, the same size is listed for all directories because each has been allocated a fixed amount of space. The FIFO file (used by two programs to communicate with one another) named drvmaxl is shown as having a size of zero because its normal state is to contain no data. The device node (used to specify the communications interface to a hardware device) named fd0hd1440 has a pair of numbers that relate to the port number and device driver program used to communicate with the hardware. These special file types are described further in Sessions 11 and 12.

Each user is placed in a group that may or may not include other users. In this example, the files are owned by sidney and are in the group named users. The only exception is fd0hd1440, which is owned by the user named root and is also in the group named root. (Now we have four things named "root"!) The default is for a user that owns a file to be in the group that owns the file, but it isn't required.

Notice the number just to the left of the user name, which is the number of links that are currently defined for this particular file. It is possible for a file to appear in more than one directory, and a count must be kept of the links so the system knows when to delete the file. This linking of files is described in Session 11.

The odd-looking letters and dashes on the far left specify the file type and the file permissions. The first character in this ten-character string specifies the file type and is one of the characters described in Table 3-1. You may encounter a letter other than those listed in the table. If you do, you need to consult the documentation for your particular implementation of UNIX. For example, an m is used to indicate the file type for a special shared memory file that is implemented only in XENIX.

Table 3-1   *Characters Indicating File Types*

Character	File Type
-	An ordinary file.
d	A directory.
c	A character special file. This is a device node used to connect to a hardware device that is capable of reading and writing one character at a time, such as a serial port or a keyboard.
b	A block special file. This is a device node used to connect to a hardware device that is capable of reading and writing blocks of data, such as a disk drive or CD-ROM drive.
l	This is a symbolic link. The actual file or directory is in another location in the file system, but the contents can be accessed by this name just as if it were local to this directory.
p	This is a pipe, also called a FIFO. One process can write data to the file while another process reads the data written to it. The reader gets the data in the same order it is written.

The next nine characters in the string display the permissions granted to various users for that file. The permission indicators appear as three groups of three characters each:

- The first group of three characters applies to the user that owns the file.
- The second group of three characters applies to members of the file's group.
- The third group of three characters applies to everyone else.

Three distinct permissions can be granted or denied. Each of these permissions are represented by one of the following three characters:

- The first character in a group of three is r, which indicates that permission to read the file is granted.
- The second character is w, which indicates that permission to write to the file is granted.
- The third character is x, which indicates that execution permission is granted.

If any of the three characters appear as a dash rather than a letter, it indicates that particular permission is denied. The following is an example of a file permissions string:

```
-rwxr--r--
```

The leading dash specifies an ordinary file. The settings for this file allow the owner of the file to read from it, write to it, and execute it as a program. Members of the group, along with everyone else, can read the file but cannot write to it or execute it.

As you might suspect, the owner of the file is normally granted more permissions than the rest of the world. For example, the following permissions string can be used if you want to write a program that anyone else can execute, but only you can change:

```
-rwx--x--x
```

This pattern indicates that the owner has been granted all permissions, but everyone else is limited to running it as a program. They can't even make copies of it because the permission to read the file has been denied.

 If you are denied access to a file, check the permissions of both the file and the directory in which it resides. Suppose for example that you try to execute a program, and you get a "not found" or "access denied" message. Although you may have execution permission for the file, you may be denied execution permission for the directory that contains it.

It is possible to change the ownership and permissions of files and directories, but it generally requires superuser powers, so the process is explained in Session 11 following the su (superuser) command.

Locating Files and Determining File Types

Part of looking around the file system is having the ability to search for a file and, once it has been found, determine its contents. The find utility can be given a file name and then be instructed to search through any number of directories to locate the file. The file utility can peek inside a file and tell you what kind of information it contains. The which utility can be used to determine what would happen if you entered a specific command.

Find

To use the find utility, you must tell it where to start looking, what to look for, and what it should do if it finds what it is looking for. In the following example, find looks in the /usr directory and all of its subdirectories for all files named willy.cpp and then lists the full path name of all of the files it finds. This example shows the command locating two files:

```
$ find /usr -name willy.cpp -print
/usr/fred/willy.cpp
/usr/simpson/devwork/pw/willy.cpp
$ _
```

You can use an asterisk as a special character in the name being sought, but because the asterisk is also a special character to your shell program (as explained in Session 8), it is necessary to prevent the shell from processing it. One technique to make certain that the shell passes the asterisk to the find command is to enclose the name inside quotes. The following command searches through the home directory and all its subdirectories for any file beginning with the letters ma:

```
$ find ~ -name "ma*" -print
/home/arthur/ns_imap/mail.xyz.net
/home/arthur/mail
/home/arthur/spool/mail
$ _
```

If you prefer, you can use the backslash character to *escape* the asterisk. The term "escape" simply refers to the insertion of a special character that forces the character that follows it to be taken literally instead of being interpreted as a special operator. The following command produces the same results as the command in the previous example:

```
$ find $HOME -name ma\* -print
```

The two previous commands differ in the way the home directory is addressed (the HOME environment variable is almost always defined) and in the way the asterisk character is included in the name. As you become more familiar with UNIX, you will find that there is more than one way to do almost everything — everyone selects their personal favorite way to do things.

You can have the find utility execute any command you could enter from the command line, and you can have it execute this command once for each file it locates. The command to delete files is rm (remove). The following find command searches the entire file system, beginning at the root, and deletes every file it finds named core.

```
$ find / -name core -exec rm {} \;
```

The syntax of this command looks a bit odd, and it is this sort of thing that has given UNIX the reputation for being cryptic, but every character on the line has a purpose. The slash immediately following the find command is the name of the root directory, which is where the search begins. For each file that it finds, -exec (instead of -print as in the previous examples) instructs find to execute the command that follows -exec. The pair of brace characters {} instructs find to insert the name of the file that it found, so the rm command is executed once for each file found. Instead of rm, you could actually include any UNIX command that can be entered from the command line.

Because different commands have different numbers of arguments, there is no way for find to know exactly where your command ends, so the command needs to terminate with a semicolon. However, just as with the asterisk earlier, the semicolon has special meaning to the shell, which makes it necessary to use a backslash character to escape the semicolon to prevent the shell from processing it.

The deletion of core files scattered around the system is not just a frivolous example. Depending on the sort of things you do, you could wind up with lots of these files. Whenever a program crashes unexpectedly, the UNIX system takes a snapshot of it and writes that snapshot to a file named core in the current directory. This core file can then be analyzed using a debugger to determine the cause of the program crash. This process is called a *post mortem*, for obvious reasons. Using core files for debugging is a technique used mostly during software development, but a core dump can happen to any program at any time. It is not uncommon for the support group at a software company to ask for the core file that dumped when the program crashed — this can lead them to the exact point of the failure without having to re-create the situation.

File

The file utility can be used to discover what is stored inside a file. You include the name of the file on the command line, and the file will be examined for content. For example:

```
$ file statement.pdf
statement.pdf: PDF document, version 1.2
$ _
```

Note that the file utility completely ignores any meaning that could be derived from the file name. It only looks at the contents of the file to make its determination. You can use an asterisk on the command line to have it identify every file in a directory, as follows:

```
$ file *
CITYWO_1.JPG:          JPEG image data, JFIF standard
Credentials1.doc:      Microsoft Office Document
DUMMI64.ZIP:           Zip archive data, at least v2.0 to extract
Documents:             directory
GWPage.class:          compiled Java class data, version 45.3
GWPage.java:           ASCII Java program text
adv660_tar:            POSIX tar archive
bear.gif:              GIF image data, version 89a, 500 x 630,
ce_install.pdf:        PDF document, version 1.3
error.bmp:             PC bitmap data, Windows 3.x format, 687 x 428 x 24
isbnInquiry.asp:       exported SGML document text
glim.html:             HTML document text
oil.dtd:               XML document text
pcheck:                ASCII text
rc.firewall:           Bourne shell script text executable
```

As you can see from the descriptions output by file, this utility is capable of determining not only the file type but, in several cases, the particular version of the file format, and even some additional information. The file utility is actually a rather small program, yet it is constantly learning about new file formats. The file command is capable of doing all this because it uses magic. Really.

A file named `magic` contains all the information required to identify the files. The `magic` file has traditionally been stored as `/etc/magic`, but you may find it as `/usr/share/magic` on some systems. Every file is made up of binary numbers, no matter what type of file it is. The `magic` file contains a huge table that specifies where to look to find values inside files that can uniquely identify them as being of a certain type. In other words, the `magic` file lists the locations and values of the magic identifying numbers. The `magic` file is amazingly comprehensive because the `file` command has been part of UNIX almost since the beginning, and everybody has always shared their magic information.

Which

Your PATH variable contains a list of directory names, each of which is searched to find any command program you are able to run. It is not uncommon to have the PATH set to search through ten or more directories for every command you enter. You can easily have duplicate commands in different locations along the path. If you want to be sure the correct command is being executed, or if you just want to find out where the command is located, you can use the `which` command. For example, if you want to know where the `date` command is located, ask `which` to find it for you, like this:

```
$ which date
/bin/date
$ _
```

It doesn't matter if other `date` commands exist in other directories along the path you have set because the `which` command locates the one that will execute when you enter its name on the command line.

Done!

REVIEW

In this session, you learn how to move about the file system and some basic techniques for locating files and directories. The underlying structure of the file system is a large tree with every branch eventually connecting to a single root. Permissions settings can be used to prevent and allow different users access to different parts of the file system.

- A set of standard directory names is used, and these names help identify the contents of a directory.
- The `cd` command can be used to move to any location in the file system.
- Special shorthand names are sometimes used for locations like the current directory and the home directory.
- Detailed permissions are defined for every file to control exactly which users are granted which permissions.
- The `find` command can be used to locate any file on the system, and then perform any desired operation on it.
- The `file` command can be used to discover the exact meaning of the contents of a file.

Sessions 11 and 12 contain more information about the UNIX file system. They discuss the file system in more detail and explore its construction and how it is used to accomplish tasks such as networking computers.

QUIZ YOURSELF

1. What is the root directory and what is its full path name? (See "The Basic File Structure.")

2. How is the /tmp directory used? (See "Some standard names.")

3. Describe the fundamental difference between absolute and relative addressing. (See "Absolute and relative path addressing.")

4. What are the three permissions that can be granted or denied on a per-file basis? (See "Using ls to Get Information About a File.")

5. What is the purpose of a core file? (See "Locating Files and Determining File Types.")

The Running Processes

Session Checklist

✔ Listing the running processes

✔ Starting and stopping processes

✔ Orphans and zombies

✔ Fork and exec

**30 Min.
To Go**

The UNIX kernel has number of processes that it keeps in execution at all times. Additionally, each user normally runs several processes at once, and UNIX is a multiuser system. This session shows you how to use the ps utility to take a peek at the processes that are running on your system. The ps program can provide a detailed snapshot of the system status, but you must know how to read its output. Therefore, this session not only describes ps, it also includes descriptions of the parent-child process relationships, the assignment of process ID numbers, and how to send signals to processes from the command line.

Listing the Running Processes

Several processes are always running, being scheduled to run, or loaded and ready to run. Some of these processes are started by the kernel to perform specific duties that keep the operating system going. Others are daemon processes that are waiting to deal with things such as printing or communication. Still others processes are user programs that are crunching data, displaying data, responding to input, or waiting for the completion of a previous request (such as reading a block of data from disk).

A standard utility named ps (process status) can be used to list all the running processes and display information about them. Exactly which processes are included in the list and what information is displayed depends on the options specified on the command line. If you enter the command without options, you get a short list and a short description of the processes that are being run from your login session, which is usually just the shell program. The -e option can be used to generate a list of all processes. The -1 (ell) option can be used to request the long form of the listing, which includes almost all of the available information. Using the -e and -1 options together gives you a fairly complete listing.

The options and display information described here are standard and can be used with ps **in nearly every system, but it seems that every version of UNIX has made its own modifications. For the most part, the information described in this session is displayed, but there is so much information available that many versions of UNIX have other options and custom formats to display them.**

Several types of information can be displayed about a process, so the ps command always lists each process on a separate line and provides column headings to identify the type of information being displayed. The following command gives you a detailed listing of every process running on your system:

```
$ ps -el
  F S   UID    PID  PPID  C PRI  NI ADDR    SZ WCHAN  TTY       TIME CMD
100 S     0      1     0  0  68   0    -   335 do_sel ?     00:00:04 init
040 S     0      2     1  0  68   0    -     0 contex ?     00:00:00 keventd
040 S     0      4     1  0  69   0    -     0 kswapd ?     00:01:01 kswapd
040 S     0    474     1  0  69   0    -   353 do_sel ?     00:00:04 syslogd
140 S     0    548     1  0  69   0    -     0 end    ?     00:06:43 nfsd
040 S     0    549   548  0  69   0    -     0 end    ?     00:00:00 lockd
040 S     0    550   549  0  69   0    -     0 end    ?     00:00:01 rpciod
140 S     0    649     1  0  68   0    -   563 do_sel ?     00:00:00 xinetd
140 S     4    667     1  0  68   0    -   630 do_sel ?     00:00:00 lpd
140 S     0    684     1  0  69   0    -  1037 do_sel ?     00:00:00 httpd
140 S     0    713     1  0  69   0    -  1260 do_sel ?     00:00:00 sendmail
140 S    29    758     1  0  69   0    -   421 do_sel ?     00:00:00 rpc.statd
040 S     0    770     1  0  68   0    -   392 nanosl ?     00:00:00 crond
100 S     0    844     1  0  69   0    -   328 read_c tty5  00:00:00 mingetty
100 S     0    845     1  0  69   0    -   328 read_c tty6  00:00:00 mingetty
100 S     0    848     1  0  69   0    -   576 wait4  tty1  00:00:00 login
100 S     0    849   848  0  69   0    -   613 read_c tty1  00:00:00 bash
100 S     0    931     1  0  69   0    -  1254 do_pol ?     00:00:00 gdm
140 S     0    936   931  0  69   0    -  1413 wait4  ?     00:00:00 gdm
100 S     0    937   936  0  70   0    -  4166 do_sel ?     02:53:59 X
100 S   502    944   936  0  69   0    -  1704 do_pol ?     00:00:02 gnome-ses
000 S   502    998     1  0  69   0    -  1959 do_pol ?     00:01:16 gnome-ter
000 S   502   1006   998  0  69   0    -   344 unix_s ?     00:00:00 gnome-pty
000 S   502  15683   998  0  70   0    -   555 wait4  pts/1 00:00:00 bash
140 S     0  21358     1  0  68   0    -   460 do_sel ?     00:00:00 pppd
000 S   502  21564     1  0  69   0    -  6424 do_sel ?     00:00:43 netscape-
000 S   502  21588 21564  0  68   0    -  4307 do_sel ?     00:00:00 netscape-
000 R   502  21720 15683  0  76   0    -   746 -      pts/1 00:00:00 ps
```

The number of processes in this list is not out of the ordinary. In a UNIX system that supports several users, it is common to have hundreds of processes running. In fact, if you use this command on your system, your list will probably contain quite a few more processes than the one shown here since over half the processes in this list were deleted.

Using the `ps -el` **command normally produces more text than can be displayed on the screen. so to make it possible to view all the text you can enter the command as follows:**

`$ ps -el | more`

You can then use the space bar or the Return key to scroll the text up the screen. Session 7 has more information on controlling command output.

The information shown in the list is from a snapshot of the processes running at a single point in time. Although all the listed processes were running when ps took the snapshot, by the time the listing was formatted and displayed, the system had moved on to something else and the status of some of the processes had changed.

The CMD (command) column on the far right displays the name of the process, which is the same as the command that was used to start the process running. Note that newest command listed — the one at the bottom of the list — is the ps process taking a snapshot of itself as it generates the listing.

The column labeled F (flags) contains information describing the current status of the process. Because you rarely actually need the information in this column, it is simply presented as flag bits. The meanings of the flags vary widely from one system to the next, but the set of flags is used to indicate such things as a process being in transition from one state to another or that a debugger has been attached to the process and is tracing its progress.

The column labeled S (status) specifies the current status of a process as a single character. The letter S indicates that a process is sleeping, waiting for something to happen. The letter R indicates that a process is currently running. This snapshot was taken by the ps process, which appears at the very bottom of the list, and is the only process with an R status because it was the only one running at the moment the snapshot was taken. If the computer had more than one hardware processor there may have been more processes with a status of R. In a computer with a single CPU there can only be one process running at any given moment. The letter Z (which stands for zombie) appears in this column if a process has died but is still hanging around trying to report its exit status. Zombies are discussed later in this session.

The UID (user ID) column specifies the owner of the process. As with files and directories, every process is owned by one user. A unique ID number identifies every user. When the ps command generates a list of running processes, users are identified with an ID number unless you specify the -f option, which causes users to be listed by name. The super user always has an ID number of 0, but the other ID numbers can be almost anything. User ID numbers are assigned by the system administrator when new users are added to the system. You can conclude, by looking at the UID numbers in the example, a user with an ID number of 502 is logged in because 502 is the UID number listed as the owner of a bash shell process, a netscape browser, and even the ps command that generated the list.

The PID (process ID) is a number that uniquely identifies a process. Every process in UNIX is assigned a unique number when it started. You can see, at the top of the list, that the process named init that has a PID of 1. The kernel starts the init process when the system boots. The init process always has a PID number of 1 and is responsible for starting all other processes. The PID numbers are assigned consecutively to processes, beginning with 1 and continuing until it reaches a maximum possible value (usually 32,767, which is the maximum value of a 16-bit number). At this point, the count wraps back around to the beginning and starts over. However, even when the numbers wrap around, no duplication is allowed because the PID must be unique in the system.

The PPID (parent process ID) column contains the PID of the parent process. Because every process (except the kernel itself) is started by another process, and every process has a unique ID number, every process has an ID number for its parent process. As you can see in the listing, the PPID of init is 0, which is the PID of the kernel. Several processes in the list have 1 for a PPID, which is normal because init has the job of starting other processes and often becomes the parent process by default. In fact, all processes can trace their heritage back to init. For example, notice that the parent of process 937 is process 936, which has the parent process 931, which has a parent process number 1.

The C (priority control), PRI (priority), and NI (nice) headings have to do with priorities assigned to various tasks. These values determine how often a process gets a slice of time and the duration of the time slices. The value under the C heading is used in special cases and deals with real-time processor utilization. The PRI value is the priority value assigned to the process — the larger the value, the lower the priority. A utility called nice can be used to specify higher or lower priority when you first start a process. The value in the NI column is the nice value that was used when the process was started.

20 Min. To Go

The ADDR (address) and SZ (size) columns provide information about the memory resident form of the process. The process sizes are usually displayed as a count of the number of 512-byte blocks that it would take to load the entire program into memory. Historically, the memory address of a running process had meaning, but with some modern computers the information may not even be available. A hardware device called the MMU (memory management unit) works as a companion to the CPU to position programs in memory and map virtual addresses to physical addresses. With all of this memory mapping occurring down inside the hardware, the kernel itself may not know where the programs are actually located.

The WCHAN (wait channel) column contains the name of the event that the process waits for while it sleeps. A process may sleep while waiting for input from a disk drive, output to a serial port, input from the keyboard, and so on. As you can see in the sample ps listing, process 936 (which is gdm, a graphics-based login prompt) is sleeping while waiting for wait4, which is keyboard input. The same is true for process 15638 (which is a shell program called bash). Process 848, a standard login prompt, is also waiting for the keyboard.

The TTY (teletype) column specifies which terminal the process is attached to. It is not required for a process to be attached to a terminal, and if a process is not attached to a terminal, a question mark is shown in the column. In the example, the processes are associated with four different terminals. Two processes are attached to tty1, two more to pts/1, one to tty5, and one to tty6. Most terminal connections have names that begin with tty because UNIX is old enough that the first terminals were teletype machines. The first terminals that didn't use paper for output were known as *glass teletypes*.

The TIME column is the accumulated amount of CPU time used by the process. The example ps listing was made on a system that had been running for about a month, so the times are relatively small. The init process, for example, had only been able to accumulate four seconds. Process 4, kswapd, is the kernel's daemon responsible for managing the swap space for all processes, only used one minute. Process 937, named X, is the X Window System process responsible for the Graphical User Interface (GUI), so it managed to accumulate almost three hours of CPU time. Process 548 is a networking daemon that is responsible for managing the shared file systems, and it is also relatively busy, having accumulated almost seven minutes.

Starting and Stopping Processes

You already know how to start a process running. All you have to do is enter the name on the command line and press Return. If the shell program can locate an executable file by the name you enter, it will be started. The process runs until it is finished, and then the shell prompts you for another command. Entering a command this way is the way things normally work, but there are some other ways to do things. It is also possible to start a process with a lower (or higher) priority setting than other processes, causing it to get a smaller (or larger) share of the CPU time. You can also run processes in the background so that you can get your shell prompt back and start issuing other commands while the process is off doing its job. This session also explains how to stop a process in case you change your mind or the process starts doing things you don't want it to do.

Background processes

To start a process running in the background, you do the same you would do to start it running in the foreground, except that you end the command line with an ampersand (&). For example, if you want to find all the files named core in the /home directory tree and have rm delete each one, you could do it this way:

```
find /home -name core -exec rm {} \;
```

If a lot of directories and files need to be searched, the command may take a long time to run, so you may want to run it in the background by adding an ampersand on the end of the command, like this:

```
find /home -name core -exec rm {} \; &
```

The shell accepts your command and spins the program off as a background task. The shell also displays a number (the PID number of the new process) and returns with a prompt. You are free to do anything else you want to do. If the process takes long enough to run that you can enter another command, you can use ps to check its status.

Priority setting with nice

If you start a process that you think may run for a while and consume a large amount of system resources, it is not necessary to let it bog down the entire system. This is especially useful if other people are logged in at the same time. It is best to be nice and have your process run so that it makes way for other processes (such as user shells) that may also be running.

Suppose, for example, that you want to use find to search through every directory on the system and delete all files named fred.workfile. This task will take some time and could slow the system down noticeably, but you can have it make way for other processes by running it like this:

```
nice find / -name fred.workfile -exec rm {} \; &
```

There are different priority settings for `nice`. The complete range is from 1 to 19, with 19 being the lowest priority. The default setting is 10. To have the `find` command run at the lowest possible priority, you can enter it this way:

```
nice -19 find / -name fred.workfile -exec rm {} \; &
```

You can also raise the priority of a process by using negative values, but you have to be the superuser to have the permission to do it. The maximum priority setting is –20. To enter a negative number, you need to use two minus signs, as in this example, which sets the value to –10:

```
nice --10 find / -name fred.workfile -exec rm {} \; &
```

Signals

One of the fundamental concepts of UNIX is the ability for one process to send a *signal* to another. When a process receives a signal, it immediately stops whatever it is doing and acknowledges the signal. If a running process does not do something to acknowledge receipt of the signal, the process is immediately terminated by the system. The process can do whatever it wants to do when it receives a signal, including simply discarding it. Actually, there is one signal a process can't discard, but that is discussed momentarily.

Quite a few of these signals are defined in UNIX, and both a number and a name identify each one. Depending on the version of UNIX, there may be 60 or more distinct signals, but rarely do you find fewer than the 19 basic signals. Table 4-1 lists the 19 common signals by both name and number. As you can see from the descriptions in the table, a process can cause a signal to be sent to itself by trying to do something it shouldn't, such as using an invalid address or executing a bad floating point operation. Sending signals is part of the mechanism by which the kernel protects itself and other processes from programs that try to break the rules. But signals have many other purposes.

A signal is a very simple thing. The only information that accompanies a signal when it arrives at a process is its identifying number.

Table 4-1 *UNIX Signals*

Number	Name	Description
1	SIGHUP	Hang up. The external connection to the process has been disconnected.
2	SIGINT	Interrupt. This signal can be generated by entering Control+C on the keyboard and is normally used to terminate the process.
3	SIGQUIT	Quit. This signal can be generated by entering Control+\ on the keyboard.

Number	Name	Description
4	SIGILL	Illegal instruction. An invalid machine level instruction was encountered while executing the program.
5	SIGTRAP	Trace trap. Used by debugging software to detect breakpoints set in a running process.
6	SIGABRT	Abort. A process may send this signal to itself by the abort() system call to cause a tidy shutdown.
7	SIGEMT	Emulation trap. Often not implemented.
8	SIGFPE	Floating point exception. Some invalid floating point operation has occurred, such as an attempt to divide by zero.
9	SIGKILL	Kill. The process is killed. The process receiving this signal cannot block it.
10	SIGBUS	Bus error. Indicates there has been some kind of hardware error.
11	SIGSEGV	Segmentation violation. The process attempted to access memory outside of its allocated address space.
12	SIGSYS	System call. An invalid system call has been made. Not implemented on all systems.
13	SIGPIPE	Broken pipe. An attempt was made to write to a pipe that had no reader at the other end.
14	SIGALRM	Alarm. The process set a timer that has expired.
15	SIGTERM	Termination. This process is instructed to terminate.
16	SIGUSR1	User signal number 1.
17	SIGUSR2	User signal number 2.
18	SIGCHLD	Child status. A child process has stopped or has been terminated.
19	SIGPWR	Power failure and restart.

Every modern UNIX system adds some of its own signals to those listed in Table 4-1. You may also find that some of the signals with numbers higher than 15 use different names than the ones shown in the table, but the ones listed are the fundamental signals that have been a part of UNIX since the early 1980s. Changes are made because of advances in the underlying hardware and in the operation and design of operating systems. In light of the fact that UNIX originated with AT&T, it is fitting that the first signal indicates that a telephone connection has been broken.

Signaling a process

**10 Min.
To Go**

Sometimes a process gets stuck and needs to be shut down. The only way to halt a process is to send it a signal. Thus, if you are running a process from the command line, you can stop it by entering Ctrl+C, which instructs the shell to send a SIGINT signal to the process. The signal immediately stops the process from running unless the process does something internally to prevent it, such as acknowledging the signal and discarding it.

> **Most processes close down cleanly upon receipt of a recognized signal. A well-written UNIX application is ready for incoming signals and responds by flushing any data it is holding to disk and closing all files before shutting down. Sadly, not all processes are well written.**

You can kill a background process as long as you know its ID number. The following command sends a SIGTERM signal to a process with a PID of 876:

```
$ kill 876
```

Although SIGTERM (signal 15) is the default signal issued from the kill command, you can send any signal you want. The following example sends a SIGHUP signal to process 876:

```
$ kill -HUP 876
```

You can also send a signal using its number. The following example sends a SIGKILL (signal 9) to process 876:

```
$ kill -9 876
```

SIGKILL is unique. It is the only signal that cannot be blocked or redirected by the process that receives it: SIGKILL always kills its target process. The disadvantage to this is that the process doesn't have the opportunity to clean up behind itself, making it possible to leave corrupt files or incomplete data on disk. If you need to kill a process, it is best to start with the friendlier form and only resort to SIGKILL if you can't get the job done any other way.

Before you can kill a process, you must have permission to do so. If the root user has started a process, only the root user can kill it. Unless two users are in the same group, one is not able to halt a process started by the other. This is both a safety and security feature, making it difficult for someone to break into the system and start processes of their own that look like system processes.

The kill command has one other feature. By using the -l (ell) option, you can get a complete list of all signals defined for your system, like this:

```
$ kill -l
```

Orphans and Zombies

Recall that every process is the child of another process, and all processes can trace their heritage back to init. Whenever a process finishes running (or is killed), a status code is sent to its parent process indicating the circumstances under which the child program died. This status code is usually a simple code that indicates either success or failure on the part of the program issuing the status. A zero indicates success while any other number indicates failure. The non-zero status code can also be a number indicating a particular kind of failure. The status code is delivered from the dying child to its parent process, which means the relationships among the processes in the tree must be maintained so that the status codes can be delivered properly.

If the parent of a process dies, the process becomes an *orphan*. The orphan process continues to run, but it must have a parent process that can receive its status report when it dies, so init immediately adopts the process. The init process listens carefully and patiently to all of its children, including the adopted ones, and dutifully accepts the status codes from each and every one as they finish their tasks and die. The init process doesn't do anything with the status code — it just throws it away — but the recently demised child process doesn't know this. The orphan happily fades away, knowing it has done its duty.

The opposite of an orphan is a *zombie*. A zombie is a child process that has died, but its parent is not listening for the status code. The defunct child remains in the process list, with the same process ID it has always had, waiting patiently for its parent to accept the status code that it is trying to send. Every process that produces children has the responsibility of continuously listening for messages from its dead child processes, even if the parent doesn't care about the concluding status of the child.

Nothing can be done for a zombie except kill its parent. Once the parent is dead, the child is adopted by init and, because init is a good parent that listens to its children, the status message is delivered and the zombie disappears. Parent processes that create zombies should be fixed so that they no longer create child processes or so that they start listening to their children when they want to report a status.

The ps command never displays an orphan because init always adopts them immediately. However, you can see zombies in the list. A zombie no longer has a process name, but it is listed as defunct. The entry looks like the following, which shows that the PID of the irresponsible parent is 21564:

```
000 S   502 21588 21564  0 68   0    -  4307         ?       00:00:00 <defunct>
```

Fork and Exec

Starting a new process on a UNIX system is not simply a matter of one program selecting another and starting it running. Starting a new process is a two-step procedure: first, the parent process clones itself, and then the clone morphs into the child process. This is a common thing for your shell program to do, because it happens every time you enter a command for the shell to execute. The following example describes the steps taken by a shell program to spawn a child process:

1. A process named ksh (a Korn shell process) with a PID of 400 wants to start find as another process because find has just been entered from the command line. To do this, ksh starts by making a fork() system call.

2. The fork() system call causes the creation of a new ksh process. These two processes are identical — same files, same data, same everything — except that they have different PID numbers. The new process has been assigned, say, 500 for its PID.

3. The original ksh looks at its PID and discovers that it is still 400. It goes on its merry way and continues to be ksh.

4. The clone ksh notices that its PID has become 500, so it knows it is the clone. It also knows that the clone must change into the new process. To make this change, it makes a system call named exec(), supplying the system call with the name of the process that the clone wants to become.

5. The system call morphs the ksh clone into find. All open files are forgotten, the old data and code for ksh is abandoned, and new data and code for find is loaded. The find code is put into execution. It is now a find process.

Done!

REVIEW

In this session, you learn how to use ps to examine the processes currently running on the system. A great deal of information is available about UNIX processes, and if you have a fundamental understanding of how the system works, the list of processes provides a fairly clear snapshot of the system's status.

- The process ID numbers link all processes into the same tree.
- The origins of all processes can be found by tracing the parent/child relationships in the process tree.
- Most of the processes are running in the background and waiting for the arrival of a command or event to begin processing.
- A user owns a process, and access to the process is controlled by permissions that are similar to the permissions used for files.
- Every running process has a priority level that can be adjusted to some extent when a process is initiated.
- A process can be sent signals to indicate certain exceptional events or to instruct the process to halt.
- Definite procedures are followed to keep the tree of processes intact whenever a process dies.

The following session starts investigating the operations of the shell in more depth. The shell is capable of making commands work better, but you must know what the shell is doing with the commands you enter. Certain characteristics and values are defined automatically when you log in, and you need to know how to set these values and how these values affect the shell and other processes.

QUIZ YOURSELF

1. What are the UID, PID, and PPID? (See "Listing the Running Processes.")

2. How can a process be started so that it doesn't block the shell prompt? (See "Background processes.")

3. What value is used to set a process at the lowest possible priority level? (See "Priority setting with nice.")

4. What is the default signal sent by the `kill` utility? (See "Signaling a process.")

5. What is an orphan process and what is a zombie process? (See "Orphans and Zombies.")

PART

I

Friday Evening
Part Review

1. What was the name of the corporation where UNIX was first written? What prevented that company from selling UNIX for several years?

2. Name at least three fundamental functions of the UNIX kernel.

3. What does UNIX do that makes it so difficult for a process to crash the system or interfere with other processes?

4. What is a UNIX shell?

5. What is Telnet?

6. What is the standard configuration of a graphic window login dialog box?

7. What would you do to add a directory full of executable programs to those available to be entered and run at the command line prompt?

8. What is a hidden file and how can you display its name?

9. What is the purpose of the echo command?

10. What is the purpose of the who command?

11. Every UNIX system has more than one directory named bin. What sort of files do they contain?

12. If you use two dots (. .) to refer to your home directory, what does that tell you about your current directory?

13. File permissions can be set specifically for the owner of a file. Who else can permissions be set for?

14. What special circumstance must be taken into consideration when using an asterisk to specify the file names to be located by the find command?

15. How does the file command determine the meaning of a file's contents?

16. What is the purpose of the ps command?

17. What is the difference between a PID and a PPID?

18. What do you need to do to request that a command be run as a background process?

19. If you need to halt a process that has a PID number of 5211, but it refuses to respond to the default kill signal, what command can you enter to ensure the kill?

20. What circumstance will cause a process to become a zombie?

☑ Friday

☑ **Saturday**

☐ Sunday

Part II — Saturday Morning

Session 5
Introduction to the vi Editor

Session 6
Introduction to the emacs Editor

Session 7
Fundamentals of the Bourne Shell

Session 8
Using the Bourne Shell

Session 9
Using Other Shells

Session 10
Regular Expressions

Part III — Saturday Afternoon

Session 11
Files and the File System

Session 12
File System Operations

Session 13
The World's Handiest Utilities

Session 14
The man Pages

Session 15
E-mail

Session 16
Writing Shell Scripts

Part IV — Saturday Evening

Session 17
Shell Scripts with Conditionals

Session 18
Shell Scripts with Loops

Session 19
Users and the passwd File

Session 20
Batch Editing

PART

II

Saturday
Morning

Session 5
Introduction to the vi Editor

Session 6
Introduction to the emacs Editor

Session 7
Fundamentals of the Bourne Shell

Session 8
Using the Bourne Shell

Session 9
Using Other Shells

Session 10
Regular Expressions

Introduction to the vi Editor

Session Checklist

✔ From line editor to screen editor

✔ Creating a new file

✔ Editing text

✔ Searching through the text

✔ Setting options

✔ A summary of vi commands

**30 Min.
To Go**

The vi (visual) editor is the standard UNIX editor and is a fundamental part of UNIX, so you will find that it is installed on every system. The purpose of a text editor is to create and modify simple text files. Editing text files happens a lot on UNIX because virtually all of the system configuration and documentation is contained in text files and programmers write source code as simple text files. In fact, almost everything you do when working with UNIX involves using a text editor.

This session describes the standard vi editor and demonstrates how some of its commands work. While vi is part of UNIX, other editors are available, such as emacs (the subject of Session 6). Exact numbers are not available, but the UNIX world seems to be evenly divided between vi and emacs with all other editors trailing far behind. The vi and emacs editors are so fundamentally different that there is no practical way to compare them — the decision to use one or the other is a matter of personal taste, based on the way you like to work. Everyone has a strong opinion about text editors. People tend to choose one editor and stay with it forever; religious wars sometimes break out over discussions about why one editor is better than the other.

From Line Editor to Screen Editor

The vi editor is what is known as a *modal* editor. During the process of editing a file, it is necessary to switch among three different modes of operation. In order to understand how and why vi works, you must first know how it developed.

The first UNIX editor was named ed. The ed editor was a line-based editor that would respond to a command instructing it to perform an action, perform the action, and then prompt you for another command. The only way to view the text (since you couldn't scroll through it) was to enter a command specifying the lines you wanted to see, and ed would display the selected lines on the terminal. This kind of editing made sense when working with terminals that printed lines on paper, but with the innovation of terminals that could position lines of text on a screen, it became technically possible to use a full-screen editor.

The conversion of ed to an interactive editor presented some interesting problems. Many different brands and models of terminals were in use, all of which used different code sequences to move the cursor, scroll text, clear the screen, and so on. A single UNIX computer often had a mixture of different types of terminals. The variety of keyboard layouts added to the problem. Some keyboards had arrow keys and function keys, and some didn't. About the only thing you could count on were keys that could produce the standard ASCII character set. This is why the Ctrl key was invented, which made it possible for terminals to produce the otherwise invisible ASCII control characters such as tab, backspace, and end-of-text. Another problem was the fact that everyone was familiar with ed — they didn't want to give up the command line capability they had all become accustomed to.

To develop a screen editor, the first hurdle was to provide the ability to control the display. Standardizing the set of cursor control sequences within the editor solved this problem. The cursor control sequences to and from the terminals were then translated into these standard sequences. The translation is performed according to a terminal description table stored in a file named /etc/termcap (terminal capabilities). Each login session specifies a configuration setting that defines its terminal type, thus informing the vi editor which set of termcap translations to use. This same translation process is still used today for dumb terminals, although most modern UNIX systems use a terminfo (terminal information) database as a more efficient way to store and retrieve the information previously stored in the /etc/termcap file.

Many applications other than vi **use** termcap **and** terminfo, **so both are always present on a UNIX system whether or not dumb terminals are present. The control-sequence mapping is performed inside a standard library package known as** curses.

The next problem to be solved was cursor navigation under control of the keyboard. It was easy enough to invent commands to scroll through the text, move the cursor, and insert text for terminals with function and arrow keys, but many terminals didn't have these keys. The only solution was to use regular ASCII characters to control the cursor, which is exactly what vi does. The vi editor responds properly to the arrow keys if you use them, and you can even assign commands to the function keys, but the regular character keys are used for navigation. Four keys control the basic cursor movements:

- Press h to move the cursor to the left.
- Press j to move the cursor down one line.

- Press k to move the cursor up one line.
- Press l to move the cursor to the right.

These four keys were not chosen arbitrarily. On the very first terminals — known as glass teletypes — the cursor movement keys were Ctrl+H, Ctrl+J, Ctrl+K, and Ctrl+L.

The last problem to solve was to devise a way to enter commands from a prompt. To do this, the bottom line of the vi display is always left blank, unless a status message is being displayed or the editor is switched into command line mode. In command line mode, a colon appears as the prompt, and the cursor is positioned to the right of the colon, waiting for input. It became necessary to add some new commands to ed to perform some actions required by the new editor. As a result the original version of ed was left intact (it is still included with every UNIX system), and an extended version of ed was created that was the basis of vi. The extended version of ed is called ex. In fact, in the middle 1980s, the vi editor was referred to as the vi/ex editor.

The ability to switch from one mode to another is accomplished by making the navigation mode the default mode and providing capabilities for switching to either of the other two modes and back to the navigation mode. Thus, there are four possible mode changes:

- **Navigation mode to edit mode** — This mode change is made by entering any one of the text insertion characters, such as i (insert at the current cursor location), o (open a new line beneath this one), 0 (open a new line above this one), or A (append to the end of the line). Some additional insertion characters are described later in this session.
- **Edit mode to navigation mode** — Press the Esc key. It's okay to press it more than once; it won't do anything while you're in the navigation mode (except possibly cause a beep).
- **Navigation mode to command line mode** — Type a colon. The cursor should immediately move to the bottom line and prompt for input.
- **Command line mode to navigation mode** — When you enter your command and press Return, the command executes, the command line is cleared, and navigation mode resumes right where it left off. If you decide not to enter a command, simply backspace over the colon prompt.

Switching modes is much simpler than it may seem from the description. After you use it for a bit you begin to see the pattern of how it all works.

Many versions of vi exist. Some are variations on the original, with changes made according to someone's preferences, or with some adjustments made so that the editor could fit the characteristics of another operating system. Some versions are the same basic editor as vi, with the addition of new commands and options.

Creating a New File

A fundamental edit session consists of opening (or creating) a file, entering and changing text, and finally, saving the file. An edit session can be started by specifying the name of the file on the command line, like this:

```
$ vi index.html
```

If the file doesn't exist, the screen clears, the cursor goes to the top line, and a message like the following appears on the bottom line:

```
"index.html" [New File]
```

The first column of each line is a tilde character (~), which is a marker indicating that the line does not exist. A blank line simply appears to be blank, but a missing line is always marked with a tilde. If the file you are editing already exists, the screen fills with the text from the file, and any leftover screen space below the text is marked with leading tilde characters. The editor starts out in navigation mode, but if there is no text, there is no place for the cursor to go. If you try the navigation keys when there is no text, the cursor does not move, and you are probably rewarded with a beep.

To insert text, enter the letter i to switch to edit mode and start typing. If you make a mistake, you can back up by using Ctrl+H or the Backspace key. Whenever you get to the end of a line, you can go to the next line by pressing the Return key. You can continue this way until you have entered several lines of text. I suggest that you create a file with some text and experiment with the commands as you go through the session. For practice, enter the following text to create a simple HTML file:

```
<html>
<head>
  <title>A bare bones home page</title>
</head>
<body>
The body contains nothing other than a line of text.
</body>
</html>
```

**20 Min.
To Go**

After you have entered all the text you need, you can switch back to the navigation mode by pressing the Esc key. You can press Esc more than once to make sure you have changed modes, because a beep usually informs you if you are already in navigation mode. There is no visible indicator to let you know which mode the editor is in, so the beep can be useful until you become accustomed to vi.

To write your text to a disk file, you can use an ex command by typing a colon and a w (write), and then pressing the Return key. The colon character switches to command line mode. After you have entered the w command, the line at the bottom of the screen looks like this:

```
:w
```

You can use another ex command to halt the editor. Simply enter a colon and a q (quit) and then press Return, as follows:

```
:q
```

The editor has a nice little safety feature to help prevent you from accidentally discarding edits. If you enter the :q command before saving your last change, nothing happens and you get a message telling you that nothing has been saved since the last change. However, if you insist, vi lets you discard the changes and quit. To insist, add an exclamation point, as in the following:

```
:q!
```

You can add the exclamation point to any of the ex commands to overcome obstacles. For example, if the permission settings on a file do not allow you to write to it, which prevents you from saving your work, you can often override the permission settings by entering the command this way:

```
:w!
```

However, if another user owns the file and you are not able to change its permissions, no amount of insisting can force vi to overwrite the existing file. Instead, you can save the text into another file by specifying another name, like this:

```
:w frammis.html
```

You can enter a single command that both saves the file and quits the editor. From the navigation mode, hold down the Shift key and enter the two characters ZZ. This immediately writes the file to disk and exits from the editor. This command is relatively safe because it is something you would probably never enter by accident.

Editing Text

When you make a change to an existing file, you start out exactly the same way you would if you were going to create the file from scratch:

```
$ vi index.html
```

This command loads the file and places the editor in navigation mode. You can use the h, j, k, and l to move around the text and place the cursor anywhere that text is displayed on the screen. If you move the cursor beyond the top or bottom of the screen, the text scrolls to make the new line visible. Entering the letter G moves the cursor to the last line of the text, even if it has to scroll several pages to get there. Using a number in front of G moves the cursor to a specific line number. For example, entering 1G moves to the first line.

A couple of other navigation characters that can come in handy are $ and ^. Entering a $ moves the cursor to the end of the current line, and entering a ^ moves the cursor to the beginning of the current line.

 Be aware that all the vi and ex commands are case-sensitive. A change of case is a complete change of command. For example, the lowercase i switches to edit mode at the current cursor location, but an uppercase I moves the cursor to the first nonblank character on the line and starts insertion mode there.

Line operations

There are two basic ways to add a new line starting from the navigation mode. If you enter the letter o (open below), an empty line is opened below the line with the cursor, and you are in edit mode ready to insert text at the beginning of the new line. If you enter the letter O (open above), a new empty line appears above the current line.

If you are in edit mode, pressing the Return key starts a new line. If you want to split a line into two lines, go into navigation mode, position the cursor on the character that you want to become the start of a new line, and enter i to switch to edit mode. Press Return to split the line. At this point, you are still in edit mode, so you can either enter some new text or press Esc.

To delete an entire line, simply place the cursor on the line and enter dd. The line disappears, and the line below it closes up to fill the space. But the line isn't gone forever. When it was deleted, a copy was stored in a location called the *yank buffer*. Whenever a line, word, character, or anything else is deleted from the text, it is copied into the yank buffer. The p command reads the text in the yank buffer and inserts it at the current cursor location. You can use the p command repeatedly to insert multiple copies of the yanked text.

One thing that seems to come up a lot in programming is the need to reverse the position of a couple of lines. To reverse two lines, place the cursor on the first of the two lines and type ddp. The dd command copies the line to the yank buffer, deletes it, and scrolls the text below the deleted line up one position so that it is now the line with the cursor. The p command then inserts the yanked line beneath the current line, causing the two lines to be reversed.

You do not need to delete a line to place a copy it in the yank buffer; you can just yank it using the yy command. Once it has been yanked, you can use p to insert a copy of it wherever you like. The three-letter sequence yyp duplicates the current line. As long as you keep pressing p, you keep getting copies of the line at the current cursor location.

You can put multipliers in front of commands to have them repeat a number of times. For example, to delete 12 lines you can enter 12dd. To yank 3 lines, you can enter 3yy. Each block of deleted or yanked lines is stored in the yank buffer (overwriting whatever was stored there before), so the p command copies back the most recently yanked text as a single block.

Any time you make a mistake and want to correct it, you can undo the most recent operation by entering u. **The original** vi **editor could only undo the most recent operation. Some of the newer versions of the editor have implemented multiple levels of undo so that repeatedly entering** u **backs out a number of edits one by one.**

By placing the cursor at the point in a line where you want to make a change, entering c$ puts you in edit mode, and whatever you type replaces everything from the cursor position to the end of the line. Similarly, c^ replaces everything from the beginning of the line to the cursor position with any text that you enter.

A convenient indention operator can be used to shift entire lines, or blocks of lines, to the left or right. Entering the character pair >> shifts the current line to the right by one tab stop. Entering the character pair << shifts the current line to the left. You can put numbers in front of the operators to shift more than one line at a time. For example, to indent the six lines starting with the one at the cursor, enter 6>>.

Word operations

The vi editor does a creditable job of detecting the beginning and ending of words, and it provides some operators you can use to manipulate words in the text. A word always starts with the character at the cursor and continues to the right until the end of the word is found. Basically, a word is a group of letters and numbers starting at the cursor and followed by a character that is not a letter or a number. In the case of a sequence of punctuation characters, everything from the cursor position to the first nonpunctuation character is taken as a word.

You can move the cursor from its current position to the beginning of the next word by entering w (word). Repeatedly entering w causes the cursor to jump from one word to the next through your document.

You can also make changes based on words. The command dw (delete word) deletes the characters from the current location to the end of the word. As in the earlier delete operations, the deleted characters are stored in the yank buffer and can be inserted anywhere with the p command. The command cw (change word) switches into edit mode, and everything you enter replaces the characters in the current word.

Numbers can be used as modifiers for both cw and dw. For example, if you enter 4cw, vi switches to edit mode, and whatever you type replaces exactly four words. When you use a number to modify a command, the display indicates where the word ends so that you know what you are replacing. Some versions of vi mark the end of the text being replaced by inserting a $ character, and other versions simply delete the characters and act as if you had entered the i command.

Character operations

To delete a single character, enter x. The editor doesn't change modes, but the character under the cursor is removed. You can precede the x command with a count of the number of characters to delete. For example, to immediately delete the five characters that begin with the one at the cursor position you can enter 5x.

When you delete a character, it is copied to the yank buffer and is restored when you enter p. Because the x command deletes the character at the cursor, and the p command inserts text directly to the right of the cursor, the xp command reverses the positions of the two characters at the current cursor position.

To overwrite a single character, enter r and the next character you type replaces the single character at the cursor. You can also use a multiplier by entering a number in front of the r command. For example, if you enter 3r the next three characters are all replaced by the single character you type.

Searching Through the Text

**10 Min.
To Go**

The slash character (/) and the question mark (?) can be used to search through the text to find a matching string of characters. The slash searches forward, and the question mark searches backward. When you enter a search command, it appears on the bottom line much like an ex command does. For example, to search forward in the text for the next occurrence of "home," enter a slash followed by the characters you want to find, and the bottom line will look like this:

```
/home
```

When you press the Return key, the search starts from the current cursor position and scans the text forward until the string of characters is found or until a "not found" message is displayed. To repeat the same search, type n (next), and the search picks up where it left off. To search in the opposite direction, use the question mark character to start the search, like this:

```
?home
```

The search is circular. When the search scan reaches the bottom of the document, it continues after wrapping around to the top. Or, if the search is moving up, it continues by wrapping around from the top to the bottom. One of the optional settings, described in the next section, is to prevent the search from wrapping around when it reaches the end of the document.

By default, all searches are case sensitive, but you can modify that situation (as well as add other search criteria) by using a regular expression.

 Regular expressions are described in Session 10.

Setting Options

A number of options can be set to change the way vi works. Each new version of vi seems to have more options available. To see all the options, along with their current settings, enter the following:

```
:set all
```

To see only the options that are currently set to something other than their default value, enter the following:

```
:set
```

You can use the :set command to dynamically change an option while you are editing. For example, the default is to have the search scan wrap around the top or bottom of the file and continue, but you can use the following command to disable wrapping:

```
:set nowrapscan
```

It can be turned on again with this command:

```
:set wrapscan
```

A number of options can be set on or off this way. The name of each setting is used to turn the option off by adding no in front of its name. For example, if you want your editor to automatically indent when writing programs, enter the command :set autoindent, or if you decide to turn off automatic indentation, enter the command :set noautoindent.

Sometimes, a specific value is associated with a command, so instead of simply indicating yes or no, it is necessary to supply a value. For example, the default tab setting is 8, but if you want to change it to 4, enter the following:

```
:set tabstop=4
```

As you become familiar with the editor, you will find that you want to have certain settings preset. This can be done by placing the commands in a configuration file in your home directory. This file is named .exrc for the traditional vi editor, but other versions of vi use other file names. For example, the very popular vim editor uses .vimrc for its configuration file name. Whenever the vi editor starts, it looks in your home directory for the file and executes the commands it finds there. The file contains a series of set commands just like you would enter them from inside the editor. For example:

```
set shiftwidth=4
set tabstop=4
set nowrapscan
```

This collection of set commands causes the shift commands << and >> to move the current line by 4 characters instead of 8, the text is displayed with tabs expanded to 4 spaces, and search scans stop when they come to the top or bottom of the text.

A Summary of vi Commands

This session describes many of the basic vi commands, and when learning a new editor these command are hard to remember. Table 5-1 lists all of the commands described in this session (plus a few others), which is certainly sufficient to perform the fundamentals of editing text. You should be aware that this list is just the tip of the iceberg. The vi editor has many more commands than the ones described here. You can read the entire list by entering man vi.

Table 5-1   *The vi Editing Commands*

Command	Action
.	Repeat the previous edit operation.
!	If possible, override any safety measures and execute the command.
$	Move the cursor to the end of the current line.
/	Start a string search forward in the text.
?	Start a string search backward in the text.
<<	Shift the current line one tab stop to the left.
>>	Shift the current line one tab stop to the right.
:w	Write the text to the file.
:q	Quit the editor.
Ctrl+U	Scroll the cursor up 12 lines.
Ctrl+D	Scroll the cursor down 12 lines.

Continued

Table 5-1 *Continued*

Command	Action
A	Insert characters starting at the end of the current line.
a	Insert characters starting at the position to the right of the cursor.
c$	Change all characters from the cursor to the end of the line.
c^	Change all characters from the cursor to the beginning of the line.
cw	Change all characters of the current word.
d$	Delete all characters from the cursor to the end of the line.
dd	Delete the current line.
dw	Delete all characters in the current word.
G	Go to the bottom (or the specified) line in the text.
h	Move the cursor one character to the left.
i	Insert characters starting at the current cursor position.
j	Move the cursor down one line.
k	Move the cursor up one line.
l	Move the cursor one character to the right.
n	Find the next string in the same search.
O	Open a new line below the current one.
o	Open a new line below the current one.
p	Insert the characters from the yank buffer into the current location.
u	Undo the previous edit operation.
w	Move the cursor to the beginning of the next word.
x	Delete the character at the current cursor position.
y$	Yank all characters from the cursor to the end of the line.
yw	Yank the characters of the current word.
yy	Yank the entire line.
ZZ	Save the file and exit the editor.

Done!

REVIEW

In this session, you learn how to use the vi editor to create text files and edit their contents. The vi editor developed from earlier forms of text editing software and evolved along with UNIX and its other standard utilities.

- During an edit session, the editor is constantly switched from navigation mode to command line mode or edit mode, and back again.
- You can use any one of several single character commands to move the cursor and scroll the text.
- At any time during the editing of text, the Esc key returns the editor to the navigation mode.
- The colon character is used to switch to the command line editing mode.
- The slash and question mark characters are used as commands to initiate searches through the text.
- Many vi commands other than those presented in this session exist, but the ones discussed here are sufficient for most text editing jobs.

Session 6 takes a look at the UNIX editor named emacs. The origin of emacs is entirely different from that of vi. The emacs editor is a child of the free software movement and was designed, from its beginning, to be a full-screen editor that uses all the keys available on a modern keyboard.

QUIZ YOURSELF

1. Why does vi not require the presence of special keys, such as the function and arrow keys? (See "From Line Editor to Screen Editor.")
2. Which four keys are used to move the cursor by one position, and which key moves the cursor in which direction? (See "From Line Editor to Screen Editor.")
3. Name two different commands that will exit the editor. (See "Creating a New File.")
4. Name two different one-letter commands that start a new line of text. (See "Line operations.")
5. Which two single-character commands are used to initiate a string search through the text? (See "Searching Through the Text.")

Introduction to the emacs Editor

Session Checklist

✔ The emacs editor takes many forms

✔ Creating, editing, and saving files

✔ Screen description and some term definitions

✔ Keys and commands

✔ Searching the text

✔ Summary of basic emacs commands

**30 Min.
To Go**

The emacs (editor macros) text editor originated as one of the first GNU free software development projects. Today, it is still free software, and it runs on many different platforms, including all flavors of UNIX along with MS-DOS and Windows.

The emacs editor is very different from the vi editor. In fact, they take almost opposite approaches to text editing. The most obvious difference is that emacs makes extensive use of the mouse, function keys, arrow keys, and other special keys on the keyboard. The emacs comes preinstalled on most current UNIX systems and is the preferred editor of many programmers.

If you haven't already selected your text editor, you may have a tough decision on your hands.

The emacs Editor Takes Many Forms

The emacs text editor is a product of the Free Software Foundation. This editor is licensed as open software and is available in source code form under the GNU public license.

The name emacs came from the fact that the program originated as a set of macros used to edit text. Down inside, the emacs editor is an interpreter of a version of the Lisp programming language, called *elisp*, that is used to execute editing commands as you enter them. When you enter a key sequence, that sequence selects a macro that is interpreted to make modifications to the text.

While it is primarily known for editing text, emacs has a number of features that enables you to use it as an environment for some of the other work you do. The following features are built into emacs:

- **Tutorial** — An interactive tutorial is provided for beginners. To run the tutorial, start emacs, press Ctrl+H, and then press T. (In emacs notation, that's C-h t.)
- **Character sets** — The emacs editor supports a number of international character sets, including Chinese, Greek, Japanese, Lao, Russian, Thai, Tibetan, Hindi, and the European variants of the Latin alphabet.
- **Word processing** — The editor can be set to recognize and operate on human language elements such as sentences, paragraphs, and pages. It can also manage outlining and formatted text, such as font enhancements, color, postscript, and multiple columns.
- **Programming** — The emacs editor can recognize and assist in the editing of the source code of different programming languages, including C, C++, and Java. From inside emacs, programmers can compile and link programs, as well as execute external programs.
- **Internet** — Software is built into emacs that can be used not only to read and write e-mail messages but to actually send and receive them. The editor also has the capability of reading and writing Usenet news.
- **Calendar** — A built-in desk calendar with a diary is included in emacs and can be used to track projects and schedule events.

The emacs editor continues to grow as free software developers and contributors continuously add features that they would like to have in their own personal editors. Add to this the fact that all emacs commands are based on macros, which makes it relatively easy for you to customize your own set of commands, and the result is a very useful text editing system that has grown in popularity.

Creating, Editing, and Saving Files

This section describes the steps necessary to create a new file, enter some text into the file, save the file to disk, and close the editor. The following command opens a new edit session for the file named index.html:

```
$ emacs index.html
```

If you are in a windowing environment, a window opens that looks like the one shown in Figure 6-1. If you are not using a windowing interface, the screen clears and emacs formats text as shown in Figure 6-2. The two layouts are identical, except for the fact that the menus are available by using the mouse in the graphic environment and the keyboard in the other. In both figures, text has already been entered (on your computer, simply type the text and press Return at the end of each line).

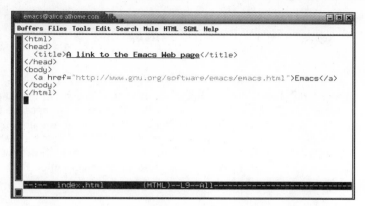

Figure 6-1   *The emacs editor as it appears in a windowing environment*

Figure 6-2   *The emacs editor as it appears in a text environment*

The appearance of the emacs editor in Figures 6-1 and 6-2 demonstrates that emacs is portable. You can use the editor on several different machines (even non-UNIX machines), and it presents the same basic interface. This portability is especially helpful to system administrators, because there is no need to learn a different editor for each type of computer.

The emacs editor can be customized to perform special functions for specific types of text files. Notice the menus called HTML and SGML that appear in the upper-right portion of the display. These two menu selections are normally not present, but in this case, they were automatically loaded and inserted because the suffix on the file name is .html, which indicates the file type. The emacs editor can dynamically load and discard editing commands because all the commands are written in the interpretive elisp language. Thus, adding a new set of commands is simply a matter of loading a collection of macros.

You are probably used to seeing control key entries written as "Ctrl+x" or "Ctrl-x." The emacs notation is shortened to "C-x." As you work with emacs, **and see how these sequences are presented on the display, you will realize the benefit of using the shorter form.**

A new file can be created in another way. You can start emacs without specifying the file name on the command line, and then specify the file name by entering the following sequence:

```
C-x C-f index.html RET
```

At the end of this command, you must press the Return key, as signified by RET in the command string. Many commands don't require a Return key, but this one does because it is the only way emacs can tell that you have finished typing the name. If the file already exists, this command loads and displays the text contained in the file. If it doesn't already exist, emacs does not actually create the file at this point — instead, when you later write the text to a file, the name you specified is the one that is used to create the file.

After the text is entered, you can write it to disk with the following character sequence:

```
C-x C-s
```

All that is left to do is close the editor. To exit emacs, enter the following two character sequences:

```
C-x C-c
```

Unless you have some unfinished operation — such as text that has been edited but not been written to disk — the emacs editor quits immediately when you enter this sequence.

Screen Description and Some Term Definitions

**20 Min.
To Go**

Figures 6-1 and 6-2 are examples of the general layout of the emacs display. The large central area of the screen is called the *window*. The text being edited is displayed in the window. During editing, a cursor marks the location in the text where the next edit is to take place. This location is known as the *point*. You can move the point around the text by using the arrow keys, the mouse, and several special emacs commands (such as M-f, which moves the point forward by one word). As opposed to a cursor, which selects a specific character, the emacs point actually indicates the location between characters, just to the left of the one selected by the cursor being displayed on the screen. This is a subtle difference, but you should be aware of it for certain operations such as splitting lines or inserting text.

The line at the very bottom of the display is the *echo area,* or *minibuffer*. It echoes command keystrokes that would otherwise be invisible. This echo is slightly delayed; as you begin entering a series of keystrokes, nothing appears in the echo area, but if you pause for a second without having completed the command, all the keystrokes you have entered will appear and the rest of the keys will appear as you type them. The result is that if you know a command well enough to enter it without pausing, the command is executed without being echoed, but if you pause during the entry of a command, the characters are echoed to verify that you are typing what you intended to type.

The echo area does more than just echo your input commands. If you enter a command that cannot be executed for some reason, an error message appears in the echo area. Some commands display information in the echo area. For example, if you enter the command sequence C-x =, the echo area displays the name, numeric value, and location in the text of the character just to the right of the point.

Immediately above the echo area is the *mode line*. The mode line provides status information. It always displays the current line number and the percentage of text that lies above the text shown in the window. The mode line also lists active modes of operation. In general, the *major mode* determines the content of the file being edited, and the *minor mode* indicates editing facilities that are turned on or off. For example, a major mode would indicate that text being edited is a programming language, or simply English text. For example, when the file named index.html was loaded, the automatic setting of HTML mode was the setting of a major mode. Examples of minor modes would be such things as having the text automatically saved at regular intervals or running a continuous spell check.

At the very top of the screen is the *menu bar*, which contains the commands that are currently available. The menu items are always available through a series of keystrokes and, if you are in a windowing environment, you can use a mouse to select from the menu. Menu items that end with an ellipsis (. . .) are commands that require you to enter some text from the keyboard before they can be executed.

To select a menu item with the keyboard, press either the control character C-` or the function key F10. Note that the control character uses the grave accent mark (also called the back tic), not the single quote character. At this point, a text window expands at the bottom of the screen that directs you through the menu selection process — when using the keyboard, the menus at the top of the screen will not actually pull down.

Keys and Commands

The emacs commands are all macros that are identified by name. For convenience in editing, special key sequences are mapped to macro names to enable you to execute commands quickly.

You enter emacs commands by typing characters while holding down the Ctrl key or the Meta key. In help messages and on the menus, emacs specifies the Ctrl key with the letter C and the Meta key with the letter M. For example, while C-x means that you should hold down the Ctrl key and press X, M-t means you should hold down the Meta key and press T. A few commands require both. For example, C-M-x means that you should hold down both the Ctrl key and the Meta key and press the letter X.

Not all keyboards are created equal. The Meta key may be labeled Edit or Alt. Thus, M-t means that you should hold down Edit or Alt and press T. An alternative to using the Meta key — in case your keyboard doesn't have one — is to press the Esc key, release it, and then press the letter.

If you are familiar with the ASCII character set, you probably know that there are only 32 control codes (characters that can be entered using the Ctrl key). By reading each individual key as it is pressed, emacs has extended the control codes to include key combinations that normally would have no meaning. For example, C-_, C-5, and C-\ are all valid emacs control characters. Also, unlike ASCII, by keeping track of the current status of Shift, emacs also differentiates between uppercase and lowercase letters. The control codes C-a and C-A are distinct.

Although commands can be executed by one or more of these specially defined keys, the commands also have names. You can also have a command that doesn't have a key sequence defined for it. You can run any command by name:

```
M-x <command name> RET
```

For example, the key sequence to scroll the screen forward is C-v, which executes the macro named scroll-up. To execute this same command by name, enter the following:

```
M-x scroll-up RET
```

If you are in the process of executing a command and you need to stop it, enter C-g. Entering C-g when no command is being executed simply produces a beep, so it is safe to use at any time.

There will come a time when you need help, and fortunately, help is available. Table 6-1 lists some, but not all, of the possible help options. To get to help, you can start the key sequence with C-h, as shown in the table, or, if you prefer, you can use the F1 key.

Table 6-1   *Useful Help Codes*

Key Sequence	Description
C-h ?	Lists all of the help options.
C-h b	Displays the complete list of key sequences and their associated macro names.
C-h c <key>	Displays the name of the command invoked by the key.
C-h C RET	Describes the coding systems (character sets) currently in use for the text.
C-h h	Displays text containing samples of all the available fonts.
C-h I	Runs the info program, which contains the entire emacs manual.
C-h t	Begins the interactive emacs tutorial.
C-h C-c	Displays the text of GNU General Public License, under which the emacs software is licensed.
C-h C-d	Displays information on getting the latest version of emacs.

Searching the Text

**10 Min.
To Go**

Text searches begin at the current point location and move either forward or backward in the text. The following command searches forward from the point until it finds the first occurrence of the string bod:

```
C-s bod
```

The search actually takes place as you enter the characters to be found. That is, when you enter B, the point moves to the next B in the text. When you enter O (given that the B that was already found is not followed by an O), the search immediately moves forward until it finds a BO. The same thing happens when you enter D. The result is a sort of command completion on the search facility that allows you to find text without entering the entire string. Once you have found what you are looking for, type RET to terminate the search. The point remains in its new position.

The same process works in the opposite direction. The following command searches from the point back to the beginning of the text:

```
C-r bod
```

If you type an incorrect character as you enter the search string, use the Del key to remove it and, if necessary, the point is restored to the position of the previous find in the text.

If you are in the midst of a search, have found a match, and want to go to the next match on the same string, just enter C-s again (or C-r depending on the direction of the search). The point will jump to the next match. Even if the search was initiated as a forward search with C-s, the C-r command can be used to execute a backward search to find the next match. Once you initiate a search in either direction, you can move backward and forward from one match to the other by repeatedly entering C-s and C-r.

There is a special kind of search string known as a *regular expression*. A string search can be initiated based on a regular expression by forming the search command this way:

```
C-M-s <regexp>
```

The form of regular expressions is discussed in Session 10. Many programs in UNIX, including the shell programs, use regular expressions for string matching.

Summary of Basic emacs Commands

The emacs editor has an amazing array of features, all of which can be configured and activated by keyboard Ctrl and Meta key sequences. Table 6-2 lists some of the basic emacs editing commands, those that are sufficient for loading, editing, and saving text files. If you decide to use the emacs editor to do your work, you will certainly learn more commands from the online help.

Table 6-2   *The Fundamental emacs Editing Commands*

Key Sequence	Description
C-a	Moves the point to the beginning of the line.
C-b	Moves the point to the left (same as left arrow).
C-d	Deletes the character at the point.
C-e	Moves the point to the end of the line.
C-f	Moves the point to the right (same as right arrow).
C-g	Abandons the current command being executed.
C-h k <key>	Displays detailed information about the actions of a key.

Continued

Table 6-2 *Continued*

Key Sequence	Description
C-h t	Begins the interactive tutorial.
C-k	Deletes all characters from the point to the end of the line.
C-M-r *<regexp>*	Executes an incremental backward search using a regular expression.
C-M-s *<regexp>*	Executes an incremental forward search using a regular expression.
C-n	Moves the point down one line (same as down arrow).
C-o	Inserts a blank line following the one with the point.
C-p	Moves the point up one line (same as up arrow).
C-r *<string>*	Executes an incremental backward search.
C-s *<string>*	Executes an incremental forward search.
C-v	Scrolls the window forward.
C-x =	Displays information on the character at the point.
C-x _	Undoes the most recent command. Same as C-x u.
C-x C-c	Exits emacs.
C-x C-f *<name>* RET	Creates a new file or loads an existing file.
C-x C-s	Writes the current text to disk.
C-x u	Undoes the most recent command. Same as C-x _.
C-x z	Repeats the previous command.
DEL	Deletes the character to the left of the point.
M->	Moves the point to the end of the text.
M-<	Moves the point to the beginning of the text.
M-b	Moves the point backward one word.
M-d	Deletes all characters from the point to the end of the word.
M-DEL	Deletes all characters from the beginning of the word to the point.
M-f	Moves the point forward one word.
M-v	Scrolls the window backward.

If you haven't done so already, I suggest that you give emacs a try. Start a file and use some of the commands in Table 6-2 to navigate from one place to another in the text and make changes. I think you will see that it is easier to use the editor than it is to read a description of how it works.

Different people edit in different ways. As you work with emacs, you will find that you use certain commands quite often, others only occasionally, and some never. Everyone I know who uses emacs has done some customization. Probably the simplest and most common form of customization is the specification of key mappings that differ from the default mappings. To change key mappings, you can enter text into a file named .emacs in your home directory. The editor reads the file and remaps the keys for you at startup. For example, the following two lines specify that C-z is to execute a macro named shell, and that C-x1 is to execute a macro named make-symbolic-link:

```
(global-key-set "\C-z" 'shell)
(global-key-set "\C-x1" 'make-symbolic-link)
```

Many other things can be customized. To see what can be altered interactively by editing the settings, enter the following command:

```
M-x customize RET
```

Done!

REVIEW

In this session, you learn how to load the emacs editor and perform some fundamental editing functions. The emacs editor is extremely flexible, with features ranging from language recognition to composing and sending e-mail.

- The emacs editor contains many options. Furthermore, because it is free software, options are constantly being added.
- The emacs editor uses all of the standard keys and many of the special keys found on a keyboard.
- Named macros do the editing in emacs, and these macros have special control character sequences defined for them so that they can be executed from the keyboard.
- The emacs editor uses its own terminology for items that appear on the display, such as the point and the echo area.

Session 7 delves further into a discussion of shells and shell operations. The operating environment and configuration settings of shells is explored. You learn that you can instruct your shell to execute commands in a variety of ways.

QUIZ YOURSELF

1. How did the name emacs originate? (See "The emacs Editor Takes Many Forms.")
2. What determines whether or not you can use a mouse to control the editor? (See "Creating, Editing, and Saving Files.")

3. Why is it necessary to press the Return key at the end of some commands but not others? (See "Creating, Editing, and Saving Files.")

4. What is another name for the echo area? (See "Screen Description and Some Term Definitions.")

5. How do you initiate a backward search? (See "Searching the Text.")

Fundamentals of the Bourne Shell

Session Checklist

✔ The command line

✔ The shell environment

✔ Command line expansion

✔ The ins and outs of commands

✔ Quoting and escaping

**30 Min.
To Go**

As discussed in Session 2, the shell is an application program that runs in much the same way as any other UNIX program. All the shells being used today are based on the original shell program written by Steve Bourne, which was initially known simply as the UNIX shell, but is now known as the Bourne Shell to differentiate it from the others. This session and the next explore the Bourne Shell. Session 9 introduces several other shells and explains how they differ from the Bourne Shell. All shells perform the same basic job, but the syntax they use is different.

The Command Line

When the shell prompt appears, you enter a command and instruct the shell to attempt to interpret and execute the command by pressing the Return key. The general form of a command is as follows:

```
command -options arguments
```

When you enter text on the command line, the shell reads the text and breaks it into words. The words are separated by spaces or tabs.

The first word is always taken to be the command. If the command is one of those built into the shell, it is executed immediately. In most cases, the command is the name of an executable program. Any other words appearing on the command line are passed on to the program as it starts running.

Each option is usually represented by a single character. If there is more than one character, they can be combined following a single hyphen, or they can be specified individually. For example, the ls command uses the -l option to specify the long form of listing file names and the -n option to specify the listing of the owner and groups by ID numbers rather than by name:

```
$ ls -l -n
```

The same command can be entered with the option letters combined:

```
$ ls -ln
```

Some options have a long form that begins with two hyphens. The ls command has a long form for the -n option but not for the -l option, so the same options can be specified this way:

```
$ ls -l --numeric-uid-gid
```

The short form and the long form do exactly the same thing, but the long form begins with a double hyphen.

The exact form of the command line varies from one program to another — partly because each program needs different kinds of information, but mainly because different people wrote the programs at different times. For example, the find command, described in Session 3, has long names for the options, but the options all start with a single hyphen. The ps command, which was discussed in Session 4, never accepts anything other than options on its command line, so it usually allows (and sometimes even requires) options to be entered without a leading hyphen.

All commands have one thing in common: silent obedience. If you enter a command and don't get a response, you know that the command executed successfully. Only two things will ever be displayed as the result of executing a command: the output that you expected, or an error message. A command will never ask, "Are you sure?"

The Environment of the Shell

When you first log in, or any other time you start a new shell program running, the Bourne Shell begins by reading a couple of files and executing the commands in them. The first file executed is /etc/profile. Because this file is executed by everyone's shells, it contains instructions and definitions that are applied system-wide. The second file that the Bourne Shell executes is named .profile and is located in your home directory. Each user has his or her own personal version of this file, so if you have some commands you wish to have executed each time you log in, this is where to put them.

The initial period in .profile's file name makes it one of the hidden files in your home directory. This particular hidden file is executed by the Bourne Shell. Other shells execute hidden files with different names, as explained in Session 9.

One of the main purposes of these shell configuration files is to define environment variables. Some environment variables are created internally by the shell itself, so they will always exist. Others are defined globally for everyone as the shells execute /etc/profile. Even more are defined in the .profile file in your home directory. And finally, you can define environment variables as you go by entering them on the command line.

Defining your own environment variables

One of the most useful things programmed into the shell is its ability to retain the definitions of environment variables that you enter from the command line or from inside a command script. The following is an example of storing an environment variable definition in the shell:

```
$ WORKDIR=/home/fred/tmp
```

To look at the value stored in a variable, you can use the echo command:

```
$ echo $WORKDIR
/home/fred/tmp
```

After this environment variable has been defined, you can precede its name with a dollar character ($) and use it anywhere you would use the directory name. For example, the following command lists all of the files in the directory /home/fred/tmp:

```
$ ls $WORKDIR
```

You can use the environment variable to build the complete path name to a file in the work directory by adjoining the names on the command line like this:

```
$ echo $WORKDIR/showsets.html
/home/fred/tmp/showsets.html
```

When using the $ character to extract the value of an environment variable, you can put braces { } around it. Using braces will help in circumstances where you need to insert variable names in the middle of strings, as in the following example:

```
$ TMPDIR=/tmp/
$ echo Workfile: ${TMPDIR}lists.html
Workfile: /tmp/lists.html
```

If there were no braces used in this example, the shell would assume that the name of the environment variable was $TMPDIRlists.html, which is not defined and would result in only a blank being echoed for the file name.

You can use the values stored in environment variables to create other environment variables, like this:

```
$ TWODIRS=$WORKDIR:$TMPDIR
$ echo $TWODIRS
/home/fred/tmp:/tmp/
```

After you have defined an environment variable, it stays defined until you either exit the shell or specifically remove the definition. To remove a definition, just define it without giving it a value, like this:

```
$ TWODIRS=
```

The standard set of environment variables

A number of standard environment variable names have special meanings, and are usually already defined when you log in. These standard names are used by the shell program, and by other programs, to perform basic operations. The system configuration files usually define most of the standard variables, but as you tune your environment, you will find that you need to define others for yourself. Any predefined variables can be easily modified when you need to change the way your shell works.

As you read through the list of environment variables that are described in this session, use either echo or env to view how they are set (or not set) for your login. Remember, you can display the list of environment variables one screen at a time with the following command:

```
$ env | more
```

**20 Min.
To Go**

The following list contains the standard set of environment variables and the ways that they are normally defined:

- CDPATH is a list of directory names separated by colons. Whenever you use the cd command to change to a directory that cannot be found locally, a search is initiated for it in the directories listed in CDPATH. For example, you could set the variable to two directories:

  ```
  $ CDPATH=/home/book/uwcc:/home/arthur/brckts
  ```

  If the uwcc directory contains subdirectories named ch01, ch02, ch03, and so on, you could switch to any one of these subdirectories with a single command. For example, no matter what the current directory is, the following command would make /home/book/uwcc/ch02 the current directory:

  ```
  $ cd ch02
  ```

- HOME is automatically set by the shell as your user login directory. Be sure you know what you are doing if you decide to change HOME because lots of utilities depend on it. Applications commonly store configuration files in the HOME directory, making it possible for different users running the same program to each have their own configuration settings. Some programs, such as mail client programs, may actually create a subdirectory in the HOME directory to store mail.

- LOGNAME is set to the login name.

- LANG is set to the name of the current locale, which specifies the language and character set used by your shell program. For example, LANG is set to en_US for U.S. English and fr_CA for Canadian French.

- MAIL is set to the name of the directory that the e-mail system uses to store incoming mail addressed to you. Utilities that retrieve mail or notify you of the arrival of new mail look in this directory to find it.

- PATH is the list of directories that the shell uses to locate the commands that you enter. If you intend to change the PATH variable setting, it is best to leave the previous setting intact and simply add your new directory. That's easy to do using the techniques described in the previous section. For example, you can use the following statement to add the directory $HOME/bin to the list of directories stored in the PATH variable:

  ```
  $ PATH=${PATH}:${HOME}/bin
  ```

  In this example, the braces are not actually required; however, it isn't a bad idea to include them whenever the expression starts to get cluttered.

- PS1 contains the command line prompt. By default, it is set to $, but almost everybody customizes it. You can turn your prompt into anything you like simply by storing a string in this variable. For example, you could change it to a simple request for a command, like this:

  ```
  $ PS1=command?
  command?_
  ```

  You can also set your prompt to the current directory, the name of the computer, the time and date, or just about anything you can think of. Some examples are given in the next session.

- PS2 is the secondary command prompt. It is normally set to the greater-than character (>), but you can change it. PS2 is used whenever you are entering a long command and need to break it, so you type the rest of the command on the next line. To continue a command on a new line, enter a backslash character (\), immediately followed by the Return key. The secondary prompt appears, and you can continue to enter your command. The following example shows how this is done with the echo command:

  ```
  $ echo This line is entered \
  >by being continued.
  This line is entered by being continued.
  ```

  In this example, the command is broken only once. However, you can break the command line as many times as you need until you press the Return key without preceding it with a backslash.

- PWD is the complete path name of the current working directory. It changes whenever you use the cd command to move to another directory.

- SHELL is the path name to the shell program itself (which is /bin/sh if you are using the Bourne Shell).

- TERM is used by programs to determine what type of terminal you are using. You may recall from Session 5 that the vi editor (along with many other programs) searches for your terminal definition in the /etc/termcap file to determine how to perform actions such as moving the cursor and clearing the screen. The name of the entry in the termcap file defining your terminal is stored in the TERM environment variable.

  Specifying the terminal type in an environment variable allows you to log in from anywhere using any kind of terminal. Once you get logged in, you only need to set the TERM variable to the correct terminal name and all the programs that perform screen operations will know where to find the instructions for doing so.

Command Line Expansion

When you enter a command, the shell checks to see whether you have entered any special characters and, whenever it finds ones, modifies the command line by inserting file names. The special characters are the asterisk (*), the question mark (?), and the square brackets ([ ]).

An asterisk matches zero or more characters of any kind. A question mark matches any single character. Characters listed between a pair of square brackets require a match with exactly one of the enclosed characters. A dash can be used to specify a range of characters. For example, [A-Z] matches any uppercase letter. If the first character following the open bracket ([) is an exclamation point (!), the next character must *not* match any of those specified. The examples listed in Table 7-1 gives you an idea of how these searches work. For a thorough understanding, you need to perform your own experiments by changing to a directory with lots of files (such as /usr/bin) and trying some of the combinations with the ls command. For example, the following command lists all file names containing the letter j:

```
$ ls *j*
```

Matches will only be made with the file names in the current directory, or in any other directory you specify. For example, if you have a file named flim.html in a directory named pages, you could list it by specifying the directory name this way:

```
$ ls pages/*.html
```

You can also use expansion on the directory name to find the same file, like this:

```
$ ls */flim.html
```

The following command lists all files that begin with F, p, S, or w:

```
$ ls [FpSw]*
```

The following command lists all files that end with a, e, i, o, or u and have second-to-last letter s or t:

```
$ ls* [st][aeiou]
```

Table 7-1   *Examples of Expressions Matching Names*

Expression	Will Match. . .	Will Not Match. . .
*X*A*	eXtrA, MIXMATCH, XA	extra, AXLE, BOX
*.html	index.html, goon.html, html.html	indexhtml, html, fred/index.html
gr	bogra, great, rugrat	booger, boorg, rugarat
*p	soup, clip, map	pam, mape, clipper
*/index.html	fred/index.html, kick/index.html	index.html, fred/deop/index.html

Expression	Will Match. . .	Will Not Match. . .
?.html	a.html, Z.html	index.html, ab.html
inde?.html	index.html, indem.html	inde.html, indexx.html
[FpSw]*	Fox, Switch, pet, wiggle	fox, aFFix, swat, PFred
*[ab]	gala, flab, ma, glib	gal, dork, abc, GALA
[aeio][rstv]*	ark, escrow, oval	axe, easy, Oval, aero
a[!rn]t	alt, act, aft	art, ant
A[a-z]*	Apple, Aardvark, Abc	apple, AArdvark, A44bc

Remember that the shell is doing this argument expansion, not the individual commands. The advantage of having the shell perform the expansion is that every program is invoked with the exact same interface. That is, when you enter a command, you always know exactly what is being passed to the program.

The Ins and Outs of Commands

10 Min. To Go

A UNIX program gets its input by reading from a stream named *standard input*. A UNIX program writes its output to a stream named *standard output*. Every UNIX program writes its error messages to another output stream named *standard error*. Under normal circumstances, standard input comes from the keyboard, and both standard output and standard error are directed to the display. All of the commands discussed so far have been run by the name of the command being entered from the keyboard. The command then executes and displays its output as lines of text on the screen. However, because every program uses these exact same streams for input and output, the shell knows what they are and can redirect them to and from other places.

For example, you can run env and redirect its output to a file named env.txt with the following command:

```
$ env >env.txt
```

The greater-than sign (>) redirects the output from the command into a newly created file. If a file by the specified name already exists, the file is deleted and replaced with a new one. To view the output that was stored in the file, you can list the contents of the file on the screen by using the more command:

```
$ more env.txt
```

The more command lists the text one page at a time and waits for you to press a key to continue. If you press the space bar, an entire new page will display. If you press the Return key, the text on the screen will scroll up by one line.

You can achieve the same result by using a pipe to connect the output of env directly to the input of more:

```
$ env | more
```

This command sends the standard output stream of env directly to the standard input stream of more. If you run this command, you will notice that the env command supplies the environment variables in what seems to be a completely random order. However, you can use the sort command to put them in alphabetical order. The first env command that was executed stored the text in a file that can now be sorted by entering this command:

```
$ sort env.txt
```

Running this command displays the same list in alphabetical order, but the list contains too many environment variables to display on one screen. This can be fixed by piping the output from sort into the input of more:

```
$ sort env.txt | more
```

This command works, but it requires the presence of the intermediate file from the previous command. To skip the intermediate step and have the whole thing execute at once, enter this command:

```
$ env | sort | more
```

There is no limit to this piping and redirecting. You can hook as many commands as you want into a long chain. In the real world, however, you seldom connect more than three, and almost never more than four.

You can also redirect the output from the end of a pipe into a file, as in the following command, to create a file named sortedenv.txt that contains a sorted list of the environment variables:

```
$ env | sort >sortedenv.txt
```

Suppose you want to create a file with sorted output from env and simultaneously have the list show up on the screen. Instead of using the greater-than (>) redirection to create the file, you would put a tee in the pipe, which sends the output to two places at once. The command looks like this:

```
$ env | sort | tee sortedenv.txt | more
```

The tee utility requires one argument: the name of a file that it will use to write the data. At the same time tee writes data to the file, it also writes it to standard output, which is piped into more and displayed on the screen.

You can also specify redirection of standard input and have it come from a file instead of the keyboard. The following command reads from the unsorted file created earlier and pipes a sorted version of the file's contents into more:

```
$ sort <env.txt | more
```

A command that reads from an unsorted file and writes the sorted results to another file looks like this:

```
$ sort <env.txt >sortedenv.txt
```

I hope that you are beginning to see the possibilities. There are hundreds of UNIX commands that can be connected together and redirected to create all kinds of custom-formatted information. Utility programs from upcoming sessions, such as grep, uniq, and awk, can be used in a pipeline to filter and modify the data as it passes through. You can use redirection to write some fairly complicated programs without doing any programming at all.

At the beginning of this section, a second output stream known as standard error was mentioned. The standard error stream is displayed on the screen just like standard output, but it is not affected by normal piping and redirection. This makes it possible for a utility in the midst of a pipeline to report an error to you. If all of a program's output was redirected to the next member of the pipe and the standard error output wasn't written to the screen, you would have no way of knowing when something went wrong.

It is possible to redirect the data from standard error into a file by tagging the redirect symbol with the number 2. And it is possible to specify all three redirections in the same command:

```
$ sort <env.txt >sortedenv.txt 2>sort.err
```

Table 7-2 contains a summary of the command line redirection operators. Notice that a couple of the operators redirect the output to a file named /dev/null, which is a UNIX special file that accepts any input fed to it and simply discards it.

Table 7-2 *Command Line Redirection Operators*

Operator	Description
>*filename*	Standard output is redirected to a new file.
>/dev/null	Standard output is discarded.
>>*filename*	Standard output is redirected and appended to the end of the named file.
<*filename*	Standard input is redirected from the named file.
A | B	The standard output from A is redirected to the standard input of B.
2>*filename*	Standard error is redirected to a new file.
2>&1	Standard error is redirected to the same output stream as standard output.
2>/dev/null	Standard error is discarded.

Quoting and Escaping

Sometimes you want to enter an asterisk on the command line and have it passed, unchanged, to the command itself. For example, if you want to use the find command to locate all the files ending with .html, you may want to enter the command this way:

```
$ find . -name *.html -print          # wrong
```

This command is formed in such a way that it should have the find command search through all the directories beneath the current directory to locate any files with the suffix .html. However, that doesn't happen. The shell processes the asterisk as a special character instead of passing it on to the find command. For example, if the local directory happens to contain a couple of HTML files named index.html and blcklm.html, the command could wind up being expanded by the shell into this:

```
$ find . -name index.html blcklm.html -print
```

This is obviously not what was intended by the person entering the command. To ensure that the unexpanded string is passed to the command, use single quotes to surround any special shell characters:

```
$ find . -name '*.html' -print
```

The shell ignores anything you put inside a pair of single quotes except another single quote character. You can also use double quotes and enter the command this way:

```
$ find . -name "*.html" -print
```

In this example, it doesn't matter whether you use double or single quotes. However, in some circumstances, differences may exist in the way they work. These differences will be explored in the context of writing shell scripts in Session 16.

If you prefer, you can also enter this command by using a backslash character to *escape* the asterisk. Placing a backslash in front of a character that the shell would otherwise process removes its powers and makes it a normal character. Actually, the shell tosses out the backslash and then takes the next character literally, no matter what it is. The command could be entered this way:

```
$ find . -name \*.html -print
```

You can use as many special characters as you like in the expression as long as you escape each one with a backslash.

Done!

REVIEW

In this session, you learn how to interact with the shell and make the shell do things you would like it to do. As you work through the rest of the sessions, you will be using the concepts described in this session.

- There is a basic format for entering a command, but this format varies widely from one command to another.
- Whenever a shell starts running, it reads and executes commands from script files that define the basic operating environment of the shell.
- An environment variable can be defined and stored in the shell. The shell returns the defined value of the variable to any process that asks for it.
- You can include asterisks, question marks, and square brackets in the text of a command and have the shell process these special characters into file names.
- Every program uses a standard form of input and output, and the shell can redirect this input and output for you.

The next session goes even further into a discussion of the Bourne Shell, exploring such topics as the ability to have a shell start other shells running to perform specific tasks.

QUIZ YOURSELF

1. What character (or characters) is used on the command line to indicate an option setting? (See "The Command Line.")
2. What are the names of the environment variables that contain the current login directory and the name of the current user? (See "The standard set of environment variables.")
3. In the matching of file names, what character is used to match any number of occurrences of any characters? (See "Command Line Expansion.")
4. What is it called when you use the vertical bar character to send the output from one command to the input of another? (See "The Ins and Outs of Commands.")
5. What techniques can you use to keep the shell from processing special characters on a command line? (See "Quoting and Escaping.")

Using the Bourne Shell

Session Checklist

✔ Running shells within shells

✔ Using built-in shell commands

✔ Setting your prompt

**30 Min.
To Go**

T his session explains some of the inner workings of shell processes. When you work with the UNIX operating system, you are viewing it and issuing command to it through the facilities provided by a shell. Every command that you issue runs inside a shell or under the control of a shell. This session explores different ways the Bourne Shell can be used to run other processes, including other shells. A few special commands that are built into the shell can be used to specify how a login session works, and even limit the types of things a user is allowed to do.

Running Shells Within Shells

It is common to run another shell process so that it can execute a command or set of commands for you. You can do this in several ways, each of which serves a different purpose. This session addresses each of these ways individually.

Running a different kind of shell

Every time you log in, your login session is controlled by the shell that has been assigned to you in the system configuration files. With root permissions, you can change your default shell (the exact way to do this is explained in Session 28), but if you do change your login to another shell, you are stuck with it until the system is reconfigured to change it back. However, because a shell is a program that can be run like any other program, you can start a different shell by entering its name on the command line. For example, if you want to switch your login session to the C Shell, enter the following command:

```
$ csh
```

The command csh is the name of the C Shell program found in the /bin directory. When the C Shell starts to run, the prompt on the command line will probably change because the C Shell has its own set of initialization files.

It could be that your login session defaults to running the C Shell. If so, you can perform the same operation in reverse by running the Bourne Shell from the C Shell. To start the Bourne Shell, enter the command sh. If you prefer, you can simply run another copy of the same shell you are using — it is possible to run any shell from inside any other shell.

While you are still in the C Shell (or whatever shell you have started), enter the following command to take a look at the value of the SHLVL environment variable:

```
$ echo $SHLVL
```

The SHLVL variable contains the number of shell levels deep that you are currently running. Enter sh and/or csh a few more times, checking the value of SHLVL each time; the number increases as you become nested deeper and deeper in a stack of shell processes. Now do the same thing in reverse: enter the exit command to stop the current shell from running and check the value of SHLVL. It should have decreased by one because the highest-level shell was killed by the exit command, and the new prompt is coming from one level closer to the login level. If you continue to type exit, the value decreases until you are back to your original shell, which has an SHLVL value of 1. If you enter exit one more time, you will be logged off (or the X window of the terminal will close).

Taking the environment variables with you

Some environment variables are local to the current shell while others are passed on, or *exported,* to any new shell that you start. You can easily determine which variables have been exported by starting a new shell process and looking at the environment variables that are defined for it. You can look at all the environment variables defined in a shell with the env command:

```
$ env | more
```

Another command, named set, is built into the shell. It lists all of the defined environment variables whether they have been exported or not:

```
$ set | more
```

All the environment variables defined so far have been local to the current shell. Defining a variable and having it exported to other processes requires a second command. The following two lines create an exported environment variable named UPPERLIMIT:

```
$ UPPERLIMIT=86
$ export UPPERLIMIT
```

After you have entered these two lines, UPPERLIMIT is defined for every program that you run and every program that your programs run.

It turns out that defining and exporting environment variables is a very handy thing. You can use this technique to run a process, or a group of processes, in an environment of their own. For example, suppose you run a program that requires some of your environment variables to be different and some new variables to be defined. Simply start a new shell, redefine the existing variables, define the new variables, export them, and then run the new program. When the program is finished, you can exit the new shell and all the temporary variable settings will disappear. The values of the variables in your original shell remain unchanged. This process is particularly useful if you store all the commands in a file and then instruct the new shell to execute everything in the file.

Starting a shell to execute commands from a file

You can store a sequence of commands in a file and have them executed by a shell as if you had entered them from the command line. To demonstrate how this works, use your text editor to create a file named oncount that contains the following two lines:

```
# Print the number of people currently logged in
who | wc -l
```

The first line is a comment that is completely ignored by the shell. Because the first column contains the # character, the shell ignores everything on the line. You can actually place the # character anywhere on the line to make it, and everything that follows it, completely invisible to the shell. Once you have created the file, you can start a new shell and have it execute the command from the file this way:

```
$ sh oncount
        3
```

The who command printed three lines. The wc -l command counted them and output the number. The oncount script reported three active logins. As it is designed to do when it executes a script, the new shell quit running when it reached the end. You can include as many commands as you like in a script. The following example script is stored in a file named logstat and demonstrates how to use more than one command:

```
# Display the date and the current login statistics
echo "Date and time:"
date
echo "Number of logins:"
who | wc -l
echo "Personal information:"
who am i
```

If you use your editor to create this file (or copy the one from the CD), you can execute the commands in the file as follows:

```
$ sh logstat
```

**20 Min.
To Go**

Much more can be done inside a script. In fact, an entire programming language is built into the shell with conditional execution, loops, and functions. In UNIX, you find shell scripts written for everything from complete applications to UNIX system configuration commands. Writing simple shell scripts is discussed in Session 16.

Logging in as another user

You don't have to log out in order to log in as someone else. All you have to do is use the su (superuser) command to create a new login shell. The command is called su because the default user name is root and it is mostly used to log in as the superuser, but you can use it to start a new session as any user. To log in as another user, you must know the password; so the default login looks like this:

```
$ su
Password:
```

If you enter the correct password, you find that you have all the powers of the superuser, but that nothing else has changed. You still have the same environment and are still working in the same directory. About the only thing that has changed is the command line prompt. The ability to jump in and out of root is very handy for executing a command that requires root permissions, such as deleting a file owned by another user or making a change to a system configuration file. You can do this type of work best by logging in as root, performing the one task, and logging out again.

You shouldn't do any more than necessary when logged in as root because every command is executed without question and with full power to do anything. For example, if you are in the root directory, the command rm -rf * will delete every file and directory on the entire disk drive.

A hyphen following the su command causes a complete change of environment. If you type the following, you get the same result as if you had logged in as the root user from the login prompt:

```
$ su -
Password:
```

After entering the password here, the environment changes completely and you find yourself in the home directory of the root user.

The default is root, but you can log in as any user by supplying the user name on the command line. To log in as a user named ben and retain your own environment, enter the following command:

```
$ su ben
```

Entering su in this form has the effect of changing the user and group ID numbers to those used by ben, but leaving everything else as it is. On the other hand, to log in as a user named ben and have the new environment initialized just as it would be from the ben login prompt, enter the command this way:

```
$ su - ben
```

Using Built-in Shell Commands

The following sections contain descriptions of some of the built-in commands that you can enter from the command line. This list does not include all the built-in commands; a number of them are designed to be used only in scripts.

The . (dot) command

The dot command is used to execute commands in a file without starting a new shell. Most of the time, it doesn't matter whether a new shell gets spawned, but in certain situations you may need to prevent this from happening. The need usually arises when you want your environment to include values that you have defined in a file. For example, you could have a file named `setblue` that contains the following:

```
BLUE=/usr/bin/lavender
BLUEMIN=89
BLUEMAX=120
export BLUE BLUEMIN BLUEMAX
```

If you start a separate shell to execute these commands, the new shell records the definitions and then quits running. Nothing changes in your environment. If you execute the command as follows, however, the new variables are defined in your current shell:

```
$ . setblue
```

After you execute the dot command, use the `env` or `set` command to check your local environment variables. The new values have been set just as if you had entered them from the command line.

Executing a script this way is called *sourcing*. I'm not sure how that name originated, but some shells use `source` as a synonym for the dot command. If you are using one of the newer Bourne Shell programs, you may be able to enter the same command this way:

```
$ source setblue
```

The unset command

The unset command can be used to remove definitions of environment variables. Certain environment variables, such as PATH, PS1, and PS2, can't have their definitions removed, but you can certainly use unset to delete any variables that you have defined yourself. You can enter the unset command from the command line, or you can put the commands in a file and "source it in," as the expression goes, by using the dot command. For example, the file named `unsetblue` contains the following three commands:

```
unset BLUE
unset BLUEMIN
unset BLUEMAX
```

The following command can then be used to remove the previously set environment:

```
$ . unsetblue
```

The type command

The `type` command is a built-in command that informs you whether another command is also built-in. You can enter a number of commands on one line and `type` will provide information about each one. For example:

```
$ type env set pwd cksum cat
env is /usr/bin/env
set is a shell builtin
pwd is a shell builtin
cksum is /usr/bin/cksum
cat is /bin/cat
```

As you can see, the `type` command identifies two built-in shell commands and provides the full path name of three utility programs.

By the way, `cksum` is a utility that provides a *cyclic redundancy check (CRC)* number for one or more files. The number will always be the same on any computer as long as the file hasn't changed, so it can be used to verify that a file has been transmitted and received without any errors. A CRC can't always catch intentional tampering, but in general, it does an excellent job.

The hash command

Whenever you enter a command and the shell locates it by looking through the directories in the `PATH` variable, the shell assumes that you will use the command in the future and thus memorizes where the command was found. This speeds things up, but it can cause problems in rare circumstances. For example, if you reorganize the disk, the shell may select the wrong command. Rarely does this cause a problem, but if it does, you can force the shell to forget where it found everything by entering the following command:

```
$ hash
```

In some shells (the C Shell, for example), this command is named `rehash`.

The odd name of this command results from the way the names of the commands have their bits scrambled to create the lookup table inside the shell.

The readonly command

Environment variables can be stored in the shell in such a way that they cannot be altered. To see a list of these variables, enter the following command:

```
$ readonly
```

You can also use the `readonly` command to convert one of the existing environment variables to a read-only variable. For example, to convert the environment variable `BLUEMAX` to a read-only variable, enter the following:

```
$ readonly BLUEMAX
```

**10 Min.
To Go**

After you have entered this command, you are prohibited from changing its value or from using unset to remove it. To get rid of a read-only variable, you must exit the shell.

The set command

Not only can the built-in set command be used to create a list of all the currently defined environment variables, it can also be used to turn flags on or off. Flags are used to modify the operation of the shell in some way. To turn the f flag on, for example, you can enter this command:

```
$ set -f
```

To turn the f flag off, use a plus sign:

```
$ set +f
```

Table 8-1 lists some basic flags, but it is almost certain that the shell you are using has more. If you want to see all the flags recognized by your shell, use the man command with the name of the shell you are using (sh, bash, csh, and so on).

Table 8-1 *The Basic Shell Flags*

Flag	Description
a	If this flag is set, every environment variable that is created or assigned a new value is automatically exported.
e	If this flag is set and a command that is being executed exits with a nonzero value — which indicates an error — the shell ceases execution immediately.
f	If this flag is set, the special characters *, ?, and [ ] will not be expanded into file names.
h	If this flag is set, the command names are hashed and their locations stored in a table for quick lookup. This setting is usually on by default.
n	If this flag is set, commands — when read from a file — are not executed. This flag can be used to check whether a script will execute.
t	If this flag is set, the shell exits after executing a single command.
u	If this flag is set, using the $ character to attempt to insert the value of an undefined environment variable will cause an error condition. If this flag is not set, undefined variables produce no characters, but no error results.
v	Setting this flag switches the shell to a more verbose mode in which it echoes commands as they are read from a script.
x	Setting this flag switches the shell to a more verbose mode in which it echoes both commands and arguments as they are executed.

The ulimit command

The shell can be used to enforce maximum limits on things such as file sizes, the number of files that can be open simultaneously, the maximum amount of CPU time a process can use, and even the amount of virtual memory that is available. A limit can be set as either a *hard* or a *soft* limit. After a hard limit is set, it cannot be increased. A soft limit can be set to any value up to the hard limit value, and a soft limit can be adjusted at any time. The soft limit value is imposed; the hard limit is just an upper bound for the soft limit. The following example shows the use of the -a option to determine your current soft limit settings:

```
$ ulimit -a
core file size (blocks)        10000
data seg size (kbytes)         512
file size (blocks)             4096
max locked memory (kbytes)     unlimited
max memory size (kbytes)       unlimited
open files                     128
pipe size (512 bytes)          8
stack size (kbytes)            8192
cpu time (seconds)             unlimited
max user processes             2048
virtual memory (kbytes)        unlimited
```

The system administrator usually sets the default limits by including ulimit commands in a global startup script used by each user's login shell. Setting the hard limit is achieved by using the -H option. The command in the following example uses the -t option to set the maximum CPU time allowed for each process to a hard limit of 30 seconds:

```
$ ulimit -H -t 30
```

After this command is executed, the shell itself, as well as any process it starts, is limited to a maximum of 30 seconds of CPU time. The time can only be expanded if the user shuts down this shell and starts another one. The soft limit can be adjusted up and down at any time, but it cannot exceed the hard limit. For example, to set a soft limit of 15 seconds, you can use the following command:

```
$ ulimit -S -t 15
```

The actual limit imposed at any given time is the soft limit. The default value for the soft limit is the value of the hard limit. When you set a limit value without specifying -H or -S, both the hard and soft limits are set to the value that you specify.

Setting Your Prompt

That's enough hard work for now. Let's have some fun. Everybody wants to set their own prompt string, and everybody has a different idea of what it should contain. Some like it very short so they can enter long commands without having to break them to the next line. Some display their login name as a prompt; some use the time, and some display the date. Personally, I like to display the complete path name of the current directory because I find it very easy to get completely lost.

To set the prompt, you only need to store the character string in the environment variable named PS1. For example, if you want to change your login prompt to your user name, followed by a colon and a space, you can type:

```
$ PS1='fred: '
```

The string is surrounded by quotes to force the entire string to become the prompt, so the space following the colon is also included. This leaves a nice space between the end of the prompt and the first character of the command that you enter. You can put the prompt back to the default setting this way:

```
$ PS1='$ '
```

There is a little utility named logname that outputs your login name, like this:

```
$ logname
arthur
```

You can use logname to make certain that you always put the correct login name in the prompt. The prompt will always be right, no matter who uses the setup script. To make the shell execute a command and return its value as a string, just enclose the command in a pair of grave accent marks (also called *back tics*). To set PS1 to the login name, you can use the following command:

```
$ PS1=`logname`
arthur_
```

This command works, but the prompt doesn't have the normal colon and space on the end. The name just butts right up against any command you might enter. To add the colon and the space, the whole thing can be enclosed in quotes, like this:

```
$ PS1='`logname`: '
arthur: _
```

You can do the same thing with any command that outputs a string. For example:

```
$ PS1='`date`: '
Thu Nov 8 15:16:09 AKST 2001: _
```

Here's my favorite. I like to know what directory I'm in, so I set up my prompt something like this:

```
$ PS1='[`pwd`] '
[/home/doc/book/uwcc/ch08] _
```

Because the whole world is on a network these days, and because it is easy to log in to other UNIX computers over the Internet using telnet, I often precede the whole prompt with the name of the current computer so I really do know where I am:

```
$ PS1='`hostname`[`pwd`] '
arlin[/home/doc/book/uwcc/ch08] _
```

You can also precede the directory name with the login name if you often use other names, such as `root`, when working on other computers.

You can make your prompt into anything. No rule says that you have to limit it to one line. And you can change it as often as you wish. I have even seen people use the prompt as a reminder note ("3 p.m. meeting" or "Pick up a loaf of bread", for example).

Done!

REVIEW

In this session, you learn several ways to manipulate the Bourne Shell.

- You can export environment variables in such a way to ensure that the environment variables defined in one shell remain defined in another.
- You can store a series of shell commands in a file and have them executed just as if they were entered on a keyboard.
- You can log in as another user without logging out.
- Commands are built into the shell that can be used to define environment variables, undefine them, make them local, make them global, and define them in such a way that they cannot be modified or deleted.
- The output of a command can be used as text by surrounding the command with grave accent marks.

Session 9 examines a number of different shells. All of these shells are built around the same basic design, but each has its own set of special capabilities.

QUIZ YOURSELF

1. What can you do to ensure that environment variables are defined in shells that you start as subprocesses? (See "Taking the environment variables with you.")
2. How can you log in as superuser without logging off first? (See "Logging in as another user.")
3. How can an environment variable be set so that it cannot be changed? (See "The readonly command.")
4. Under what circumstances would you want to use the `hash` command? (See "The hash command.")
5. How can you set your prompt to display the current working directory? (See "Setting Your Prompt.")

Using Other Shells

Session Checklist

✔ How to select a shell

✔ Introduction to the C Shell

✔ Introduction to the Korn Shell

✔ Introduction to the Bourne-Again Shell

✔ Other shells

**30 Min.
To Go**

Because the shell is a separate program — instead of an integral part of the operating system — a number of shells have been developed over the years. This session provides an introduction to some of the more common UNIX shells. It's hard to tell which shell is used the most, but four of them are tied for the lead: the Bourne Shell, the Korn Shell, the Bourne-Again Shell, and the C Shell.

How to Select a Shell

The particular shell you decide to use depends on several factors. One important factor is which shell is being used by the people that you are working with. If everyone on your project is using a certain shell, it is best for you to use that shell so the things you do will be compatible. Most commands work the same in one shell as they do in another, but small differences here and there can cause problems. The worst of these problems is the kind that doesn't notify you that something is wrong. For example, if a change is made to the system-wide initialization script of the commonly shared shell, and you are using a different shell, you will fail to get the update. This could cause you to do work in the wrong directory or even on the wrong computer. This situation could even cause all your mail to be misdirected and files to be lost.

Another factor is the learning curve you must go through after switching to a new shell. To reduce the odds of this happening, you should try to select a shell that is available on many different computers. If you learn all the peculiarities of a certain shell, making a sudden switch to another shell can be an inconvenience.

Everybody has personal preferences, including the people who write shell programs. You have opinions too, which will make the flavor of one particular shell more appealing to you than others. The Bourne Shell is the original UNIX shell. The Korn Shell (ksh) and the Bourne-Again Shell (bash) are both extensions of, and compatible with, the basic Bourne Shell (sh). The original C Shell (csh) is only partially based on the Bourne Shell and has been extended into a shell called the TC Shell (tcsh), which is the C Shell with some features added. Because the TC Shell is completely compatible with the C Shell, it is also frequently referred to as the C Shell. To determine which shell you are running, enter the following command, which responds with the full path name of the shell you are using:

```
$ echo $SHELL
```

If the shell's default prompt is being used, it can indicate which shell is running. The Bourne and Korn Shells use $ as their default prompt. The Bourne-Again Shell defaults to bash$. The default prompt of the C Shell is %, and the TC Shell uses >.

Fortunately, you can easily switch from one shell to another. The previous session discussed how easy it is to start a new shell running, but if you want the change to be something other than temporary, you need to tell the system and have your login configuration changed. To switch to a different shell as your login shell, you can use the chsh (change shell) command. Before you make the change, you need to known which shells are available, so the -1 (ell) option can be used to display a list of them:

```
$ chsh -1
/bin/bash
/bin/sh
/bin/tcsh
/bin/csh
```

To switch to another login shell, enter the chsh command without an argument and respond to the prompts. For example, if you are logged in as lance, a switch from the Bourne Shell to the C Shell looks like this:

```
$ chsh
Changing shell for lance
Password:
New shell [/bin/sh]: /bin/csh
Shell changed.
% _
```

Your password is required to prevent someone from changing your shell behind your back. As with all UNIX passwords, it is not echoed to the screen as you enter it. At the prompt for the new shell, you enter the path name in the same form chsh listed it for you earlier. When that is done, you will be using the C Shell whenever you log in. Note that the prompt for the new shell name includes the current shell name; if you simply press Return, no change is made.

Introduction to csh and tcsh, the C Shell

The original Bourne Shell appeared in 1979. The C Shell, which was the first alternative to the Bourne Shell, appeared a couple of years later. The C Shell was written by Bill Joy at the University of California, Berkeley to be part of the Berkeley System Distribution (BSD) version of UNIX. The C Shell uses a command syntax that somewhat resembles the C programming language; this similarity is intended to help C programmers more easily use the system. The C Shell and BSD introduced some features that have since become integrated into most other shells and most other systems.

The C Shell brought several new things to the party, but one of the most popular was the use of the tilde character (~) as a synonym for the home directory. Every shell seems to have adopted this shorthand form of addressing the home directory because it comes in handy in so many situations. With the tilde character representing your home directory and the dot character representing the current directory, some commands can be greatly shortened. For example, if you are currently in a directory other than your home directory, you could copy the file named grimace.html from your home directory to the current directory with the following command:

```
$ cp ~/grimace.html .
```

The syntax of the cp command is cp *input output*. The input file is in the home directory (the tilde), and the output location is the current directory (the period). Because no file name is specified for output, the same name as the input is used, so a duplicate of the file named gramice.html appears in the current directory.

Startup and shutdown

The C Shell has a number of files it executes when you log in and out. Every C Shell begins by executing /etc/csh.cshrc and /etc/csh.login, which are global files executed at the startup of every C Shell on the system. Next, the files .cshrc and .login, which are located in the home directory of the user, are executed. If it is the TC Shell instead of the C Shell, the .chsrc file is ignored and .tcshrc is used instead.

If the shell is not a login shell (that is, if it is a subshell being started to run a process), it doesn't execute /etc/csh.login or .login. The reason for this is to provide a place to put any commands that need to be executed only during the user login.

When you log out, the commands found in the files /etc/csh.logout and ~/.logout are executed, making it possible to close ports, make log entries, or perform any other necessary cleanup tasks.

Environment variables

Environment variables work about the same as they do in the Bourne Shell, with minor differences in the way you define them. To define an environment variable in the C Shell, you must use the set command, like this:

**20 Min.
To Go**

```
% set PXCOLOR=green
```

The names of the standard variables are also different than they are in the Bourne Shell. For example, the name of the home directory is stored in cwd instead of PWD. If you understand the variables defined in the Bourne Shell, you should have no problem understanding the ones in the C Shell. The PS1 and PS2 variables are named prompt and prompt2, but they work the same as they do in the Bourne Shell. For example, enter the following to create a custom prompt:

```
% set prompt="Yes? "
Yes? _
```

C Shell command history

As you use the C Shell by entering commands, the shell records the commands and stores them in a history list so that you can use them again. This is especially useful when you need to repeat a long command or if you need to make a small change to a command and execute it again. You can see your command history by using the history command:

```
% history
    1  ls
    2  cd /home/fred/temp
    3  ls
    4  find . -name clomp.c -print
    5  env | more
    6  set BLUEMAX=44
    7  history
```

The last command shown in the list is always history because it is the command that created the list. Each command in the history is identified by a unique number. If you see the command you wish to repeat, you can use an exclamation point to select it by its number. The following example repeats the find command:

```
% !4
```

If you have been at the keyboard for a while, don't be surprised if the list scrolls off the screen. The default is for the shell to memorize the last 100 commands, which are all listed when you make a request to see them. It is usually okay if the list scrolls off the screen because the last 20 or so commands are left on the display, and you are usually interested in the most recent ones. To look farther back in the list, you can pipe the output into more:

```
% history | more
```

You can shorten the length of the history list (or lengthen it) by setting the history environment variable. The following command limits the list to the ten most recent entries:

```
% set history=10
```

If you remember the command name but don't want to go to the trouble of typing all the arguments you passed to it, you can use the name alone to execute it again. For example, to execute the most recent find command in your history list, you could type

```
% !find
```

The command is executed as if you had entered the entire line. Actually, you don't have to enter the entire command because the shell moves back through the history list until the characters you type match the beginning of a command. For example, you could also execute the most recent `find` command by entering the following:

```
% !fi
```

The following is shorthand for repeating the last command:

```
% !!
```

It can be frustrating to enter a long command and find that you have made a spelling error or some other simple mistake and need to type the whole thing again. Instead, you can make a quick fix and submit the corrected command by modifying the command stored in the history list. For example, suppose you enter the following command:

```
% fidn /home -name "*.html" -exec grep monkey {} \; | more
```

The moment you hit the Return key, you get the message that the `fidn` command was not found. Instead of typing that whole mess over again, you can enter the following:

```
% ^fidn^find^
```

The shell makes a quick text substitution (changing `fidn` to `find` in the most recent command in the history list) and resubmits the edited version of the command. By the way, the `grep` command in this example is used to search through text to locate a matching string. The `grep` command is covered in detail in the next session.

Aliases

In a manner similar to the way it memorizes environment variables, the C Shell maintains an internal list of aliases, which can be set, unset, and viewed using the built-in `alias` command. Whenever you enter a command, the first word of the command line is checked to see if it is defined as an alias. If it is, the alias string is substituted in the command before the command is executed.

One of the more commonly used aliases is for `ls`. The `ls` command has many options and is used quite often, which makes it a good candidate for an alias. For example, I like my `ls` command to show all the hidden files (the ones that start with a period), and I also like to have the file names tagged with the file type. The `-A` option includes the hidden file names, and the `-F` option marks the names of directories and executable files. The following command defines an alias that uses both of these flags:

```
% alias ls 'ls -AF'
```

After this alias is defined, the `-A` and `-F` options are used every time you enter `ls`. You can specify other flags whenever you enter the command, but they are simply added to the ones that are defined in the alias.

The `-F` flag on `ls` causes a slash / character to be displayed at the end of all directory names and an asterisk * to be displayed at the end of executable program names.

You can do more with aliases than just set simple options. The following alias lists only the hidden file and directory names:

```
% alias hidden 'ls -d .[a-zA-Z]*'
```

The hidden alias uses the -d option on ls, which causes it to list directories by name instead of listing the contents of directories. This alias lists any file names that start with a dot and have a letter as the second character. The reason the alias is written to require a letter as the second character is to omit the directory names . and .., which are synonyms for the current directory and the current parent directory.

To get a list of currently defined aliases, use the alias command without an argument:

```
% alias
```

If you decide to get rid of an alias, you can use the unalias command, like this:

```
% unalias hidden
```

Aliases originated with the C Shell, but they proved to be so useful that most of the other shells have adopted them. Even if you are not using the C Shell, try entering the alias **command to see if you have any aliases defined.**

Introduction to ksh, the Korn Shell

The Korn Shell, written by David Korn, is based on the Bourne Shell. It includes some of the features that were introduced in the C Shell and adds some features of its own. The Korn Shell has both aliases and history, but they operate a bit differently.

If you are accustomed to working with the Bourne Shell, switching to the Korn Shell will hardly be noticed. The Korn Shell was intended to be a direct replacement for the Bourne Shell, and has been installed this way quite successfully (by being installed as /bin/sh in the place of the Bourne Shell). The Korn Shell uses the same initialization files, /etc/profile and ~/.profile, as the Bourne Shell.

But differences do exist between the Korn Shell and the Bourne Shell. For example, the type command in the Bourne Shell works the same way as the one in the Korn Shell but is called whence. Also, the Korn Shell has aliases that work like the ones in the C Shell.

Korn Shell command history

The command history of the Korn Shell works a little differently than the command history of the C Shell. You can think of the history of commands in the Korn Shell as a large text document, and your current prompt is asking for new text to append to the bottom line of the document. The rest of the document is made up of the text of the commands you have been entering. Moving back to a previous command is a matter of moving the cursor to the command you want. Of course, you can only see one command at a time — as if you are editing in a tiny window that is only one-line tall.

Editing the command history is simple because you are probably already familiar with the editing commands. Two sets of edit commands are built into the Korn Shell. You can select the emacs edit keys by issuing the following command:

```
$ set -o emacs
```

Or, you can select the vi editing keys with the following command:

```
$ set -o vi
```

If you select the emacs mode, you are ready to move around through the command lines, edit them at will, and select the line containing the command that you want to execute. C-p is the emacs command that moves you to the previous line, so you simply enter C-p until you get to the command that you want to use. If you want to edit the line, you have at your disposal all of the emacs commands for inserting, deleting, and changing characters. When the line is exactly the way you want it, just press the Return key to execute the command.

If you select vi as your command editor, you need to press the Escape key to put you into vi navigation mode. This allows you to move up and down through the commands, edit the one you want to use, and press Return to execute the command.

When you modify a command, you feel like you are invoking your favorite editor, but that isn't the case. These commands are all built into the Korn Shell. All you do when you set the mode is determine which keystrokes are mapped to the edit commands.

Functions

**10 Min.
To Go**

You can combine a collection of command line statements into a single block, assign a name to the block, and have that name become a new command consisting of all the commands in the block. Such a named block of commands is called a *function*. A function takes the following general form:

```
function name {
    list of commands
}
```

A function definition can be entered directly from the command line. The shell knows the syntax of a function, so it continues to prompt for more lines (by using the secondary prompt) until you have entered the closing brace. For example, the following series of commands defines a function named homehide that displays a count of the number of hidden files in your home directory:

```
$ function homehide {
>ls -Ad ~/.* | wc -l
>}
$ _
```

After you enter the function definition, homehide becomes a command built into the shell. If you want to verify that it has been defined, you can look at the text of the function by entering the set command with no arguments. The set command not only lists all of the environment variables, it also lists the full text of all the currently defined functions.

If you look at the content of the homehide function, you can see why you may want to avoid entering the entire command every time. The -A option causes the files selected by ls to include all of the hidden files. The -d option specifies that the file search is not to descend into subdirectories but, instead, limit itself to the names found in the named directory. The expression ~/.* restricts the selection to names in your home directory that begin with a period (which are the hidden files). The output of ls is piped into wc, which is specified with the -l option so it only outputs a count of the number of lines fed to it.

Anything that can be entered from the command line can also be entered from a file. For example, the following function definition is contained in a file named dcount.function:

```
function dcount {
    echo "Number of files in current directory:\c"
    /bin/ls | wc -l
    echo "Number of hidden files in current directory:\c"
    /bin/ls -Ad .* | wc -l
    echo "Number of logins:\c"
    who | wc -l
    echo "Number of processes:\c"
    ps ax | wc -l
}
```

Recall from Session 4 that the options for the ps command are customized for each version of UNIX; otherwise, this function will run perfectly anywhere. To be defined in your current shell, the function needs to be sourced into your current shell with the following command:

```
$ source dcount.function
```

The dcount function outputs count values. The \c at the end of each quoted string on the echo commands causes the string displayed by echo to not have a newline character at its end, so the numbers are displayed on the same line as the text. The result looks like this:

```
$ dcount
Number of files in current directory:     53
Number of hidden files in current directory:     66
Number of logins:     3
Number of processes:     76
```

The UNIX newline character is the ASCII Carriage Return character — the same one that your keyboard generates with the Return key. The newline character in UNIX generates both a carriage return (moving the cursor to the left) and a line feed (moving the cursor down one line).

Introduction to bash, the Bourne-Again Shell

As you might suspect from its name, the Bourne-Again Shell is based on the Bourne Shell. The Bourne-Again Shell (most often called bash) is the product of the Free Software Foundation, and was copyrighted as free software in 1989. It was originally designed and written to be part of a free implementation of the UNIX operating system, and this is exactly what has happened. The Linux operating system uses bash as its default shell.

The Bourne-Again Shell is not only completely compatible with the Bourne Shell, it also incorporates many of the features of both the C Shell and the Korn Shell. As in the Korn Shell, bash keeps a history of the command lines, and you can use either emacs or vi to select and edit them into new commands. You can also define and use both aliases and functions in bash.

Because bash is based primarily on the Bourne Shell, as is the Korn Shell, and because bash has all the capabilities of the Korn shell as well as those of the C Shell, it seems to have replaced the Korn Shell on many systems. Fundamental differences in syntax (especially in the writing of scripts) between the C Shell and the other shells has resulted in the C Shell's continued popularity. The fact that bash is free, and is also a direct replacement for both Bourne and Korn, makes it very popular.

The bash shell has taken the idea of initialization files to a new height by having several of them. Like the Bourne and Korn Shells, it starts by executing the /etc/profile script. It then looks in the user's home directory for ~/.bash_profile, ~/.bash_login, and then ~/.profile. If it is not a login shell, it uses ~./bashrc instead of ~/.bash_login. If it is a login shell, it executes ~/.bash_logout when you log out.

Other Shells

New shells are always being written and old shells are always being modified in a seeming quest for the perfect shell. Many shells exist, and many arguments rage on about what should be included in a shell and how things should work. Every shell has its roots in the Bourne Shell, but each one also has its own flavor and its own extensions. The following list contains the most well-known shells:

- **Ash** (ash) — This is an open source version of the bash shell that has some of the features removed and, as a result, is much smaller and runs scripts faster. It can be renamed and installed as /bin/sh (replacing the Bourne Shell) and used to execute scripts while bash continues to be used as the interactive shell.

- **Remote Shell** (rsh) — The Remote Shell allows you to run a shell locally while you are logged in to a remote system over an Internet connection. Commands allow you to mix remote and local operations. For example, you can run a command on the remote machine and redirect its output to a file on your local disk. An example of remote logins is found in Session 25.

- **Secure Shell** (ssh) — The SSH Secure Shell is a commercial product that encrypts the data passed between the shell and the computer. This shell is primarily used for the security of remote connections in virtual private networks, remote system administration, and file transfers of sensitive data.

- **Windowing Korn Shell** (wksh) — This is a Korn Shell with windowing designed to work in the X Window System.

- **Zsh** (zsh) — Designed for interactive use, this shell incorporates features from bash, ksh, and tcsh. If you want a shell with many features, zsh is what you are looking for.

If you decide to embark on your own search for the perfect shell, you must be able to switch from one shell to another. To switch to a new shell using chsh, the shell's name must be listed in the file named /etc/shells. However, if you intend to experiment with a strange shell, you may want to create a login just for that purpose because you may find yourself at the "point of no return." The mechanics of adding a new user, and assigning a default shell to the user, are explained in Session 19.

Done!

REVIEW

This session introduces you to some of the shells available on UNIX, highlighting those that are most well known and widely used.

- The chsh command can be used to change your default login shell.
- The C Shell introduced new features, such as command histories, command aliases, and the tilde as a synonym for the home directory.
- The Korn Shell combines the Bourne Shell with features from the C Shell.
- The Korn Shell adds the ability to define functions that are stored in the shell, much like environment variables.
- The Bourne-Again Shell is free software that combines the features of the Bourne Shell, the C Shell, and the Korn Shell.
- Many shells are available, many of which are designed for special purposes.

The following session takes a closer look at regular expressions and the applications that use them.

QUIZ YOURSELF

1. What is the process for editing the previous command in the C Shell? (See "C Shell command history.")
2. What is the purpose of an alias? (See "Aliases.")
3. The Korn Shell was derived from the Bourne Shell to add features from what other shell? (See "Introduction to ksh, the Korn Shell.")
4. Where is the definition of a function stored? (See "Functions.")
5. What is the purpose of the remote shell (rsh)? (See "Other Shells.")

Regular Expressions

Session Checklist

✔ Expression construction

✔ Grepping

✔ Advanced grepping

✔ The flags of grep

**30 Min.
To Go**

Regular expressions have become a very important part of UNIX. This session takes a more detailed look at regular expressions in general and the grep (get regular expression) utility in particular. The grep utility enables you to search through files to find words, phrases, and just about any collection of textual characters.

Expression Construction

A *regular expression* is a pattern defined by a string of characters. This pattern is used as a rule for matching, and thus locating, specific strings of characters in the names of files, or in the text within files.

You might think that something with a name like *regular expression* would have some solidity to its structure and a clear, consistent definition. Regular expressions have some basic structures in common, but there are some irregularities. Regular expressions have existed as part of various UNIX utilities since the very first shell. However, because each utility implements its own regular expression processor, details about the structure of regular expressions vary from one program to another. The difference in regular expression rules results partially from the fact that each program is trying to achieve something slightly different from the others. For example, the emacs and vi editors have special regular expression forms that allow you to match character strings found at the beginning or end of a line. The regular expression processor for a shell's command line doesn't know anything about matching line positions because it only matches patterns found in file names.

UNIX has a reputation for having cryptic commands. The primary reason for this reputation is the existence of regular expressions. If you come across a command in a script or in a manual that contains a regular expression, or if you look over someone's shoulder as they type an expression into a command line, it can seem very cryptic. But regular expressions really aren't as difficult as they look because you only need to write them — you seldom have to read one. A regular expression is a form of shorthand that you use to talk to a program. For example, instead of saying, "List the file names that are exactly five characters long and that start with J followed by a digit 1, 2, or 3 stored in subdirectories that end with the letters inc," you can use shorthand, like this:

```
$ ls *inc/J[123]???
```

If you are not accustomed to regular expressions, that still looks cryptic. The truth is, an expression of this sort seldom slips full-blown from the user's fingers to the keyboard. It comes about in steps. For example, you would normally create the above expression by entering several different ls commands. Your first attempt may have been to list all the files contained within directories that have names ending with inc:

```
$ ls *inc/*
```

That works, but if the list of names turns out to be too long, the list can be shortened by making the expression more specific and by limiting it to the names that start with J, as in the following:

```
$ ls *inc/J*
```

That also works, but the expression matches file names that you don't want. Therefore, you can refine the command further to list only those file names that have the digit 1, 2, or 3 following the J:

```
$ ls *inc/J[123]*
```

The final step would be to eliminate the rest of the unwanted files from the list by replacing the trailing asterisk with three question marks, which requires exactly three characters following the J and the digit 1, 2, or 3. We have now built the expression that I showed you at the beginning of this section:

```
$ ls *inc/J[123]???
```

Grepping

In my opinion, UNIX programmers and administrators use three utilities more than all others. The most used command is ls. The second most used is the text editor. My guess for the third most used is grep (get regular expression). The concept behind grep is really simple, but grep turns out to be one of the most useful commands in UNIX. All this program does is read through a file (or a group of files) and search for strings that match a regular expression.

The grep utility expects the command line to contain the regular expression followed by the list of files to search. For example, the following command reads through the

/etc/services file looking for the string http and, by displaying each line that contains a match, displays the port number assigned to the http protocol for your local Web server:

```
$ grep http /etc/services
http        80/tcp      www www-http    # WorldWideWeb HTTP
http        80/udp      www www-http    # HyperText Transfer Protocol
https       443/tcp         # MCom
https       443/udp         # MCom
http-alt    8008/tcp
http-alt    8008/udp
```

The /etc/services file contains all the local port assignments for the Internet. In this example, the http protocol of the Web is shown to be using port 80 for both tcp and udp connections. The specified grep pattern also matches https (the secure http protocol) and http-alt (an alternate Web port used for special purposes).

For more information on ports and protocols, see Session 29.

You can just as easily have grep search through more than one file. For example, if you have a Web site made up of a collection of HTML files and if you know that somewhere among them is a link to the emacs editor's Web site, you can find the link this way:

```
$ grep emacs *.html
gnu.html:<li><a href="manual/emacs/emacs_toc.html">emacs</a>
wcc.html:<li><a href="http://www.gnu.org/emacs">The emacs editor</a>
```

The requested pattern turns up links in two separate files. The file named gnu.html contains a link to a local page named manual/emacs/emacs_toc.html, and the file named wcc.html contains a link to the Internet site of the emacs editor. Using grep this way enables you to detect duplicate entries or verify that an entry doesn't appear anywhere in your files.

Whenever you are searching through more than one file, grep lists the file name on each line of output. If you search only one file, grep omits the file name. If you want, you can use the -H option so that the file name is always included in the output.

The file /etc/passwd is a configuration file that contains information about users. If you want to know more about who UNIX thinks you are, use your login name to enter a command such as the following:

```
$ grep herbert /etc/passwd
herbert:x:502:500:H G Wells:/home/herbert:/bin/sh
```

The output informs you that herbert has the user ID number 502 and is a member of the group with an ID of 500. His real name is H. G. Wells, he uses /home/herbert as his home directory, and he uses the Bourne Shell (/bin/sh). Session 19 further explores these configuration files.

If you enter a grep command without specifying any file names, grep searches the text that you pipe into it for pattern matches. For example, if you use the -aux options on the ps command, it lists all of the running processes in a long format that includes the user names. You pipe this output into grep to display all the processes being run by a specific user. The following command lists only the processes being run by root:

```
$ ps -aux | grep root
```

If you enter this command, you will notice that the very last process in the list is actually not a root process. It is the grep process that you are running to output the list, and it is a match because the name root appears somewhere on the line. The line that displays the grep process looks something like the following:

```
arthur   24790  0.0  0.0  2412  600 pts/2    S    11:21   0:00 grep root
```

The output of one grep can be piped into the input of another grep. For example, suppose that you want to find a line among your HTML files where you use the word local in a page title. You grep for the word local and find that it appears in many places other than the title of a page, so you need to refine your search. What you really need to find are the places where the word local and the word title appear on the same line. To do so, you can use the following command:

```
$ grep local *.html | grep title
```

The first grep command reads through all the HTML files and outputs only the lines that contain the word local. The output from the first grep command is used as input into the second command, which throws away everything except the lines containing the word title. I applied this command to my Web site and got the following output:

```
bckup.html:    <title>Home is a local place</title>
```

Advanced Grepping

When you use one or more of the special characters to form a regular expression for your search, you need to surround the expression with single or double quotes to prevent the shell from processing it. The following example is incorrect:

```
$ grep *.jpeg index.html            # wrong
```

The intention of this command is to list the lines containing file names ending in .jpeg, but it won't work. Instead, the shell takes a look at the command and expands *.jpeg into a list of all the file names that end in .jpeg in the current directory. To prevent this from happening and to cause the expression to be passed on to grep, enter the command this way:

```
$ grep '*.jpeg' index.html
```

You can use a regular expression for both grep and the shell in the same statement. For example, if you want to find all the file names ending in .jpeg in all the HTML files, you could use the following command:

```
$ grep '*.jpeg' *.html
```

Another reason for using quotes is to allow for the inclusion of spaces in the expression, as shown in the following:

```
$ grep 'in an open' *.html
as found in an open source implementation of the
```

If the quotes were removed from this example, the shell would split the arguments up, and grep would look for the word in inside files named an and open, as well as inside all the HTML files.

Regular expression operators

The basic regular expression characters summarized in Table 10-1 are similar to, but not the same as, those recognized by the shell. Notice that most of the operators don't actually match characters — most of them modify the matching characteristics of the preceding item in the expression. Any character not listed in this table is a literal match for itself.

Table 10-1   *The Regular Expression Operators*

Operators	Description
.	Matches any single character.
*	The preceding item is matched zero times or one time.
?	The preceding item is matched zero times or one time.
+	The preceding item is matched one or more times.
[ ]	Matches one of the characters inside the brackets.
[^]	Matches any character except those inside the brackets.
^	Matches the start of a line.
$	Matches the end of a line.
\	The escape character. Any character following a backslash is included literally and must be matched exactly.
\{m\}	The preceding item is matched exactly m times.
\{m,\}	The preceding item is matched m or more times.
\{m,n\}	The preceding item is matched a minimum of m and a maximum of n times.
\<	Matches the beginning of a word. That is, the character preceding this expression operator character cannot be a letter, digit, or the underscore character.
\>	Matches the ending of a word. That is, the character following this operator cannot be a letter, digit, or the underscore character.

A period matches any single character. For example, if you want to find every four-letter word beginning with H and ending with k, the expression would be H..k. The period is not a special character to the shell, which makes it convenient if you want to match text that contains spaces. For example:

```
$ grep in.an.open *.html
as found in an open source implementation of the
```

An asterisk character can be used as a multiplier to allow the character preceding it to be repeated any number of times. The asterisk is a special character to the shell, so any expression that uses it should be surrounded by quotes. The following expression matches jimy, jimmy, and jimmmy, but it doesn't match jim or jmy. It will match jiy because the asterisk modifies the m for "zero or more" matches.

```
$ grep 'jim*y' *.html
```

Placing brackets around a collection of characters matches a single character in the text with any one of the characters in the brackets. For example, the expression h[ei]ll matches both hill and hell, but not hall. If you insert a caret character as the first character in the brackets, the action is reversed. That is, the expression h[^ei]ll matches both hall and hull, but not hill or hell.

The following expression matches any nonzero digit:

```
[123456789]
```

You can use a shortcut to do the same thing. A hyphen can be used to indicate a range of characters. The following expression, just like the previous one, matches any nonzero digit:

```
[1-9]
```

Because the expression matches just one character, the multiplier can be used with it to allow it to repeat and match any number of nonzero digits, like this:

```
[1-9]+
```

You can combine several ranges into a single expression. The following expression matches any digit, any uppercase character, or any lowercase character:

```
[0-9A-Za-z]
```

The following expression uses a multiplier to match any string that begins with a letter followed by a string of several digits, and then ends with a lowercase letter:

```
[A-Za-z][0-9]*[a-z]
```

A caret character can be used inside the brackets to reverse the matching action. The following will match any kind of punctuation character, but will not match a letter or a digit:

```
[^0-9A-Za-z]
```

The only characters that have special powers when they are used inside square brackets are the closing square bracket, the hyphen, and the caret. An asterisk, for example, would only be a match for an actual asterisk character in the text. The closing square bracket, the hyphen, or the caret can only be taken as literal characters if they are included in specific ways:

- **A hyphen** is taken as a literal character if nothing follows it other than the closing bracket.
- **A closing square bracket** is taken as a literal character if it is the first character in the list.
- **A caret** is taken as a literal character if it does not come first in the list.

For example, the following expression matches any one of the letters A, B, or C, and also matches a right square bracket, a hyphen (minus sign), or a caret:

```
[]AB^C-]
```

The caret character takes a different meaning when placed outside of square brackets and at the very beginning of the entire expression. When a caret is used this way, the expression matches text only at the beginning of a line. For example, the following command only matches lines that begin with the characters <center>:

```
$ grep '^<center>' *.html
```

Anything at the front of a string that would otherwise match — even a single space or tab — will prevent the match.

The dollar character is similar to the carat, but it matches the end of a line instead of the beginning. The following example matches the characters nto only if they come at the very end of a line:

```
$ grep 'nto$' *.html
```

You can combine these two into one expression to match an entire line. The following command finds all lines in the HTML files that consist of <hr> and nothing else:

```
$ grep '^<hr>$' *.html
```

If you want to search a file for one of the special characters, you need to precede it with the escape character. Placing a backslash in front of a bracket or a caret takes away its special powers and reduces it to a literal match. For example, if you want to search through all of your HTML files to find an exact match on the string [0], then you need to escape the bracket characters so that the match can be made, as follows:

```
$grep '\[0\]' *.html
```

You can use this same technique if you want to search for a backslash, asterisk, or period. For example, if you want to locate a backslash followed by an asterisk, you can enter the following command:

```
$ grep '\\\*' *.html
```

The first backslash acts as the escape for the second backslash, making it a literal character to be matched. The third backslash acts as the escape for the asterisk.

If you want to be very specific about the number of times an item is repeated, you can specify the number of repetitions. By placing a number between \{ and \}, the item must occur exactly that number of times. The following expression matches jimmy, but does not match jimy or jimmmy:

```
jim\{2\}y
```

If you want a character to be matched an unlimited number of times, but you want to impose a minimum, insert a comma following the number specifying the minimum. The following expression matches jimmy, jimmmy, jimmmmy; and so on, but it does not match jimy:

```
jim\{2,\}y
```

Finally, you can set both a lower limit and an upper limit by specifying two numbers. The following expression matches jimmy, jimmmy, and jimmmmy; but does not match jimy or jimmmmmy:

```
jim\{2,4\}y
```

Anything in an expression that matches exactly one character can be repeated by numbers. You can place any of the repeating expressions after a set of square brackets, because a set of square brackets only matches one character. For example, the following expression matches a string made up of all digits and commas, as long as the string is at least two characters long and no more than eight:

```
[0-9,]\{2,8\}
```

**10 Min.
To Go**

Other versions of grep

In most cases, when you use grep, you are searching for an exact match on a string of characters that doesn't contain any of the regular expression operators. It also turns out that using software that matches regular expressions is not as efficient as using software that performs a simple string match. The fgrep (fast grep) utility is a version of grep that only has exact matching, but otherwise works just like grep. For example, the following command finds all occurrences of the word center in a collection of HTML files:

```
$ fgrep center *.html
```

The only advantage to using fgrep is to speed things up when you are searching a lot of files.

Another version of grep is called egrep (extended grep). The modern versions of egrep are not as extended as they once were because most of the extensions now also exist in grep. But some differences exist. The characters \{, and \} used in grep are written as {, and } in egrep. A vertical bar can be used as an OR operator to allow a match to be made by two or more expressions. For example, if you want to search all of the HTML files for every <b> tag and every <i> tag, you could use the following:

```
$ egrep '<i>|<b>' *.html
```

The Flags of grep

You can use a few option flags to make grep act differently. I find that the -l (ell) option is one of the most useful. This option limits the output to the names of the files that contain at least one match for the expression. For example, if you want to get a list of the names of all the HTML files that contain href, and thus contain a link to another page, you can use the following command:

```
$ grep -l href *.html
```

This command lists the names of all the files but not the actual lines in the files.

The -L option does just the opposite by listing the names of all the files that do not contain a match. To get a list of all the Web pages that do not contain a link to another page, enter the following command:

```
$ grep -L href *.html
```

You can also get a count of the lines with matches. The following command uses the -c option to list the names of the files that contain a match, along with the number of matching lines in each file:

```
$ grep -c href *.html
```

The keywords in an HTML file are not case-sensitive; as far as a Web browser is concerned, the words HREF and href mean the same thing. However, everything in UNIX, including grep, is case-sensitive so, if you use grep to find all of the links in an HTML file, you could miss a few unless you use the -i option to request that the match ignore case. The following command outputs a list of all the files that contain href, Href, HREF, or any other combination of upper- and lowercase:

```
$ grep -il href *.html
```

Table 10-2 provides a summary of the most common flags. Depending on the version of grep you are using, additional flags may be available, but the flags in the table are universally available. Many different versions of UNIX have adopted the GNU version of grep because it is quite portable and has many options. If you are using the GNU grep, you may want to take a look at its man page to see what other flags you can use besides those listed here.

Table 10-2 *The Most Commonly Used grep Flags*

Flag	Description
-c	Output only the file names and a count of the number of matches in each file.
-E	Use the pattern matching of egrep.
-F	Use the pattern matching of fgrep.
-I	Ignore case when matching letters.

Continued

Table 10-2 *Continued*

Flag	Description
-H	Insert the name of the file at the end of each output line even if only one file is being searched.
-h	Do not insert the file name at the beginning of each output line.
-L	Output only the names of the files that do not contain a match.
-l	Output only the names of the files that contain a match.
-n	Precede each output line with its line number in the file.
-s	Suppress error messages about nonexistent and unreadable files.
-v	Output only the lines that do not match the pattern.

Done!

REVIEW

In this session, you learn how to use the regular expressions defined in grep to locate text in a file or a group of files. Programs such as vi and emacs also use regular expressions. Programs such as sed and awk, which are covered in Sessions 20 and 21, use regular expressions to search through files and make changes.

- Although all regular expressions are commonly used to match text, the forms of these expressions vary from one application to the next.
- The grep utility program can be used to search multiple files for complex regular expression matches.
- You can pipe output from other applications through grep to filter and refine the data that is displayed.
- The grep utility provides a large number of special operators for the construction of regular expressions, and grep also has several flags that can be used to modify its actions.
- The fgrep and egrep utilities do the same job as grep but have features of their own.

The next session takes a closer look at the UNIX file system. Operations such as mounting and unmounting CD-ROM and floppy disk drives are explained. The next session also contains an expanded explanation of file permissions and how to achieve such things as changing file user and group ownership.

QUIZ YOURSELF

1. What is the procedure for constructing a complicated regular expression? (See "Expression Construction.")

2. How can you use grep to discover a home directory and the default shell of a user? (See "Grepping.")

3. When using a regular expression with grep, what can you do to keep the shell from processing the special characters? (See "Advanced Grepping.")

4. Under what circumstances would you want to use fgrep? (See "Other versions of grep.")

5. How can you make grep list only file names instead of each line on which it finds a match? (See "The Flags of grep.")

PART

II

Saturday Morning

1. Why is the vi editor called a modal editor?

2. In the vi editor, what is the yank buffer?

3. Which vi editor command can be used to undo an edit action?

4. In the notation used in the emacs editor, what does C-x C-c mean?

5. What does the term Meta key refer to in emacs?

6. When working in a windowing environment, what action do you need to take to activate the mouse for the emacs editor?

7. In the emacs editor, the object that indicates your current location in the text is not called a cursor. What is it called, and how does it differ from a cursor?

8. In the Bourne Shell, what command would define an environment variable named LASTDIR to contain the string /home/max/prev?

9. The ls command lists all the file names from the current directory, and the wc -w command produces a count of the number of words passed to it. How would you write a single command to count the number of files in the current directory?

10. What command would you enter to get a list of all the files in the current directory that have names beginning with J and containing the characters va?

11. What is sourcing a script?

12. What are two different ways to remove the definition of an environment variable?

13. What is a command that uses the date utility to store the current date and time into an environment variable named TSTAMP?

14. The Bourne Shell and the Korn Shell use the same initialization scripts when they start. What are the names of these files?

15. How would you define an alias named lhome that always lists the files in your home directory?

16. How would you define a function named lhome that always lists the files in your home directory?

17. In the Korn Shell and the Bourne-Again Shell, it is possible to set the command editing mode to one of two editors. What are these editors, and how are the modes set?

18. What command can you enter that tells you which HTML files in the current directory contain the word color?

19. How can you list all the lines in a file named HamNum that contain a word beginning with the letter J followed by one or more digits?

20. How can you list all the lines in a file named HamNum that end with either the three letters nto or nxo?

PART

III

Saturday Afternoon

Session 11
Files and the File System

Session 12
File System Operations

Session 13
The World's Handiest Utilities

Session 14
The man Pages

Session 15
E-mail

Session 16
Writing Shell Scripts

Files and the File System

Session Checklist

✔ Setting file permissions

✔ Adjusting file timestamps

✔ Working with files and directories

✔ Changing file ownership

✔ Linking files

**30 Min.
To Go**

This session takes a look at files and directories by introducing several utilities that can be used to create, destroy, duplicate, and change the characteristics of files and directories. The three primary file utilities are mv, cp, and rm. Each has special options that can be used to modify their behavior. You can use these utilities on existing files and directories, and other utilities are available to create new files and directories. One of the most important topics covered in this session is managing file permissions to provide a security barrier.

Setting File Permissions

You may recall from Session 3 that when you use the ls command to display the attributes of a file, the information is formatted as a single line with the permissions displayed on the left:

```
$ ls -l onxyz
-rwxrwxrwx    1 arthur    users        7669 Nov 20 07:17 onxyz
```

The permissions information is composed of ten characters organized as shown in Figure 11-1. The first character designates the file type. (A hyphen denotes a regular file.) The next nine characters specify the permissions granted to the owner (user) of the file, the permissions granted to the other members of the owner's group, and the permissions granted to everyone else.

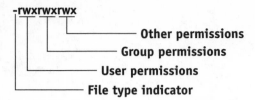

-rwxrwxrwx
— Other permissions
— Group permissions
— User permissions
— File type indicator

Figure 11-1   *File type and permissions indicators*

The command to change file permissions is chmod (change mode). To change permissions, you must specify whose permissions you want to change and which access permissions you want to enable or disable. The following example gives the user permission to execute a file named onxyz:

```
$ chmod u+x onxyz
```

The letter u specifies that the user's permissions are being modified. You can also specify g for group and o for other. The plus sign indicates that the permission is being turned on. To turn a permission off, use a minus sign. The x specifies that the execution permission is being turned on. Use r to alter the read permissions and w to alter the write permissions. You can use these letters singly or in combinations. For example, to turn on both read and write permissions for both the group and others, use this command:

```
$ chmod go-rw onxyz
```

If you want to set the permission setting for the user, the group, and the others to the same value with a single command, you can use the three letters ugo. The following command allows all three to execute the file onxyz:

```
$ chmod ugo+x onxyz
```

You can also refer to all three (user, group, and others) by using the letter a. The following command is identical to the previous one:

```
$ chmod a+x onxyz
```

Instead of using a plus or minus, you can use an equals sign to set permissions exactly. For example, the following command enables read and execute permissions while disabling the write permissions for the group and others:

```
$ chmod go=rx onxyz
```

The result you get from this command is the same as if you had used go+rx in one chmod command followed by go-w in another.

Understanding the octal form of file permissions

If you prefer to think in numbers instead of letters, you can use octal digits to change permissions. Each of the nine permissions settings can be represented by a single bit (1 for on and 0 for off), so nine binary bits match with the nine permissions settings.

An octal digit between 0 and 7 can be used to represent any one of the possible three-bit patterns, as shown in Table 11-1. The permissions flags consist of three groups of three bits each, so it is possible to represent all of the possible access permissions with just three octal digits.

Table 11-1 *Converting Permissions Settings*

Letters	Binary	Octal
- - -	000	0
- - x	001	1
- w -	010	2
- w x	011	3
r - -	100	4
r - x	101	5
r w -	110	6
r w x	111	7

This means that another way of writing r-xr--rwx is 547.

Using an octal number as the argument of the chmod command allows you to set all the permissions bits at once to any pattern you like. The following command enables read, write, and execute for the user and, in the same command, enables read and execute permissions while disabling write permissions for the group and others:

```
$ chmod 755 onxyz
```

No matter what the permissions settings were before the previous command was issued, the new set of permissions looks like this:

```
-rwxr-xr-x
```

Setting initial file permissions

The same permissions that apply to files also apply to directories. You must have write permission to the directory before you can add a new file to it or make a change to any of the files stored in it. Also, you must have directory read permission if you want to read any of the files the directory contains, or even to get a list of the names of its files.

Whenever you enter a command that creates a new file, the program that creates the file imposes the pattern of permissions. For example, when you use the vi editor to create a new file, the editor sets the following permissions for the new file:

```
-rw-rw-rw-
```

This pattern is a reasonable default because it awards read and write permissions to everyone but doesn't assume the file should be executable. You can prevent a program from assigning certain permissions by using umask, which is a value stored in the shell. If you enter the umask command without anything else on the command line, you can look at your current umask setting:

```
$ umask
022
```

The setting is displayed in the form of three octal digits that represent nine bits corresponding to the nine permissions settings, as with the chmod command. Whenever a new file is created, the umask bits that are set to 1 specify which permissions are not set by the application, even if the application tries to set them. The umask bits acts as a mask over the settings preventing an application from setting certain permissions bits. The value 022 prevents write access from being assigned to the group and to others because those umask bits are set to 1. For example, using the value 022 as your umask setting causes vi to set permissions on new files to the following:

```
-rw-r--r--
```

The value 022 is used as an example here because it is the most common default setting. This setting prevents anyone other than yourself from making changes to your new files. You can set your umask value to anything you want. For example, the following command sets umask to prevent an application from giving any permissions at all to others but allows any permissions to be set for the user and the group:

```
$ umask 007
```

The umask setting affects files only at the moment of their creation. After a file has been created, the owner has no problem changing a file's permissions.

If you want to experiment with umask, you can do so by using the touch command, which creates a new empty file with read and write permissions for everyone. The following sequence of commands and responses demonstrates how umask modifies the initial settings:

```
$ umask 000
$ umask
000
$ touch testfile1
$ ls -l testfile1
-rw-rw-rw-    1 arthur    users            0 Nov 20 08:36 testfile1
$ umask 077
$ umask
077
$ touch testfile2
$ ls -l testfile2
-rw-------    1 arthur    users            0 Nov 20 08:37 testfile2
```

In this series of commands, the umask value is initially set to 000, which is verified by entering the umask command a second time without an argument. The value 000 has the effect of disabling umask. The touch command is then used to create a file named testfile1. The umask value is set to 077, which completely masks the setting of any permissions for the group and others, which results in testfile2 granting read and write permissions only to the owner of the file.

Adjusting File Timestamps

A file has two timestamps. The one most often seen is the *modification* time, which is the time and date the file was last modified or, if it has never been modified, the time and date the file was created. The other timestamp is the *access* time, which is the last time a process read something from the file. The modification time is the more useful of the two timestamps, so it is generally referred to as the file's timestamp. The long form of ls normally displays the modification time, like this:

```
$ ls -l onxyz
-rwxrwxrwx    1 arthur    users         7669 Nov 20 07:17 onxyz
```

You can use the -u option to request that ls display the time that the file was last accessed, as in the following command:

```
$ ls -ul onxyz
-rwxrwxrwx    1 arthur    users         7669 Nov 23 11:21 onxyz
```

The access time is always the same as or later than the modification time. If you modify a file, both timestamps are adjusted. In the previous examples, the file named onxyz is executable, so it is possible that the file was executed, which would account for the difference in its modification and access timestamps.

You can update the modification timestamp to the current time with the touch command as follows:

```
$ touch onxyz
```

The file already exists, so instead of being created, it simply has its modification timestamp changed to the current time. With the -a option you can use the touch command to update the access time as follows:

```
$ touch -a onxyz
```

Working with Files and Directories

This section describes some of the fundamental commands that can be used to make modifications to the file system. If you have the appropriate access permissions, you can use these commands to rename, relocate, create, and delete files and directories.

Changing file names

The mv (move) command can be used to change the name of a file as follows:

```
$ mv oldname newname
```

But, as its name implies, mv can be used for more than simply renaming a file — it can also be used to move a file from one location to another. It doesn't matter whether the old and new locations are in the same directory or on completely separate disk drives. For example, to move a file from one directory to another, you can use the following command:

```
$ mv glolist.html /usr/home/pagers/oldlist.html
```

This command moves the local file named glolist.html to the directory named /user/home/pagers and names it oldlist.html. The new name does not have to be different from the old name. If you name only a directory as the target, the mv statement moves the file to that directory without changing the name of the original file. The following example is the same as the previous one, except that only the location of the file changes — its name stays the same:

```
$ mv glolist.html /usr/home/pagers
```

The more recent versions of the mv command can move anything. If you name a directory as the source (the first argument), the entire directory tree is moved to the new location (the second argument). This is a relatively new addition to mv, so the version that you are using may not have this capability.

The mv command is quite smart about the way it does things. If a file or directory is being moved to a new name within the same directory, it simply changes the name listed in the directory. If the move is to another directory on the same physical disk drive, mv simply removes the name of the item being moved from the original directory and adds it to the new one. If the move is to a different physical disk drive, mv copies everything to the new location and then deletes the original.

Before you can move a file or directory, you must have the proper permissions. You can always move a file that you own. If the move is an attempt to overwrite an existing file, then you must have permission to do so. You are notified if you don't have permission to replace a file. You can use the -i and -f flags to control the way mv overwrites files:

- **mv -i** — This command activates an interactive prompt. If an existing file is to be overwritten, you are prompted before the file is deleted. You must enter y to confirm that you want the file overwritten.

- **mv -f** — This command forces target files to be overwritten. If you don't have permission to overwrite a file but you would be able to use chmod to change the permissions, the mv command will overwrite the file and not mention that it had to change the permission. Without this option, the mv command requests confirmation before overwriting every file.

Duplicating files

The cp (copy) command is very similar to the mv command, except that the original file is always duplicated, leaving the original completely unchanged. The mv command leaves the timestamp unchanged, but the cp command, which always creates a new file, sets the timestamp on the new file to the current time. Three flags are available to control cp:

- **cp -i** — This command activates an interactive prompt. If an existing file is going to be overwritten, you are prompted before the file is deleted. You must enter y to confirm that you want the file overwritten.

- **cp -r** — If the item being copied is a directory, the directory and all its contents (files and subdirectories) are duplicated. Without this option, no directory will be copied.
- **cp -p** — The original timestamp and permissions settings are preserved in the new files and directories. Without this flag, the timestamps are set to the current time, and umask is applied to the setting of permissions on the new files.

Deleting files

The rm (remove) command is the last of the three basic file manipulation utilities. It can be used to delete a single file or a complete directory tree. In order to delete a file, you must have write permission for it. If you don't, you must either be the owner of the file or the superuser. You can use the following options to control the way rm works:

- **rm -f** — If a file is write-protected and you are either the owner of the file or the super user, the file is deleted. Without this flag, the file could still be deleted, but you are asked to confirm the deletion of each write-protected file.
- **rm -r** — If the item that you try to delete is a directory, this option deletes the entire directory tree, including all of its files and subdirectories. If you do not have permission to delete one or more files in the tree, they (and the path to them) are left intact, and all others are removed.

Creating directories

The mkdir command creates a new directory. For example, if you want to create a directory named workdir in the current directory, you can do so with the following command:

```
$ mkdir workdir
```

The mkdir default permissions on a newly created directory allow read, write, and execute for everyone, but the umask value modifies the settings for new directories just as it does for new files. You can override both the default and the umask value by specifying the octal mode flags on the mkdir command. By using the -m option, the flag settings can be specified in the character form or as octal digits, just as they are on the chmod command. The following command creates a directory and assigns only read and write permissions for user, group, and others:

```
$ mkdir -m 666 workdir
```

If you want to check the permission settings, to verify that they are set the way you intended, you must use the -d option with the ls command:

```
$ ls -ld workdir
drw-rw-rw-    1 arthur    users       4096 Nov 21 11:37 workdir
```

Without the -d option, the ls command attempts to list the members of the directory instead of listing the directory itself.

You can use the mkdir command with the -p option to create several directories defining a complete path. The following command creates the directory named bay, as well as the directories mls and resid if they don't already exist:

```
$ mkdir -p mls/resid/bay
```

The rmdir command can be used to remove a directory, but only if the directory is empty. Like mkdir, you can use the -p option with rmdir to cause the command to delete all of the empty directories along a path. The following command removes the bay directory if it is empty. Then, if that leaves the resid directory empty, resid is also deleted. Finally, if deleting resid leaves mls empty, mls is also deleted:

```
$ rmdir -p mls/resid/bay
```

Changing File Ownership

The chown (change owner) command can be used to transfer the ownership of a file from one user to another. For example, if you have a file named onxyz and you want to change the ownership to fred, you can do so with this command:

```
$ chown fred onxyz
```

Be aware that this process is a one-way street because you must either be the owner of the file or the superuser to change the ownership of a file. After you give the file to fred, you can't get it back.

The chgrp (change group) command works in much the same way as chown. The syntax of the two commands is the same, except that chgrp requires a group name and chown requires a user name. To change the group of a file named onxyz to a group named pdq, enter the following:

```
$ chgrp pdq onxyz
```

Every user is the member of a group. A user creating a file is assigned as the file's owner, and the group that the user belongs to is assigned as the file's group. However, nothing requires that the owner of a file and the file itself must belong to the same group.

The same set of permission restrictions that apply to chgrp also apply to chown. If you are allowed to change owner, you can change the group.

 A system configuration setting can be made to prevent you from changing ownership of your files. If you attempt to change the ownership of a file and get the error message Operation not permitted, **then only the superuser can change file ownership. In this day of high-security risks, this limitation is imposed more often than not.**

Linking Files

10 Min.
To Go As you may recall from the earlier discussion of the mv command, you can move a file from one directory to another simply by removing its name from one directory and inserting it

into another. The file itself remains in the same location and is not changed in any way. In other words, every file exists as an unnamed entity of its own somewhere on disk, and it is only a directory that assigns it a name and keeps track of its location.

Figure 11-2 shows a diagram representing a directory named /home/fred that contains three files. The file named onxyz is located on the disk at location 106, and this number is stored in the directory along with the name. In the same way, the directory has the disk location of sig as 492 and exrc as 881. The files can be anywhere on the same disk as the directory as long as the directory contains the correct location numbers.

/home/fred

onxyz	106
sig	492
exrc	881

106	file data...
492	file data...
881	file data...

Figure 11-2 *A directory contains the disk addresses of its files.*

Nothing prevents two or more directories from referring to the same disk location, causing the same file to appear simultaneously in more than one directory. In fact, the file contains no information about its name, so the same file can be listed in multiple directories under different names, as shown in Figure 11-3. The exact location on the disk where these directories and files are stored is not important.

/home/fred

onxyz	106
sig	492
exrc	881

106	file data...
492	file data...
881	file data...

/home/arthur

onxyz	106
oldsig	492
grpsig	492

/root/work/lfiles

sig	492
exrc	881

Figure 11-3 *A file can have different names and appear in multiple directories.*

In Figure 11-3, the file at disk location 106 is named onxyz in both the /home/fred directory and the /home/arthur directory. The file at location 492 appears under the name sig in both the /home/fred directory and the /root/work/lfiles directory, and it also appears twice with two different names in the /home/arthur directory. Each of these directory entries has an owner and a set of permissions.

These kinds of links are easy to create by using the ln (link) command. The first argument is the existing directory entry, and the second argument is the new one you wish to create. If the directory of /home/fred contains the files shown in Figure 11-3, you can create the new directory entries in /home/arthur with the following commands. The first name is that of a directory entry that already exists, and the second is the name of directory that is being created:

```
$ ln /home/fred/onxyz /home/arthur/onxyz
$ ln /home/fred/sig /home/arthur/oldsig
$ ln /home/fred/sig /home/arthur/grpsig
```

After linking these files, a small change appears in the information displayed by ls for the file /fred/onxyz:

```
$ ls -l /home/fred/onxyz
-rwxrwxrwx   2 arthur   users        7669 Nov 23 11:21 onxyz
```

The number 2 that appears immediately in front of the name of the owner is the number of links to the file. If another link were to be created, such as one in the /root/work/lfilse directory in Figure 11-3, the number would change to 3 because of the presence of three links to the file. These directory links are all equivalent. The links could have been created in any order, and the result would have been the same. The original link is no different from any of the others, and even if the original link were deleted, the file would still exist and be accessible through any of its other links.

It is not possible to create this type of link to a file on another disk drive or in another partition of the same drive, because the location of the file in the directory is nothing more than an offset from the beginning of the disk, and the current disk drive is assumed. This direct address form is known as a *hard link*. Another kind of link, called a *symbolic link*, can be used to span disk drives.

Figure 11-4 shows how a symbolic link is constructed. The directory entry named onxy is a hard link to a local file containing data, just as before. The directory entry named lanhom is also a link to a file on the local directory, but instead of the data for the file itself, there is special link information that contains everything necessary to locate the actual file data on another disk drive.

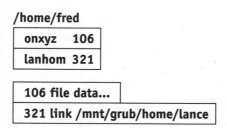

/home/fred

onxyz	106
lanhom	321

106 file data...
321 link /mnt/grub/home/lance

Figure 11-4 *Files on other disk drives can be linked through special disk entries.*

If the -s option is used on the ln command, it specifies that the link be symbolic. The symbolic link in Figure 11-4 can be created with the following command:

```
$ ln -s /mnt/grub/home/lance /home/fred/lanhom
```

The ln command is creating a new file on the local disk to act as the indirect link, so it sets the permissions according to umask. If the umask setting is all zeroes, the ln command awards read, write, and execute permissions to everyone. The file that is created is a special link file, so it shows up with an l (ell) as the file type if you look at it with ls:

```
$ ls -l lanhom
lrwxrwxrwx   1 fred    users      6 Nov 20 13:07 lanhom -> /mnt/grub/home/lance
```

After you have created a symbolic link, you can treat it just about the same as any other directory entry. You can use the mv command to rename the link or the cp command to duplicate the contents of the file or directory that the link points to. The newly created duplicate file or directory is then a hard link to new data. You can use the rm command to remove only the symbolic link and leave the data intact.

As a safety measure, the rm -r command does not delete the entire tree of files and directories inside a symbolically linked directory. This prevents the unexpected destruction that could occur if you decided to remove an old directory system that contained a forgotten symbolic link buried somewhere deep inside.

Done!

REVIEW

In this session, you learn how to use command line utilities to manage files and directories. The ability to set levels of permissions on each individual file makes the UNIX file system extremely secure.

- The chmod command can be used to control file and directory access permissions.
- The three basic commands — cp, mv, and rm — fulfill the basic needs of file and directory management.
- File ownership can be modified using the chown and chgrp commands.
- Every file has a timestamp that is updated every time the file itself is updated.
- The name of a file is the property of the directory, not of the file itself, so it is possible to assign any name to a file. It is also possible for the same file to appear under many different names.

The following session explores the file system further, describing, for example, how you can combine multiple disk drives into a single file system by mounting the drives as directories. The next session also explores the internal form of a UNIX file system based on i-nodes. The session also provides an introduction to the special files used for communicating with hardware devices.

QUIZ YOURSELF

1. Why are octal digits used on the chmod command instead of regular base 10 digits? (See "Understanding the octal form of file permissions.")

2. What two things determine the file permissions settings for a newly created file? (See "Setting initial file permissions.")

3. What command can be used to delete an entire directory tree and all its files? (See "Deleting files.")

4. What makes it possible for the same file to appear under different names in different directories? (See "Linking Files.")

5. What is the difference between a hard link and a symbolic link? (See "Linking Files.")

File System Operations

Session Checklist

✔ Device nodes

✔ Hard disk file systems

✔ Other file systems

✔ Internal file system structure

**30 Min.
To Go**

This session takes a closer look at file systems and explains how devices, including disk drives, are attached to UNIX in such a way that your processes can easily access them. You can connect a device to UNIX and allow your software to read from it and write to it as if it were a file. In particular, any number of disk drives can be included so that the combination of drives appears to be one large file system with multiple directories. A clever file system mechanism allows disk drives with fixed-size blocks to contain files that dynamically expand as needed.

Device Nodes

In order to read data coming in from a device, or write data to a device, you need to have two pieces of information: the *interrupt* (the ID that specifies the hardware port connecting the computer to the device) and the software *device driver* that knows how to communicate with that particular type of device. The kernel maintains a table of device drivers that are installed on the system and indexes the table by assigning each driver its own ID number. The result is that numbers identify both the driver and the interrupt (also called the *port*). The number for the device driver is called the *major number*, and the number for the port is called the *minor number*.

UNIX assigns an alias name to identify a particular major and minor number pair, which effectively assigns a unique name to each device. Naming conventions are used to construct alias names, and these conventions can play a part in helping you identify the devices.

Naming conventions vary among different versions of UNIX, but certain conventions seem to be universal. For example, an alias beginning with the letters hd is usually used to identify an Integrated Drive Electronics (IDE) hard drive, sd is often used to indicate the device is a Small Computer System Interface (SCSI) hard drive, and st could indicate a SCSI tape drive. An alias that starts with tty or with cu is always a terminal.

Aliases are stored in a directory in the same fashion as file names, which means that you can use ls to view information about an alias. A directory entry is known as a *special file* or a *device node*. Every UNIX system stores the device nodes in the directory named /dev. Every device node is either a *character* node or a *block* node. Examples of character devices are keyboards and terminal display screens that can read and/or write only one character at a time. A character device is also called a *serial* device. Examples of block devices are disk drives and CD-ROMs that can read and/or write a block of bytes in a single operation.

Some devices can act as both character and block devices. An example of this is a tape drive, which can transfer entire blocks of data or one byte at a time. A device node is either one type or the other so, to have the flexibility of using both character and block mode for the same device, it is necessary to have two device nodes in the /dev directory. Both device nodes have the same minor number, but may have different major numbers.

Device nodes and files are very different, but they do share certain characteristics. Depending on permissions settings and the capabilities of the device, device nodes can be opened, read from, and written to just like a file. This kind of raw I/O is not used very often, but there are cases where it is necessary. For example, the print spooler formats data for output and writes it directly to the device node /dev/lp.

The terminal device node

You can use the tty command to determine the device node of your terminal, and then you can use ls to display its characteristics:

```
$ tty
/dev/tty1
$ ls -l /dev/tty1
crw--w----   1 arthur   tty          4,   1 Nov 22 12:27 /dev/tty1
```

The timestamp for a device node is updated each time a program writes to it, so every character that appears on your screen updates the timestamp. The major and minor numbers appear where ls normally displays the size of a file. This particular terminal has a major number of 4, which indicates the device driver for this terminal type, and a minor number of 1, which indicates where the terminal is physically connected to the computer.

The permission settings for a device are the same as they are for a file. Instead of a hyphen for a regular file or d for a directory, the letter c indicates that this is a character type device node. Had this been a block device node, the type would have been indicated by the letter b.

For a terminal, the owner of the device node is changed to become the user that is logged in at the moment, but the group always remains tty. The shell, and any other program run by the current user, is thus able to read from the keyboard and write to the screen because the program and the terminal have the same owner and thus have the owner's privileges. And any member of the tty group can write to the screen — a capability that comes in quite handy for sending messages as described in Session 13.

Hard disk drive device nodes

When UNIX is installed a hard disk drive can be divided into partitions, and each partition has its own device node. You can easily determine the names of these device nodes by using the df (disk free) utility. The purpose of df is to tell you how much space is available on a disk drive, but it also reports the total size of the drive, how much of it is used, and the name of the device node. For example, the output of df can look like the following:

```
$ df
Filesystem        1k-blocks      Used Available Use% Mounted on
/dev/hda5          6056164    3342140   2406384  59% /
/dev/hda1            23302       4205     17894  20% /boot
/dev/hdb1          3845592    1807108   1843136  50% /home
```

This computer has three disk drives, with device nodes named hda5, hda1, and hdb1. All of these drives are different sizes. At 6GB, the hda5 drive is the largest, with just over 3GB (59 percent) being used. The hda1 and hdb1 drives are assigned the directory names /boot and /home. The hda5 disk drive is being used as the root directory, which is simply named /. One drive always has the name /.

More information on mounting and naming disk drives is provided in the next section. If your computer is on a local area network, you may see the names of some of the other computers in the first column. These names are Network File System (NFS) links to directories on hard drives of other computers. NFS is described in Session 25.

When you use ls to look at these device nodes, you get the following output:

```
$ ls -l /dev/hda5 /dev/hda1 /dev/hdb1
brw-rw----  1 root     disk      3,   5 Mar 23  2001 /dev/hda5
brw-rw----  1 root     disk      3,   1 Mar 23  2001 /dev/hda1
brw-rw----  1 root     disk      3,  65 Mar 23  2001 /dev/hdb1
```

The letter b on the left indicates that these are all block device nodes. They have the same major number, which indicates they all use the same device driver, but each one is unique because it has its own minor number. The superuser is the owner and has read and write permission. The node is a member of the disk group, and the group is also awarded read and write permission, but access is prohibited to other users. Thus, unless you log in as root, you can only access the disk drive through the device driver (which is a member of the disk group).

Looking at the device node alias names provides a bit more information. The hd prefix on the name indicates that the devices are IDE hard disks. There are two physical drives named hda and hdb (these are the *raw* names of the devices). When a disk drive is formatted, it is often broken into partitions, each with its own device node. The first and second partitions on hda have the device node names hda1 and hda2. The drive hdb has only one partition, so the entire formatted area of the disk drive is accessed through hdb1. It is possible to read from and write to the drives through the raw device node names hda and hdb, but these are for raw access and used for such operations as formatting the drive or making mirror-image copies of an entire drive.

Pseudo terminal device nodes

If you are logged in through the X Window System by using a graphics window, then the terminal device node output by the `tty` command starts with the letters pt, as in the following example:

```
$ tty
/dev/ptys0
```

The prefix pt indicates that you are using a *pseudo terminal* instead of a physical terminal. The device node of a pseudo terminal makes connection to an X application that uses a window and the keyboard to simulate a terminal. Input from the keyboard is directed through the pseudo device node to the application. In turn, the application sends the text to be displayed to the X server, which displays it on the window. This application is called a *terminal emulator* because it does in software everything that a regular terminal does in hardware. As with a regular terminal, the terminal emulator runs a shell program that prompts you for input, and the shell program executes commands that result in output being directed through the same device node as the pseudo terminal. Session 26 provides more information on this process.

Several pseudo terminals can be open on the same screen, and a device node uniquely identifies each one. The first terminal window you open is named /dev/ptys0, the second is named /dev/ptys1, and so on. The actual node names vary from one UNIX system to another, but they almost always begin with pt and end with a number or letter to make each one unique. The /dev directory (or one of its subdirectories) contains enough of these nodes to accommodate several pseudo terminals for each user logged in to the system.

The newer versions of X dynamically create pseudo terminal nodes as they are needed. Each time a new pseudo terminal is opened, a new device node is created for it in a directory named /dev/pts (or something similar). These nodes are simply named 0, 1, 2, and so on. If your system works this way, and if you are using the first pseudo terminal opened on the system, your response to the `tty` command looks like this:

```
$ tty
/dev/pts/0
```

Some special device node names

**20 Min.
To Go**

As you look through the /dev directory on your system, you will see several nodes with special names. For example, the node named /dev/console is usually included as another name for /dev/tty0. Background processes send error messages, and other text, to the device node named /dev/console. This means that you could create a new version of /dev/console to redirect all console messages to another terminal.

You also see names such as /dev/cdrom and /dev/floppy that are not actually device nodes, but are *links* to device nodes. These links are created by using the ln command, the same way the file links were created in the previous session. After the proper device node for your CD-ROM drive is configured for your system, a link can be created so the applications can refer to the device node by a generic name. For example, if your CD-ROM is connected through the device node /dev/hdc, a link to it can be created that looks something like this:

```
$ ls -l /dev/cdrom
lrwxrwxrwx   1 root  root     8 Aug  9 15:09  cdrom -> /dev/hdc
```

Most systems are installed with the links already in place, so you can refer to device nodes using names like /dev/tape, /dev/mouse, and /dev/floppy.

The device node /dev/null is in a class of its own. It accepts any input you feed to it, and simply throws the input away. It's surprising how often /dev/null comes in handy. For example, you may have a program named blset that generates more error messages than data, and you want to get rid of the error messages so you can find the data. You can run blset and redirect the error output stream to the null device like this:

```
$ blset 2>/dev/null
```

All standard error output text is redirected to /dev/null, and the standard output text is displayed on the screen.

Creating a device node

In the unlikely event that you are actually required to create a new node, you can use the mknod (make node) command. You must specify the major number, the minor number, whether it is block or character, and the alias name. For example, the following command creates a character node named xxy0 that has a major number of 88 and a minor number of 44:

```
$ mknod xxy0 c 88 44
```

As with the creation of files, the original permissions settings for device nodes are controlled by umask and can be modified by using chmod. You can also specify the settings by using octal digits with the -m option:

```
$ mknod -m 666 xxy0 c 88 44
```

Hard Disk File Systems

Before you can use a hard disk, its file system must be mounted. This is done by creating an empty directory on the disk and then associating that directory with a device node in such a way that accessing the directory actually accesses the mounted file system. Starting from scratch, the following steps are required to install a disk drive:

1. **Low-level format** — Formatting organizes the disk into sectors and cylinders. It is done at the factory and seldom needs to be repeated.

2. **Partition** — The entire drive can be used as a single unit for a single file system, but at times you may need to split it up, so you can use parts of it as if they were separate drives. The primary disk drive on a UNIX system will normally need to be split up to create swap space and possibly some other partitions.

3. **File system format** — Each partition on the drive must be formatted with its own file system. More than one kind of file system is available on every UNIX system, and you can format each partition with a different file system if you wish. For

example, the original System V primarily uses the s5 file system, but it also provides ufs, which is more efficient for large files. Solaris also supports ufs and has its own file system, called vfs. Linux supports a number of file systems, including its own ext2 and ext3. Almost all UNIX systems support the DOS file system, variously named fat, dos, msdos, or pcfs. All file systems look the same to your shell and your applications because they are always accessed through a device driver that takes care of the details of reading and writing.

4. **Mount** — The root partition is mounted first by having the name / assigned to it. The other partitions, no matter which disk drive they are on, are mounted by having other directory names associated with their device nodes. To assign a directory name to a disk drive, an empty directory is first created somewhere in the root file system; that name is then associated with a drive by using the mount command. Any access to that directory name will actually access the disk drive mounted there. Any number of drives can be added to the system by simply creating new directory names and mounting the hard drive partitions on them.

5. **Configure** — If you want the file system to be permanently mounted, the system must be instructed to mount it whenever the system boots. To do this, the name of the device node and its mount point are added to the system configuration file. This file is usually named /etc/fstab or /etc/vfstab. Session 30 provides more details about the file system mounting process.

The previous five steps cover disk management in very general terms. As the saying goes, "The devil is in the details," and every version of UNIX has its own characteristics. Different file systems and device node naming conventions are used, as well as different commands to format the drives.

The command that you use to create a new file system in a disk partition depends on the version of UNIX you are working with. For example, the Solaris command is newfs and the System V command is makefsys. The following command creates a Linux file system on the partition addressed by the device node /dev/hdb3:

```
$ mkfs /dev/hdb3
```

If you do not specify a particular type of file system, the default system for that version of UNIX is used. If you want to specify a particular file system, use the -t option like this:

```
$ mkfs -t PCFS /dev/hdb3
```

To share files on a machine that can be booted under two operating systems, you only need to make certain that the selected file system is supported by both operating systems so that you can mount the system and access the files directly.

The mount command is used to attach a file system to a directory. After the device node is mounted on the directory name, the disk drive addressed by the device node can be accessed just as if it were physically a part of the file system. The following commands can be used to mount the device node /dev/hdb3 as the directory /usr/games:

```
$ mkdir /usr/games
$ mount /dev/hdb3 /usr/games
```

You can remove the mounted file system with the umount command as follows:

```
$ umount /dev/hdb3
```

Other File Systems

The mount command can be used to list all of the currently mounted devices. The following list was generated by a Linux system:

```
$ mount
/dev/hda5 on / type ext2 (rw)
none on /proc type proc (rw)
usbdevfs on /proc/bus/usb type usbdevfs (rw)
/dev/hda1 on /boot type ext2 (rw)
/dev/hdb1 on /home type ext2 (rw)
none on /dev/pts type devpts (rw,gid=5,mode=620)
alice:/home on /mnt/alice type nfs (rw,addr=192.168.0.4)
/dev/hdc on /mnt/cdrom type iso9660 (ro,nosuid,nodev,user=arthur)
/dev/fd0 on /mnt/floppy type msdos (rw)
```

Each line contains information on a mounted device that includes the name of the device node, the directory being used as the mount point, and the type of file system. You will rarely deal with anything other than disk drives, but you should be aware that there are other kinds of things that are mounted.

For most file systems, the indicator at the far right is rw (read-write), but a CD-ROM is ro (read-only). Other codes are listed on the right having to do with access permissions and ownership. The list of possible codes is extensive and can be found in the man page for mount.

The proc file system has no device node because it is a very special case — it provides direct access to kernel facilities and information. For example, the ps command uses information found in the proc file system to get the list of running processes. Access to the usbdevfs (Universal Serial Bus) is provided because it is mounted in the proc directory. The devpts file system is another special case — it is the set of virtual terminals that are dynamically created and destroyed as X pseudo terminals are created and destroyed and as terminal windows are opened and closed.

One entry in this list has the file system type nfs (Network File System), and the item mounted is actually a directory on the disk of another computer. The name of the remote computer is alice, the name of the remote directory is /home, and the name of the local mount point is /mnt/alice. NFS is an internet protocol, so it can be used to mount the directories of any computer that can be reached through an IP address and is willing to share its files. Once a remote disk drive is mounted this way, it acts just like a local drive (except its speed is limited by the speed of the internet link).

The following is a typical example of a list of mounted devices on a Solaris system:

```
$ mount
/ on /dev/dsk/c0t3d0s0 read,write,suid,largefiles
/var on /dev/dsk/c0t3d0s1 read,write,suid,largefiles
/proc on /proc read,write,suid
/dev/fd on fd read,write,suid
```

The exact format varies among different versions of UNIX, but the information provided is basically the same.

Floppy drives

To use a floppy drive, you need to mount it just like any other disk. The name of the floppy's device node varies from one version of UNIX to the next. I have seen it named /dev/floppy, /dev/fd0, and /dev/diskette. In most cases, one of these generic names is either a link to, or a duplicate of, something with a name that more specifically defines the type of floppy drive, such as /dev/fd0h1440. You will normally find several names of this form to indicate the different types and sizes of floppies.

Whenever you insert a floppy disk, you must use the mount command to mount the disk to a directory. The disk must be formatted and must contain a file system before it can be mounted. You can use the same commands that you use for a hard drive to format a floppy disk. You insert the floppy and perform low-level formatting, and then use the mkfs or newfs command to create whatever file system you like.

After the disk is formatted, the mount command makes the disk's file system available at whatever directory you specify. If you are not using the default file system, you need to know what type of file system you are mounting. For example, if you are mounting a DOS formatted floppy onto the directory named /mnt/floppy, you can enter a command like the following:

```
$ mount -t msdos /dev/fd0 /mnt/floppy
```

This example uses the device node /dev/fd0, but you will need to use the node on your system that has a minor number specifying a device driver responsible for DOS-formatted floppies. Once you have a floppy disk mounted, it works the same as any other file system, except that it is smaller and probably slower.

**10 Min.
To Go**

CD-ROM drives

A special file system, defined as ISO standard 9660, is used for CD-ROMs. Because ISO standard 9660 is an independent and open standard, UNIX, Macintosh, DOS, and Windows can read all CD-ROM drives.

Like a floppy disk, a CD-ROM disk must be mounted before it can be accessed. Most modern systems have a facility that automatically mounts a CD-ROM when it is inserted into the drive. A daemon process is installed to watch the device node for signs of activity. When the CD-ROM is inserted into the drive, the daemon automatically mounts the disk. The daemon can be configured to attempt to execute a program named autorun on every CD-ROM that it mounts. Unfortunately, no standard has been defined for the name or content of the executable file.

Internal File System Structure

Files stored on disk in a UNIX system are expandable. Whenever a file needs to be extended, some disk space must be allocated and attached to the end of the file. The file cannot simply be expanded in place because another file may be right behind it. To overcome this, each segment of a file is linked to the next segment, and the individual segments can be stored anywhere on the disk.

You can think of the file system of a disk as a huge collection of numbered post office boxes where every box is the same size. Whenever you open a file, you are allocated one of these boxes. You store information in the box until it is full. When you try to put something into a full box, the post office sticks a note in the box with the number of another empty box. The note stays in your original box, and you start stuffing the second box. If the second box fills up and you need more space, the post office inserts a note with a new box number and off you go to a new box. This continues until you have stored all your data in a series of boxes that are linked together by their addresses (or until the post office runs out of empty boxes).

When you come back to retrieve your data, you start at the first box and read everything it contains. You find the note that gives you the next box number and read everything the second box contains. You move from box to box until you find the one that doesn't contain a note sending you to another box, at which point you have come to the end of the file.

Organization by inodes

You may recall from Session 11 that an entry in a directory contains the name of a file and a number that indicates the actual location of the file on disk. That number is the location on disk of an *inode*. The inode (pronounced eye-node) is the mechanism that organizes the addresses of the blocks of data that make up the file. Each file uses one inode, and a number identifies each inode. You can use the ls command with the -i option to list the inode numbers for the members of a directory. In the following example the -F option is also used so that the directories will be indicated:

```
$ ls -iF
 382533 books.html     378485 gcc.html     382001 money.html
 382522 curios.html     90995 index.html   382527 research.html
   4535 ed2go.html     382534 java.html    382528 rounds.html
 152323 folks.html     410276 manual/
```

Some of the inode numbers are sequential, which may indicate that the files were created at the same time. Sequential numbering is not guaranteed, however. When a file is deleted, its inode is made available for reallocation. When a file system is created, a fixed number of inodes are allocated and stored on the drive, but there are many thousands of them so there is rarely a need to create a file system that contains more than the default.

Figure 12-1 shows a typical layout for organizing and allocating data blocks. The inode begins with a header that includes the file name, the file permissions, the owner's ID, the number of bytes in the file, and so on. Following the header, a list of disk locations comprises the main body of the inode. The first few each contain the address of a single block of data. Next, there is a list of addresses of indirect blocks, each of which contains another list of block addresses. If the file is large enough, you will have double indirect blocks that each contains a list of addresses of indirect blocks, and triple indirect blocks that contain addresses of double indirect blocks.

All inodes are a fixed size, and one is used whenever a file is created. As you write to the file, it begins to fill up from the top. When you start writing, the first block is allocated and its disk address stored in the top of the list in the inode. As you continue to write to the file, the second block is allocated, then the third, and so on. If the file becomes large enough, indirect blocks start to be allocated. An indirect block may hold the address of only two blocks, as shown in Figure 12-1, but it can usually hold many more addresses. If your file continues to expand, the system begins to allocate double indirect blocks, then triple indirect blocks. Each of these indirect blocks can contain the address of a number of other blocks, which makes a single inode capable of managing an extremely large file. This progressive increase of indirection allows the inode to remain small for a small file, but allows it to expand to handle huge files. It is not uncommon for a single inode to be capable of handling single files in excess of 200GB.

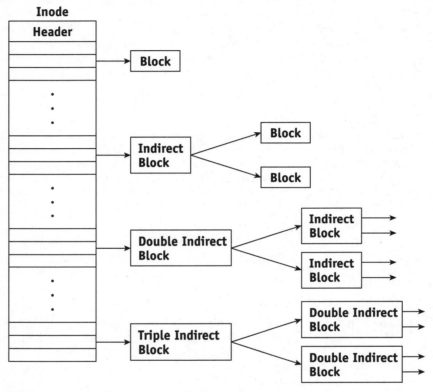

Figure 12-1   *A diagram of an inode*

The inodes are a fixed part of the file system. When you use the mkfs command to create a file system on an empty disk, it is the inodes that are created. Also, at the beginning of the disk, an area called the *superblock* is created. The superblock is responsible for maintaining a list of the available inodes and the other blocks that are doled out to you as you need them. The superblock normally keeps a list of free blocks and free inodes for immediate allocation but usually maintains most of them as links to prevent using too much space on the disk.

The superblock, inodes, indirect blocks, and data blocks can be organized in many different ways. The main differences among file systems are the size of individual blocks, the pattern of linking indirect blocks, the method of selecting the next block to be used, and how the free blocks are tracked.

Synchronizing

A running UNIX system can have many processes running with each one of them writing to its open files from time to time. This output is normally buffered (held in memory) until there is enough to fill an entire block on disk, and then the entire block is written in a single operation. This is the most efficient way to do things. You may recall from the discussion of dynamic allocation in Session 1 that a program running on a busy system will have some of its data swapped out to disk to provide space for other processes to run. It is possible that the data swapped to disk is not as up-to-date as the data stored in memory. The following command causes all of this buffered data to be immediately written to disk, thus synchronizing the system:

```
$ sync
```

Issuing this command not only flushes any data held in memory, it also updates all of the superblocks and inodes. It is seldom necessary to issue this command because the system keeps track of shared files, and a sync command is included in the system shutdown procedure.

Done!

REVIEW

In this session, you learn about some of the internals of the UNIX file system, and some of the basic operations you may need to perform on the file system.

- A device node is a special kind of directory entry that includes descriptive information about a hardware device and how you can communicate with it.
- Two kinds of device nodes exist: those that read and write blocks of data, and those that read and write one character at a time.
- UNIX has all the utilities necessary to construct a file system on a hard disk and to mount the disk so that it becomes part of the file system.
- A UNIX file system uses an inode as the underlying structure of a file, and the inode contains the structure necessary to efficiently manage very small and very large files.

The following session describes a set of very useful utility programs that are a part of UNIX. Of the hundreds of commands included as part of UNIX, these are some of the most useful.

QUIZ YOURSELF

1. What are the two kinds of device nodes? (See "Device Nodes.")
2. What command lists the disk drives and displays the percentage of each drive that is being used? (See "Hard disk drive device nodes.")
3. What is a pseudo terminal? (See "Pseudo terminal device nodes.")
4. What does it mean to mount a disk drive? (See "Hard Disk File Systems.")
5. How can you get a listing of all the mounted devices? (See "Other File Systems.")

The World's Handiest Utilities

Session Checklist

✔ Viewing text files

✔ Sorting and selecting

✔ Date and time

**30 Min.
To Go**

UNIX has hundreds of utility programs. The majority of these utilities are used for special situations, but some are used often enough that they become something you can't live without. The previous sessions introduced a few of the most indispensable utilities (1s, cd, pwd, the text editor, and so on), and this session adds a few more to that list. Because everyone works in a different way, anyone else's list of must-have tools would be very different. These are some of my personal favorites.

Viewing Text Files

Most of the files on your disk are plain ASCII text files. Although binary executable programs are common, and you may be using some kind of database, most of the data you work with is stored as plain text. Many executable programs are actually editable text scripts, and virtually all of the UNIX configuration files are text files. The result of all this is that you frequently need to look at the contents of a text file. You can always use your editor to look at the contents of a text file — and this method provides maximum flexibility and control — but some utilities are available that may be more convenient if you only want to take a quick look into a file.

Looking with more

The more command has been used in previous sessions to prevent the output of a command from scrolling off the top of the screen. For example, if a directory contains so many files that you can't see their descriptions on one screen, you can pipe the list into more:

```
$ ls -l | more
```

The list scrolls up the screen and stops before the first line disappears. You can scroll up one line at a time by using the Return key, or you can scroll up one full screen with the space bar. You can also scroll forward by pressing d or Ctrl+D. Pressing q causes more to exit immediately.

You can also use more and a file name to display a file's contents. The following command displays the contents of /etc/printcap, which is always a very large file because it contains definitions for the many different types of terminals that can be connected to your UNIX system:

```
$ more /etc/printcap
```

Enter this command and you will see one screen full of text. Press the space bar or the Return key to move forward in the file and press q to exit. Because the input to the more command is a file and more can determine how large the file is, a prompt appears at the bottom of the screen, telling you what percentage of the file has already been viewed. For example, the following prompt indicates that you have already scrolled past 14 percent of the file:

```
--More--(14%)
```

The more utility has some special commands. Entering an equals sign will display the current line number. You can enter a slash followed by a regular expression string to search forward in the file. For example, the following command searches forward for a string match and scrolls forward to display the text containing the match:

```
/intosh
```

After a string is found, enter n to search for the next matching string. If this seems reminiscent of vi, you're right. In fact, inside more, entering the letter v causes the vi editor to take over — with the same page of text showing — so that you can immediately start editing the file. Enter the letter h to list all of these more commands and others.

Looking with less

The utility named less is a later version of more, and it does everything that more does and even more. Even though less has more options and commands than more, some people still like more better than less.

The primary difference between these two utilities is that less enables you to move both forward and backward through a file, while more only enables you to move forward. You can use less exactly the same way you use more to look at the text coming piped from another command, like this:

```
$ ls -l | less
```

and you can enter the name of a file on the command line this way:

```
$ less /etc/termcap
```

After a screen full of text has appeared, press the letter h to see a help screen listing several different keys that can be used to move backward and forward through the file. Notice that some tasks can be accomplished in several ways. For example, you can use any one of five different keystrokes (e, Ctrl+E, j, Ctrl+N, and Return) to move the text forward by one line. The reason for all the different options is so that you can pick a set that makes sense and is easy to remember. For example, the keys that scroll up and down in vi also scroll up and down in less.

File peeking with head and tail

If you only need to look at the beginning of a file, you can use the head command. For example, the following command lists the first ten lines of the file named index.html:

```
$ head index.html
```

You can change the number of lines displayed to something other than the default of ten lines by using the -n option. For example, if you want to list only five lines, enter the following command:

```
$ head -n 5 index.html
```

The head command is most useful if you need to look at the beginnings of several files. The following command lists the first ten lines of each HTML file in the current directory:

```
$ head *.html | more
```

The head command inserts the file name in front of the ten lines of text from each file. It is best to pipe this command through more (or less) — if you have more than one file, the text will scroll off the display until only lines from the last couple of files are visible.

The tail command displays the other end of the file. The following command displays the last ten lines of the file named index.html:

```
$ tail index.html
```

As with head, you can use the -n option with tail to display a specific number of lines. The following example displays the last 17 lines of the file:

```
$ tail -n 17 index.html
```

It turns out that tail is generally more useful than head because of an extra trick it can perform. Suppose you have a program running that occasionally writes a line of text to a file named scanner.log. The following command lists each line as it is written to the file:

```
$ tail -f scanner.log
```

When you enter this command, the tail utility immediately displays the last ten lines of the file, but tail doesn't stop running. It becomes a sort of daemon process that sits and waits for more text to be written to the file and displays each new line as it is added to the file. As a result, you have a real-time copy of the log file scrolling up your screen.

The things cat can do

The cat (concatenate) command reads a file and echoes it to the standard output. To list the entire content of a text file to the display, enter a command such as the following:

```
$ cat index.html
```

The contents of the file scroll by on the screen until it has all been shown, and then cat quits. It is possible to redirect the output, which makes it possible to duplicate a file, as in the following example:

```
$ cat index.html >index.copy
```

You can name several files on the command line and cat lists all of them, one after the other, without pause. Redirection makes it possible to use cat for some special operations. For example, you can combine several files into one file by redirecting the output of cat as follows:

```
$ cat *.html >allpages
```

The result of this command is that the HTML files in the current directory are concatenated into one large file. In fact, it is this concatenation ability that gave cat its name. The cat command is a little like echo. Both cat and echo are very simple programs that perform very simple tasks, but they can be extremely useful in certain situations.

Dumping a file byte by byte

The term *dump* has a special meaning in UNIX. Dumping something (a program, a file, data stream, or whatever) is to put it in such a form that you can examine the raw data bit by bit. The od (octal dump) utility dumps its input in forms that you can use to analyze the content of every byte. Input can be piped into od, but its input most often from a file.

The od command can dump any file, but the following text file (containing the non-displayable ASCII characters tab, escape, and backspace) can be used to demonstrate the readability of the output formats:

```
The quick brown rumor jumped
over the lazy gray fact.
Tab=
Escape=
Backspace=
```

The tab, escape, and backspace characters are not visible text, so they don't show up in the listing, but they are present in the file. To prove it, the od command can be used with the -c option to display each byte as a character:

```
$ od -c quick.text
0000000   T   h   e       q   u   i   c   k       b   r   o   w   n
0000020   r   u   m   o   r       j   u   m   p   e   d  \n   o   v   e
0000040   r       t   h   e       l   a   z   y       g   r   a   y
0000060   f   a   c   t   .  \n   T   a   b   =  \t  \n   E   s   c   a
0000100   p   e   =  033  \n   B   a   c   k   s   p   a   c   e   =  \b
0000120  \n
0000121
```

The characters are displayed 16 per line, and each line begins with the hexadecimal address of the first character in the line. Printable characters appear as themselves. Certain special characters show up in their encoded format: \n is the newline (carriage return) character, \t is tab, and \b is backspace. Any byte that is not displayable and does not have an encoding shows up as three octal digits. In this example, the escape character appears in its octal form as 033.

 A list of all the special-character encodings appears in Session 16.

If you prefer to see each byte of the file listed as a pair of hexadecimal digits, you can use the -x option, like this:

```
$ od -x quick.text
0000000 6854 2065 7571 6369 206b 7262 776f 206e
0000020 7572 6f6d 2072 756a 706d 6465 6f0a 6576
0000040 2072 6874 2065 616c 797a 6720 6172 2079
0000060 6166 7463 0a2e 6154 3d62 0a09 7345 6163
0000100 6570 1b3d 420a 6361 736b 6170 6563 083d
0000120 000a
0000121
```

Dumps can be displayed in other formats, and it is possible to combine formats to get more than one view of the dump. For example, you can intermix characters and hexadecimal digits by using -xc as the command line option. The od command is very old — you can spot the older UNIX commands because they work in octal — and every version of UNIX has added some formatting options to od. I have my personal favorite format, and you can see how it can be generated in one of the C programming examples in Session 16.

Sorting and Selecting

The sort utility rearranges the lines of text files to put them in a particular order. The default is to sort the lines in *lexicographic* order. Lexicographic order is similar to alphabetical order, but it has some odd twists. For example, digits come before letters and uppercase letters always come before lowercase letters, which means the letter Z comes before the letter b. Punctuation is sort of sprinkled around. The hash and the ampersand characters come before the digits, the question mark comes after the digits but before uppercase letters, the open and close brackets come after uppercase but before lowercase letters, and the tilde character comes at the very end. Lexicographic sorting is ordering by the numeric ASCII values of the characters, so if you look at an ASCII chart, you will see the sorting order.

The sort command gets its input from a file or from standard input and writes the result to standard output. The following command sorts the lines of text in unsorted.text and lists them on the screen:

```
$ sort unsorted.text
```

The following command sorts the content of the unsorted.text file and stores the results in a new file named sorted.text:

```
$ sort unsorted.text >sorted.text
```

You can use multiple files as the input to sort, and the text from all of the files is combined into a single sorted output stream:

```
$ sort file1.text file2.text file3.text >sorted.text
```

If you intend to use several files as input to the sort command, and you know that the individual files are already sorted, you can use the -m option to merge the files without sorting them. Merging files is much faster that sorting files.

The sort command can be used in other ways. For example, the -r option reverses the order of the sort. The default is to compare the entire line of text for sorting, but options are available that allow you to specify which characters within the line are compared.

The uniq (unique) command reads through a text file and removes all lines that are identical to the line preceding them. If the file is sorted, all duplicate lines are back to back, and uniq deletes all but one in the series of identical lines. For example, HTML has a standard format, so you have a number of repeated lines in a collection of HTML files. To determine the exact number of duplicate lines, start by using the wc command to count the total number of lines, as in the following example:

```
$ sort *.html | wc
   1469    5099    54230
```

The wc (word count) utility lists the number of lines, words, and characters found in the file. To remove the duplicated lines and then count only the unique lines, you can pass the sorted output through uniq and then send the sorted stream into wc to produce the count:

```
$ sort *.html | uniq | wc
   709    4717    50771
```

Removing the duplicates reduces the number of lines from 1469 to 709 showing the files contain 760 duplicate lines. This shows that there is a lot of redundancy in HTML.

If you want to know exactly which lines have been removed, you can redirect the output of each of the above commands to files, and then use the diff command to compare the two files and get a complete list of the lines that uniq deleted. The diff command, which is described in Session 28, lists the lines of text that make two files different.

These procedures for counting lines of text are examples of using a group of simple commands to perform more complicated tasks. You could carry the examination further by piping the output of diff through uniq to derive a list that contains only one copy of each of the deleted duplicate lines.

Date and Time

A computer runs on a clock that ticks continuously and is used for everything from placing the date and timestamp on a file to determining how long a process has been running. One of the evil truths of computing is that, somehow, no matter how accurate the clock is supposed to be, the system clock either runs fast or slow. Because everything is controlled by time, it is important that the clock be kept reasonably accurate.

The UNIX clock is the count of the number of seconds since January 1, 1970, so setting the time and the date are the same thing. The value is a 32-bit number with positive values representing time after January 1, 1970, and negative values representing time before January 1, 1970. The oldest date possible is in the year 1902. The clock will run out early in the morning of January 19, 2038. Y2K returns.

The clock in a UNIX system is only accurate to one second. Facilities exist that can be used inside programs to measure fractions of seconds, but that is only needed in special circumstances. By most definitions of the term *real time*, UNIX is not a real time system. The best description I have heard is that UNIX is a *near time* system. UNIX runs multiple tasks seemingly all at once, but each task is regularly stopped for short periods of time to allow other tasks to run. Real time UNIX systems do exist but, like all real time operating systems, they run on hardware specifically designed to support real time operations.

Accessing the system clock

**10 Min.
To Go**

The date utility can be used to display the current date and time or to set the internal system clock. You must have superuser power in order to set the clock.

The following is an example of the default date display format:

```
$ date
Thu Nov 29 16:34:52 AKST 2001
```

Setting the System Clock

The following sequence of commands can be used to set both the date and the time:

```
$ su -
password:
% date Nov 29 16:18:16
% exit

$ _
```

Before you attempt to change the clock on your system, it would be a good idea to look at the documentation for date. The date command varies in subtle ways from one version of UNIX to the next. Most versions accept the date and time in a fairly loose format. Some require you to use an -s option with the date command in order to set the clock. For example, the following date command uses an -s option to set the time, but leaves the date unchanged:

```
% date -s 16:34:45
```

You can specify how you want the display string to look by setting up a series of formatting parameters, which are listed in Table 13-1. The string of formatting characters must be surrounded by quotes and preceded by a plus sign. For example, the command that re-creates the default format looks like this:

```
$ date '+%a %b %e %T %Z %Y'
Thu Nov 29 16:34:52 AKST 2001
```

Any characters inside the quoted string that are not preceded with a percent sign are displayed as literals, as in the following example:

```
$ date '+DATE %m/%d/%y%nTIME %H:%M:%S'
DATE 11/29/01
TIME 16:34:52
```

As shown in Table 13-1, enough formatting characters are available that you should be able to create any date format that you can think of. Notice the term *locale* that is mentioned in the table. UNIX is used internationally, and the standard date formats differ from one place to another. In particular, the standard U.S. format for the date is dd/mm/yy, and the European format is mm/dd/yy. If you want to see your current locale setting, execute the locale command to display the information on the screen.

Table 13-1 *Formatting Characters Recognized by the date Command*

Formatting	Displays
%a	The three-letter abbreviation of the name of the day of the week.
%A	The full-length name of the day of the week.
%b	The three-letter abbreviation of the name of the month. This is the same as %h.
%B	The full-length name of the month.
%c	The format of the date and time suitable to the locale. This is the default format.
%d	The two-character day of the month, ranging from 01 to 31.
%D	This is the same as %m/%d/%y.
%e	The two-character day of the month, ranging from 1 to 31. The single-digit values are preceded by a space.
%h	The three-letter abbreviation of the name of the month. This is the same as %b.
%H	The two-digit hour, ranging from 01 to 23.
%I	The two-digit hour, ranging from 01 to 12.
%j	The three-digit day of the year, ranging from 000 to 366.

Formatting	Displays
%m	The two-digit month of the year, ranging from 01 to 12.
%M	The two-digit minute, ranging from 00 to 59.
%n	A newline character to break the format to the next line.
%p	The two-character meridian indicator. Either AM or PM.
%r	This is the same as %I:%M:%S %p.
%R	This is the same as %H:%M.
%S	Two-character seconds, ranging from 01 to 61. The value 61 allows for leap seconds.
%t	A tab character.
%T	This is the same as %H:%M:%S.
%U	The two-digit week number of the year, ranging from 00 to 53. Sunday is the first day of the week.
%w	The single-digit day of the week, ranging from 0 to 6. Sunday is 0.
%W	The two-digit week number of the year, ranging from 00 to 53. Monday is the first day of the week.
%x	A date format suitable for the locale.
%X	A time format suitable for the locale.
%Y	The four-digit year.
%Z	The name of the time zone.

Watching the clock

To time a process, enter the command time in front of the command that starts the process running. The time utility starts its clock, runs the command, and reports the duration after the command has finished. For example, if you want to know how long it takes the find command to search through the /home directory tree for a file, you can enter the following command:

```
$ /usr/bin/time find /home -name fred -print
0.61user 0.88system 1:03.89elapsed 2%CPU
```

Three different times are printed. The *user time* (0.61 seconds) is shown first and is the total amount of time actually used by the code inside the find program. The *system time* (0.88 seconds) is shown second; and it is the amount of time that kernel code (system calls) was being executed. The last time shown (03.89 seconds) is also called the wall clock time and is the total elapsed time according to the system clock in the computer. In this example, 0.88 seconds was spent in the system calls and only 0.61 seconds on the code of find itself, because the find utility has to make a quite a few system calls to get all the directory listings for all the subdirectories in the tree. The sum of the user and system times, about 01.49 seconds, is the total amount of CPU time used by the command. The overall time lapsed (the wall clock time) is about one minute and four seconds, which is much longer than the user and system times combined because the process was repeatedly interrupted to allow other processes to run. As displayed in the output, the process used an average of only 2 percent of the total CPU time while it was running.

The exact format of the output from this command varies. You usually get information on how much memory space was used, the number and size of the swaps, and possibly some other data. You may have noticed that /usr/bin/time was entered, rather than time. It is possible for a time command to be built into the shell, and if you enter time without specifying the path, the system looks no further than the shell to locate the command. The following example uses the time command built into the Bash Shell:

```
$ time find /home -name fred -print
real    1m4.083s
user    0m0.610s
sys     0m0.700s
```

As you can see, both commands work the same way and produce virtually the same results.

Done!

REVIEW

This session explores some of the more useful utilities in UNIX. You may find others that serve you better for certain tasks, but the ones described here have been around since the early days of UNIX and have proven to be useful.

- The more and less commands can be used to control the viewing of a file or a stream of text.
- The head and tail commands can be used to get a quick look at the beginning or end of a file.
- The cat command echoes its input to standard output.
- The od command dumps its input to standard output by formatting the display of each byte.
- The sort command reorders the text from one or more files.
- The date utility can be used to read the system clock.

The following session discusses more utilities. In particular, two of these utilities can be used to read UNIX documentation. Access to the documentation is essential for even the simplest of commands because special situations come up and require special options to handle them.

Quiz Yourself

1. How can you switch from more into the vi editor while keeping your place in the file? (See "Looking with more.")

2. Why does the less command provide so many commands that do the same thing? (See "Looking with less.")

3. On what basis does the sort utility order lines of text? (See "Sorting and Selecting.")

4. What is the smallest unit of time measurable by the UNIX clock? (See "Date and Time.")

5. What is meant by user time, system time, and elapsed time? (See "Watching the clock.")

The man Pages

Session Checklist

✔ Viewing UNIX documentation with man

✔ The options of man

✔ Viewing UNIX documentation with xman

✔ Getting help from other sources

**30 Min.
To Go**

This session explains the fundamental documentation system of UNIX and how you can use it. Documentation is one of the most important parts of UNIX — or any other system. It doesn't matter how good or how useful something may be; if you don't know it exists or you can't figure out how to make it work, it's the same as if it doesn't exist.

Viewing UNIX Documentation with man

UNIX documentation is stored in files that can be quickly formatted and displayed by using the man (manual) command. The files that contain the documentation are known as *man files,* or *man pages.* For quick lookup, the files bear the same name as the item they document. For example, if you want to see the documentation for grep, you enter the following command and the man utility looks among the document files for one with a name that matches:

```
$ man grep
```

The man command looks in several subdirectories and uses the first file it finds with a name that matches the one on the command line. A default list of directories is searched. This default search path normally includes directory names such as /usr/share/man, /usr/contrib/man, /usr/local/man, and /usr/X11R6/man. You can instruct man to ignore the default directory list by setting the MANPATH environment variable to a list that you prefer. The following example specifies the three directories for man to search:

```
$ MANPATH=/usr/share/man:/usr/local/man:/home/arthur/man
$ export MANPATH
```

If you set the MANPATH environment variable, the contents of the variable completely override the default, and no other directories will be searched. The directories are searched in the order that they are listed in the environment variable, which can be an important detail because man stops searching after the first match is found.

 A directory containing man documents is always named man. **The installation of a software package will often create a** man **directory of its own and fill it with man pages to document the application. If you use the** find **command to search your entire system for directories named** man, **you may uncover some documentation you didn't know was available.**

Inside each of the man directories, the man files are divided into the categories shown in Table 14-1. This division is not nearly as tidy as the description of the list would indicate. For example, the date command displays the current time and is a perfect fit for Section 1 (user commands). But the date command can also be used to set the system clock, which means that it should go in Section 8. The section names that are listed in the table are standard, but other section names exist that are not so consistent. On some systems, you will find section names such as 2b and 3x. You may also encounter section names like n for new and o for old.

Table 14-1   *Sections Used to Organize man Pages*

Section	Description
1	User commands — the UNIX commands that can be executed from the command line.
2	System calls — the kernel system calls that are available for a programmer to use inside an application.
3	Subroutines — the standard library functions that are available for a programmer to use inside an application.
4	Devices — descriptions of both the hardware devices and the device nodes.
5	File format — the descriptions of the internal formats of the standard UNIX configuration and data files.
6	Games.
7	Miscellaneous.
8	System administration — the utility programs used to configure and control the system.

Any man directory can include pages from any or all of these sections. You can use MANPATH to specify which directories are searched, and if you want to limit the search to a specific section, you can do so from the command line. If you precede the name of the man page by the ID of its section, only that section will be searched in each of the man directories. For example, the time command, discussed in the previous session, is a user command found in Section 1, but a kernel system call named time (for use inside programs) is also documented in Section 2. The man utility always finds the command in Section 1 unless you tell it to look elsewhere, like this:

```
$ man 2 time
```

An example man page

20 Min. To Go

You can use a UNIX command called nohup (no hang-up) to run a program in such a way that it will not be halted if you log off or send it a simple kill signal. The following man page, which describes nohup, is part of the documentation for HP-UX, Hewlett-Packard's version of UNIX. Some of the content is specific to HP-UX, but the layout of the man page itself is standard across all systems.

A man page always prints the name of the item being described on the top line and includes its section ID in parentheses. The text of the man page is formatted by a set of macros, and the macros used to format it for screen display are different from the ones used to format it for print. The following example is obviously formatted to be printed because lines of text that include a page number appear periodically and are followed by another heading that marks the beginning of a new page.

```
nohup(1)                                                              nohup(1)

NAME
      nohup - run a command immune to hangups

SYNOPSIS
      nohup command [arguments]

DESCRIPTION
      nohup executes command with hangups and quits ignored.  If output is
      not redirected by the user, both standard output and standard error
      are sent to nohup.out.  If nohup.out is not writable in the current
      directory, output is redirected to $HOME/nohup.out; otherwise, nohup
      fails. If a file is created, the file's permission bits will be set to
      S_IRUSR | S_IWUSR.

      If output from nohup is redirected to a terminal, or is not redirected
      at all, the output is sent to nohup.out.

EXTERNAL INFLUENCES
   Environment Variables
      LC_MESSAGES determines the language in which messages are displayed.

      If LC_MESSAGES is not specified in the environment or is set to the
      empty string, the value of LANG is used as a default for each
      unspecified or empty variable.  If LANG is not specified or is set to
      the empty string, a default of "C" (see lang(5)) is used instead of
      LANG.

      If any internationalization variable contains an invalid setting,
      nohup behaves as if all internationalization variables are set to "C".
      See environ(5).
```

International Code Set Support
    Single- and multi-byte character code sets are supported.

EXAMPLES
    It is frequently desirable to apply **nohup** to pipelines or lists of
    commands. This can be done only by placing pipelines and command
    lists in a single file, called a shell script. To run the script
    using **nohup**:

        nohup sh file

    nohup features apply to the entire contents of *file*. If the shell
    script file is to be executed often, the need to type **sh** can be
    eliminated by setting execute permission on *file*. The script can also
    be run in the background with interrupts ignored (see *sh*(1)):

        nohup file &

    file typically contains normal keyboard command sequences that one
    would want to continue running in case the terminal disconnects, such

Hewlett-Packard Company   - 1 -   HP-UX Release 11.00: October 1997

nohup(1)   nohup(1)

    as:

        tbl ofile | eqn | nroff > nfile

WARNINGS
    Be careful to place punctuation properly. For example, in the command
    form:

        nohup command1; command2

    nohup applies only to *command1*. To correct the problem, use the
    command form:

        nohup (command1; command2)

    Be careful of where standard error is redirected. The following
    command may put error messages on tape, making it unreadable:

        nohup cpio -o <list >/dev/rmt/c0t0d0BEST&

    whereas

        nohup cpio -o <list >/dev/rmt/c0t0d0BEST 2>errors&

    puts the error messages into file **errors**.

EXIT STATUS
    The following exit values are returned:

        126   The command specified by command was found but could
                   not be invoked

```
         127          An error occurred in the nohup utility or the specified
                      command could not be found

         Otherwise, the exit status of nohup will be that of the command
         specified.

SEE ALSO
     chmod(1), nice(1), sh(1), signal(5).

STANDARDS CONFORMANCE
     nohup: SVID2, SVID3, XPG2, XPG3, XPG4, POSIX.2

Hewlett-Packard Company              - 2 -   HP-UX Release 11.00: October 1997
```

The structure of a man page

The body of the document is divided into specific pieces with section headings. Some of these headings are standard, but any heading name can be inserted or deleted as appropriate. The most common headings are as follows:

- **NAME** — This is always the first section of a man page. It contains a description of the software's purpose, which is in general terms and usually limited to a single sentence.

- **SYNOPSIS** — The synopsis shows the syntax of the command or system call. This section is often quite simple, as in the nohup example, but complicated commands can have multiple options that require several lines. If you are familiar with a command, this synopsis may be all you need to remind you how to use it.

- **DESCRIPTION** — This section is usually the largest part of the man page. Along with a full description of the purpose of the software, you will find descriptions of the options and internal operations. This section often contains detailed descriptions and information listed in tables and alphabetized subheadings.

- **EXAMPLES** — This section provides one or more examples showing the use of a command. This section is especially important if the syntax is complicated or the software being described has numerous options. If a command is complicated, a simple example can get you started and you can modify the command line to make the command do what you want. If you are unfamiliar with a command and this section provides examples, be sure to read it because the fact that examples are provided indicates something that is out of the ordinary.

- **FILES** — Many commands are controlled by settings found in configuration files. Some commands use work files for temporary storage, have a default file name that is used for output, or read the data from system configurations files. The file names are listed in this section.

- **RETURN VALUE** — For system calls and subroutines, this section specifies the type of possible data returned to the calling program.

- **DIAGNOSTICS** — If a command has a set of different code values that it returns to indicate its status, or if error messages can be displayed, they are described in this section. This section is often named ERRORS.

- **ENVIRONMENT** — Some commands are affected by the setting of environment variables and the values stored in configuration files. This section is sometimes named `CONFIGURATION`, or `EXTERNAL INFLUENCES`.

- **NOTES** — Special situations are often associated with a command. For example, there may be something that the description of a command implies it should do, but that the command really doesn't do. In certain circumstances, you should not use a command because it may do more harm than good. This section can also be named `WARNINGS`, or `EXCEPTIONS`. Originally, this section was named `BUGS`, but UNIX has become more aware of its image and no longer admits that it has bugs.

- **SEE ALSO** — A command may have other commands that are related to it in some way. There may also be other commands that do the same thing or that use the same files. This section lists each related command along with its man page section ID.

- **ACKNOWLEDGEMENTS** — This section contains background information. It often contains the company and/or individual that originated the software. If appropriate, it also lists the names of companies and individuals that have modified or maintained the software, and the person responsible for the man page.

The Options of man

Like most other command line utilities, man has options. A couple of these options, such as -f and -k, are so useful that they have been assigned command names of their own.

If you want to look at the one-sentence description at the top of a man page, you can use the -f option, as in the following command:

```
$ man -f hosts
hosts        (5) - The static table lookup for host names
```

The -f option is so useful that it has become a command of its own, named whatis. The whatis command can be used in place of man -f, as in the following example:

```
$ whatis time
time        (1) - time a simple command or give resource usage
time        (2) - get time in seconds
```

One of the benefits of using whatis to get a definition is that you get a list of all entries by that name no matter what section of the documentation they are found in.

Suppose you don't know the name of the command that you want to use, but you know a word that is probably in the one-line description at the top of its man page. If you use the -k option, man looks through all of the descriptions and lists the ones that contain the specified word. For example, if you want to learn what is available to set up a PPP (Point-to-Point Protocol) telephone dialer, try the following command:

```
$ man -k ppp
ppp-watch   (8) - daemon to make PPP interfaces act more like other interfaces
pppd        (8) - Point to Point Protocol daemon
pppdump     (8) - convert PPP record file to readable format
pppstats    (8) - print PPP statistics
wvdial      (1) - PPP dialer with built-in intelligence
```

This list includes several programs dealing with PPP connections, and even one dialer. Other man pages may deal with the subject, but if they do not include the three letters "ppp" in the description, they do not show up in this list. However, even if you don't find exactly what you want, you can continue your search by looking under the SEE ALSO heading of one of the listed items.

The man command with the -k option also has a name of its own. The command apropos in the following example is a synonym for man -k:

```
$ apropos ppp
```

Several other useful options are available, but there is no need to describe them here because you can see them for yourself by entering the following command:

```
$ man man
```

Viewing UNIX Documentation with xman

10 Min. To Go

A program named xman is installed on many UNIX systems, which enables you to access the man pages through a Graphical User Interface (GUI). The xman program uses the X Window System, so it runs whether you are using Gnome, CDE, KDE, Motif, or any other UNIX windowing environment. You can find more information about the X Window System in Session 26. If X is installed in the standard way, the program can be found among the other X programs as /usr/bin/X11/xman. The xman program can be started from the command line, or if you make frequent use of it, you can add it as one of the menu or icon selections. This program is designed to run continuously as a very small window to be available quickly whenever you need it. You can start it from the command line like this:

```
$ xman &
```

The main window of xman is shown in Figure 14-1. This window is only used as a launcher for the window that shows the man pages, which provides the convenience of having more than one man page displayed at once.

Figure 14-1 *The xman control window*

One interesting thing about the buttons on the main window is that you have to double-click them to make them work. This is not a flaw; it is part of the design of the widgets (buttons, menus, and so on) at the time xman was written. The xman utility is not new; it dates from the very early days of GUI interfaces and uses the Athena widget set that was designed at MIT as part of the original version of X. All widgets operated this way and had this flat appearance until the early 1980s, when the Motif widget set introduced the beveled edge buttons that are used by almost everyone today. The Athena widgets may not be as attractive as some of their newer cousins, but they are much simpler and they work much faster.

You can see a pair of pull-down menus at the top the xman display window, shown in Figure 14-2. Under the Options menu, you can request an alphabetical list of all commands or search for a single command by name. The Sections menu can be used to select one of the man page sections, which displays the complete list of available documentation for a selected section. Once the list of commands is displayed, you can select the commands with the mouse. In fact, using xman is the only way I know of to get a complete list of the available man pages.

Figure 14-2   *A man page displayed in an xman window*

The scroll bar on the left of the window in Figure 14-2 probably works a bit differently than others you are accustomed to. The left mouse button scrolls the text down one page, the right mouse button scrolls the text up one page, and the middle mouse button can be used to drag the scroll bar from one position to another.

If you want to know more about xman, run it and read the information displayed when you select the Help button (or when you first select the Manual Page button).

Getting Help from Other Sources

Probably the greatest source of information on the UNIX system is word-of-mouth. UNIX has a great oral tradition, so if you have access to someone with UNIX experience, don't hesitate if you need to ask a question. Anyone who has worked with UNIX for a while will be more than happy to share whatever knowledge they have. It's sort of a cult thing. You will actually be doing the person a favor — we like the opportunity to be a wizard from time to time.

The Internet

An enormous amount of information is available on the Internet. The Internet grew up on UNIX systems, so you can find complete technical documentation for both of them. Much of the available information has been converted to a format that can be viewed on the Web. You can find all the man pages in HTML or PDF format for almost every version of UNIX. A good search engine will find several pages on any UNIX subject. Which search engine is best is a matter of opinion, and depends to a large degree on the type of information you are searching for. I seem to have the best luck with the following search engines:

- Google, at www.google.com
- Teoma, at www.teoma.com
- Wisenut, at www.wisenut.com

Besides the Web, another good source of information is the hundreds of newsgroups that pertain to particular aspects of UNIX. The amount of traffic and the high level of expertise make them quite useful. The same is true of the hundreds of mailing lists that are available.

If you need to keep up with a particular topic, in most cases you can subscribe to a mailing list on the subject. Often, a good Web site on the topic that you are interested in suggests mailing lists on the topic. Or you can go to a Web site that maintains a directory of mailing lists. No single directory lists them all (the Internet is not that organized), but certain directories can be used effectively, such as:

- Tile Net, at http://tile.net/lists
- Publicly Accessible Mailing Lists, at http://paml.net
- L-Soft, at http://www.lsoft.com/lists/listref.html

The info utility

If you are using Linux, another source of documentation is available. The info utility works something like man. For example, if you want to use info to find out about nohup, enter the following command:

```
$ info nohup
```

The primary difference between info and man are the keys that you use to move around the document. The control keys for man are based on the keys used with more, and the keys for info are the ones you find in emacs. If you use the emacs editor and have become familiar with its navigation keys, you should be able to start using info right away. If you are not familiar with emacs, you may need to study the Help information for info before you will be able to read the documents.

Done!

REVIEW

In this session, you learn how to use man to locate and read UNIX documentation.

- The man command searches through several different directories of documentation to find the item that you request.

- The standard layout of a man page is constructed by selecting from a set of standard headings.
- A program named xman enables you to access the man pages through a Graphical User Interface (GUI).
- You can use a Web browser to find the man pages on the Internet.

The following session discusses the UNIX e-mail system, with a primary focus on the client e-mail programs that users employ to read, edit, and send e-mail.

QUIZ YOURSELF

1. How do you enter the man command so that the search is limited to one particular section of the documentation? (See "Viewing UNIX Documentation with man.")

2. What is the first heading in every man page? (See "The structure of a man page.")

3. What special functions do the commands apropos and whatis provide? (See "The Options of man.")

4. What makes the Graphical User Interface of the xman utility so plain? (See "Viewing UNIX Documentation with xman.")

5. On a Linux system, what other utility can be used to view much of the documentation? (See "The info utility.")

E-mail

Session Checklist

✔ E-mail and the Internet

✔ Communicating with other users

**30 Min.
To Go**

This session introduces you to the basic and standard set of e-mail utility programs available on UNIX. Several programs can be used to read and send e-mail. They all perform basically the same task and, because the underlying mechanism is basically the same, you can freely switch from one to another.

A primitive (but easy to use) messaging system can be used to transmit messages to another user or to establish a conversation between two users.

E-mail and the Internet

Opinions differ on which specific event was the birth of the Internet. Some say the Internet was born when the first documents outlining its design were produced or when programming first began. Others say it was born the first time Internet software was installed on more than one computer and a connection was made between them. However, most people agree that the birth of the Internet occurred when the first message was sent from one computer to another. That was e-mail.

Since that first message, e-mail has become very important — so important, in fact, that when something disrupts it, even for a few minutes, it has quite an impact on us.

The Internet is very flexible and allows e-mail to be originated, routed, distributed, and received in many different ways. Different types of e-mail programs can be used to send and receive messages. An *e-mail client*, a program that is used to both transmit and receive messages, is built into most Web browsers and included in many of the office suites of software.

The following paragraphs describe the three most fundamental e-mail programs: mail, elm, and pine. They are all in wide use today because they have some special talents that their younger GUI cousins no longer have. Primary among these features is the ability to issue an e-mail message from a single command line on a terminal or from inside a script.

Using mail

A very early version of an e-mail client is the program named mail. This program is quite simple, but it is its simplicity that makes it so useful. It works from the command line in such a way that you can send a short message to someone by typing the command, address, and message on one line.

The simplest way to use mail is to send a message to a user on the local computer. Because the message is not going over an internet link to a remote computer, you do not need to include an at sign (@) in the address — mail assumes that you mean the local computer, so you only need the user name. For example, if your login name is fred, you can send yourself a message using the following command:

```
$ mail fred
Subject: Just testing
This is the body of the test message being sent to myself
just to see if the mail will go through.
.
Cc:
```

You specify the recipient's address on the command line, and are prompted for a subject line to include as part of the header of the message. You can enter as many lines of text as you like. You can signal the end of the message by entering Ctrl+D, which is the ASCII end-of-file character, or by entering a line that consists of nothing but a period, as in this example. Finally, you are prompted to enter an optional address to which a copy of the message will be sent. After you press the Return key, the message is sent, and you are back to the command line prompt.

To use the mail utility to read the message you have sent to yourself, you can enter the mail command without any arguments. The message is listed, as in the following example:

```
$ mail
Mail version 8.1 6/6/93.  Type ? for help.
"/var/spool/mail/fred": 1 message 1 new
>N  1 fred@arlin.xyz.   Mon Dec  3 08:27  14/456  "Just Testing"
```

This example shows only one message, but there can be several messages in the list. A number identifies each message. To display and read the message, simply enter its number, as in the following example:

```
Message 1:
Date: Mon Dec 3 08:27:39 2001 -0900
From: Fred <fred@arlin.xyz
Subject: Just testing
This is the body of the test message being sent to myself
just to see if the mail will go through.
```

Messages are always addressed by number. You can use the d command to delete a message by number. For example, to delete message number 4, enter the following command:

```
& d 4
```

Other mail commands can be used to read, save, delete, edit, forward, and otherwise manage your incoming mail, and you can find descriptions of all of these commands on the man page for mail. But reading mail this way is not what has kept the mail utility in business. As e-mail has become more important, better ways have been devised to handle incoming messages. The real power of the mail utility is its ability to quickly send a simple message. For example, you can pipe a short message into mail and have it instantly sent, like this:

```
$ echo The meeting has been cancelled | mail herbert
```

That's all there is to it. The mail program has been given a message and an address, so it transmits immediately. If the user you want to reach is on another computer, the same process works, but you have to supply the full address:

```
$ echo The meeting has been cancelled | mail herbert@mngrv.xyz.com
```

Occasionally, you need to send someone a text file. The following example shows how you can quickly pipe a file named x15.xpec into mail and have it sent:

```
$ cat x15.spec | mail -s "Updated rocket spec" herbert@mngrv.xyz.com
```

The -s option is used to specify the subject line. In UNIX, there are always at least two different ways to do the same thing. The following command uses redirection instead of a pipe to achieve exactly the same result as the previous example:

```
$ mail -s "Updated rocket spec" herbert@mngrv.xyz.com <x15.spec
```

You can have mail send the same message to more that one recipient by naming all of the recipients on the command line. The following command sends the same message to four recipients:

```
$ mail herbert sam william@blorg.zimmish.com martha
```

If you find that you repeatedly send messages to the same group of people, you can assign an alias name to the list of addresses. The .mailrc file in your home directory can be used to define aliases. For example, adding the following line to the text of the .mailrc file creates an alias called group for the mail recipients in the previous example:

```
alias group herbert sam william@blorg.zimmish.com martha
```

After you have defined the alias group, you can send a message to every member in the alias list by entering the following command:

```
$ echo We are going to skip lunch today | mail group
```

If you use the .mailrc file to define the alias, you are the only one that can use it because it is in your home directory. However, you can create an alias that everyone can use by using the /etc/aliases file to define the alias. The alias works the same way, but the format of a line in /etc/aliases is slightly different than a line in .mailrc. The following is an example of defining an alias in the /etc/aliases file:

```
group: herbert, sam, william@blorg.zimmish.com, martha
```

The /etc/aliases file has its own man page, which you can read by entering this command:

```
$ man 5 aliases
```

20 Min. To Go

Using elm

The e-mail program named elm was written to provide a friendlier mail-reading user interface to the original mail program. It retains the capability of sending mail from a single command line entry. Also like mail, you can pipe text into elm and have it mailed, as in the following example:

```
$ echo The meeting has been cancelled | elm herbert
```

You can also redirect files into elm and have them mailed immediately, as shown in the following example:

```
$ elm -s "Updated rocket spec" herbert@mngrv.xyz.com <x15.spec
```

The elm mailer provides a simple way to quickly edit and send a message. If you start elm with the name of a recipient, or a list of recipients, you are prompted for a subject line and the addresses of additional recipients. The following example shows this process:

```
$ elm braxon@xyz.net
                        Send only mode [ELM 2.5]
To: braxon@xyz.net
Subject of message: Slim to none
Copies to: _
```

It doesn't matter whether you enter addresses in the Copies to: field. When you press the Return key, elm invents the name of a file to hold the body of the message and uses your editor to open the file. You can specify which editor you would like elm to use by naming it in an environment variable, like this:

```
EDITOR=vi
export vi
```

If you intend to use elm to send messages, you should define the EDITOR environment variable as part of the startup profile of your shell so that it always selects the editor of your choice.

You will want to set other environment variables if you decide to use elm interactively. You will certainly need to set the TMPDIR variable, which is required to send attachments. The other variables are all described in the elm man page.

After you have finished editing the text of your message and have saved the file, exiting the editor causes elm to clear the screen and display a screen like that shown in Figure 15-1. At this point, you can proceed in several ways:

- Press the letter y or the Return key to send the message and end your elm session.
- Press the letter e to return to the editor to change the text of the message.
- Press the letter a to be prompted for a file to be added as an attachment.
- Press the letter n to exit elm without sending the message.

If you press the letter a, the screen layout shown in Figure 15-2 is displayed so you can attach one or more files to the message. In the figure, the first attachment listed is the main body of the message and the other two are files of different types that have been added. You can add an attachment in one of two ways: by simply entering the file name or by entering a period to display a directory listing, which enables you to move from one directory to another to select the file.

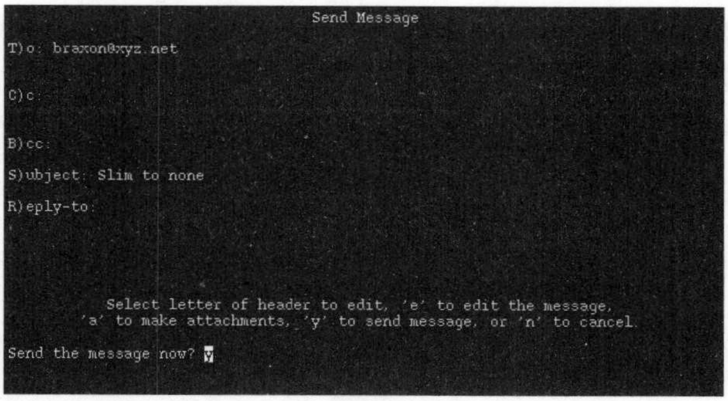

Figure 15-1   *The main elm screen, used to send messages*

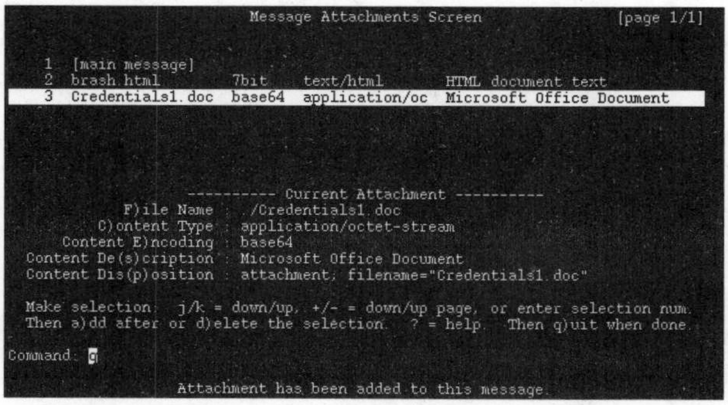

Figure 15-2   *The elm screen, used to attach files to an outgoing message*

Entering the elm command without any arguments clears the display and shows a screen formatted like that shown in Figure 15-3. This layout, and the operations that are available, demonstrate elm's heritage from mail. Like mail, the list of existing messages is displayed, with each message tagged as being new or old, and you can select a message by number.

```
      Mailbox is '/var/spool/mail/braxton' with 4 messages [ELM 2.5 PL5]

N   1     Dec 04 * Arthur                 (13)    Slim to none
NM  2     Dec 04 * Mail Delivery Subs     (67)    Returned mail: see transcript for
N   3     Dec 04 * Maglimit               (463)   The lunch problem
N   4     Nov 30 * fred                   (103)   Updated schedule




      You can use any of the following commands by pressing the first character;
   d)elete or u)ndelete mail,  m)ail a message,  r)eply or f)orward mail,  q)uit
      To read a message, press <return>.  j = move down, k = move up, ? = help

Command:
```

Figure 15-3   *The main elm screen, used to read and send mail*

The elm mailer improves on mail in several ways. The fact that elm handles attachments is very important because e-mail isn't just for simple messages any more. The ability to use the editor of your choice (instead of the rudimentary line editor in mail) is also a great advantage to those of us who have already trained our fingers. The elm interface is much simpler because elm uses screens instead of simple responses on the command line. The result is that elm has a more window-like look and feel that guides the user through the necessary steps.

Using pine

The pine editor is partially derived from elm, but pine takes a different approach. You can start pine from the command line by providing it with the address of a recipient and by piping, or redirecting, a text message into it, but pine doesn't automatically send the message. Instead, it clears the screen and formats it to resemble the screen shown in Figure 15-4. From this screen you can edit the text, add attachments, and send the message.

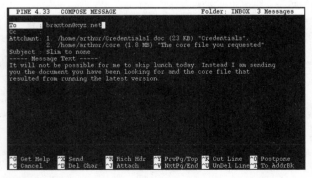

Figure 15-4   *The pine screen, used to compose and send e-mail messages*

In Figure 15-4, you can see the command keys displayed across the bottom of the screen. The caret character (^) is used to indicate the Ctrl key, so ^X means Ctrl+X. The pico text editor can be used from the command line just like any other editor, but a version of it is built into pine for editing messages. It is a simple editor and has its own man page.

When you start pine without specifying a recipient, the screen clears and the main screen is displayed, as shown in Figure 15-5. As you can see, pine has a much more window-like interface than the earlier e-mail programs. You can use the arrow keys to navigate around the screen or make a menu selection by entering a letter. The pine mailer includes an address book that can be used to store e-mail addresses and has a menu selection that you can use to specify configuration settings from inside the program.

```
 PINE 4.33    MAIN MENU                      Folder: INBOX  3 Messages


          ?     HELP            -  Get help using Pine

          C     COMPOSE MESSAGE -  Compose and send a message

          I     MESSAGE INDEX   -  View messages in current folder

          L     FOLDER LIST     -  Select a folder to view

          A     ADDRESS BOOK    -  Update address book

          S     SETUP           -  Configure Pine Options

          Q     QUIT            -  Leave the Pine program



     Copyright 1989-2001  PINE is a trademark of the University of Washington.
                    [Folder "INBOX" opened with 3 messages]
 ? Help                        P PrevCmd                    R RelNotes
 O OTHER CMDS > [ListFldrs] N NextCmd                       K KBLock
```

Figure 15-5   *The main pine screen*

As you can see, option keys are defined at the bottom of the screens shown in Figures 15-4 and 15-5. This format of displaying keys is consistent throughout pine, and you need to refer to them because the purposes of the keys are not consistent from one screen to the next. For example, to return to the main menu from the folder list, you use the < character. However, to return to the main menu from the setup screen, you enter the letter E. To exit the composition screen, you must enter Ctrl+C. The arrow keys can be used to navigate around every screen — a fact not specified on the display.

The pine e-mail program has a lot of users. People who have been working in a UNIX environment for a few years have become familiar with pine. It takes practice, but after you use pine for a while, it becomes very easy to work with. Using pine does not limit your options because mail is still available to send quick messages from the command line.

Communicating with Other Users

**10 Min.
To Go**

UNIX provides a very fast way to communicate with other users. You can send a message in such a way that it is written directly to another user's terminal. At least, you can if the other user permits it.

Granting and denying message permissions

You have complete control over whether others are allowed to send messages to your terminal. To determine whether incoming messages are allowed on your terminal, use the tty command to determine the device node for your terminal, and then use ls to check the permissions as follows:

```
$ tty
/dev/pts/1
$ ls -l /dev/pts/1
crw--w----  1 arthur   tty    136,   1 Dec 4 13:47 /dev/pts/1
```

The permissions flags on this terminal show that the person logged in has read and write permissions (as would be expected) and that group members have write permission. If the group has write permission, the terminal can receive messages from other users. You can use the mesg command to change the permissions setting that controls the receipt of messages. You can turn messaging off to your terminal with a single command, as follows:

```
$ mesg n
$ ls -l /dev/pts/1
crw-------  1 arthur   tty    136,   1 Dec 4 14:33 /dev/pts/1
```

The n option turns off the device node's permission bit that allows other users to write to your terminal. To turn messaging back on, enter the following command:

```
$ mesg y
```

Instead of using ls to look at how the access bits are set, you can run mesg without an argument to determine whether the setting is y or n. The following example shows that messages are allowed on the terminal:

```
$ mesg
is y
```

Sending a message

To send a message, you need to know how and where the recipient is logged in. To find out who is logged in to which terminal, use the finger command without an argument, as in the following example:

```
$ finger
Login    Name     Tty      Idle  Login Time
maglin   Maglin   pts/0    4:25  Nov 27 08:24 (:0)
maglin   Maglin   pts/1          Nov 27 08:24 (:0)
fred     Fred     tty3           Nov 30 11:42 (:0)
root     root     tty1     16d   Nov 18 11:15
```

This list shows four active logins, and that the same person is logged in on two terminals. The actual wall time each user logged in and how long the terminal has been idle are also listed. The idle time is the time that has elapsed since the last keystroke. You can usually tell from the idle time whether someone is at the terminal. For example, you can be fairly certain that there is no root user at the tty1 terminal because there hasn't been a keystroke for 16 days. The two maglin logins are at pseudo terminals, and one of these terminals hasn't been used for over four hours. The best bet that the fred login has to actually contact someone is to send a message to `maglin` on `/dev/pts/1`. The `write` command can be used to send the message:

```
$ write maglin pts/1
Do you think it is about time for lunch. Or are
you going to skip it again?
```

You can type as many lines as you want. When you are done typing, enter Ctrl+D, which is the ASCII character EOF (end of file). If you want to get the attention of the person at the other end, you can type Ctrl+G, which is the ASCII character BEL (bell). This causes some terminals to emit a beep and others to flash the screen.

Receiving and responding to a message

If you have messaging enabled, and you receive a message, something like the following appears on your screen:

```
Message from fred on tty3 at 14:35
Do you think it is about time for lunch. Or are
you going to skip it again?
EOF
```

You don't need to do anything unless you wish to respond. The EOF at the end of the message means that the originator entered Ctrl+D and has thus exited from `write`. However, until that EOF arrives, an opening exists for a two-way communications link. To respond, use `write`, as in the following message:

```
$ write fred tty3
Lunch is a good idea. Now? -o
```

The two parties can then write back and forth, and the lines are intermixed on each terminal. That little `-o` at the end of the line is not necessary — it's the traditional way of saying "over."

A utility named `talk` is more sophisticated than `write`, but it works much the same way. The `talk` utility splits the screen and allows you to write on the bottom half while the incoming messages are displayed on the top half. The problem is that `talk` may not work because it doesn't have a standard for its interface and it isn't installed on every UNIX system.

Sending a message with wall

The utility named `wall` does the same thing that `write` does, with two exceptions. First, you can type as many lines of text as you want and none of them are sent until you enter Ctrl+D. Second, instead of sending the message to a person specified on the command line, `wall` sends the message to everybody that is logged in. For example, the following message will be displayed on every terminal that permits messages and has someone logged in:

```
$ wall
This is to notify everyone that since no one is skipping lunch
we are going to stay one hour later tonight.
```

Done!

REVIEW

In this session, you learn how to use the basic UNIX e-mail utilities and the internal messaging system.

- The simplest e-mail program is named `mail`, which is controlled entirely by commands entered from the command line.
- The `elm` e-mail program is an upgrade of the `mail` program and provides a more formatted interface for the user.
- The `pine` e-mail program is not operated from the command line, but it provides a very complete window-like interface.
- The programs named `write` and `wall` can be used to send messages directly to other users.

In the next session, some additional capabilities of the shell program are discussed. It is possible to write shell scripts that perform very complicated tasks. A well-written shell script can be made portable across all versions of UNIX.

QUIZ YOURSELF

1. Describe two ways to get the text of your message into the `mail` utility. (See "Using mail.")
2. Why are there two files that can be used to establish alias lists for `mail`? (See "Using mail.")
3. What do you need to do to specify which text editor is used to create mail when using `elm`? (See "Using elm.")
4. What can be done to prevent messages from others being displayed on your terminal? (See "Granting and denying message permissions.")
5. What two things do you need to know to send a message to another user? (See "Sending a message.")

Writing Shell Scripts

Session Checklist

✔ Simple scripts

✔ Command line arguments

✔ Environment variables

**30 Min.
To Go**

This session introduces shell programming. It shows you how to create a script file and configure it to be executable. A default shell is always available, but a script should specify which shell program should be used for its execution. Arguments can be passed from the command line to a shell script. A shell program can set and use both local and global environment variables.

Shell programming is important in UNIX, because it makes it possible to combine any number of commands to create a new command. At first, the syntax seems very simple, but as you become more familiar with it, you will see that it is really quite flexible and powerful. Shell scripts are often hundreds of lines long and perform very complicated tasks.

Simple Scripts

You may find that you frequently enter a particular group of commands from the command line. Instead of repeatedly typing the commands, you can put them in a file and have them run from there. A file of this type is known as a *shell script* (sometimes just called a *script*). A script is nothing more than a text file that contains a list of one or more commands and their arguments, and you can run the script just like any other program. In effect, the script becomes a new command. The commands found in shell scripts are the same as those that you have been entering from the command prompt and, as you will soon see, others are designed to work only inside scripts. The following paragraphs explain how scripting can be accomplished by describing the creation of a shell script that contains a single command.

The following command line displays the number of currently active logins:

```
$ who | wc -l
```

The who command lists all of the logins, one per line, and then the output from who is piped into the wc -l command, which simply outputs a count of the number of lines piped to it. The result is a display of the number of active logins. If you want to use this command line frequently, and you don't want to enter the entire command every time, you can use a text editor to create a file containing the command. For example, if you create a file named lon that contains the command line, you can run the command by entering

```
$ sh lon
```

This command starts a new copy of the Bourne Shell and directs it to read and execute the commands found in the file named lon. This is the same shell program you have been using all along to display prompts that allow you to enter commands, but this time it is run from the command line and supplied with an argument. Instead of prompting you for input, the shell executes the commands found in the file and then quits. This technique of running scripts works, but there is a better way. Using the chmod command, you can change the mode of the script so you can execute it directly:

```
$ chmod u+x lon
```

You may recall from Session 3 that the chmod command makes the file executable by the user, so it can now be executed directly from the command line just like any other program. All you have to do is enter the file name, like this:

```
$ lon
```

When you enter the name of the file, the shell detects that the file is executable and also determines that it is a text file, so the shell assumes that the file is a shell script and acts accordingly. This new lon command always shows you the number of active logins.

A potential problem still exists. As you know from previous sessions, the syntax required for commands can vary from one shell to another. Fortunately, all of the shells have agreed on a convention that allows you to specify — inside the script itself — which shell is to be used to interpret the commands. For example, the following script is always run by the Bourne Shell:

```
#!/bin/sh
who | wc -l
```

The following script is always run by the C Shell:

```
#!/bin/csh
who | wc -l
```

In this example, the body of the script is the same, but many commands are different among the different shells. Fortunately, all of the shells agree on the convention of having the first line specify the program (usually a shell) that will execute the commands in the script. This convention means you can write your shell script using whatever syntax you prefer and it will always be interpreted by the correct shell program. In fact, you can specify any program you like, and that program will be run and will have the text of the script fed to it. For example, if you were to write a Perl language script, all you need to do is specify the name of the Perl interpreter. Keep in mind that the interpreter you want to use must be named on the first line of the script, and the first two characters of the line must be #!.

> You should *always* specify the correct shell in the first line of every script you write. This makes it very easy for you to write scripts that everyone can run. If you write your script designed to run using the Bourne Shell, it will work just fine for anyone using the C Shell, the Korn Shell, bash, or any other shell. And, in return, if people using other shells follow the same convention, you can use any of their scripts.

There is one more piece to a complete script: you should include a comment to describe what the script does. Any line that begins with the hash character # is a comment line and is ignored by the shell (the first line beginning with #! is a special case). You can insert comment lines anywhere in your script. After adding a comment to our simple script, it looks like this:

```
#!/bin/sh
# Displays the number of active logins
who | wc -l
```

Command Line Arguments

**20 Min.
To Go**

A collection of predefined variables provides your script with any command line arguments the user specifies when the script is run. The arguments are simply named $1, $2, $3, and so on, up to $9. You can actually have more than nine arguments, but there is a trick to reading them, which is described later. The following shell script displays the first two argument strings entered on the command line:

```
#!/bin/sh
# showtwo -- display the first two arguments
echo $1
echo $2
```

This script displays the first two arguments, but ignores the rest. The following example shows what happens when you enter three arguments on the line:

```
$ showtwo apple pear plum
apple
pear
```

As with any other UNIX program, the arguments on the command line must be separated by spaces. You can always group two or more command line entries into a single argument by putting them in quotes, as shown in the following example:

```
$ showtwo "apple pear" plum
apple pear
plum
```

Using the arguments

Suppose you want to create a simple backup utility that is capable of copying a specified file from the current directory into a subdirectory named `safety`. The following script will do that:

```
#!/bin/sh
# save - copy a file to a safety directory
mkdir safety 2>/dev/null
cp $1 safety/$1
```

The `mkdir` command makes certain that the directory exists. If it does, an error message that you don't care about is output from `mkdir` and redirected to the `/dev/null` device, as described in Session 12. The `cp` command copies the file into the new directory.

If you want to put the `safety` directory someplace else, you can specify it that way in the script. For example, if you want it to be in your home directory, you can write the script this way:

```
#!/bin/sh
# save - copy a file to a safety directory
mkdir /usr/fred/safety 2>/dev/null
cp $1 /usr/fred/safety/$1
```

You don't really need to create a subdirectory for this simple kind of backup. Instead, you can save the file under another name in the same directory, as in the following script:

```
#!/bin/sh
# back - make a safety backup of a file
cp $1 $1.backup
```

This script will make a duplicate of a file, with the new file having the same name as the original file, but the suffix `.backup` appended to it. The name of the new file is constructed by combining the argument $1 with the suffix. For example, the backup name of a file named `fred.text` would be `fred.text.backup`. In scripts, it is quite common to mix the arguments with other text, environment variables, and even other arguments in order to create new names.

You can see how a script like this could be very handy if you are involved in managing a collection of files, such as occurs in the maintenance of a Web site. Suppose you want to make changes to some HTML files, but you want the ability to go back to the original files if anything goes wrong. Before you make any changes, you can use this script on the files that you are going to modify. After you make the changes, you can revert back to the original files by simply deleting the new files and renaming the backup files to their original names (which, of course, you could do with another script). If, on the other hand, you decide to keep the changes, just delete the backup files.

I have a simple script named `crazy` that I use before making any changes that might cause problems. The script is named `crazy` because it allows me to recover whenever I do something crazy. The script creates a subdirectory named `crazy` and copies all the files from the current directory into the subdirectory. The script looks like this:

```
#!/bin/sh
# crazy -- duplicate all files in this directory
```

```
mkdir crazy 2>/dev/null
cp * crazy
```

After this script has run, changes can safely be made to any of the files in the current directory. If the changes work out, the following command will delete the `crazy` directory and its contents:

```
$ rm -rf crazy
```

If the changes don't work out, the original files can all be restored with the following command:

```
$ cp crazy/* .
```

Using all the arguments

It is convenient to be able to enter a number of arguments on the command line of a script. The following script makes backup copies of three files:

```
#!/bin/sh
# save3 - copy three files to a safety directory
mkdir safety 2>/dev/null
cp $1 safety/$1
cp $2 safety/$2
cp $3 safety/$3
```

This works, but it's a bit clumsy. This script only works if you specify exactly three file names on the command line — it won't work for two, and it won't work for four. If you specify four file names, the last one will be ignored. If you only specify two file names, the last statement in the script will execute with no name stored in $3. A better thing to do is write the script so that it will work for any number of files entered on the command line. This requires that the script be able to determine how many arguments are entered on the command line and have the script adjust itself to handle that number. Fortunately, certain special built-in variables, listed in Table 16-1, provide the information.

Table 16-1 *Predefined Variables in a Bourne Shell Script*

Term	Description
$#	The number of arguments that were entered on the command line.
$-	The flags that were specified on the command line or that were defined by the set command.
$?	The value that was returned from the most recently executed program.
$$	The process ID number of the current shell program.
$!	The process ID number of the most recently spawned background process.

The echo command can be employed within a script called `showvars` to demonstrate the values of the shell's internal variables:

```
#!/bin/sh
# showvars - demonstrate the built-in variables
echo Number of arguments: $#
echo Process ID of this shell: $$
date &
echo Process ID of date: $!
ls /etc/passwd 2>/dev/null
echo Return code from ls: $?
ls /etc/notfound 2>/dev/null
echo Return code from ls notfound: $?
```

If you run the `showvars` script with three arguments on the command line, you get output that looks something like this:

```
$ showvars a b c
Number of arguments: 3
Process ID of this shell: 26878
Process ID of date: 26879
Sat Apr 14 20:09:53 AKDT 2001
/etc/passwd
Return code from ls: 0
Return code from ls notfound: 1
```

The value of $# is 3, which indicates that $1, $2, and $3 all have an argument from the command line stored in them. Whenever a script is executed, a separate process is run to actually execute the commands in the script, and every process has its own ID number. This example shows that the process ID number of that shell is 26878, the value found in the $$ variable.

Whenever a separate process is started from inside the shell, its process ID number is stored in the variable named $!. The process ID number is the same PID discussed in Session 4. In this script, the date process is run — it is run in the background because it has the & character following it — and is shown to have a process ID number of 26879. Notice that the ID number of date is one greater than the ID number of the shell running the script — this happens because ID numbers are allocated sequentially and date was the next process to be started after the start of the shell. ID numbers are not always sequential, because other processes could have been started elsewhere in the system.

There is a reason to be interested in all these ID numbers. It is not uncommon for a script to send a signal to another process by using the kill command (as described in Session 4), and the ID number is needed to do that. Of course, we could get the number by using the ps command from inside the script, just like we did from the command line in Session 4, but it gets a bit complicated to separate the process ID from the rest of the text.

Whenever a process stops running, it generates a code number. This number is known as an *exit code*, *status code,* or *completion code.* In almost all cases, a completion code of 0 indicates successful termination, while any other number is some sort of error indicator. In its simplest form, a process completes with either 0 to indicate success or 1 to indicate failure. In the `showvars` script, the ls command is executed once to succeed (because it finds at least one file it is instructed to list) and once to fail (because it cannot find any file it is instructed to list). In each case, the value of the completion code is stored in the variable named $?.

One shell script can execute another by using exactly the same command you would use on the command line. A shell script, by default, has a completion code of 0. If you want to specify some other value for the completion code, you can do so by using an exit **command similar to this:**

```
exit 5
```

The exit **command not only specifies the completion code, it also causes the shell script to quit immediately, even if the command is somewhere in the middle of the script.**

Using the built-in variables, and a couple of other tricks, you can write a script that makes a backup copy of all the files named on the command line:

```
#!/bin/sh
# saveall - copy named files to a safety directory
mkdir safety 2>/dev/null
until [ $# = 0 ]
do
    cp $1 safety/$1
    shift
done
```

The until/do/done block repeatedly executes the list of commands between do and done as long as the conditional expression it is testing at the top of the loop is false. In this case, the condition is false only if the special value $# is equal to zero — that is, if the count of arguments from the command line is zero. There are two statements inside the loop. The cp statement copies the file and the shift statement moves the command line arguments one position to the left. To make room for the arguments to be shifted to the left, the value of the argument $1 is omitted. Omitting $1 results in one less argument and $# is thus reduced by one. For example, assume that the following command, which has three arguments, is entered:

```
$ saveall frammis.c flowdoc.txt makefile
```

In this case, the original value of $# is 3 and the value of $1 is frammis.c. After execution of the shift command, the value of $# is 2 and the value of $1 is flowdoc.txt. Another execution of the shift command sets $# to 1, and the value of $1 becomes makefile. A final execution of shift sets $# to 0, indicating that no arguments are left. With this technique, your script can process hundreds of arguments from the command line.

Session 17 has more information on looping inside scripts, and more information on creating conditional expressions. Loops in shell scripts can be created by setting up loop counters, by executing the loop once for each name in a list of names, or even by executing the loop once for each file in a directory.

Using Environment Variables

Environment variables can be used to store such information as argument strings and process ID numbers. However, it is more common to invent and use environment variables of your own, or to use one or more of the variables that are predefined in your environment.

Using the existing variables

Quite a few environment variables are set each time you log in. This is not only achieved through the system scripts, but also by the local configuration scripts in your home directory.

Any environment variable that has been defined and exported is available inside your scripts. For example, the save script from earlier in this session could be rewritten as hsave to save the files in your home directory as follows:

```
#!/bin/sh
# hsave - copy a file to a save directory
mkdir $HOME/safety 2>/dev/null
cp $1 $HOME/safety/$1
```

The environment variable HOME normally contains the complete path to the home directory of the user. In this example, the HOME path is combined with a subdirectory name to create the complete path to a backup directory.

The names are easily combined in this example because slash characters and spaces surround them. If you find yourself in a situation where it is necessary to put names together in some ambiguous way, you can use the characters { and } to isolate the variables. The commands in the hsave script could just as well have been written this way:

```
mkdir ${HOME}/safety 2>/dev/null
cp ${1} ${HOME}/safety/${1}
```

You won't need to use the braces often, but in some situations, there is no other way. For example, if you have an environment variable named PREFIX and you wish to combine its value with the characters MMM to make one large name, you may find yourself entering the following:

```
mkdir $PREFIXMMM 2>/dev/null          # wrong
```

If the name of the environment variable and the string run together, the name is unrecognizable. Using the braces, you can construct the string you are after as follows:

```
mkdir ${PREFIX}MMM 2>/dev/null
```

If you want to see a list of all the environment variables that are currently defined, you can use the env command. There are enough of them that the list will scroll off the screen, so you will need to see more as follows:

```
$ env | more
```

Personally, I like to have the variables listed in alphabetical order, which can be done by entering the following command:

```
$ env | sort | more
```

Setting environment variables

You can invent and set your own environment variables in a script just like you can set them from the command line. All you need to do is think of a good name and set it to a value. Here is a simple example:

```
#!/bin/sh
NUMSET=88
echo $NUMSET
```

This script creates and sets the value of NUMSET. Environment variables are set to a string of characters. Even though NUMSET looks like it holds a number, it is actually holding the two-character string 88. Here is another simple example:

```
#!/bin/sh
ONSET="This is what it holds"
echo $ONSET
```

You must use quotes whenever there is a space in the string being stored in the variable, but the quotes themselves are not included as part of the string stored in the variable.

The ONSET and NUMSET variables are local to the script. That is, they are defined for this one script, but they do not become defined for other programs or other scripts that are started by this script. To make ONSET globally available to all the subprocesses that the script starts (including other script processes), you must use an export statement. For example:

```
#!/bin/sh
ONSET="This is what it holds"
echo $ONSET
export ONSET
```

You can use other environment variables as all or part of the string stored in a new environment variable. For example, the following command uses the value stored in HOME to build a new environment variable named BDIR:

```
BDIR=$HOME/safety
```

You can even run a program and store its output in an environment variable. For example, the utility program hostname outputs the name of your local computer. In the following code, the hostname program is run and the name of the host is stored in an environment variable named HNAME:

```
HNAME=`hostname`
```

The tic marks surrounding hostname are not regular single quote marks. They are quote marks that tilt to the left and are called *reverse quotes*, *back tics*, or *grave accent* marks.

 The string stored in an environment variable can be as long as you want. It can also contain special characters such as tabs and newlines.

Done!

REVIEW

In this session, you learn the basic structure and operation of a shell script.

- A shell script is a collection of command line instructions that are stored in a text file.
- A shell can be instructed to run the commands in a script by entering sh and using the name of the script as an argument, or the script can be executed directly from the command line if its execution permissions are set.
- Special predefined shell variables contain information from outside the script, such as the number of arguments on the command line.
- Environment variables can be defined and used inside a script.

The following session has more information on writing scripts. One of the most important capabilities of scripting is conditional execution, which allows a script to adapt its actions to fit the current circumstances.

QUIZ YOURSELF

1. A shell script is a simple text file. What must you do to configure a shell script so you can run it like a program? (See "Simple Scripts.")
2. If you create a special script that needs to be executed by a shell program named /bin/tcsh, what can you do to make sure that the correct shell is used? (See "Simple Scripts.")
3. One or more arguments can be entered on the command line. What is the name of the environment variable that contains the second argument? (See "Using the arguments.")
4. The $ character is used to read the string contained in an environment variable, and the variable name itself can optionally be enclosed in some special characters. What are these characters? (See "Using the existing variables.")
5. What command is used to make an environment variable available to the current script's subprocesses? (See "Setting environment variables.")

1. If you have a file in the current directory named `limwid`, what command would you enter to configure the file so that only you can read the file and write to the file, but execution permission is granted to anyone?

2. What does an `umask` value of 033 mean?

3. What is the difference between a hard link and a symbolic link?

4. What happens if you enter the `mount` command without supplying any arguments on the command line?

5. What is the difference between a dumb terminal and a pseudo terminal?

6. Give one example each of a character device and a block device.

7. Why must a file system be created on a disk drive before it can be mounted?

8. What is the most important thing you can do with `less` that you cannot do with `more`?

9. How accurate is the UNIX clock, and what program do you use to set it?

10. What is meant by lexicographic order?

11. What is the difference between the utility programs `man` and `xman`?

12. What can you do to change the directories that the `man` utility searches to locate requested documents?

13. Under what circumstances is it important to be able to limit a search to a single section of the man pages, and how is it done?

14. What is the name of an e-mail program that can accept the text of outgoing messages being piped or redirected into it from the command line?

15. If you are sending e-mail and you do not use an at-sign (@) in the recipient's address, where is the recipient assumed to be located?

16. When using `mail` from the command line, what can you do to have the same e-mail sent to more than one recipient?

17. What is the difference between the commands `write` and `wall`?

18. Write a shell script named pback that creates a subdirectory named pageback and copies all of the HTML files from the current directory into pageback.

19. Write a shell script named today that outputs only the name of the day of the week.

20. Write a shell script named allfiles that stores the names of all the files of the current directory in an environment variable named FNAMES.

PART

IV

Saturday Evening

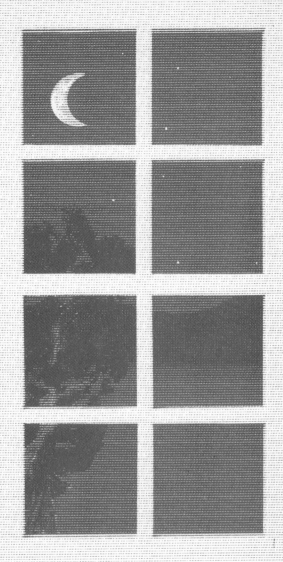

Session 17
Shell Scripts with Conditionals

Session 18
Shell Scripts with Loops

Session 19
Users and the passwd File

Session 20
Batch Editing

SESSION

Shell Scripts with Conditionals

Session Checklist

✔ Testing for true or false

✔ Testing for a pattern match

✔ Completing the script

✔ Adjusting your environment with a script

**30 Min.
To Go**

This session explains the basics of having a shell script make decisions about what it is supposed to do. You can control the actions of a shell script by specifying file names or keywords as command line arguments when you start the script running. The command that does the conditional testing is very simple, but it does have an odd sort of syntax about it.

Testing for True or False

As mentioned in the previous session, in scripts, the value of the exit code of the most recently executed command is stored as an environment variable and can be retrieved by using the expression $?. The following script displays the exit codes for both a successful command and a failed command:

```
#!/bin/sh
# statls - display exit codes for success and failure
ls misfil
echo The exit status of ls: $?
ls
echo The exit status of ls: $?
```

If the statls script is in a directory that does not contain a file named misfil, the output looks like this:

```
ls: misfil: No such file or directory
The exit status of ls: 1
statls
The exit status of ls: 0
```

The first ls command searched for a file that did not exist, so it resulted in a failure code of 1. The second ls command succeeded and exited with 0. The first and third lines of the output came from ls itself.

Another way of interpreting the status codes is to treat zero as true and any nonzero value as false. This is exactly the way the conditional expressions work in a shell script. The shell keyword if uses the return code from a command to determine whether the result is true or false. For example, the following script uses the exit code from ls to determine whether the file named misfil was found in the current directory:

```
#!/bin/sh
# ifls - check whether a file exists
if ls misfil
then
     echo The file exists
fi
```

If the exit status of the ls command results in true (that is, if its exit code is zero), the statements between then and fi will be executed. On the other hand, if the ls command produces a false result (that is, if the exit code is not zero) the script skips over everything and continues with the line following fi (fi is if spelled backward, indicating the end of an if block).

The if and then commands are usually written on a single line, like this:

```
if ls misfil; then
```

This form works because a semicolon has special meaning to the Bourne Shell. The text following a semicolon is treated as a separate command, just as if you had put it on a line by itself. A then statement always follows an if statement, so the two are almost always on the same line with a semicolon between them.

While the ls command can be used to test for the presence or absence of a file, another program, named test, is more suited for the job. test was designed to test a file and produce status codes of either true or false (0 or 1). More than that, it has options that can be used to query files for specific characteristics. The following example uses test with the -f option, which results in true only if the file tested is a regular file (not a directory or a device node):

```
#!/bin/sh
# regtest - test for a regular file
if test -f $1; then
     echo $1 is a regular file
else
     echo $1 is not a regular file
fi
```

The `regtest` script accepts the name of the file on the command line, so it can be used to test any file. This example also introduces the new keyword `else`, which is used to specify a list of statements that are to be executed if the result from `test` is false.

The `test` command has several options. In the previous example, `test` with the `-f` option results in true only if the argument is a regular file. You can also use the `-d` option, which reports true only if the name is that of a directory. The following script tells you whether the name on the command line is a regular file or a directory:

```
#!/bin/sh
# regdirtest - detect whether the parameter is the
#              name of a file or directory
if test -f $1; then
    echo $1 is a regular file
elif test -d $1; then
    echo $1 is a directory
else
    echo $1 is neither a regular file nor directory
fi
```

This script introduces the new keyword `elif`, which is part of the `if` syntax. The statements in the `elif` list are executed only when the `if` is false but the `elif` statement is true. You can use as many `elif` statements as you need to test all the possible cases.

A summary of the if command

The general syntax of the `if` statement is as follows:

```
if expression; then
    statement list
elif expression; then
    statement list
elif expression; then
    statement list
    .
    .
    .
else expression; then
    statement list
fi
```

Only one of the statement lists is executed. The `elif` statements and the `else` statements are optional.

The then keyword can be on the same line as the `if`, or it can be on the line following it. The following example reformats `regdirtest`, but is still valid and works exactly the same way as the previous example:

```
#!/bin/sh
# regdirtest2 - detect whether the parameter is the
#               name of a file or directory
if test -f $1
then
```

```
    echo $1 is a regular file
elif test -d $1
then
    echo $1 is a directory
else
    echo $1 is neither a regular file nor directory
fi
```

You can nest if statements one inside the other. This is necessary only if you have an else for each of the if statements, which you can't do with elif. The following example is yet another version of regdirtest that has an else statement for both of the if statements:

```
#!/bin/sh
# regdirtest3 - detect whether the argument is the
#               name of a file or directory
if test -f $1; then
    echo $1 is a regular file
else
    echo $1 is not a regular file
    if test -d $1; then
        echo $1 is a directory
    else
        echo $1 is not a directory
    fi
fi
```

Indention is important for the sake of readability. Also, if you make a mistake in the structure of the script, the indention will help you find where things are mismatched.

A summary of the test command

20 Min.
To Go

The test command can either be a separately executed program, or it can be implemented as part of the shell. Because test is used so frequently, it is becoming more common to include it as part of the shell, which is more efficient than loading and executing a program.

The test command is used often enough in writing shell scripts that an alternate syntax has been devised for it. The shell recognizes the pair of bracket characters [ ] as a sort of shorthand for test. The following expression checks for the existence of a file named fred:

```
if test -f fred;
```

You can write exactly the same thing by using brackets:

```
if [ -f fred ];
```

I find the brackets a bit easier to read, but, in general, the syntax is a matter of personal preference. Any place you need to use test, you can use the brackets instead. The following is another form of the regdirtest script:

```
#!/bin/sh
# regdirtest4 - detect whether the argument is the
#               name of a file or directory
if [ -f $1 ]; then
```

```
    echo $1 is a regular file
elif [ -d $1 ]; then
    echo $1 is a directory
else
    echo $1 is neither a regular file nor directory
fi
```

As shown in Table 17-1, quite a few operators can be used to construct the expression that tells test what to do. You can check whether a file is in any one of several states, as well as compare the size of integer numeric values and compare the character content of strings.

Table 17-1 *Logical Expressions Used by test*

Expression	Returns True if. . .
-r *filename*	the file can be read by the user running the script.
-w *filename*	the file can be written to by the user running the script.
-x *filename*	the file can be executed by the user running the script.
-f *filename*	the file exists and is a regular file. With the C Shell and BSD version of test, this is true if it exists and is any kind of file other than a directory.
-d *filename*	the file exists and is a directory.
-h *filename*	the file exists and is a symbolic link to another file.
-c *filename*	the file exists and is a character device node.
-b *filename*	the file exists and is a block device node.
-p *filename*	the file exists and is a named pipe file.
-u *filename*	the file exists and its set-user-ID bit is set.
-g *filename*	the file exists and its set-group-ID bit is set.
-k *filename*	the file exists and its sticky bit is set.
-s *filename*	the file exists and has a size greater than zero.
-t *number*	the number is a file descriptor of an open file, and the file either reads from or writes to a terminal.
-z *string*	the length of the string is zero.
-n *string*	the length of the string is greater than zero.
String1 = *string2*	the length and content of string1 and string2 are identical.
String1 != *string2*	the length and content of string1 and string2 are not identical.

Continued

Table 17-1   *Continued*

Expression	Returns True if. . .
String1	string1 is not the null string.
number1 -eq *number2*	number1 is equal to number2.
number1 -ne *number2*	number1 is not equal to number2.
number1 -lt *number2*	number1 is less than number2.
number1 -gt *number2*	number1 is greater than number2.
number1 -le *number2*	number1 is less than or equal to number2.
number1 -ge *number2*	number1 is greater than or equal to number2.
! *expr*	expr is false. Returns false if expr is true.
expr1 -o *expr2*	either expr1 or expr2 is true.
expr1 -a *expr2*	both expr1 and expr2 are true.

The -u flag tests whether the *set-user-ID bit* is set. If this bit is set for an executable file, the execution permissions of the program are switched to those of the file's owner during the time the program is actually executing. The executable file can have any owner, but it is most common for programs to be owned by root, which makes it possible for any user to run a program that requires root permissions to do its job. Note that the user running the program is not granted root permissions; it is only the program that is granted the permissions while it is running. The -g option tests for the *set-group-ID bit*, which operates the same way as the set-user-ID bit, but with the group instead of the user.

The -k flag tests whether the *sticky bit* is set on a directory. If it is set, and the permissions of the directory are set to allow the creation and deletion of files by more than one user, the only user that can actually delete a file from the directory is the one that created it. That is, you can delete your own files, but not the files belonging to anyone else. This is useful when you need to make a directory accessible to more than one user, but need to prevent users from damaging or deleting each other's files. An example is the standard /tmp directory that is used by many applications as a work area to hold temporary files.

Testing for a Pattern Match

It is possible to check for a match on a regular expression to determine which statement to execute next. The case statement matches a word against a list of regular expressions and, if a match is found, executes the statements following the regular expression. The general syntax of the Bourne Shell's case statement looks like this:

```
case word in
regexpr1)
    command list 1
  ;;
```

```
regexpr2)
    command list 2
    ;;
    .
    .
    .
esac
```

The *word* is first tested for a match against the regular expression *regexpr1*. If a match is found, *command list 1* is executed and the next statement executed is the one following the esac statement. On the other hand, if *regexpr1* is not a match, *regexpr2* is tried. This process continues until one of the expressions is a match, or the execution flow simply drops through past the esac statement without anything having been executed. The following is a summary of the rules:

- The expression testing begins at the top and moves down the list until a match is made or the bottom is reached.
- Only one match can be made, and only one block of statements can be executed.
- If no expression matches the word, no code is executed.
- Multiple expression patterns can be defined for one block of statements by using the vertical bar (|) as the OR operator.

The following script checks the input parameter against a set of regular expressions:

```
#!/bin/sh
# comsel -- Select one from a set of commands
case $1 in
show)
    echo The word $1 selected by show
    ;;
sho*)
    echo The word $1 selected by sho\*
    ;;
*x* | *y*)
    echo The word $1 selected by \*x\* \| \*y\*
    ;;
[qQ]*)
    echo The word $1 selected by \[qQ\]\*
    ;;
*)
    echo The word $1 did not make a selection
    ;;
esac
```

In this example, the case statement uses the first parameter supplied on the command line as the word to be used in matching. The first selection must match the word show exactly. The second selection matches any word beginning with the letters sho. The third selection matches any word containing either an x or a y. The fourth selection matches any word beginning with either q or Q. The last selection is the standard form used for the default entry because it is a match for anything. The following output of the script demonstrates how matches are made:

```
The word show selected by show
The word shoxxx selected by sho*
The word xshow selected by *x* | *y*
The word quit selected by [qQ]*
The word Q selected by [qQ]*
The word quox selected by *x* | *y*
The word fred did not make a selection
```

The word quox could have been matched in more than one place but, because only one selection can be made, the first match found is the one that was used. Notice that when the echo command is used to print the output lines, it is necessary to use the backslash character to escape certain characters because they have special meaning for the shell. A command that is issued inside a script has exactly the same characteristics as one that is typed on the command line.

**10 Min.
To Go**

Completing the Script

A complete script contains certain things that make it friendlier to use and easier to understand in the future. A script should specify the shell that will be used to run it and have some kind of comment explaining what it does. All the scripts to this point in the session have had those things, but there are some other important things that they don't have. A script should specify its return status code so it can be included as part of a test in another script. A script should also act in some reasonable way if it expects a parameter on the command line and doesn't find one, or finds something that it doesn't know how to handle.

The following script displays information about the file named on the command line:

```
#!/bin/sh
# fwhat - Determine whether the first parameter is the name
# of a regular file. If it is a regular file, report on
# the settings of its access flags.

if [ "$1" = "" ]; then
    echo No file name specified.
    exit 1
fi

if [ ! -f $1 ]; then
    echo $1 is not a regular file.
    exit 2
fi

echo -n $1 is
if [ -r $1 ]; then
    echo -n " readable,"
else
    echo -n " not readable,"
fi
```

```
if [ -w $1 ]; then
    echo -n " writeable,"
else
    echo -n " not writeable,"
fi
if [ -x $1 ]; then
    echo " and executable"
else
    echo " and not executable"
fi
exit 0
```

The `exit` statement causes a script to set its status code value and cease execution immediately. The first thing this script does is compare the parameter string to a zero-length string, and, if they are equal, it announces the fact that no file name was specified and exits with a status code of 1. The script then tests to make sure the parameter is the name of a regular file and, if not, exits with a status code of 2. These first two tests and their `exit` commands take care of the possible error conditions. The only other `exit` is at the very bottom of the script, which sets the status code to 0, indicating success.

Once the preliminaries are over, other tests are used to construct the output message. The `-n` option on the echo command instructs it to not output a newline on the end of the output string so that any subsequent output is appended onto the same line. The result is that the information appears as a single statement, as in the following examples:

```
$ fwhat /bin/sh
/bin/sh is readable, not writeable, and executable
$ fwhat fwhat
fwhat is readable, writeable, and executable
$ fwhat fred
fred is not a regular file
$ fwhat
No file name specified
```

A Script to Adjust Your Environment

Generally, when you run a script, you want it to go off, do its job, and report the results back to you. During the course of doing its job, the script may set several new environment variables and change some of those that have already been set. It is best for a script not to disturb your operating environment because it can be inconvenient (to say the least) to have your environment scrambled every time you run a command. For this reason, any environment changes made during the execution of a script are discarded when the script ceases execution.

But there are times when you want these changes to affect your current environment. For example, the following script makes a modification to the environment variable named MANPATH. You may recall that MANPATH is the list of directories that man searches to find a requested man page. If you have a lot of man page directories installed on your system, you

may want the capability to change the places man looks so it only looks in document directories that pertain to what you are doing. The following script makes such a change:

```
# setman - Set the MANPATH list of directories according to
#    the parameter. If the value of the parameter is not
#    known, make no change. No other environment variables
#    are modified.
#    NOTE: For this script to work, it must be sourced.

case $1 in
normal)
    MANPATH=/usr/share/man:/usr/local/man:/usr/man
    ;;
perl)
    MANPATH=/usr/lib/perl5/man
    ;;
x)
    MANPATH=/usr/X11R6/man
    ;;
none)
    unset MANPATH
    ;;
esac
```

This script sets MANPATH to the selected directories, but it only works if it is executed
without starting a new shell, like this:

```
$ source setman perl
```

Or, depending on the way your shell works, you can use the dot command to do the same
thing, as in the following command:

```
$ . setman perl
```

Sourcing the script is the same as setting the environment variable from the command
line. You may notice that this script does not have a line at the top specifying which shell
is to be used to run it — it has no choice but to run in the shell that sources it. Also, no
exit command is included in the script because entering exit from the command line
closes your shell and logs you out.

Done!

REVIEW

In this session, you learn how to write shell scripts that make decisions and act differently
depending on data passed to them. Scripts can also make decisions based on the values
found in environment variables and the results produced from running applications.

- Conditional execution of statements is achieved when the if statement responds to
  an expression that is either zero for true or nonzero for false.

- The test utility evaluates an expression and terminates with either 0 or 1, depending on the results of the expression.

- The brackets [and] can be used as a synonym for test.
- The case statement is used to select one from among several blocks of executable statements.
- Every script should begin with !# and end with exit, except when it shouldn't.

In the next session, the discussion moves from conditional execution to repeated execution. Loops can be created inside a shell script in various ways. The test command can be used to determine the number of times a loop is repeated.

Quiz Yourself

1. Why is it necessary to insert a semicolon following the expression of an if statement? (See "Testing for True or False.")

2. What is the difference between else and elif inside an if statement? (See "Testing for True or False.")

3. What is the difference between using brackets ([ ]) and using test? (See "A summary of the test command.")

4. In a case statement, what happens if none of the regular expressions match the word being tested? (See "Testing for a Pattern Match.")

5. What is the regular expression that is used as the default selection in a case statement, and why must it be last? (See "Testing for a Pattern Match.")

Shell Scripts with Loops

Session Checklist

✔ Loop while true

✔ Loop until true

✔ Loop for a count

✔ Processing command line options

**30 Min.
To Go**

This session explains how to loop through a set of commands. There are many reasons why a script may need to loop, but a loop is most commonly used to process a list of files or the list of parameters from the command line. As these items are processed, values are often stored in environment variables so they can be referred to and used later in the script. Loops can be constructed in three ways. A script can loop *while* a condition is true, *until* a condition is true, or *for* each member of a list of names.

Loop while True

The following represents the basic syntax of the while loop:

```
while expression
do
     statement list
done
```

This layout is very similar to that of the if statement. The expression can be any command that produces an exit status. As long as the exit code of the expression is zero (indicating true), the statements between the do and done keywords are executed.

The execution of a while loop is really quite straightforward. It begins with the evaluation of the expression on the while statement. If the result is not zero, the body of the while loop is not executed, and the flow of execution is transferred to the statement that follows the done keyword. On the other hand, if the result is zero, execution is transferred to the first statement that follows the do keyword. When the statements that follow the do statement have been executed, the done keyword causes execution to jump back to the while statement, where the expression is evaluated again and the whole process starts over.

 The statements in the statement list, between do **and** done, **must do something that eventually makes the expression at the top of the loop false. If they don't, the loop will never end, forcing you to kill the process.**

The most common thing done with a while loop is dealing with the list of parameters that comes in from the command line. You may recall that the first parameter is $1, the second is $2, and so on. The shift command causes the $1 parameter to be discarded and all the others shifted over by one position so that $2 becomes the new $1, $3 becomes the new $2, and so on. The following script uses a shift command inside a while loop to display a list of the parameters from the command line:

```sh
#!/bin/sh
# showparms - output a list of all the parameters from
#           the command line.
while [ "$1" != "" ]
do
    echo $1
    shift
done
exit 0
```

This script outputs the parameters one per line, like this:

```
$ showparms iliamna redoubt augustine
iliamna
redoubt
augustine
```

The following script takes all of the parameters on the command line and outputs them, separated by commas, on a single line. This script could actually be useful because a comma-separated string is a popular form of data input that is accepted by quite a few programs.

```sh
#!/bin/sh
# encomma - Output all of the parameters on the command
#      line as a comma separated string.
echo -n $1
shift
while [ "$1" != "" ]
do
    echo -n , $1
    shift
done
echo
exit 0
```

In the encomma script, you must output the first parameter before starting the loop because it is the only one not preceded by a comma. The -n option is used on echo to prevent the addition of a newline at the end of each parameter. This means that you must have a terminating echo command after the loop to output the single newline character. The following command shows how this script can be used to create a comma-separated list of all the file names in a directory:

```
$ encomma *
catparms, encomma, ispass, keepalive, showparms
```

Keeping a loop running

Situations arise when you don't want a loop to stop. If, for example, you have an Internet connection that disconnects after just a few minutes of inactivity, and you want to automatically produce some kind of activity that keeps the connection alive, you could use the following script:

```
#!/bin/sh
# keepalive -- produce activity on an Internet link
#        so it will not time out and be dropped.
while true
do
    sleep 300
    ping -c 2 belugalake.com >/dev/null
done
```

This script uses one of the two simplest commands in UNIX. The true command always produces an exit code of zero. The other simple command, named false, always produces an exit code of one. The expression on the while statement is always true, so the loop can only be ended by a signal. The sleep command pauses for the number of seconds specified — in this example, 300 seconds, or 5 minutes — before continuing on to the ping statement. The ping command sends a short message to the named Internet host and times the response delay. Normally, the ping command runs until it is stopped and prints out the duration of each message's round-trip, but in this script the -c option is used to limit it to pinging twice and then quitting. Also, the output from ping is discarded by being redirected to /dev/null because the goal is to produce some activity on the line, no matter how long it takes. When ping is done, the loop goes around again, and after another 5-minute pause, there is another ping.

If you start this script from the command line, you can kill it by entering Ctrl+C, which sends a SIGTERM signal to the process and halts it. Generally, any process you run from the command line can be halted with Ctrl+C. If you run it as a background process, you need to send a kill signal to its process ID number.

Prompting and looping

Session 19 explores the format of the /etc/passwd file, which contains all of the login names and other login information. The following script takes advantage of the fact that the /etc/passwd file contains all of the login names. It prompts the user to enter a name and then reports whether or not the name is in the /etc/passwd file. It will continuously prompt for names and report their absence or presence in the file until either `quit` or Ctrl-D is entered.

```
#!/bin/sh
# ispass - Prompt the user for a name and check whether that
#     is listed in the password file. Continue to prompt for
#     names until the name "quit" is entered, or until
#     either Ctrl-D or Ctrl-C is entered.
echo -n "Name: "
while read NAME
do
    if [ "$NAME" = "quit" ]; then
        exit 0
    fi
    if grep "$NAME" /etc/passwd >/dev/null 2>/dev/null
    then
        echo $NAME is in the password file
    else
        echo $NAME is not in the password file
    fi
    echo -n "Name: "
done
echo
exit 0
```

The `read` command stops and waits for input from the keyboard. It accepts all the characters you type until you press the Return key. It then takes the name you entered and stores it in the `NAME` environment variable. If `read` is successful in getting your input, it has an exit code of zero. On the other hand, if it reads an end-of-file condition, it exits with a nonzero status. Because the `read` command is used as the expression on the `while` statement, the body of the loop executes only if `read` has successfully gotten a string of characters from the keyboard.

At the top of the loop, the script checks to see if the user has entered `quit`, and if so, the script exits. If the `quit` command is entered, the exit code from the script is set to zero because responding to a command to quit is not an error.

The `grep` utility exits with a status code of zero if at least one regular expression match was found. This script only needs to know whether `grep` matched something in the password file, so the output from `grep` is discarded.

Loop until True

The `until` keyword works exactly the same way as the `while` keyword, except that the loop is executed as long as the expression is false instead of true. The syntactic structure of `until` is the same as `while`:

```
until expression
do
    statement list
done
```

The following script uses an until loop to combine all the parameter strings from the command line into a single string, stores the new string in an environment variable, and then uses echo to display the contents of the environment variable:

```
#!/bin/sh
# catparms - combine all the parameters on the command line
#           into an environment variable as a single string
#           with no spaces.
ALLPARMS=$1
shift
until [ $# = 0 ]
do
    ALLPARMS=${ALLPARMS}$1
    shift
done
echo $ALLPARMS
exit 0
```

The environment variable is initialized with the value of the first parameter, and the parameters are immediately shifted so the second parameter is in the first position before the loop begins. The expression on the until keyword compares the number of remaining parameters to the value zero, which is false as long as at least one parameter is left in the list. This means the loop executes once for each parameter, continuing until the expression becomes true. Inside the loop, a new value is stored into ALLPARMS that consists of the previous value of ALLPARMS combined with the current parameter — as a result, the string stored in ALLPARMS gets longer each time the loop executes. You can make a string containing all the file names in a directory as follows:

```
$ catparms *
catparmsencommaispasskeepaliveshowparms
```

In short, you can use until any place you can use while by simply reversing the result of the expression. Based on the comparison operators listed in Table 17-1, the following two statements are identical:

```
while [ 42 -lt $MAXVAL ] ...
until [ 42 -ge $MAXVAL ] ...
```

Looping for a Count

Unlike other languages you may already be familiar with, the for loop does not establish a counter and then increment or decrement it by a value. In most cases, the numeric value would not be useful inside the loop because the shell language does not have indexed arrays, so it is not possible to use an index to select one member of a collection. Instead, the for loop breaks out each item in a string of space-separated items and iterates through the body of the loop once for each item.

The following script displays the ten integer values that are presented to it as a list:

```
#!/bin/sh
# prnums - Display a list of integers
for NUM in 1 2 3 5 4 6 7 8 9 10
do
    echo -n " $NUM"
done
echo
exit 0
```

Executing this script displays the following output:

```
$ prnum
 1 2 3 5 4 6 7 8 9 10
```

You may have noticed that the numbers are out of order. The loop has nothing to do with the numeric values, only with the order in which they appear as space-separated strings following the in keyword. Each time through the loop, one of the strings is set into the environment variable NUM to make it available inside the loop.

Instead of being specified explicitly, the list is normally created from the parameters on the command line or the execution of some command. For example, the following script uses ls to select the list of file names displayed by the loop:

```
#!/bin/sh
# showzi - List the names of all the files in the
#     /usr/bin directory that have 'zi' in their names.
ZILIST=`ls /usr/bin/*zi*`
for FNAME in $ZILIST
do
    echo $FNAME
done
exit 0
```

This script begins by executing the ls command inside a pair of back tic marks, which stores its output into the environment variable ZILIST. Using ZILIST as the list on the for statement, the loop is executed once for each member of the list. Running the command results in something like the following:

```
$ showzi
/usr/bin/bunzip2
/usr/bin/bzip2
/usr/bin/gunzip
/usr/bin/gzip
/usr/bin/pbmtozinc
/usr/bin/unzip
/usr/bin/zip
/usr/bin/zipsplit
```

A utility named basename can be used to remove the directory names from a full path name and just leave the file name. The loop in the showzi script can be modified in such a way that `basename` is applied to each file name before it is displayed, which changes the loop to the following:

```
#!/bin/sh
# showzi2 - List the names of all the files in the
#    /usr/bin directory that have 'zi' in their names.
ZILIST=`ls /usr/bin/*zi*`
for FNAME in $ZILIST
do
    echo `basename $FNAME`
done
exit 0
```

This new version employs the back tic marks again so the output of `basename` is displayed by `echo`, causing the output to look like the following:

```
$ showzi2
bunzip2
bzip2
gunzip
gzip
pbmtozinc
unzip
zip
zipsplit
```

Because `for` loops are often used to process each of the individual command line parameters, a shorthand form of the `for` command is available for that purpose. If you omit the `in` keyword of the `for` command and simply put an environment variable name in its place, the environment variable magically contains one of the command line arguments each time through the loop. For example, the following script displays each of the parameters on a separate line:

```
#!/bin/sh
# listparms - Display the command line parameters.
for PARM
do
    echo $PARM
done
exit 0
```

In my opinion, this form of the loop is much simpler, but it is rarely used. Most scripts use a `while` loop with `$1` and `shift`, as described earlier in this session. I think this is because most people write a script by copying another script that is somewhat similar and making the necessary changes so that it works differently. That's the way I do it.

A popular extension has been implemented in many Bourne and Bourne-like Shells today, which enables you to set up an environment variable as a counter using the following format:

```
for (( COUNTER = 1 ; COUNTER < 5 ; COUNTER++ )); do ...
```

Processing Command Line Options

The getopts command is capable of extracting the option settings from the command line to simplify the task of setting flags and environment variables inside your script. This command even checks the syntax of the command line to make certain all the provided options are valid. The following script demonstrates how to use getopts to extract the options from the command line while leaving the rest of the parameters intact:

```
#!/bin/sh
# showopts -- Display the options set on the command line.
while getopts abo:p: OPLETTER
do
    case $OPLETTER in
    a)
        echo Option a selected
        ;;
    b)
        echo Option b selected
        ;;
    o)
        echo Option o set to $OPTARG
        ;;
    p)
        echo Option p set to $OPTARG
        ;;
    \?)
        echo $USAGE
        exit 1
        ;;
    esac
done

shift `expr $OPTIND - 1`

for PARM
do
    echo $PARM
done
exit 0
```

At the beginning of the script, the getopts command is used as the controlling expression of a while loop. Whenever the getopts command is executed (which happens at the top of each iteration of the while loop), it exits with a 0 if it finds an option flag and with a 1 if it does not. This causes the loop to execute once for each option found on the command line, with the option letter stored in the environment variable OPLETTER.

The valid letters accepted as options are specified in the list passed to the getopts command. In this example, the valid flags are -a, -b, -o, and -p. Both the o and p are followed by colons in the defining string, so they must be followed by a word (or quoted string) on the command line.

Inside the `while` loop, a `case` statement branches according to the letter stored in OPLETTER. Under normal circumstances, the script would set internal variables to represent the options that were selected, but this example just echoes a line declaring that the option was specified. In the case of the `-o` and `-p` options, a word or string is also present, which `getopts` stores in an environment variable named OPTARG.

The last selection in the `case` statement is the only one executed if `getopts` detects a syntax error on the command line. The USAGE environment variable contains a brief explanation of the error, which is customarily followed by a brief summary of the correct syntax and, perhaps, a brief summary of the purpose of each option.

Following the `while` loop is a `shift` command. Until now, the `shift` command has only been used to move the parameters one position to the left in the list. The default is to shift one position, but you can specify the number of positions to shift. For example, the following statement shifts the parameters three positions to the left:

```
shift 3
```

The `getopts` command stores the number of the first parameter that does not set options in an environment variable named OPTIND. For example, in the following command, parameters $1 and $2 are both option flags, so the value of OPTIND is set to 3:

```
listopts -a -b gladhand
```

To omit the flag-setting parameters from the list, the list must shift two positions to the left, which is one less than the value stored in OPTIND. Fortunately, a small utility named expr can calculate arithmetic expressions provided for it on the command line and output the result as a string of one or more digits. For example, the following command will display the number 23:

```
expr 40 / 2 + 3
```

The script uses the following expr statement to subtract one from OPTIND, resulting in the number of positions that the parameter list needs to be shifted:

```
expr $OPTIND - 1
```

To have the result of the calculations specified as the argument to the `shift` command, back tics are used to cause expr to be executed and its output appear on the command line:

```
shift `expr $OPTIND - 1`
```

Experiment with the showopts script to see what combination of arguments it accepts and what it does not accept. It handles all of the following without reporting an error, but it may not do exactly what you would like or expect in all cases because `getopts` will only detect option flags that come before anything else on the command line:

```
showopts -a
showopts -a -o handsome -p munchy
showopts -abp quibble frothing spindle
showopts -a grillwork -b
showopts -ofreckle -pwhipstitch
```

Done!

REVIEW

In this session, you learn how to use scripts that process collections by looping through the same code as often as necessary. The following points are covered:

- The `while` command repeatedly executes a block of code as long as an expression is true.
- The `until` command repeatedly executes a block of code as long as an expression is false.
- The `for` command executes a block of code once for each item in a list.
- The `showopts` command extracts the options entered on the command line.

The following session moves away from writing programs and explores more of the internal workings of the system. In particular, it provides an explanation of stored user information, such as passwords, user ID numbers, and groups.

QUIZ YOURSELF

1. What is the sequence of execution of the statements in a `while` loop? (See "Loop while True.")

2. What is the purpose of the `shift` command in a loop? (See "Loop while True.")

3. What simple expression can be used to cause a loop to never stop execution? (See "Keeping a loop running.")

4. What is the difference between a `while` loop and an `until` loop? (See "Loop until True.")

5. What are the names of the environment variables used by `getopts` to store information about options entered on the command line? (See "Processing Command Line Options.")

Users and the passwd File

Session Checklist

✔ The keys to the system
✔ Passwords

**30 Min.
To Go**

There is nothing more important to the security of a system than its passwords. This session explores the way passwords are stored in the system and how users and groups are managed in order to provide password protection for files and directories.

The Keys to the System

A small collection of text files stored in the /etc directory control system access. Not only do they define the available access portals, they act as the primary points of defense against intrusion into the system. These simple little files contain all the names and passwords for every possible method of accessing the system, whether that is a user login or a utility for transferring files or sharing printers.

/etc/passwd

In the /etc directory, you find a file named passwd that contains login names, passwords, home directories, and other information about users. Each line of the file contains a series of fields that defines a login account. The format of each line from the file is shown in Figure 19-1.

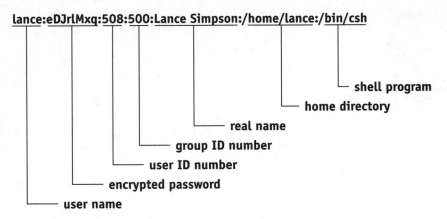

Figure 19-1 *The format of a line in /etc/passwd*

The fields in each line of the /etc/passwd file are separated by colons. The following list describes the content of each field:

- **user name** — The user name is the string entered in response to the login prompt. It is the unique identifier for the user throughout the session. The program that prompts for the login name reads this file to get the rest of the defining information about the user logging in.

- **encrypted password** — The program that prompts for the login name reads the information found in this field and uses the information to validate the password entered by the user. The password is the primary mechanism for security in every UNIX system.

- **user ID number** — Each user has an ID number that can be used as a synonym for the user name. Both the ID number and the user name are unique within the system, so if you know one, you can find the other from this file.

- **group ID number** — Each user has one group ID number. Any number of users can be assigned to the same group. The group ID number is used to assign group access permissions to files, directories, and devices.

- **real name** — The real name of the user is a convenience because login names tend to be obscure nicknames, such as blot or herbert36. This is actually a free-form text field that can contain anything. It can be left empty by simply putting the two colons back to back.

- **home directory** — Once the login has succeeded, the home directory becomes the current directory. It is traditionally the private domain of the person logging in, but it can actually be any directory on the system. This is the name that gets stored in the HOME environment variable.

- **shell program** — This is the shell program that is to be run once the user logs in. If none is specified, /bin/sh is assumed.

Several programs use the information in the /etc/passwd file, so it must be readable by everyone. If you want to take a look at the definition of your login in the file, use the grep command like this:

```
$ grep fred /etc/passwd
fred:x:513:500:Fred Kenai:/home/fred:/bin/sh
```

You can always find a root login in the /etc/passwd file that looks something like the following:

```
root:x:0:0:root:/root:/bin/sh
```

The root user has a user ID of 0 and a group ID of 0. Other than that, there is nothing special about the /etc/passwd entry — it can be assigned any home directory and use any shell.

/etc/group

The user ID numbers are relatively easy to manage because they are all defined in the /etc/passwd file along with the user names. Having them both in one file makes them easy to track to verify that every user name and every user ID number is unique.

The group ID numbers do not need to be unique in the /etc/passwd file because any number of users can belong to the same group. Each group number is defined by being assigned a name in the /etc/group file, which is a text file with each line formatted like the example in Figure 19-2.

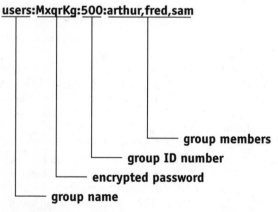

Figure 19-2   *The format of a line in /etc/group*

As in the /etc/passwd file, the fields in each line of the /etc/group file are separated by colons. The following list describes the content of each field:

- **group name** — The name of the group defined by this line.
- **encrypted password** — It is not required that a group have a password, but it is possible to have one because group membership provides access to files and directories.
- **group ID number** — The number that is stored in the /etc/passwd file to identify group membership for a user. The ID number and the group name are unique, so if you know one, you can find the other from this file.

- **group members** — A list of the users in the /etc/passwd file that are members of this group.

The format of the /etc/passwd file allows for only one group ID number, so a user can be a member of only one group at a time. You can, however, use the newgrp command to dynamically move from one group to another while you are logged in, as demonstrated by the following example:

```
$ newgrp dbusers
Password:
```

If you enter the correct password, your login session is switched to the named group. The only change of consequence is that the new group ID is used to calculate file permissions. The command line prompt usually changes to act as a reminder that you have changed groups. To change back to your original group, enter newgrp without an argument.

Because security has become such a concern, you will find some variation in the formatting of these files as different versions of UNIX make their own modifications and extensions. For example, some systems have moved the list of user names into the shadow file, which is described in the next section.

/etc/shadow

**20 Min.
To Go**

The previous examples of lines from the /etc/passwd and /etc/group files show encrypted passwords in the files. Some systems still store the passwords this way, but most modern UNIX systems have switched to using a *shadow* file to contain the passwords as an extra level of security.

Passwords are based on a trap door encryption. That is, you can encrypt a password, but you can't decrypt one — the encryption algorithm only goes one way. This type of encryption is fine for a password, because there is never a need to decrypt it. You only need to use the same algorithm to encrypt a newly entered password and then compare the result against the encrypted version stored in the file; if they match, the password is correct. This is an effective line of defense because no one can break in by unscrambling the encrypted password.

It turns out that the encrypted password being stored in the /etc/passwd file leaves a hole in security. The /etc/passwd file must be readable by everyone because it is used by so many programs to determine such things as the user ID number, group membership, and home directory. This allows anyone to get a copy of the /etc/passwd file, and thus get a copy of all the password encryptions. And this makes it possible to set up a simple program to test the entire dictionary against a private copy of the encrypted passwords in an attempt to happen upon a match. As computers became faster, it became possible to test all possible letter combinations against an encrypted password. Eventually, using this technique, any password could be cracked.

The solution is to hide the passwords in another file. The file holding the passwords is known as the shadow file and is normally named /etc/shadow. The shadow file is only readable by its owner, which is root. This means that no one can read the passwords unless they have root access, and if they already have root access, nothing can be gained by cracking the passwords in the shadow file.

You can tell by looking at the data in the /etc/passwd file whether the actual password is in a shadow file because the password field displays an x rather than an encrypted password. The shadow file is a text file, and each line has the format shown in Figure 19-3.

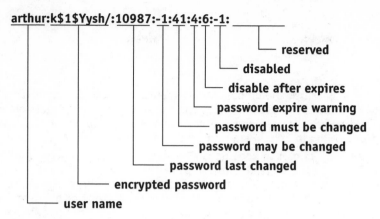

arthur:k1Yysh/:10987:-1:41:4:6:-1:

- reserved
- disabled
- disable after expires
- password expire warning
- password must be changed
- password may be changed
- password last changed
- encrypted password
- user name

Figure 19-3   *The format of a line in /etc/shadow*

The fields in each line of the /etc/shadow file are separated by colons. The following list describes the content of each field:

- **user name** — The same name found in the /etc/passwd file.
- **encrypted password** — The encrypted form of the password.
- **password last changed** — The day that the password was last changed. The date is a count of the number of days since January 1, 1970.
- **password may be changed** — The number of days before the user has permission to change the password. A value of -1 means it can be changed any time.
- **password must be changed** — The number of days from the time the password is set until the password expires and must be changed.
- **password expire warning** — The number of days prior to the password expiring that the user is to be warned of the expiration date.
- **disable after expires** — The number of days after the password expires that the account is to be automatically disabled.
- **disabled** — The date that the account was disabled. The date is a count of the number of days since January 1, 1970.

As you can see, the shadow file is more than simply a container for encrypted passwords. It also contains dates and day counters that can be used to force the users to change their passwords from time to time, under the threat of having the account disabled. The super-user can modify the settings that control password changes with the utility named chage. A user can use the same utility with the -l (ell) option to determine the current settings for the current login account, as in the following example:

```
$ chage -l fred
Minimum:             -1
Maximum:             41
Warning:             4
Inactive:            6
Last Change:         Jan 31, 2000
Password Expires:    Apr 12, 2000
```

```
Password Inactive:   Apr  8, 2000
Account Expires:     Apr 18, 2000
```

Passwords

A number of UNIX security measures should be taken to guard your system from attack. Some of these measures are discussed in Session 28, but the most important points of security in the entire system are the passwords. In particular, the root password is crucial because it allows someone to log in and do anything they want in the system.

The UNIX system itself does its part in keeping the passwords secure by encrypting them and storing them in a file that can't be read. The one place the system breaks down is in password selection. People like to select passwords that they can actually remember, so they have a tendency to use words they know, such as the name of their street or building, the name of the login account, or even the word "password."

Setting your password

The command to change passwords is passwd. You can change your own password by entering the command and responding to the prompts, as in the following example:

```
$ passwd
Current password:
New password:
Retype new password:
```

None of the password information is echoed to the display. You are first required to enter your existing password (few things are more embarrassing than leaving your terminal momentarily unattended and having some prankster change your password). The new password must be entered twice to help prevent you from changing your password to something you didn't intend by making a typo (one of the few things more embarrassing than having a prankster change it).

Only the superuser can change the password of another user. The change is made by naming the user on the passwd command line, like this:

```
$ passwd fred
Changing the password for user fred
New password:
Retype new password:
```

Notice that it is not required of the superuser to enter the current password in order to make the change. This means you can always go to the system administrator to get yourself out of one of the embarrassing situations mentioned earlier.

Cracking passwords

Several different approaches can be used to find a password. Some are better than others, but all have been used successfully at one time or another. The simplest technique is called *brute force*. It requires setting up a program that runs continuously and tries every possible combination of characters one after the other. Often, this technique begins by using commonly used passwords, then dictionary words, then pairs of dictionary words, and then finally steps through all possible combinations of letters.

The UNIX login procedure prevents brute force from being applied directly to the system. You may notice that if you accidentally enter the wrong user name or password at login, there is always a slight pause before you are prompted to try again. This pause thwarts automated brute force attempts because, with such a long period of time between guesses, it would take forever to try them all. This same pause occurs with the su command when you get the password wrong.

The password encryption algorithm adds a bit of *salt* to each password. A couple of extra characters, called the salt, are added to each password before it is run through the encryption algorithm. The actual characters added vary from one system to the next, which means that the encryption of identical passwords on different systems results in different encryption strings. This prevents someone from simply encrypting the entire dictionary and doing a lookup on the encryptions to find the passwords.

The ultimate goal for anyone trying to break into a system is to get the root password, but they may be able to get what they want by logging in as someone else. For example, if they crack a user's password, they gain access to the /etc/passwd file of the local computer, and possibly several other computers on a network. The /etc/passwd file can be searched for specific vulnerabilities. For example, some user name besides root logs in with a user ID of zero, which would mean that this login has superuser permissions, and it may have an easier password to crack than the root user.

The /etc/passwd file is not limited to human logins — it is also used by services to log in, often to communicate with a local daemon, so entries with passwords exist for things like ftp and mail. These facilities often contain vulnerabilities that can be attacked if their passwords are cracked. Session 28 provides more information about this form of attack.

Selecting a good password

The following list contains tips for choosing passwords that keep your system secure:

**10 Min.
To Go**

- Don't use a short password. The longer a password, the more time it takes to break it. The absolute minimum is six characters, but a password should contain eight characters or more. Modern systems don't impose a maximum length.

- Include some digits and punctuation in the password. This makes the dictionary cracking technique useless and means that a brute force attack must try several million more combinations before a hit.

- Mix upper- and lowercase letters so at least a couple of letters are in each case.

- Don't use a word that you can find in the dictionary. At the very least, you should make up a word, but it would be best to use a string of seemingly random characters.

Of course, if you follow these suggestions, you could come up with a perfect password that is all but impossible to remember. I use mnemonic sentences that I can recite while entering the password, where the words of the sentence remind me of each character in the password. For example, the sentence "The speech went on forever and ever" could represent the password "TSwo4frnfr." Or what about using "I8almtIsh" for the sentence "I ate a lot more than I should have"?

System Administration

Adding, removing, and modifying the capabilities of users is primarily achieved by modifying the /etc/passwd file. It will involve managing the /etc/group file if you will be adding or deleting group names. Most versions of UNIX today provide an interactive utility that you can use to manage all of these files, but there are always the standard command line utilities that can be used as well. The following is a brief introduction to the command line utilities that manage the content of the two files. You must be logged in as root to use these utilities.

You can use the groupadd command to create a new group. For example, the following command creates a new group named dbuser with an ID number of 515:

```
$ groupadd -g 515 dbuser
```

The -g option is used to specify the ID number of the group. If you don't specify an ID number, the group is assigned the smallest available number that is greater than 500. Generally, group numbers lower than 500 are reserved for system accounts.

To create a new user, you need to supply the information to be stored in the /etc/passwd file. The following example creates an entry for a new user with an ID of 210 in the group with the ID number of 515. In this example, the user's login name is fred, and the real name is Fred Lance. The home directory is /home/fred and the default shell is /bin/sh.

```
$ useradd -u 210 -g 515 -c "Fred Lance" \
> -d /home/fred -s /bin/sh -m fred
```

A lot of parameters are required, so the backslash character was used to continue the command to the next line. Creating a new user this way requires that you also create the home directory. It would also be a good idea to populate the home directory with a default startup file for the shell — for this example, the file would be named .profile because that is the startup file of the Bourne Shell.

You also need to assign a password to the user using the passwd command described earlier. It is normal to assign some kind of temporary password to new accounts until the users can get logged in and select their own passwords.

You can disable a login without removing it by making a small change to the /etc/passwd file. Simply replace the password (whether or not it is shadowed) with an asterisk. This prevents logins, and only the superuser can enable the login account again by assigning a new password to it. You can do this with the text editor, or you can use the userdel command. For example, to remove access to the login account named fred, enter the following command:

```
$userdel fred
```

To completely remove a login from the /etc/passwd file, along with the home directory and all the files it contains, enter the userdel command with the -r option, as in the following example:

```
$ userdel -r fred
```

To remove a group named dbuser, enter the following command:

```
$ groupdel dbuser
```

Deleting a group does not change the ID number on the files that have been assigned to the group. It is necessary to scan through all of the files to find the ones that are in the deleted group. An example of such a scan using find and awk can be found in Session 21.

Done!

REVIEW

In this session, you learn about the internal structure of the UNIX password system.

- The login information for all users is stored in /etc/passwd.
- The encrypted passwords are stored in a file named /etc/shadow.
- Certain controls can be imposed on users to control how passwords are changed.
- Care must be taken in choosing passwords to prevent system break-ins.

The following session explores the sed batch editor. This editor can be used to write simple editing scripts and then have the edits applied to collections of files. Other simple editing commands, such as tr and cut, are also explored.

QUIZ YOURSELF

1. How is the home directory and the default shell assigned to a user? (See "/etc/passwd.")
2. In what form are passwords stored internally? (See "/etc/passwd.")
3. Why are passwords stored in a shadow file? (See "/etc/shadow.")
4. How would you go about changing your own password? (See "Setting your password.")
5. What are the characteristics of a good password? (See "Selecting a good password.")

Batch Editing

Session Checklist

✔ Making text substitutions with tr

✔ Editing files with sed

**30 Min.
To Go**

his session is about a couple of tools that you may not use as often as some of the others, but when you need one of them, nothing else will do. This session is the first of two sessions on batch editing. The ability to specify text editing commands and have them automatically applied to one or more files can save you a lot of time — and save you from a lot of really boring work.

Making Text Substitutions with tr

The tr (translate) utility reads the text from standard input, makes the requested character translations, and writes the translated text to standard output. To demonstrate how tr works, the examples in this section use a text file named inlet that contains the following text:

```
"Walk a little faster," said the walrus to the snail.
The time has come to talk of cabbages and kings.
```

The following command reads the text from the file and translates every occurrence of a to x, b to y, and c to z, and then writes the results to standard output:

```
$ tr 'abc' 'xyz' <inlet
"Wxlk x little fxster," sxid the wxlrus to the snxil.
The time hxs zome to txlk of zxyyxges xnd kings.
```

The translation character strings are enclosed in quotes to prevent the shell from responding to a character that has special meaning for it. The letters of the first string are used to match characters in the text, and when a match is found the letter in the text is replaced with the corresponding character from the second string. It doesn't matter how many times each letter in the text appears — they are all translated. If you want to save the results to a file, you only need to redirect the output.

The `-d` option can be used to delete all occurrences of specific characters. The following command applied to the `inlet` file produces output with the specified characters missing:

```
$ tr -d 'abc' <inlet
"Wlk  little fster," sid the wlrus to the snil.
The time hs ome to tlk of ges nd kings.
```

The `-s` option can be used to reduce any number of repeated characters to a single character. This is most often useful for removing extra spaces found in text, but it can be applied to any sequence of characters. For example, the following command deletes the double letters from the words in the `inlet` file:

```
$ tr -s 'tb' <inlet
"Walk a litle faster," said the walrus to the snail.
The time has come to talk of cabages and kings.
```

Certain expressions can be used to specify groups of letters in a way that is very similar to the syntax of a regular expression. For example, the following command changes all lowercase letters to uppercase:

```
$ tr 'a-z' 'A-Z' <inlet
"WALK A LITTLE FASTER," SAID THE WALRUS TO THE SNAIL.
THE TIME HAS COME TO TALK OF CABBAGES AND KINGS.
```

The rot13 Algorithm

A very simple encryption algorithm called `rot13` has been popular over the years for sending messages. It's a simple-minded encryption, and it's not that hard to crack, but you have to be familiar with it or you could spend some time trying to figure out what the character jumble is all about. The `rot13` algorithm simply rotates the alphabet by half its length (thus the 13), which means that it can also be used as its own deciphering tool. The `rot13` algorithm successfully obscures text, and you will see it used in discussion groups to mask plot spoilers or something that could be offensive. The scrambled message is usually accompanied by a note that explains that the content is something you may not want to read.

The following shell script is a `rot13` utility that can be used to both encrypt and decrypt text piped through it:

```
#!/bin/sh
#  rot13 -- Rotate letters 13 characters forward.

tr 'a-zA-Z' 'n-za-mN-ZA-M'
```

For example, the encryption of the file inlet looks like this:

```
$ rot13 <inlet
"Jnyx n yvggyr snfgre," fnvq gur jnyehf gb gur fanvy.

Gur gvzr unf pbzr gb gnyx bs pnoontrf naq xvatf.
```

You can prove to yourself that the rot13 script is the reverse of itself. Enter the following command to see that the text is displayed unmodified, because it is rotated by 13 characters twice, returning it to its original form:

```
$ rot13 <inlet | rot13
```

Editing Files with sed

The sed (stream edit) editor reads text from the standard input, edits it according to a set of commands (in a script or on the command line), and writes the result to the standard output. If the editing script is simple enough, it can be included on the command line, but a more complicated script can be stored in a file.

The most common form of a sed command is to replace all occurrences of a particular string with another string. For example, the following command replaces every occurrence of the string bull with the string steer and saves the edited version to outfile:

```
$ sed 's/bull/steer/g' <infile >outfile
```

The s function being used with the g option works on the principle of search and replace on every occurrence of a string. A search is made for a string, and whenever a match is found the string is replaced with another string. The surrounding characters are ignored, so the above example not only changes bull to steer, it also changes bullock to steerock. Fortunately, the search string is a regular expression, so you can prevent the conversion of bullock by skipping instances of bull that are followed by an o with the following command:

```
$ sed 's/bull[^o]/steer/g' <infile >outfile
```

This type of operation is very useful, but there is a bit more to sed than simple text replacement.

The name of the input file can be included on the command line without the < redirection symbol in front of it and sed assumes that it is the name of the input file. My personal preference is to include the < to make the line easier to read.

Internals and addressing

The sed editor operates on one line at a time. The editing functions are first loaded and stored. The editor then reads a line of text and stores it in an internal register called a *pattern space*. The editing functions are then applied to the text stored in the pattern space. If more than one editing function has been stored, each function is applied in turn. After all the functions have been applied, the line is written from the pattern space to the output. A new line is read from the text and the process repeats.

Some of the editing functions use a secondary register, called the *hold space*, that can be used to store text to be used by subsequent editing functions. This makes it possible to extract text from one location and insert it into another.

The general syntax of the definition of an editing function is as follows:

```
[ address [ , address ] ] function [ arguments ]
```

The addresses are often line numbers, which means you can have an editing function applied to a single line or to a specific block of lines. A function is not applied to the line loaded into the pattern space if its address does not fall within the address range of that function.

- If no address is specified, the function is applied to all lines.
- If one address is specified, the function is only applied to the line that matches the address.
- If two addresses are specified, the function is applied to every line from the line that matches the first address through the line that matches the second address.

For example, the p function prints the line in the pattern space to the output, so the following function outputs only the third line of the text:

```
$ sed '3p' <insed
```

All lines in the pattern space are written to the output at the end of editing, so the preceding command with the p function adds a new line to the output text by duplicating the third line. The following command adds three lines to the output text by duplicating lines 3, 4, and 5:

```
$ sed '3,5p' <insed
```

You can also use regular expressions to create line addresses. The syntax of a regular expression for a line address is as follows:

```
/expression/
```

The / character can be replaced by something else if you precede the first one with a backslash, so you can choose something that doesn't appear in the expression itself. The following example replaces the slashes with question marks. The following command duplicates any line in the insed file that contains the word bull:

```
$ sed '\?bull? p' <insed
```

The following command uses a pair of addresses to duplicate every line from line 2 through the next line that contains the letter b followed by two letters and then an l (ell):

```
$ sed '2,/b..l/ p' <insed
```

The selection made by an address can be reversed by placing an ! character in front of the function. For example, the following command duplicates every line except lines 2 through the next line containing the word bull:

```
$ sed '2,\XbullX !p' <insed
```

As a special case, the $ symbol is the address of the last line of the input file.

Storing commands in a file

Most of the editing you do with sed is quite simple and can be included on the command line in the form of a single function, but there are times when you want to perform several operations in a single edit. The best way to do this is to put the functions in a file and have sed execute them from there. For example, the following set of functions replaces all occurrences of bull with steer, as well as compresses every occurrence of two spaces in a row into a single space:

```
s/bull[^a-z]/steer/g
s/  / /g
```

Because sed normally assumes that its input is text to be edited, the -f option is required to specify the name of a file containing edit commands. If the commands are stored in a file named bscript, the script can be applied to the file insed with the following command:

```
$ sed -f bscript <insed
```

You can have as many functions as you want in a script, and each will be applied in the order that they appear to every line of text that the function addresses. The previous script could have been written as follows:

```
s/bull/steer/g
s/steerock/bullock/g
s/  / /g
```

In this example, the first line changes bullock to steerock in the pattern space, but the second line changes it back again.

The reason for using sed is to make global changes, and quite often these changes need to be made in multiple files. Say, for example, you are using a software tool to create Web pages, but for some reason it insists on using a particular color and you can't persuade it to change. The following script changes the color it produces to the one you prefer in all the HTML files in the current directory:

```
#!/bin/sh
# recolor -- Change color CC6600 to 336633 in
#    every .html file in this directory
```

```
FLIST=*.html
for FNAME in $FLIST
do
    if sed 's/#CC6600/#336600/g' <$FNAME >$FNAME.new
    then
        mv $FNAME $FNAME.back
        mv $FNAME.new $FNAME
    else
        echo Error processing $FNAME
    fi
done
exit 0
```

The script loops once for each file with an .html suffix on its name. Recall that any command in a script is executed by a shell, so the regular expression *.html works the same in a script as it does from the command line. The sed editor is applied to each file and has its output written to another file of the same name with the suffix .new appended to it. If the exit code from sed is zero, you know that the new file was successfully created and that no errors occurred during the editing process — it doesn't indicate that some text was actually changed. On successful completion, the original file has the suffix .back appended onto its name, and the new file takes the place of the original. After you run a script like this for a while and start trusting it to do the right thing, you can remove the line that creates the backup.

 To create or make changes to a script that modifies valuable files, it is best to make a copy of the files in another directory and work on the script there. A tiny error in a script like this may scramble your directory in ways you can't imagine until it happens.

A simple modification to the recolor script changes it to make the same edits on all the files in the current directory and in all its subdirectories. It is only a matter of changing the method of gathering up the file names, like this:

```
FLIST=`find . -name "*.html" -print`
```

The find command looks in the current directory and all subdirectories to construct the list of file names. Each file name coming from the find command includes its full path, so each of the files is addressed and edited in its own directory, and each backup file is stored in the same directory as the original file.

The sed editing functions

Only two of the sed editing functions have been looked at so far, but quite a few more are available. The editing functions are summarized in Table 20-1.

10 Min. To Go

Table 20-1 *The sed Functions*

Function	Description
a	Append text to the end of the text stored in the pattern space. The text is entered on a line (or lines) following the function. For example: ``` a \ this is the appended text ```
b	Skip to the label in a script defined on a colon (:) function. For example: ``` b lblname ``` If no label is specified, the branch is to the end of the script.
c	Change the text by deleting the entire line in the pattern space and replacing it with the inline text. The text is entered on a line (or lines) following the function. For example: ``` c \ this is the replacement text ```
d	Delete all of the text in the pattern space, read a new input line, and restart the script from the top.
D	Delete the text in the pattern space up to the first newline character, and restart the script from the top. If some text remains in the pattern space, do not read a new line.
g	Replace the contents of the pattern space by copying the contents of the hold space into it.
G	Append the contents of the hold space onto the contents of the pattern space.
h	Replace the contents of the hold space by copying the contents of the pattern space into it.
H	Append the contents of the pattern space onto the contents of the hold space.
i	Insert text by writing it to the output. The text is entered on a line (or lines) following the function. For example: ``` i \ this is the inserted text ```

Continued

Table 20-1   *Continued*

Function	Description
l	List the contents of the pattern space to the output by folding long lines and formatting nondisplayable characters as octal digits.
n	Copy the pattern space to the output and read a new line.
N	Read a new line from the input and append it to any text that may already be in the pattern space. A newline character is inserted between them.
p	Copy the contents of the pattern space to the output.
P	Copy the contents of the pattern space up to the first newline character to the output.
q	Quit immediately.
r	Read a file and write its entire contents to the output, then read another line from the input.
s	Replace the characters matched by a regular expression with another string of characters. The syntax of the function is `s/regexp/string/flag` Any character you choose can be used in place of the / characters by using a backslash character in front of the first one. More than one flag can be specified. If the g flag is specified, every substitution is made instead of just the first one on the line. If the p flag is specified, the pattern space is written to the output if a substitution is made. If the w flag is followed by a file name, the pattern space is appended to the end of the file if a substitution is made.
w	Append the pattern space to the end of the named file. The syntax of the function is `w filename` On the first execution of the w function, any existing contents of the file are destroyed.
x	Swap the contents of the pattern space and the hold space.
y	Replace the occurrence of each character in string1 with the corresponding character in string2 (this works like `tr`). The syntax of this function is `y/string1/string2/` The length of `string1` and `string2` must be the same.

A few one-liners

The sed editor is a member of a group of UNIX utilities that are famous for *one-liners*. A one-liner is a command that is complete in a single line but performs some useful task. In many cases, the task performed is surprisingly complex.

There are things you can do to wind up with a text file that has leading blanks in front of every line. This happens a lot when you copy text from a Web browser. The following command removes all spaces from the beginning of every line in the file:

```
$ sed 's/^[ ]*//' <file
```

The following script inserts a blank line following every line in the text file. Unless you copy something into the hold space, it remains empty. The G command adds a newline character before it appends the contents of the hold space to the pattern space, so the following command double-spaces a file:

```
$ sed G <file
```

The following command performs a case-insensitive search for the word unix (or Unix, or uNix) and replaces it with UNIX:

```
$ sed 's/[Uu][Nn][Ii][Xx]/UNIX/g' <file
```

The following command changes primp to pamper only in the first three lines:

```
$ sed '1,3s/primp/pamper/g' <file
```

The following command changes primp to pamper from the beginning of the file to a line that contains the word pompous:

```
$ sed '1,/pompous/s/primp/pamper/g' <file
```

The following command removes all blank lines from a file:

```
$ sed '/^$/d' <file
```

This works because the caret ^ character matches the beginning of a line and the dollar $ matches the end of a line; so if the beginning is next to the end, it is a blank line.

You can use a semicolon in a sed command line to specify two functions on the same line, which has the same effect as specifying them as two separate functions in a script. A semicolon is used in the following script to create a command that first deletes all leading spaces from a line and then deletes the line if it has no other characters:

```
sed 's/^[ ]*//;/^$/d' <file
```

In Session 1, I mentioned that UNIX has a reputation for being cryptic. The format of the editing commands for sed (and for several other utilities) is the reason for this reputation. If you spend much time working with UNIX, it won't be long before you come across a script with statements in it that look like streams of random punctuation marks. When that happens, take a look at the command at the beginning of the line — it will either be some utility that is described in the man pages or the name of another script. It may even be an old friend like tr or sed, but it will always be decipherable if you take a minute to think about it. You have enough knowledge to do that. And it gets easier with practice.

REVIEW

In this session, you learn how to use the tr and sed commands to modify text files.

- The tr command can translate any one character into any other character.
- The sed command can be used to change any string of characters found in a file to any other string of characters.
- The sed command is capable of addressing specific lines by line number or by searching for a regular expression match.
- The sed command has a large number of editing functions that can be applied to text. Some of them deal with more than one line at a time, but each edit function works primarily with a single line.

The next session explores another batch text editor that is similar to sed in operation but is much more flexible and provides much more detailed control over the editing process.

QUIZ YOURSELF

1. How can tr be used to delete specific characters from a file? (See "Making Text Substitutions with tr.")
2. How many internal registers does sed have that can be used to contain a line of text? (See "Internals and addressing.")
3. Under what circumstances would you want to store your sed editing functions in a separate file? (See "Storing commands in a file.")
4. What would cause a sed function that makes the changes you want to also make changes that you do not intend? (See "Storing commands in a file.")
5. The s function in sed substitutes one string of characters for another. What happens if you do not include the g flag with it? (See "The sed editing functions.")

PART

IV

Saturday Evening

1. Write a shell script that accepts two words on the command line. If the two strings are identical, display only one of them; otherwise, display them both.

2. Write a shell script that looks at the name on the command line and responds with the output string `Web page` if the name ends with `html` or with `htm` and with the output string `applet` if the name ends with `class`.

3. Write a shell script that copies a file name entered on the command line to the `/tmp` directory only if the file is executable.

4. In a well-written script, what do you expect to see as the first line and as the last line?

5. Under what circumstances will the following script print `Eureka!`?

```
#!/bin/sh
if [ -d $MUGGLES ]
then
     echo Eureka!
fi
exit 0
```

6. Write a shell script that displays all of the parameters entered on the command line.

7. Write a shell script that displays all of the files in the `/tmp` directory.

8. Store a list of words in an environment variable named `MYLIST`, and then write a shell script that displays the words, each on its own line.

9. Write a script that changes the permissions of all files in the current directory that end with `scpt` so that they are executable by everyone.

10. What is the purpose of the `sleep` command?

11. What is the name of the file that contains the name of the user's home directory?

12. Why must the `/etc/passwd` file remain readable by anyone?

13. What is the difference between a group ID number and a user ID number?

14. What is a shadow file?

15. Why is using DoorKnob for a password not a good idea?

16. Compose a tr command that translates every letter Z into a Q, and every letter J into a P.

17. Compose a sed command that deletes the fourth line from a file named infour and writes the results to a file named outfour.

18. Compose a sed script that changes every occurrence of the word rain to the word snow but does not change the words train or raindrop.

19. Write a shell script using sed to replace all occurrences of the word Internet with the word internet for all files in the current directory. Assign the output files the same name as the input files, but store the output files in a subdirectory named lowcase.

20. Compose a sed command that deletes everything in a file from the beginning of the file through the first line that contains the word dragon.

☑ Friday

☑ Saturday

☑ Sunday

Part V — Sunday Morning

Session 21
Batch Editing with awk

Session 22
The Perl Programming Language

Session 23
Writing and Compiling a C Program

Session 24
More Handy Utilities

Session 25
A Few Daemons

Session 26
The X Window System

Part VI — Sunday Afternoon

Session 27
Archiving and Compressing Files

Session 28
Security

Session 29
Network Security and the Apache Server

Session 30
When UNIX Boots

PART

V

Sunday Morning

Session 21
Batch Editing with awk

Session 22
The Perl Programming Language

Session 23
Writing and Compiling a C Program

Session 24
More Handy Utilities

Session 25
A Few Daemons

Session 26
The X Window System

Batch Editing with awk

Session Checklist

✔ Introduction to awk

✔ The pattern and the action

✔ Getting input

✔ Formatting with the print statement

✔ Formatting with the printf statement

✔ The beginning and the end

✔ Control flow

✔ One liners

30 Min. To Go

This session is a brief introduction to the awk programming language, which is a text processing language that can be used in much the same way as sed. However, awk has more flexibility than sed.

This session provides an introduction to the basic form of an awk program. You'll find much more to the awk language than is presented here, but if you decide to use awk, you will find that adding to your knowledge will be an easy thing to do because everything hangs on the basic structure described in this session.

Introduction to awk

The awk language is designed to extract data from text files in order to do such chores as changing the format of the data, checking its validity, locating items, performing calculations, and printing reports. Instead of being a general-purpose language, awk specializes in this specific kind of data processing. Several facilities that are built in to awk greatly simplify input and output. Not every programming problem can be solved with awk, but it is a very good tool to have when certain kinds of problems need to be solved. It can be used for many different tasks, but it seems to be most useful in extracting information from files.

One curious thing about awk is the way it got its name. The names of most UNIX utilities are derived from the function they perform, but awk gets its name from the initials of the three people that designed it: Alfred *Aho*, Peter *Weinberger*, and Brian *Kernighan*. But you will also find it under other names. Some new features were added to the language in 1985, resulting in a UNIX System V version named *nawk*. The GNU open source version is named *gawk*.

Another curious thing about awk is how easily it can introduce someone to programming. It can be used as a scripting language, much like the shell scripting language, making it possible for a nonprogrammer to write useful awk programs almost from the very beginning. Because awk uses some of the more advanced syntactic constructs, it encourages an awk script writer to move on to more advanced programming techniques. Some of its syntax is very similar to C, so for some people it has been a good introduction to programming in C, C++, and Java.

More than in any previous session, you need to work through the examples in this session. This is because awk is more of a programming language than anything that has been dealt with so far, and the only way to learn a programming language is to use it.

The Pattern and the Action

When awk reads a line of text, it automatically breaks it into separate fields. The first field is named $1, the second is named $2, and so on. If you want to use the entire line in your program, you can refer to it by the name $0. The default is for awk to break a line into fields by spaces and tabs, but you can set options to specify other separators.

An awk program consists of one or more lines; each line specifies a pattern to be matched and an action to be taken whenever a match is made. The basic syntax looks like this:

```
pattern { action }
```

Each time awk reads a line of text and breaks it into fields, the pattern is checked against the fields for a match, and if a match is found, the action is executed. If the awk program is made up of more than one pattern/action line, they are all applied to each input line.

The best way to show how this works is with an example. The test data that is used throughout this session is a file named contribs that contains a list of names (each name representing someone who has contributed money to a charity), the amount they have pledged, and the amount they have contributed so far:

```
Frank 100 23
Simpson 75 75
Willow 50 10
Lita 100 0
Spate 50 25
```

The following awk command reads the file and lists the names and the amounts contributed so far:

```
$ awk '$3 > 0 { print $1, $3 }' contribs
Frank 23
Simpson 75
Willow 10
Spate 25
```

In this example, a pattern matches only if field 3 (the amount contributed so far) is a number, and the number is greater than zero. For each line that matches the pattern, both the name and the amount are printed. As in previous commands, the awk script must be included in quotes to keep the shell from processing the special characters on the line.

The following command prints a list of the amounts due from those that have not contributed the full pledge amount:

```
$ awk '$2 - $3 > 0 { print $1, $2 - $3 }' contribs
Frank 77
Willow 40
Lita 100
Spate 25
```

If the pattern matching is omitted, all the lines qualify. For example, the following produces a list of all the names and how much they have pledged:

```
$ awk '{ print $1, $2}' contribs
Frank 100
Simpson 75
Willow 50
Lita 100
Spate 50
```

The following command lists the names of those that have not yet contributed:

```
$ awk '$3 == 0 { print $1 }' contrib
Lita
```

The == operator is a test for equality and is true only if the two values are the same.

Storing an awk Program in a File

If you have an awk program that you use repeatedly, or that is made up of more than one line, you can store it in a file and execute it from there. For example, the following two-line program is stored in a file named flist. This program lists the names of the contributors and inserts a line containing the word "done" immediately before the name of anybody that has fulfilled their pledge:

```
$2 == $3 { print "...done..." }
$3 > 0 { print $1 }
```

Each of these two lines have their patterns matched against each line of output, so it is possible to have one line execute both actions. Using the same input data as before, the command and its output looks like the following:

```
$ awk -f flist contribs
Frank
...done...
Simpson
Willow
Spate
```

Formatting with the print Statement

20 Min.
To Go

The print command can be used to output any string of data. If there is more than one item to be included on the output line, they should all be separated by commas in the print command. A single space is inserted between the fields on the output line.

The following two print statements are identical:

```
{ print }
{ print $0 }
```

If no arguments are included on the line, $0 is assumed. Both of these statements echo the entire input line to the output.

In the previous examples, you have seen how names like $1 and $2 are used to print specific fields. And you have seen how they can be used in arithmetic. There is also a number named NF that is the total number of fields that were extracted from the line. The number named NT is the same as the number of the last field of the current line — that is, if there are a total of three fields, using $NT is the same as using $3. The following command prints the total number of fields and then prints the first and last field.

```
{ print NF, $1, $NT }
```

The NR variable contains the current line number. The following awk command outputs a version of the input text with the lines numbered:

```
$ awk '{ print NR, $0 }' contribs
1 Frank 100 23
2 Simpson 75 75
3 Willow 50 10
4 Lita 100 0
5 Spate 50 25
```

You can insert text in the list of fields being displayed in the output by using the print command, as in the following expression:

```
$ awk '$3 < $2 { print "Contributor", $1, "owes", $2 - $3 }' contribs
Contributor Frank owes 77
Contributor Willow owes 40
Contributor Lita owes 100
Contributor Spate owes 25
```

Formatting with the printf Statement

The purpose of awk is to select and output data formatted in such a way that it can be easily understood, either by a human or by another program. For this reason, the `printf` command provides a simple, flexible syntax that enables you to carefully format the data for those times when you need a specific layout.

The `printf` statement has the following syntax:

```
printf(format,value,value,...,value)
```

A *format* is a string of text that specifies the appearance of the output line including specifying the places where the fields are to be inserted. In the following example, the `printf` statement specifies that each line of output consist of the character string `Pledge amount of` followed by the donor's name, the word `is`, and the amount pledged:

```
$awk '{ printf("Pledge amount of %s is $%.2f\n",$1,$2) }' contribs
Pledge amount of Frank is $100.00
Pledge amount of Simpson is $75.00
Pledge amount of Willow is $50.00
Pledge amount of Lita is $100.00
Pledge amount of Spate is $50.00
```

If you have done any programming in C, you will recognize this example immediately. The fields listed following the format definition string (which is enclosed in quotes) are each inserted at the place where a percent % sign appears in the format. The characters immediately following the percent sign determine how the data from the field is to be interpreted and, possibly, converted. The `%s` format command simply inserts the field as a string of characters. The `%.2f` format instructs `printf` to interpret the field as a floating point number, and to print its value formatted with two places to the right of the decimal. The `$` immediately preceding the `%.2f` is treated as a literal character because it is not followed by a digit.

A newline character, written as `\n`, is at the end of the format string. If you do not place a newline at the end of a format string, the next output string will be appended onto the end of the same line.

The following command lists all the contributors sorted with the ones that pledged the largest amounts first:

```
$ awk '{ printf("%7.2f   %s\n",$2,$1) }' contribs | sort -r
 100.00   Lita
 100.00   Frank
  75.00   Simpson
  50.00   Willow
  50.00   Spate
```

The formatting string `%7.2f` formats a number in no less than seven characters with two of the digits to the right of the decimal in such a way that the decimal points all appear in the same column.

The Beginning and the End

The awk language selects lines to be processed by matching patterns. If no pattern is specified, a match is made for every line. To force a match on an imaginary line that comes before the first line, use the special pattern BEGIN. To force one match following the last line, use the special pattern END. These two pattern matches can be used for any number of things, but they come in particularly handy in formatting readable output. Using BEGIN as a pattern causes its action to be executed only once, and it will be executed before the first line of text is read. The END pattern is also matched only once, but its action is executed only after all the input text has been processed. The following script uses both BEGIN and END:

```
BEGIN { printf("    Name    Pledge      Paid\n\n") }
{ printf("%8s   %6.2f   %6.2f\n",$1,$2,$3) }
END { printf("  ------------------------\n") }
```

Using the formatting string %8s causes the formatted name to be a minimum of eight characters long, with blanks inserted on the left as necessary. This script, named btlist, formats the data from the contribs file with column headers and a terminating underline as follows:

```
$ awk -f btlist contribs
    Name    Pledge      Paid

   Frank    100.00     23.00
 Simpson     75.00     75.00
  Willow     50.00     10.00
    Lita    100.00      0.00
   Spate     50.00     25.00
  ------------------------
```

Now that you can print headings and summaries, the use of variables to contain the values makes it possible to print things like totals and averages. The following script named summit uses a pair of variables to keep running tallies and display the total amount pledged and total amount received so far:

```
{ pledged += $2 }
{ total += $3 }
END { print "Pledged:",pledged," Received:",total
      print "Average pledged:",pledged / NR
      print "Average received:",total / NR }
```

The summit script contains a couple of new things. First, variables do not need to declare a variable before they are used. A variable comes into existence when you first mention it, and it starts off empty, which for arithmetic acts the same as zero. Second, the += operator adds the quantity on the right to the variable on the left. The same script could have been written this way:

```
{ pledged = pledged + $2 }
{ total = total + $3 }
END { print "Pledged:",pledged," Received:",total }
END { print "Average pledged:",pledged / NR }
END { print "Average received:",total / NR }
```

Running either form of the `summit` script produces the following:

```
$ awk -f summit contribs
Pledged: 375    Received: 133
Average pledged: 75
Average received: 26.6
```

Variables are not just for storing and calculating values — they can also be used to store and build strings from data found in the input. The following simple script combines all the input names into one line and displays the line at the end:

```
{ all = all $1 " " }
END { print all }
```

The variable `all` begins with nothing in it, and for each line of the text, it is combined with the characters from the first field (the person's name) along with a single blank. Running this script outputs the following single line of text:

```
$ awk -f namelist contribs
Frank Simpson Willow Lita Spate
```

Conditions and Loops

The action portion of an awk statement can use the keyword `if` for conditional execution, and the keywords `for` and `while` for looping. Again, if you are familiar with C, this syntax will be familiar.

The following example uses the `if` statement to guard against division by zero in calculating and listing what percentage of each pledge has been received:

```
{ if ( $2 > 0 )
    print $1, $3 / $2
  else
    print $1, "made no pledge"
}
```

The conditional expression in the parentheses is evaluated and, if true, the first statement is executed. If the expression is false, the `print` statement following the `else` is executed.

The following script stores all the names and the pledge amounts in arrays and then, at the end, displays them all:

```
{ name[NR] = $1 }
{ pledge[NR] = $2 }
END { for (i = 1; i <= NR; i = i + 1)
        print name[i], pledge[i]
    }
```

The output from running this program looks like the following:

```
Frank 100
Simpson 7
```

```
Willow 50
Lita 100
Spate 50
```

Just like other variables, you do not need to declare an array before you store something into it. The value NR is the line number, which makes it an ideal index for storing a value from each line into an array. Inside the parentheses of the for statement, the value of i is initially set to 1. At the end of the awk program, the value of NR retains the line number of the last line read (making it a total line count), so it is perfect for setting the maximum number of times to loop. Each time through the loop, the value of i is incremented to become the index of the next name and pledge value in the arrays.

The following example does the same thing as the previous example, except it uses a while loop instead of a for loop:

```
{ name[NR] = $1 }
{ pledge[NR] = $2 }
END { i = 1
      while( i <= NR) {
          print name[i], pledge[i]
          i = i + 1
      }
    }
```

The value of i, which is initialized to 1, is compared to NR and is incremented inside the loop. As long as the expression in the parentheses is true, the loop continues to execute.

One Liners

It is possible that awk is the king of one-line programs. You can find a number of Web sites dedicated to awk one liners. The awk language does so much of the detail work that it is quite common to write tiny programs that are very useful. A couple of the following programs are actually longer than a single line, but all of them do a lot of work in very little code.

The following prints the total number of lines:

```
END { print NR }
```

The following prints all lines that are not blank:

```
NF > 0 { print }
```

The following prints the total number of bytes used by all the files in the current directory:

```
ls -l | awk '{ sum += $5 }; END { print "Bytes:",x }'
```

The following prints the last field of every line:

```
{ print $NF }
```

The following prints every line that has more than three fields:

```
NF > 3 { print }
```

The following prints the number of fields in each line, followed by the line itself:

```
{ print NF, $0 }
```

The following deletes the first field from each line and then prints the line. The resulting output is the entire line with the first field missing:

```
{ $1 = ""; print }
```

The -F option instructs awk to use something besides spaces to separate the fields. The following command separates fields by colons, and lists all the users that have the group ID number 502:

```
awk -F: '$4 == 502 { print $1 }' /etc/passwd
```

A built-in function awk named length() returns the number of characters in a string. The following program uses the length() function to print all lines that are longer than 80 characters:

```
length($0) > 80 { print NR, $0 }
```

The following prints the number of characters in the longest line:

```
{ if (length($0) > maximum) maximum = length($0) }
END { print maximum }
```

Using the built-in function named rand(), which returns a random number from 0.0 to 1.0, the following prints a random number between 0 and 10:

```
BEGIN { print 10 * rand() }
```

The following prints all the fields of each line in reverse order:

```
{ for (i = NF; i > 0; i = i - 1)
    printf("%s ",$i)
  printf("\n")
}
```

Done!

REVIEW

This session discusses the fundamental syntax of the awk programming language. There is quite a bit more to the language than the overview presented here, but with a man page on your screen or a manual at your elbow you will have no problem writing useful awk programs.

- Every awk statement starts with a pattern to match values in the input line and ends with one or more actions to be taken whenever a match is found.

- When awk reads a line of input, it breaks the input down into separate fields with the names $1, $2, $3, and so on.

- Like all other UNIX utilities, the input and output of awk data can both be piped and redirected.

- Special patterns BEGIN and END have their actions executed before any line is read and after all lines have been read, respectively.

- The awk language is so terse, and so much work is done for you, it is common to write one and two line programs that are quite useful.

The next session continues the discussion of programming by introducing the Perl programming language. Perl has become very useful on the Internet for producing Web pages on demand, but the design of the language allows it to be used for almost any task.

Quiz Yourself

1. Every statement in an awk program is made up of what two things? (See "The Pattern and the Action.")
2. Under what circumstances do you need to store an awk program in a file? (See "Storing an awk Program in a File.")
3. What values are stored in the variables NF and NR? (See "Formatting with the print Statement.")
4. Why is it usually necessary to insert a newline character at the end of an output string formatted by the `printf` statement? (See "Formatting with the printf Statement.")
5. What do the pattern names BEGIN and END match? (See "The Beginning and the End.")

The Perl Programming Language

Session Checklist

✔ Introduction to Perl

✔ Using variables and arrays in Perl programs

✔ Creating subroutines

✔ Comparing data to control conditional execution

✔ Constructing loops and accessing command line arguments

**30 Min.
To Go**

Perl has become very popular for processing text. You can use it to do the same sort of things you can do with awk, but Perl is much more flexible and has the ability to do many things that require a more general-purpose language. Unlike the sed and awk scripting languages described in previous sessions, the Perl language is very large. It is not possible to describe the entire language (that would take the rest of the book), but the material covered in this session will get you started writing simple Perl applications.

Introduction to Perl

Perl (Practical Extraction and Report Language) is an interpreted scripting language designed primarily for string manipulation. The syntax of the language draws from the Bourne Shell, C, sed, and awk.

Perl is best known as the language that generates Web pages on the Internet. When you enter a request for a specially designed page, such as the pages that search engines provide or a detailed product information sheet from a catalog company, it is quite likely that the Web page was the output of a Perl program. This type of program is called a CGI (Common Gateway Interface) program. A large percentage of CGI programs are written in Perl.

UNIX system administration is the second area in which Perl shines. One of the reasons it is so popular for system administration is that it has so many built-in functions that can be used to communicate with the operating system. Perl has all the capabilities of sed, awk, and shell scripts — and, being more of a general-purpose language, Perl is capable of doing much more. Because Perl is more general-purpose it requires a bit more knowledge about programming before you can tell it what to do.

A simple Perl program

A Perl program is a script stored in a text file just like a shell or an awk script. The language syntax is completely free form, so it doesn't matter where you insert tabs or start new lines. Just as with the shell scripts, the hash (#) character is the comment character, so anything following it on the same line is ignored. Perl statements are terminated by semicolons.

The following is a very simple Perl program stored in a file named perlhi:

```
#!/usr/bin/perl
print "Hello, world\n";
```

You can execute this program with the following command:

```
$ perl perlhi
Hello, world
```

The first line identifies the file as a Perl script. Because the # character represents the beginning of a comment to Perl, it is possible to execute a Perl script directly from the command line in the same way you would execute a shell script. Your shell looks at the first line and uses the program /usr/bin/perl to execute the script. To be able to do this, the Perl script file must be executable, which you can set with the following command:

```
$ chmod a+x perlhi
```

You can then enter this name of the script as a command, like this:

```
$ perlhi
Hello, world
```

Creating a simple Web page

Knowing just this little of the language, you can already write a very simple CGI program that produces a Web page that can be displayed in a Web browser. The following example is stored in a file named demopage.cgi:

```
#!/usr/bin/perl
# demopage -- This Perl script generates a simple
#    Web page containing only a title heading.
print "Content-type: text/html\n\n";
print "<html>";
print "<head>";
print "<title>Perl-Generated HTML</title>";
print "</head>";
print "<body>";
print "<hr>";
```

```
print "<h2><center>Hello, world!</center></h2>";
print "<hr>";
print "</body>";
print "</html>";
```

This example has no dynamic data; it is made up entirely of print statements that write the HTML code. Under normal circumstances, it would have code to read the arguments passed to it from the Web server, then to read data from files to include in the formatted Web page.

To make the script work on a Web server, you must have Perl installed on the computer and must place this script in a location with a name that the Web server recognizes as a script to be interpreted. In the case of the Apache server, the default directory is named cgi-bin. The Apache server executes the script as a shell command, so the shell reads the first line and discovers the name of the interpreter assigned to run the script. As the Perl script is run, its output is piped into the Web server as the text of a Web page that is transmitted over the Internet to the Web browser that requested it. Figure 22-1 shows this sample page as it is displayed by the Mozilla browser.

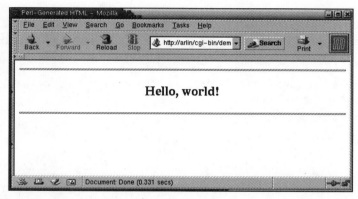

Figure 22-1   *A Web page generated by Perl*

Variables

You can store string values in variables and access them later in other parts of the program. The following Perl script stores values in a pair of variables and displays them inside a string:

```
#!/usr/bin/perl
$vehicle = "truck";
$speed = 35;
print "The $vehicle was going $speed MPH.\n";
```

The dollar ($) characters inside a quoted string indicate that the value of the variable named is to be inserted into the string. Notice that one of the variables holds a string of characters while the other contains a number. Because both variables store their contents as a string of characters, there is actually no difference between them. Some languages require that variables be declared before they are used, but this is not the case with Perl. Executing the previous script produces the following output:

```
The truck was going 35 MPH.
```

A print statement that produces the same output can be written by listing the items in a comma-separated list, like this:

```
print "The ",$vehicle," was going ",$speed," MPH.\n";
```

By using an at sign (@) instead of a dollar ($) sign, you can create an array of variables. As with all Perl variables, an array does not have to be declared ahead of time because it is dynamically allocated as you put data into it and will continuously extend itself to contain whatever you store in it. The following program stores three values in an array and displays them all on one line:

```
#!/usr/bin/perl
@word[0]="humbug";
@word[1]="piglet";
@word[2]="mangrove";
print "@word\n";
```

The members of the array are all displayed on the same line and separated by spaces:

```
humbug piglet mangrove
```

The entire array can be initialized in one statement, and then each member of the array displays on its own line, as in the following example:

```
#!/usr/bin/perl
@word=("humbug","piglet","mangrove");
print "$word[0]\n";
print "$word[1]\n";
print "$word[2]\n";
```

Because each print statement is terminated with a newline character (\n) each word appears on a separate line, like this:

```
humbug
piglet
mangrove
```

**20 Min.
To Go**

Subroutines

A *subroutine* is a collection of one or more executable statements that are grouped together and assigned a name by the sub keyword. You can use a subroutine to store code that you use frequently in various places. The following example stores different values in a variable named value, and then calls on a subroutine to display each of them:

```
#!/usr/bin/perl
$runnum = 100;
&showrunnum;
```

```
$runnum += 50;
&showrunnum;
$runnum /= 3;
&showrunnum;

sub showrunnum {
    print "The value is $runnum\n";
}
```

The variable named runnum is initially set to 100, and the subroutine showrunnum is called to display the current value stored in it. Notice that a call to a subroutine is indicated by having an ampersand precede the subroutine name. The += operator adds 50 to the value, and showrunnum is called to display the new value. Finally, the /= operation divides runnum by 3 and showrunnum is again called on to display the value. The output of this program looks like the following:

```
The value is 100
The value is 150
The value is 50
```

The next section explains the trick necessary to pass values to a subroutine.

Conditional Execution

Perl variables all have the same internal structure — each one is a string of characters. But these strings can also be treated as numbers. This makes variables flexible and easy to work with, but in some circumstances ambiguities creep in. If you are adding or subtracting variables, they are obviously being treated as numbers, but if you are going to compare the variable $widget with $limburger, the question arises as to whether you wish to compare them as numbers or as strings. To solve this problem, Perl uses two sets of comparison operators, which are listed in Table 22-1. One operator compares the two values as strings, and the other operator converts the strings to numbers and compares the values. Any variable can be evaluated as a number — if it contains no digits, it evaluates as zero.

Table 22-1   *String and Numeric Comparison Operators*

Operation	Numeric Value	Character String
Equal to	==	eq
Not equal to	!=	ne
Greater than	>	gt
Greater than or equal to	>=	ge
Less than	<	lt
Less than or equal to	<=	le

The following example demonstrates the difference between comparing variables as character strings and as numeric values:

```perl
#!/usr/bin/perl
$vstring1 = "0";
$vstring2 = "X";
if($vstring1 eq $vstring2) {
    print "As strings '$vstring1' is equal to '$vstring2'\n";
} else {
    print "As strings '$vstring1' is not equal to '$vstring2'\n";
}
if ($vstring1 == $vstring2) {
    print "As numbers '$vstring1' is equal to '$vstring2'\n";
} else {
    print "As numbers '$vstring1' is not equal to '$vstring2'\n";
}
```

Running this script results in the following output:

```
As strings '0' is not equal to 'X'
As numbers '0' is equal to 'X'
```

The first result is no surprise because the character strings are not equal. The second comparison required that the strings be converted to numbers before the comparison, and they both translated into zero because one of them contains the digit 0 and the other contains no digits (which defaults to zero).

The previous example demonstrated the format of an if and else statement. The braces { and } are required around the statements that are to be executed depending on the result of the test. The following program, which is a redesign of the previous program, uses a different form of the if statement. This example does the comparing in a subroutine, which makes it easier to compare several different variables:

```perl
#!/usr/bin/perl

$vstring1 = "0";
$vstring2 = "X";

&docompare($vstring1,$vstring2);
&docompare("000","0");
&docompare("882",882);
&docompare(50 + 1,51);
&docompare($vstring1+10,"10");
&docompare("blivit","skimbo");
&docompare($vstring1,$vstring2 + 10);

sub docompare() {
    ($st1,$st2)=@_;
    if($st1 eq $st2) {
        print "The strings '$st1' and '$st2' are identical\n";
    } elsif($st1 == $st2) {
        print "The strings '$st1' and '$st2' are the same number\n";
```

```
    } else {
        print "The strings '$st1' and '$st2' are not the same\n";
    }
}
```

The subroutine named docompare() does a comparison of two variables that are passed to it. Each call to docompare() specifies a different pair of values to be compared. The various forms of the parameters used in the calls to docompare() demonstrate how easily Perl allows you to convert between strings and numbers. Every variable is a string right up until the moment you do some arithmetic on it, at which point it turns into a number. As soon as the arithmetic is over, it turns back into a string.

When you pass arguments to a subroutine, they show up in the subroutine in an array that has the unlikely name of @_. The first parameter passed is @_[0], and the second is @_[1]. For convenience, the following statement copies the two parameters into local variables:

```
($st1,$st2)=@_;
```

The first parameter is stored in $st1 and the second in $st2. This statement is a shorthand form of the following two statements:

```
$st1 = @_[0];
$st2 = @_[1];
```

The form of the if statement in docompare() is slightly different than the if statement in the previous example. The docompare() subroutine uses elsif to make a second comparison if the first one fails. If the second comparison is also false, the else statement is executed. A single if statement can be followed by as many elsif statements as you need to test the possible conditions.

This example produces the following output:

```
The strings '0' and 'X' are the same number
The strings '000' and '0' are the same number
The strings '882' and '882' are identical
The strings '51' and '51' are identical
The strings '10' and '10' are identical
The strings 'blivit' and 'skimbo' are the same number
The strings '0' and '10' are not the same
```

In the Perl tradition of providing several ways to do the same thing, there is a special form of the if statement that makes the test for true or false following the statement it controls. For example:

```
print "There are too few!\n" if $count < $minimum;
print "There are too many!\n" unless $count <= $maximum;
```

The first print statement executes only if $count is less than $minimum, and the second print statement executes only if $count is greater than $maximum. Notice also the introduction of the unless keyword, which is simply the inverse of if; the unless statement only executes if the expression is false.

Looping

Looping is no exception to the Perl tradition of providing several ways to do everything. Most loops are based on the number of members in an array. A special expression, which uses the hash (#) character, can be used to return the number of members of an array. The following example contains a for loop that prints all the members of an array:

```perl
#!/usr/bin/perl
@words = ("plunge","magpie","wormwood","hips","scandal");
for($i = 0; $i < $#words; $i++) {
    print "$words[$i]\n";
}
```

The expression $#words is the number of members of the @words array. The variable $i is used as a counter that is initialized to zero, tested against the number of members of the array, and incremented by one at the bottom of each loop.

You can also define a for loop using a pair of dots as the range operator, as in the following example, which performs exactly the same function as the previous loop:

```perl
for $i (0 .. $#words) {
    print "$words[$i]\n";
}
```

Notice that the $i variable appears right after the for keyword, and the lower and upper bounds of the loop are inside the parentheses separated by a pair of dots. If you don't like this way of doing things, you have another option:

```perl
for $oneword (@words) {
    print "$oneword\n";
}
```

In this form of the for loop, a member of the array @words is stored in the variable $oneword for each iteration through the loop.

Using the default variable name, the following loop does the same thing in an even shorter form:

```perl
foreach (@words) {
    print "$_\n";
}
```

If you don't specify the name of a variable on the foreach command, it uses one named $_ by default. This means you can use $_ inside the loop to display a member of the array. In fact, the $_ variable is the default for a number of Perl commands, including print, which leads us to the following form of the same loop:

```perl
foreach (@words) {
    print;
    print "\n";
}
```

This loop also prints all of the names from the array. However, it was necessary to add an extra `print` statement so that each member of the array was on a separate line to create output in the same format as all the previous versions.

The following example demonstrates another form of looping that uses the `while` keyword:

```
$i = 0;
while ($i < $#words) {
    print "$words[$i]\n";
    $i++;
}
```

This final version of the loop executes continuously as long as the expression in the parentheses is true. In this example, the variable `$i` is set up as a counter to be compared to the number of members of the array and is incremented inside the loop.

Command line arguments come into the program as an array, so you can either dole them out into separate variables or read the array members directly inside a loop. The command line argument array is named @ARGV, and it works much the same way as parameters in a subroutine. If you want to store the command line arguments in variables, you can do it in the following way:

```
$cvar1 = @ARGV[0];
$cvar2 = @ARGV[1];
```

Or, you can do it one statement, as follows:

```
($cvar1,$cvar2) = @ARGV;
```

The following example uses a loop to display each command line argument on a separate line:

```
#!/usr/bin/perl
for $arg (@ARGV) {
    print "$arg\n";
}
```

Done!

REVIEW

In this session, you learn how to write simple Perl programs. Although Perl is a complicated language, this session gives you enough information to get started.

- The Perl language is based on interpreting scripts stored as text files.
- Perl has only one type of variable, and it can be treated as a string or as a number. Variables are automatically converted from strings whenever an arithmetic operation is performed.
- Subroutines have access to the global variables, but you can also pass arguments directly to a subroutine.
- Loops can be defined in different ways using the keywords for, foreach, and while.
- Command line arguments appear as an array named @ARGS.

The following session examines the C programming language and the tools available in UNIX to compile and run application programs. Some of what you find in the next session will be familiar because much of the syntax of both awk and Perl originated from the C language.

QUIZ YOURSELF

1. The Perl language has become a fundamental part of the World Wide Web by doing what? (See "Introduction to Perl.")
2. What must you do to make a Perl script directly executable from the shell command line? (See "A simple Perl program.")
3. In what form are all variables stored? (See "Variables.")
4. What operator would you use in a comparison to determine whether one number is larger than another? (See "Conditional Execution.")
5. How do the command line arguments arrive inside a program? (See "Looping.")

Writing and Compiling a C Program

Session Checklist

✔ Writing simple programs in C

✔ Examining a hexadecimal dumping program

✔ Using source files to build a complete C program

✔ Core files

**30 Min.
To Go**

The UNIX operating system is written in C, so this session reaches to the very core of UNIX. The C programming language was originally devised to translate the code of UNIX into a higher-level language. Since that time, many variations on the basic syntax of C have appeared, such as C++, Objective C, and Java. This session is a very brief introduction to C, but it gives you an idea of how C fits into UNIX.

Hello, World

A C program is a collection of functions. The functions that make up a C program can all be in the same file, or they can be in a number of different files that are all compiled and linked together to create a program. Whenever a C program executes, it always starts with a function named main(). Every C program must contain a main() function.

The following is the classic beginning C program:

```
main()
{
    printf("hello, world\n");
}
```

Running this program simply prints the line of text hello, world, including the newline character, to the standard output. Before a C program can be run, however, it must be compiled into an executable form. By convention, the names of files that contain the source code for C programs end with a .c suffix. If you create a file named helloworld.c that contains the text of this program, it can be compiled with the standard UNIX compiler named cc (C compiler) by entering the following command:

```
$ cc helloworld.c
```

 The name of the cc command may vary from one system to the next. For example, the GNU compiler that has become popular is called gcc. All of these compilers work basically the same way, but you need to check the documentation of your system to determine the exact name.

The result of compiling the program is a file named a.out. That is the default name of the file output by the compiler unless you specify some other name on the command line. If the compiler finds no errors in your source file, the a.out file it produces is a complete program and can be executed as follows:

```
$ a.out
hello, world
```

I strongly suggest that you get your C compiler working before you read any further. If you are going to be working with UNIX, you will eventually need to compile a C program. It may be one of your own, or it may be one that you have gotten from another location. It is becoming more common for software to be distributed in the form of source code, so you need to know how to compile it when you get it. The reason for this form of distribution is that the source code can be compiled on any computer that has a C compiler, but the format of the executable code is unique to a specific version of UNIX and a specific computer architecture.

A more complete version of hello world

Much has happened since the original hello world program was written. A number of improvements and changes have been made to C, and the improved version of the language has become an ANSI standard.

 ANSI (American National Standards Institute) is an organization founded in 1918 solely for the purpose of establishing and managing standards. Among the many services it provides today, it coordinates its efforts with other standards organizations to maintain international computing standards.

The following is an example of a more robust version of the hello world program:

```
#include <stdio.h>

int main(int argc,char *argv[])
{
    printf("hello, world\n");
    return(0);
}
```

The #include statement causes the C compiler to read the text of the named file as if it had been inserted with a text editor. The .h suffix on the file name means that it is a *header* file, which is intended for inclusion this way. It is inside the stdio.h file that the format of the parameters passed to printf() are specified. As the name implies, the stdio.h file contains definitions for all the functions necessary for performing standard input and output. These pre-declarations are necessary for the C compiler to detect errors in the way you call the functions, instead of waiting for errors to appear when the program is running.

The declaration of the main() function is preceded by the keyword int to specify the type of data that it will return at its conclusion. This is the standard UNIX return code that can be detected in a shell script to determine whether a command has completed successfully. In this example, the value specified on the return statement is always 0, so this program will always report success.

The command line arguments are stored in argc and argv, and are explained in the next section.

Handling command line arguments

The following program simply echoes everything entered on the command line to the standard output:

```
#include <stdio.h>

int main(int argc,char *argv[])
{
    int i;

    for(i=0; i<argc; i++)
        printf("%d: %s\n",i,argv[i]);
    return(0);
}
```

In C, variables must be declared at the top of the function in which they are to be used. In this example, an int (integer) variable named i is declared. The int variable is used as the loop counter in the for loop.

The number stored in argc (argument count) is the number of arguments entered on the command line, while the arguments themselves are stored in the array of strings named argv (argument vector). The variable named argv is declared as an array (the [ ] characters) of *pointers* (the asterisk) to data of the char data type. A pointer to a char data type can be the address of a single character or, as in this case, the address of the first character of an array of characters. Each pointer in the array holds the address of the first character of one of the arguments from the command line.

The loop executes once for each item on the command line. By storing this source in a file named listargs.c, the program can be compiled and run as in the following example:

```
$ cc listargs.c
$ a.out a b strum slipper
0: a.out
```

```
1: a
2: b
3: strum
4: slipper
```

The parameter showing up at index 0 is the name of the program itself. If a.out had been renamed to listargs, the name listargs would have appeared at index 0. It can be quite useful for a program to know the name under which it was started. For example, take a look at the definition of the file named /bin/view:

```
$ file /bin/view
/bin/view: symbolic link to vi
```

Thus, you can start the vi editor under the name view. Starting the vi editor this way causes it to open files as read-only and prevents you from saving any changes to the text. It's a good safety measure to use when you need to look at a file, but you want to be careful not to change it. Many of the UNIX utilities are actually the same as some other program, just running under a different name. You may find, for example, that your version of unzip is a symbolic link to zip, and the program determines what to do by the name that was used to start it running.

A Hexadecimal Dumping Program

**20 Min.
To Go**

Session 13 introduced the UNIX od utility that can be used to output the numeric value of each byte of a file. The program described here is named hd, and it outputs the values of the bytes in a file in hexadecimal format and simultaneously displays the character defined by the value in each byte.

This program demonstrates that C gives you much more detailed control over data than awk or Perl. But there is a penalty to be paid. Because of the level of control you have over every byte of data, there is more programming to be done.

```
 1 #include <stdio.h>
 2
 3 /* hd.c
 4    A program that reads a file and outputs each
 5    byte in both hexadecimal and character format.
 6    If a byte has no character representation, it
 7    is displayed as a period. */
 8 int main(int argc,char *argv[]) {
 9     int i;
10     int j;
11     int k;
12     FILE *file;
13     int inChar[16];
14     int inCharacter;
15     int endOfFile = 0;
16     char tempString[10];
17     char outString[80];
18     unsigned long majorCount = 0L;
19     int minorCount = 0;
```

```
20
21      if(argc < 2) {
22          fprintf(stderr,"Usage: hd <file>\n");
23          return(1);
24      }
25
26      file = fopen(argv[1],"r");
27      if(file == NULL) {
28          fprintf(stderr,"Unable to open %s\n",argv[1]);
29          return(2);
30      }
31
32      while(!endOfFile) {
33          for(i=0; i<16; i++) {
34              inCharacter = fgetc(file);
35              if(inCharacter == EOF) {
36                  endOfFile = 1;
37                  break;
38              }
39              inChar[i] = inCharacter;
40          }
41          if(minorCount == 0) {
42              printf("           ");
43              for(k=0; k< 16; k++)
44                  printf("  %1X",k);
45              printf("\n");
46          }
47          if(++minorCount > 15)
48              minorCount = 0;
49          sprintf(outString," %08X",majorCount);
50          majorCount += 16L;
51          for(j=0; j<16; j++) {
52              if(j < i)
53                  sprintf(tempString," %02X",inChar[j]);
54              else
55                  sprintf(tempString,"   ");
56              strcat(outString,tempString);
57          }
58          strcat(outString,"   ");
59          for(j=0; j<16; j++) {
60              if(j < i) {
61                  if(isprint(inChar[j]))
62                      sprintf(tempString,"%c",inChar[j]);
63                  else
64                      sprintf(tempString,".");
65              } else {
66                      sprintf(tempString," ");
67              }
68              strcat(outString,tempString);
69          }
70          printf("%s\n",outString);
71      }
```

```
72
73      fclose(file);
74      return(0);
75 }
```

C doesn't use line numbers. The numbers attached to the listing of hd.c were added to make it easy to locate parts of the program from the text.

- **Line 1** is an #include statement for the stdio.h header file, which defines the facilities for input and output.

- **Lines 3 through 7** are all comments. Anything between /* and */ is ignored by the compiler. You can put comments anywhere in your program.

- **Lines 9 through 19** declare the variables that are used in this program.

- **Line 21** checks to make sure you have at least two arguments on the command line (the name of the program itself and the name of a file to be dumped). If no file is named on the command line, the fprintf() function is called to write the message to standard error, and the program exits with a status code of 1.

- **Lines 26 through 30** open the file by calling fopen() and storing the file *handle* in the variable named file. The FILE data type is actually not the handle — it is a structure that contains the handle and some additional information. From this point on, all input from the file is through the handle. If the file fails to open for some reason, a message explaining the problem is written to standard error and the program terminates with an error status.

- **Line 32** is the top of the main loop that does the input and output. Each time through the loop, 16 bytes of data are read and formatted as a single line of output.

- **Lines 33 through 40** read 16 bytes of input while checking for an end-of-file condition on each byte. The fgetc() function reads a single byte from the input each time it is called. If less than 16 bytes are read before the end of the file is reached, the break keyword exits the loop. After the loop has finished, as many as 16 bytes of input data are stored in the character array named inChar.

- **Lines 41 through 48** insert column headings above the first line, and above every sixteenth line after that. The variable minorCount is a counter of output lines that is used to determine whether to insert the column headings.

- **Lines 49 and 50** begin construction of the output line by formatting the file offset address in hexadecimal format at the beginning of the character array outString. The sprintf() function formats and writes data to a character array the same way printf() writes to standard output. The variable majorCount contains the offset from the top of the file of the first byte being displayed on the line.

- **Lines 51 through 57** append the hexadecimal values of the bytes onto the output string. The sprintf() function is used to format the byte values in tempString. strcat() is then called to append tempString onto the end of outString. In this loop, the loop counter j is compared against the value of i, which contains the number of bytes actually in the inChar array.

- **Lines 59 through 69** loop through the 16 bytes in inChar and append an ASCII form of each byte value to the output line. The isprint() function is used to determine whether the byte value represents a visible character. If it does, the sprintf() statement uses %c to format the output as a character (instead of the %X that was used earlier to format bytes as hexadecimal digits) and adds it to the output line.

- **Line 70** sends the fully constructed output line to standard output.
- **Lines 73 and 74** are executed after the loop has completed. The file is closed and the program returns a zero exit code to indicate success.

The following sequence of commands compiles hd.c, renames the executable file hd, and uses it to dump the listargs.c program described earlier in this session:

```
$ cc hd.c
$ mv a.out hd
$ hd listargs.c
           0  1  2  3  4  5  6  7  8  9  A  B  C  D  E  F
00000000  23 69 6E 63 6C 75 64 65 20 3C 73 74 64 69 6F 2E    #include <stdio.
00000010  68 3E 0A 0A 69 6E 74 20 6D 61 69 6E 28 69 6E 74    h>..int main(int
00000020  20 61 72 67 63 2C 63 68 61 72 20 2A 61 72 67 76     argc,char *argv
00000030  5B 5D 29 0A 7B 0A 09 69 6E 74 20 69 3B 0A 0A 09    []).{..int i;...
00000040  66 6F 72 28 69 3D 30 3B 20 69 3C 61 72 67 63 3B    for(i=0; i<argc;
00000050  20 69 2B 2B 29 0A 09 09 70 72 69 6E 74 66 28 22     i++)...printf("
00000060  25 64 3A 20 25 73 5C 6E 22 2C 69 2C 61 72 67 76    %d: %s\n",i,argv
00000070  5B 69 5D 29 3B 0A 09 72 65 74 75 72 6E 28 30 29    [i]);..return(0)
00000080  3B 0A 7D 0A                                        ;.}.
```

This output displays the file offset address of each byte (in the column on the left and the headings across the top), the hexadecimal value of each character (in the center), and each character itself (on the right). The hexadecimal value 0A is the newline character, and 09 is a tab.

A Complete C Program

C programs can get quite large. The UNIX kernel is a C program, as are the vi and emacs editors. It is normal to write a large program as separate source modules and then link all the modules together into one program. The previous examples are written as single source modules, and the cc command simply compiles and links it into an executable program. If you have multiple source files, each one is first compiled into an *object* file, which contains the executable code for one part of the program. All these object files are then linked together to create a single executable file.

Multiple source files

The following source file is the main module of a program that converts UNIX-formatted text files to DOS/Windows formatted text files and DOS/Windows formatted text files into UNIX formatted text files:

```
/* reform.c */
#include <stdio.h>
int unixform(FILE *inFile,FILE *outFile);
int dosform(FILE *inFile,FILE *outFile);

int main(int argc,char *argv[]) {
    FILE *inFile;

    if(argc < 2) {
```

```
        fprintf(stderr,"Usage: reform [-d | -u] [<file>]\n");
        return(1);
    }

    if(argc > 2) {
        inFile = fopen(argv[2],"r");
        if(inFile == NULL) {
            fprintf(stderr,"Error opening input file %s\n",argv[2]);
            return(1);
        }
    } else {
        inFile = stdin;
    }

    if(!strcmp(argv[1],"-d"))
        dosform(inFile,stdout);
    if(!strcmp(argv[1],"-u")) {
        unixform(inFile,stdout);
    }
    return(0);
}
```

At the top of the program, the functions unixform() and dosform() are declared to specify their return types and the type of data that is to be passed to them. These two functions do the job of converting text, and are fully defined in other source files.

The command line requires the presence of a -d or -u flag to specify whether the format of the output file is to be in DOS or UNIX format. If a second argument is present, it is assumed to be the name of the input file. If no file named is on the command line, the input comes from standard input. Inside a C program, the data from standard input is read just like data from a file. The variable inFile contains the handle of the input data, so it contains the return value of a call from fopen(), which opens an input file, or it contains a copy of stdin, which contains the handle of standard input. In C, standard output is named stdout, standard input is named stdin, and standard error is named stderr. All three of these are defined in stdio.h, so this program has access to them.

Once the source of the input has been determined, a function named dosform() is called if the -d flag was specified, or unixform() is called if -u was specified. The source code of unixform() is stored in a file named unixform.c and looks like the following:

```
/* unixform.c */
#include <stdio.h>
void unixform(FILE *inFile,FILE *outFile)
{
    int character;

    while((character = fgetc(inFile)) != EOF) {
        if(character != '\r')
            fputc(character,outFile);
    }
}
```

The unixform() function is quite simple because DOS text ends with two terminating characters and UNIX text ends with only one. To convert the text, you only need to remove the carriage return character (written as '\r' in C) and leave the newline characters in place. The fgetc() function is called to read a single character. Every character that is not '\r' is written to the output. This continues until the input character is EOF (end of file), indicating that there is no more input.

The text conversion performed by reform.c is the same one performed by the FTP (File Transfer Protocol) program when transferring files across the Internet. FTP utilities always have an option to have files transferred as binary or text format. If you select the text format, and the transfer is to or from a Windows computer, the text will be translated. That is why transferring binary files in text mode scrambles the data.

The dosform() function works basically the same way as the unixform() function, except it inserts line termination characters instead of deleting them. The source code of dosform() is stored in a file named dosform.c and looks like the following:

```
/* dosform.c */
#include <stdio.h>
void dosform(FILE *inFile,FILE *outFile)
{
    int character;
    int prevCharacter;

    while((character = fgetc(inFile)) != EOF) {
        if((character == '\n') && (prevCharacter != '\r'))
            fputc('\r',outFile);
        fputc(character,outFile);
        prevCharacter = character;
    }
}
```

Each line of DOS text ends with the two-character sequence \r, followed by \n. Whenever an \n, which is C encoding for newline, is found that was not preceded by \r, the \r' character needs to be inserted in front of it. To do this, you must keep track of the previous character, which is done by storing it in prevCharacter at the bottom of the loop.

Compiling separate source files

Now that the three separate source files are ready, they each need to be compiled separately and then linked together. The cc command has flag settings that you can use to specify what you want it to do. The -c option is used when you want to compile a program to produce an object file instead of attempting to link it into an executable file. The -o option is used to name the output files — they can't all be named a.out. The following sequence of commands creates the three object files:

```
$ cc -c -o dosform.o dosform.c
$ cc -c -o unixform.o unixform.c
$ cc -c -o reform.o reform.c
```

**10 Min.
To Go**

The cc command not only recognizes files that have a .c suffix as being source, but it also recognizes the .o suffix as being an object file, so you can link the three object files together into an executable program this way:

```
$ cc reform.o unixform.o dosform.o -o reform
```

This time, the -c option was not specified, so the output file is an executable program. The -o option was used to name it reform.

The reform program is quite friendly in the way it converts files because you don't have to know the format of the text of the input file — if a file is already in the requested format, it won't be changed. The program can be run to translate the original hello world program to DOS text format with the following command:

```
$ reform -d helloworld.c >doshello.c
```

To verify that it worked, enter the following two commands to compare the content of the files:

```
$ hd helloworld.c
         0  1  2  3  4  5  6  7  8  9  A  B  C  D  E  F
00000000 6D 61 69 6E 28 29 0A 7B 0A 20 20 20 20 70 72 69   main().{.    pri
00000010 6E 74 66 28 22 68 65 6C 6C 6F 2C 20 77 6F 72 6C   ntf("hello, worl
00000020 64 5C 6E 22 29 3B 0A 7D 0A                        d\n");.}.


$ hd doshello.c
         0  1  2  3  4  5  6  7  8  9  A  B  C  D  E  F
00000000 6D 61 69 6E 28 29 0D 0A 7B 0D 0A 20 20 20 20 70   main()..{..    p
00000010 72 69 6E 74 66 28 22 68 65 6C 6C 6F 2C 20 77 6F   rintf("hello, wo
00000020 72 6C 64 5C 6E 22 29 3B 0D 0A 7D 0D 0A            rld\n");..}..
```

Notice that the DOS form of the text file terminates each line with the 0D 0A pair, whereas the UNIX text terminates each line with only 0A.

A better way to compile

You can manage the compiling and linking of multiple source files much more easily by using a utility named make. This utility reads a script containing the commands and relationships among the files and uses the information to compile and link programs. The make utility also checks the dates of the files so it only compiles programs you have edited since the last compilation. The make utility also knows all about cc and the flags that it needs to perform its various chores.

The default name of the make script is makefile or Makefile. The following is a makefile that compiles and links reform:

```
reform: reform.o dosform.o unixform.o

reform.o: reform.c
dosform.o: dosform.c
unixform.o: unixform.c
```

```
clean:
    rm -f reform
    rm -f *.o
```

As makefiles go, this is a very simple one. The first line names a *target* to be produced. You can always spot a target because it begins in the first column and is followed by a colon. The names following the colon are called the *dependencies*. The target can be constructed from the files listed as its dependencies. Notice that the dependencies are also listed as targets with dependencies of their own. The processing of this script begins with make attempting to create the target named reform. To do this, it must first create the dependencies, so it looks for targets named reform.o, dosform.o, and unixform.o and uses their dependencies to create the three of them. If make has no instructions for the creation of a dependency, it looks on disk to see if the files exist. The make utility knows how to create .o files from .c files by executing the cc command. The make utility then uses the .o files to create reform. If you store the make script in a file named either makefile for Makefile, the following statement compiles all the modules and links the program:

```
$ make
```

This command works because make defaults to creating the first target in the makefile, which is reform. You can specify a target in the makefile other than the default by naming it on the command line as follows:

```
$ make clean
```

The clean target does not compile anything. In fact, it does just the opposite. The commands following it clean up the directory by deleting all the object files, and even the executable program.

The make utility is almost as old as UNIX and it has some peculiarities. For example, in the clean target of this makefile, the rm statements must all be preceded by tab characters. If you use spaces, the makefile will not work. I can tell you the secret to creating makefiles quickly and easily: Copy an existing makefile that works and change it to do what you want. After you have done this a few times, you will begin to see how it all fits together and be able to write them from scratch.

Core Files

When you are running a program and something goes terribly wrong, you may get a message that a *core* file has been created. This means that your program broke a rule and was summarily executed by the kernel, and that a raw unmodified image of the program (as it appeared in memory at the time of its crime) has been written to a file named core. The program is said to have *dumped*, or *dumped core*.

The following program dumps a core file every time you run it:

```
int main(int argc,char *argv[]) {
    char *neverland = 0;
    char ch;
```

```
        ch = neverland[0];

        return(0);
    }
```

The character pointer named neverland is assigned the absolute address of zero, which by definition, is a location that is not accessible from inside a program. An attempt is made by the program to read a character from that location, and a segmentation fault occurs. This means that a segmentation fault signal (the SEGFAULT described in Session 4) is sent from the operating system to the program, which, unless your program does something very clever to prevent it, dumps a core file of its image and stops the program.

Having a core file enables you to use a debugger to perform a postmortem by loading the source code of the program and the core file it produced. When you first start the debugger, you are taken directly to the spot in the source that was being executed when everything went black.

These core files have a tendency to be very large and should be removed unless they are going to be used. It is normal for a system administrator to have a script that runs once a week to search all the disks for core files and remove them. The moral of this story is that you should never name one of your files core.

Done!

REVIEW

This session introduces C programming. The C programming language is used to write the UNIX utilities and most of the UNIX kernel itself.

- The standard C compiler on UNIX is named cc, but other compilers with other names are available.
- The C language has become an ANSI standard.
- A C program must be compiled into an executable form before it can be run.
- Every C program starts with a main() function that is passed the command line arguments in an array of character strings.
- C has the ability to manipulate the lowest level bits and bytes of data.
- C programs of any size are written as a collection of source files, which are all compiled separately and linked together to form a complete program.
- The make utility reads a script and interprets it to determine which modules need to be compiled and which ones are included in the linking of a program.

This session concludes the discussion of programming. Session 24 discusses the command line utilities that haven't been described so far, such as printf, which makes it possible to format output from a shell script, and top, which displays a list of the running processes and the processes that are using the most CPU time.

Quiz Yourself

1. What is the name of the default output file of the cc compiler? (See "Hello, World.")

2. What is stored in the variables argc and argv? (See "Handling command line arguments.")

3. Inside a C program, how does a program access data from the standard input and write data to the standard output and standard error? (See "Multiple source files.")

4. What is the default name of the command script read by the make utility? (See "A better way to compile.")

5. If you discover a file on disk named core, what is it? (See "Core Files.")

More Handy Utilities

Session Checklist

✔ Comparing two files

✔ Comparing two text files

✔ Comparing three text files

✔ Merging file differences

✔ Displaying the calendar

✔ A view from the top

**30 Min.
To Go**

This session examines a few more of the UNIX utilities. Several of these utilities can be used to compare the contents of files. It is even possible to automatically generate editing scripts that can convert one file to another. A very useful calendar program is available, as well as a utility that monitors the system status and keeps you constantly updated.

Comparing Two Files

The cmp command compares the two files that you name on the command line. If the files are identical, cmp produces no output and terminates with an exit code of zero. If the files are not identical, cmp outputs the location of the first byte that differs and terminates with an exit code of one, as in the following example:

```
$ cmp sample1.c sample2.c
sample1.c sample2.c differ: char 89, line 6
```

These two files are byte-for-byte identical for the first 88 bytes, but byte number 89 is different. The line number has meaning only if the files being compared are text files. The number of the byte that differs is always measured from the top of the file, not from the beginning of a line. The comparison is always on byte values — the only thing that cmp knows about text files is how to count newline characters.

The cmp command can be used to compare any kind of file. The following example compares two binary executable files and reports that their first 24 bytes are identical:

```
$ cmp /bin/vi /bin/awk
/bin/vi /bin/awk differ: char 25, line 1
```

You can get more information on the differences between two files by using the -l (ell) option as follows:

```
$ cmp -l sample1.c sample2.c
    89 162 145
    90 145 170
    91 164 151
    92 165 164
    93 162  50
    94 156  60
    95  50  51
    96  60  73
    97  51  12
    98  73 175
cmp: EOF on sample2.c
```

There is one line of output for every byte that differs. The first column is the location of the difference, the second is the byte value in the first file, and the third is the byte value in the second file. The bottom line is output when one file is longer than the other. If two files are supposed to be identical, but one has been chopped off on the end making it shorter than the other, the EOF line is the only message you will get, even if you don't use the -l option.

Comparing Two Text Files

You can compare text files line by line and have the difference listed by using a utility named diff. The listing that comes out of diff not only includes information on the differences, it also includes editing instructions that can be followed to convert one file into the other. For example, in the following series of commands, a file named index.html was copied to newindex.html, and the vi editor was used to make some changes in newindex.html for diff to detect. The diff command then reads the two files, compares them, and lists the changes that were made:

```
$ diff index.html newindex.html
25d24
< <li><a href="research.html">Research</a>
29a29,30
> <li><a href="mogrify.html">Mogrify</a>
> <li><a href="heimlich.html">Heimlich</a>
62c63
< <h2>Show Bizz</h2>
---
> <h2>Show Biz</h2>
```

The arrow that appears in the first column of the output indicates which file contains the line of text being displayed. The left-pointing arrow indicates the file on the left (the first one listed on the command line), which is index.html, and the right-pointing arrow indicates the file on the right, which is newindex.html.

The lines with the numbers on each side of a letter are editing commands that can be used to convert one file to the other. Following each edit command is one or more lines of text that needs to be inserted or deleted. Using the line number on the left and by obeying the edit commands, a (add), d (delete), or c (change), the index.html file can be converted to the newindex.html file. The command 25d means that line 25 should be deleted from the input on the left. The command 29a means that the following line, or lines, should be added (inserted) as new lines 29 and 30. The command 62c means that line 62 of the right file should be replaced with the line from the left file (the replacement lines are the ones immediately following the command).

The numbers on the right make the commands reversible. By using the numbers on the right instead of the ones on the left, and by interpreting a as d and d as a (the c command works the same in both directions), the file on the right can be converted to the one on the left.

Comparing Three Text Files

When more than one person is working on a project, it is inevitable that two people will make modifications to copies of the same file at the same time. For example, suppose you have a Perl script that performs some task, and you decide to make a couple of improvements to it. To do this, you make your own personal copy of it and start to experiment. At the same time, someone else makes their own copy and makes their own changes to it. After all the improving is done, you wind up with two different sets of changes and, to keep them both, you must be able to determine exactly what changes were made to each of the two new files. You can look at all three of them (the original and the two modifications) at once with the diff3 command by naming all of them on the command line in this order:

```
$ diff3 mine original yours
```

For example, if a file named index.html has two newer versions named myindex.html and yourindex.html, you can see the differences among them with the following command:

```
$ diff myindex.html index.html yourindex.html
====1
1:28c
  <li><a href="wintering.html">Wintering</a>
2:27a
3:27a
====1
1:47a
2:47,48c
3:47,48c
  <li><a href="shopping.html">Shopping</a>
  <li><a href="curios.html">Curios</a>
====
1:52c
```

```
   <li><a href="money.html">Money</a>
2:53,54c
   <li><a href="money.html">Money</a>
   <li><a href="jobs.html">Jobs</a>
3:53c
   <li><a href="jobs.html">Jobs</a>
```

This output lists only the lines that are different and identifies places where changes were made. Each area of change is separated by four equal signs. If only one of the files is different from the original in each area of change, its number is shown at the end of the four equal signs. The numbers represent the position of the files on the command line: number 1 indicates mine, number 2 indicates original, and 3 is for yours.

Each area of change contains editing commands for specific changes made in each of the three files. An editing command takes one of the following formats:

```
n : line a
n : line c
n : line , line c
```

The value of *n* is the number (1, 2, or 3) representing one of the three files. The value of *line* is the number of the line (or lines) affected by the change. The letter a indicates that text is to be inserted after the specified line number. The letter c indicates that the specified line (or range of lines) is to be changed by being replaced with the line that follows. This format is a bit terse and cryptic when you first see it, but it becomes surprisingly clear with a bit of practice.

Merging File Differences

**20 Min.
To Go**

You can merge changes that have been made to different copies of a file in four different ways. The first, and obvious, method is to use a text editor to update the contents of one file with the changes that showed up in the other. This can be a useful approach if the changes are small and obvious, but it is often a bit more complex than that. It's best to automate the process by using one of the three following techniques.

Merging two files with diff

The diff command can be used to generate a script that contains only the commands necessary to reproduce one file by editing another. For example, if you have a file named index.html and you edit it to create newindex.html, you can create a batch editing script that instantly converts index.html into newindex.html. This technique is often used inside file archiving software, making it possible to keep multiple generations of text files (usually the source code of programs) by only keeping the original version of the text and a collection of small editing scripts. The original version of the source can be automatically edited to produce the second version, which can then be edited into the third, then into the fourth, and so on until the latest version (or whichever is the desired version) is produced. Maintaining a collection of files this way allows you to retrieve any of the previous versions by storing only small editing scripts instead of the entire files.

A program that executes this kind of script is a batch editor named ed. You can work with ed from the command line, or you can write the editing scripts by hand. The problem is that the commands are a bit cryptic, so this sort of editing is normally done using scripts generated by some other program, such as diff.

To request that diff create a script, the -e option is included on the command line:

```
$ diff -e index.html newindex.html >escript
```

You can now delete newindex.html — you can always use escript to re-create it with the following sequence of commands:

```
$ cat escript >edscript
$ echo '1,$p' >>edscript
$ cat edscript | ed - index.html >newindex.html
```

The first cat command makes a copy of the edit script, and the echo command appends an editing command line to the end of the copy. It is necessary to modify the ed script by appending the editing command 1,$p to its end. The command 1,$p instructs ed to print the first line (line number 1) through the end of the document (indicated by $) to the standard output.

The second cat command pipes the modified edit script into ed. The ed command has a hyphen as its first argument, which means it accepts all editing commands from standard input. The name of the file to be edited follows the hyphen. The last line of the edit commands instructs ed to print the edited text, which is redirected into the file named newindex.html. The deleted file has been re-created.

A single line version of this command sequence — one that does not create an intermediate file to hold the edit commands — can be written as follows:

```
$ (cat escript;echo '1,$p') | ed - index.html >newindex.html
```

You may recall that two shell commands can be included on the same line if they are separated by a semicolon. Also, putting them both in parentheses makes the two commands act as a single command as far as the standard output from them is concerned. The cat command lists the script to standard output, and the echo command follows it with a final line containing the four characters 1,$p.

Merging three files into one

The diff3 command can be used to compare three files and to generate a script that can be used with ed to generate one file that includes all the changes. The process is very similar to that used for diff, but this editing is done for an entirely different purpose. If two people have made changes to the same file, the process of creating a new version of the file that incorporates both sets of changes can be automated.

If you use the -e option with diff3, you can create an ed script that incorporates the changes. If the original file is named oldfile, and the new (but different) versions are named myfile and yourfile, the script can be constructed this way:

```
$ diff3 -e myfile oldfile yourfile >escript
```

The script is applied to myfile to create a completely new file that contains all the changes that were made. The following command can be used to apply the script:

```
$ (cat escript;echo '1,$p') | ed - myfile
```

As long as the differences are mutually exclusive, this approach works perfectly. However, if there is a single instance of the same line being modified in different ways in the two files, then some kind of decision must be made. A utility that addresses this problem is described in the next section.

Interactively comparing and merging two files

The sdiff utility can be used to merge the modifications from two files into a single file that incorporates the modifications from both files. If there is a conflict between the two files, you are prompted to make a decision. The lines from each file are displayed side by side, separated by a space. If a new line has been added to the file on the left side, a < character appears in the space, and no text appears on the right. If a line has been added to the file on the right side, a > character appears in the space, and no text appears on the left. If the lines on the left and right are different, a bar (|) character appears between them.

You can use sdiff to simply examine the differences between the files:

```
$ sdiff -s myfile yourfile
```

The -s option skips all the lines that are identical. If you want to merge the two files into one named newfile, you can use the sdiff command with the -o option:

```
$ sdiff -o newfile myfile yourfile
```

Or, if you want to look at all the lines that are different in both files, you can enter the command with both options:

```
$ sdiff -os newfile myfile yourfile
```

This command merges the two files myfile and yourfile into newfile. If there are no editing conflicts, it proceeds right through both files and produces the merged version. Each time a decision must be made, you get a percent (%) prompt. To proceed, you must enter one of the command letters listed in Table 24-1.

Table 24-1　*Decision Commands for sdiff*

Command	Result
l (ell)	The line on the left is sent to the output.
r	The line on the right is sent to the output.
s	Do not display identical lines. This is the same as using the -s option.
v	Display identical lines. This is the default if the -s option is not used.
e l (ell)	Start the text editor with the text from the left column.

Command	Result
e r	Start the text editor with the text from the right column.
e b	Start the text editor with the text from both the left and right columns.
e	Start the text editor with a blank line.
q	Quit.

Using these commands, you can choose either of the two lines being displayed, or you can create an entirely new line to be used. Toggling the display of identical lines on and off has no effect on the output file. If you choose to edit the text of a line, once you exit the editor, the text from it is sent to the output file.

The Calendar

10 Min.
To Go

There is a simple command line calendar that is very quick and easy to use. Enter the following command to look at the current month:

```
$ cal
      March 2002
Su Mo Tu We Th Fr Sa
                1  2
 3  4  5  6  7  8  9
10 11 12 13 14 15 16
17 18 19 20 21 22 23
24 25 26 27 28 29 30
31
```

If you need to see the calendar for an entire year, just enter the year to have all twelve months scroll up the screen. You must enter the year as a four-digit number, because this calendar starts with year 1 and goes through year 9999 — at which time we will have a Y10K problem. The calendar is quite accurate across the range of years that it deals with. You can specify both a month and year to view the calendar for any one month in the past or future, as in the following example:

```
$ cal 9 1752
    September 1752
Su Mo Tu We Th Fr Sa
       1  2 14 15 16
17 18 19 20 21 22 23
24 25 26 27 28 29 30
```

This shows that in September of 1752 the days 3 through 13 are simply missing from the calendar. That was the year the calendar was adjusted for the errors that had been creeping in since the calendar was first devised. The leap year pattern we use today was implemented to keep it correct after that.

A View from the Top

A utility named top displays a continuously updated listing of the system load and all of the running processes. The top utility displays the same sort of information as ps, but in a form that keeps you more up to date and gives you a fairly good picture of what is happening in the system over a period of time. When you enter the top on the command line, the screen clears and columns of names and figures fill the screen, as shown in Figure 24-1. The data on the screen is constantly updated to reflect the current status of the system.

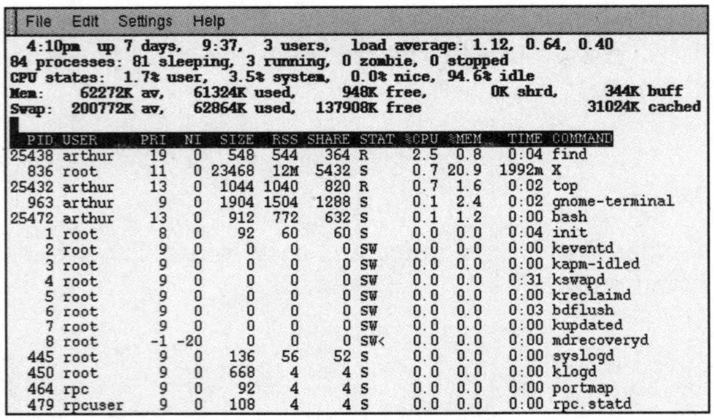

```
 File  Edit  Settings  Help

  4:10pm  up 7 days,   9:37,   3 users,   load average: 1.12, 0.64, 0.40
84 processes: 81 sleeping, 3 running, 0 zombie, 0 stopped
CPU states:   1.7% user,   3.5% system,   0.0% nice, 94.6% idle
Mem:      62272K av,   61324K used,    948K free,       0K shrd,    344K buff
Swap:    200772K av,   62864K used,  137908K free                31024K cached

  PID USER     PRI  NI  SIZE  RSS SHARE STAT %CPU %MEM   TIME COMMAND
25438 arthur    19   0   548  544   364 R     2.5  0.8   0:04 find
  836 root      11   0 23468  12M  5432 S     0.7 20.9  1992m X
25432 arthur    13   0  1044 1040   820 R     0.7  1.6   0:02 top
  963 arthur     9   0  1904 1504  1288 S     0.1  2.4   0:02 gnome-terminal
25472 arthur    13   0   912  772   632 S     0.1  1.2   0:00 bash
    1 root       8   0    92   60    60 S     0.0  0.0   0:04 init
    2 root       9   0     0    0     0 SW    0.0  0.0   0:00 keventd
    3 root       9   0     0    0     0 SW    0.0  0.0   0:00 kapm-idled
    4 root       9   0     0    0     0 SW    0.0  0.0   0:31 kswapd
    5 root       9   0     0    0     0 SW    0.0  0.0   0:00 kreclaimd
    6 root       9   0     0    0     0 SW    0.0  0.0   0:03 bdflush
    7 root       9   0     0    0     0 SW    0.0  0.0   0:00 kupdated
    8 root      -1 -20     0    0     0 SW<   0.0  0.0   0:00 mdrecoveryd
  445 root       9   0   136   56    52 S     0.0  0.0   0:00 syslogd
  450 root       9   0   668    4     4 S     0.0  0.0   0:00 klogd
  464 rpc        9   0    92    4     4 S     0.0  0.0   0:00 portmap
  479 rpcuser    9   0   108    4     4 S     0.0  0.0   0:00 rpc.statd
```

Figure 24-1 *A screen display of top*

The display in Figure 24-1 is updated at regular intervals. The default is to update it once every five seconds, but the delay can be adjusted to a shorter or longer period. It is even possible to set the delay to 0, which causes a continuous update. As you can see by looking at the top of the screen, this particular system was booted just one week ago. There are currently 84 processes, 3 of which are actively running. The majority of the processes are sleeping, waiting for some sort of input before they do something. Most of the processor time is being spent idling, which implies that the running processes are spending most of their time waiting for input and output. Two rows of numbers display the current allocation of memory and swap space.

Most often, the top utility is run to discover information about processes or about one process in particular. If a system seems to be bogging down, running top tells you immediately whether you have a process that is running away and using up all the CPU time. If you have a runaway, the value in the %CPU column causes it to come to the top of the list. It is not unknown for a runaway process to use 97 percent of the CPU time, which leaves almost no time for anything else to happen. In the example shown here, the top process itself takes up more time than the other processes, but it is using less than 1 percent.

The process with the most accumulated time is X (which is the X server), but this large accumulation of time is reasonable. The X server's time has been accumulating since the computer was booted, and it does have the responsibility of doing all the graphics.

You should test-drive top on your system to get the feel of it. After you get top running, it will respond to several one-letter commands. Some of the most useful of these commands are listed in Table 24-2.

Table 24-2 *Interactive Commands for top*

Command	Description
h or ?	Display a list of all the interactive commands.
k	Kill a process. You are prompted for the PID number of the process and then for the signal number. The default signal is 15 (SIGTERM), but you can also use 9 (SIGKILL) for a more abrupt and sure termination.
r	Re-nice a task. You are prompted for the PID number of the process and then for a new nice number, which is used to increase or decrease the priority of the process.
N	Sort the process list by PID number, with the smallest number first.
A	Sort the process list by age, with the youngest process first.
P	Sort the process list by CPU usage, with the largest percentage first. This is the default sort order.
M	Sort the process list by memory usage, with the largest process first.
T	Sort the process list by the cumulative time, with the largest time value first.
u	Show only the processes of a specific user. You are prompted for a user name. Entering a blank name displays the process of all users, which is the default.
s	Set the delay between updates. You are prompted for a number of seconds. You can use decimals to specify fractions of seconds. Entering 0 causes top to continuously update. The default is 5.
q	Quit.

When using utilities that format the screen to display continuously updated data, the screen can become garbled. If you need to have the entire screen cleared and displayed again, enter Ctrl+L.

Done!

REVIEW

In this session, you learn how to make comparisons among files and reconcile their differences. You also become familiar with the UNIX calendar and the top utility, which monitors the system load.

- The cmp utility can be used to determine whether two files are absolutely identical.
- The diff utility can be used to expose the line-by-line differences between two text files.
- The diff3 utility can be used to expose the line-by-line differences among three text files.
- The ed utility can be used to reconcile differences detected by diff and diff3.

- The sdiff utility can be used to reconcile differences in files when the edits conflict.
- The cal utility can display the calendar for any year or any month of any year.
- The top utility continuously tracks the system status.

The following session looks into some of the processes that lurk in the background, waiting to receive a message so that they can spring into action.

QUIZ YOURSELF

1. In the output of the diff utility, what do the characters < and > indicate? (See "Comparing Two Text Files.")
2. What is the purpose of comparing the text in three files? (See "Comparing Three Text Files.")
3. The diff and diff3 utilities generate editing commands for which editor? (See "Merging two files with diff.")
4. Why can't the merging of files be entirely automatic? (See "Interactively comparing and merging two files.")
5. What is the minimum interval at which top can be set to update the display? (See "A View from the Top.")

Session Checklist

✔ The Internet services daemon

✔ The Network File System daemon

✔ The scheduling daemon

✔ The printer daemon

**30 Min.
To Go**

This session is about daemons. A daemon sits and waits for a message to come to it, and when a message comes, the daemon leaps into action and performs the requested task. When the task is completed, the daemon goes quietly back into the wait mode. UNIX has lots of daemons. When you use the ps command to list all the processes, anything that is not part of the kernel or is not a process being run by a user is most likely a daemon. You can spot many of the daemons because their names end with the letter d. It is not uncommon for there to be over a hundred daemons just waiting for something to do.

The Internet Services Daemon

The daemon responsible for managing many of the Internet services is named inetd and is normally started when the system boots. The inetd daemon also starts other daemons, as they are needed. The inetd daemon listens for remote connection requests coming in through the Internet connection. When a connection request is received, inetd starts the service that matches the request as specified in the configuration file /etc/inetd.config. The advantage of this technique is that several Internet services can be provided by one daemon process listening to the port instead of several daemons actively checking the content of the incoming messages. For example, if your system is configured to allow 30 simultaneous FTP connections, you don't need to have 30 FTP daemons running unless you actually have 30 FTP active sessions. One inetd daemon can listen to the port and start a new FTP process to match each connection request.

It is not required that an Internet daemon be started through inetd. For example, a Web server should probably be left out of the inetd configuration files and run on its own to receive incoming HTTP protocol messages.

The inetd daemon handles few simple protocols directly instead of starting another process to do it. For example, an incoming message with the echo protocol is a request for a simple response, which inetd provides. The discard protocol is a request for no action to be taken and nothing — not even an error message — to be returned. The daytime protocol returns the current time in text format, and the time protocol returns the current time as a count of the number of seconds since January 1, 1900.

The Network File System Daemon

NFS (Network File System) enables you to mount and use disk drives from other computers in the same way as the ones that are physically attached to your local computer. With NFS, every computer on the network has access to the same collection of disk drives in exactly the same way. When you first start working with NFS mounted disk drives, it feels like some kind of magic is going on somewhere, but the trick is really quite simple once you see how it is done.

A file system can only do a certain number of things. You can read files, write files, and list information about the files. If these same capabilities are provided for a remote disk, it acts just like a local disk. Figure 25-1 is a diagram of the way access works for a local disk. Whenever you issue a command from the keyboard that requires disk access, the command passes the request to the kernel. The kernel then passes the message to the device driver, which retrieves the information from the disk and returns it to the kernel. The kernel passes the information back to the process that requested it, and the process uses the information however it wishes. Figure 25-1 shows the ls process, which displays the names of the files on the screen.

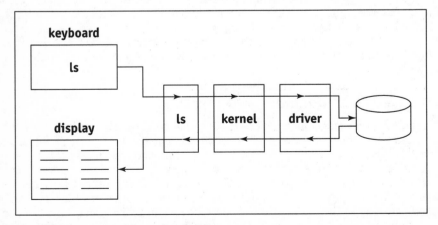

Figure 25-1   *Accessing a local disk*

The process required to access a remote disk is the same as that for a local disk, with the addition of some intermediate steps.

Figure 25-2 is a diagram of the procedure to access a remote disk drive. A command entered at the keyboard that requires remote disk access transmits the request to the kernel, just as it would if it were accessing a local disk. The kernel forwards the request to the device driver of the disk but, in this case, the device driver is named nfs. Instead of communicating with a local disk drive, the nfs driver transmits the request over an internet link to another computer. On the remote computer, an NFS daemon process named nfsd receives the request. The nfsd daemon acts as any process local to that computer in making a disk access request and passes the original request to the kernel. The kernel uses the local driver to retrieve the information from the disk drive and returns it to the nfsd driver. The nfsd driver returns the information through the internet link to the nfs driver on the original computer. The information is then passed back through the kernel to the requesting process, which uses the information any way it wants.

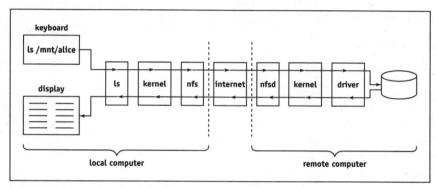

Figure 25-2   *Accessing a remote disk*

As you can surmise from Figure 25-2, some configuration must be performed on both systems before this kind of remote access will work. Aside from the basic TCP/IP permissions settings to make an internet connection, the local computer needs to have the nfs device driver running and associated with the proper remote disk drive. As described in Session 30, the mount command is used to start the nfs drivers. The remote computer must have an nfsd daemon process configured to receive incoming disk requests. Daemons are normally started at boot time, which is also explained in Session 30.

As you may suspect, this explanation glosses over a few details. For one thing, the communication between the nfs driver and the nfsd daemon uses the RPC (remote procedure call) system. The RPC system works by having the nfsd daemon register itself with the RPC daemon so that the nfs drivers can find the appropriate nfsd daemon and learn how to send a message to it. The RPC system provides many advantages. For example, when a process crashes, a computer is rebooted, the network connection is lost, or one of any number of other possible mishaps occur, the two processes will find each other automatically through the RPC registry as soon as things get back to normal. All this happens by having an RPC daemon process keep track of which processes are running and ready to communicate. The RPC system serves many purposes other than NFS disk access.

The result of all these daemons talking to one another is that every command you can use to access your local disk can also be used to access a remote disk. The only difference is a possible difference in speed of the response from the disk.

The Scheduling Daemon

A daemon named cron reads a list that contains commands and the times they should be started. The cron daemon then sits back with its pocket watch waiting for one of the commands to come due. When the time comes, cron starts a process in the background by issuing the command and then goes back to waiting for the next command to come due. Any user can add commands to the list of commands scheduled by cron.

When the cron daemon first starts running, it looks in the directory named /var/spool/cron for files that contain instructions about starting processes. The names of the files in this directory are the same as the login names in /etc/passwd, which provides cron with the information needed to assign ownership and permissions to each command as it is executed.

Any user can schedule processes to be run by using the crontab utility. Whenever a user makes a change to the list of jobs to be scheduled, the cron daemon is notified and the daemon rereads the entire directory of files and reschedules everything. You must store all of the commands you want to schedule in a single file. Each line of the file is formatted into six fields as follows:

    m h d mo dw command

The six fields in each line contain the following information:

- *m* **(minute)** — The minute of the hour from 0 to 59.
- *h* **(hour)** — The hour of the day from 0 to 23.
- *d* **(day)** — The day of the month from 1 to 31.
- *mo* **(month)** — The month of the year from 1 to 12.
- *dw* **(day of the week)** — The day of the week from 0 to 6, with Sunday being 0.
- *command* — Everything else on the line is assumed to be the command.

Each of these entries can consist of a single value, several values separated by commas, or simply an asterisk. An asterisk tells cron to choose every valid value, such as every day of the week or every month. Table 25-1 lists examples that demonstrate how the settings that precede the command work.

20 Min.
To Go

Table 25-1   *Setting crontab Times*

Setting	Means
0 0 1 * *	At midnight the first day of every month.
0 0 * * 5	At midnight every Thursday.
30 6,18 * * *	Every day at 6:30 a.m. and 6:30 p.m.
0 10 * * 1	Every Monday morning at 10:00 a.m.
0 12 * * 1-5	Monday through Friday at noon.
0 17 1,15 * *	The first and fifteenth of each month at 5:00 p.m.
5,35 * * * *	Five minutes and thirty-five minutes after every hour of every day.

The file that contains the list of times and instructions is called a *cron file*. The individual tasks listed in the cron files are called *cron jobs*. The `crontab` utility can be used to create and maintain your list of cron jobs. First, you must create the cron file using your text editor. You can name the file anything you want. For example, you could insert the following command to have all the core files removed from your home directory and its subdirectories:

```
15 3 * * 6 find . -name core -exec rm -rf {} \;
```

This command will run each Sunday morning at 3:15 a.m. to locate all of the core files in the current directory tree and remove them. The current directory tree is always the home directory of the user that owns the cron file. If you name the file containing this command `mycron`, the command can then be added to the schedule with the following command:

```
$ crontab mycron
```

To verify that it was actually added to the schedule, you can use the `-l` (ell) option:

```
$ crontab -l
15 3 * * 6 find . -name cron -exec rm -rf {} \;
```

If you decide you don't want this command to be scheduled any more, you can remove all of your scheduled commands with the `-r` option:

```
$ crontab -r
```

The only way you can modify your cron file commands is to replace all of the existing commands with new ones. This is not really a problem because the stored version of your cron file can always be retrieved, modified, and restored this way:

```
$ crontab -l >mycron
$ vi mycron
$ crontab mycron
```

If the command you run produces any output, it is mailed to you. This is a handy method of being notified that your cron job ran as scheduled, and you can tell from the content of the message whether or not the job ran properly.

The root user commonly performs regular file backups with a cron job. Backup is a process that is often forgotten, so it is handy to be automatically notified of its success or failure. If you want, you can specify the address where the output from a cron job is to be mailed. The following pair of cron commands executes scripts for a full backup every Sunday night and a partial backup on the other nights. The output is mailed to the address `arthur@xyz.net`:

```
0 23 * * 1-6 partbackup | mail arthur@xyz.net
0 23 * * 0 fullbackup | mail arthur@xyz.net
```

If you want, you can write the results of the full backup to a log file and discard the partial backup information completely, as in the following example:

```
0 23 * * 1-6 partbackup >/dev/null 2>&1
0 23 * * 0 fullbackup >>/home/back/logfile 2>&
```

Recall that the redirection command >> appends text to the end of the file instead of overwriting it.

A command named at can be used to quickly schedule one or more commands to be executed once at a later time. For example, if you are using a utility that notifies you when mail arrives, and you need to be reminded of an appointment, you can enter the following command:

```
$ at 3:15pm
at> echo It is now 3:15, so hurry
at> EOF
```

When you enter the at command and specify a time, you get a prompt to enter a command. In fact, you continue to get prompts for more commands until you enter Ctrl+D to mark the end of the file, which causes at to respond with EOF and schedule your cron job. Any output from the command is mailed to you, so at 3:15 you receive a message to hurry up. Entering the time on the at command is almost free form. All of the following are valid:

```
at 0815am Jan 24
at 8:15 am
at now + 1 day
at now next day
at 5 pm Friday
```

The Printer Daemon

A printer daemon, usually named lpd or lpsched, runs constantly and accepts print jobs from any process that needs to send text to a printer. One or more printers may be connected to the local machine, and several other printers may be accessible over the network. All of these printers are reached through the same daemon.

The printer daemon is sometimes called the *print spooler*, or simply *spooler*, because of the way it handles print jobs to keep multiple simultaneous jobs from interfering with one another. When you run a program that writes text to the printer daemon, nothing is actually sent from the daemon to the printer until the program originating the text has sent everything it is going to send and closes its connection with the daemon. At the time the connection is closed, the daemon will have stored the entire body of text to be printed. Only then does the daemon start to send the text to the printer. The print job is said to have been *spooled* to the printer.

The print spooler can be receiving several print jobs simultaneously and spool all of them. As each job is completed, the job is sent on to the printer by being appended to a print queue for a specific printer. Of course, print jobs can come from the spooler faster than they go out through the printer, so you may find several print jobs queued and waiting for the printer. The default order for this queue is the order in which the print jobs finish spooling, but utilities exist that can be used to change the order, or even cancel, the jobs in the queue.

If text is to be printed on a remote printer (that is, a printer that is physically connected to another computer) the print spooler on the local computer forwards the text of the spooled print job to the spooler on the remote computer. It could be that the text is not spooled locally — it may simply be sent line by line to the remote spooler, just as it would from any other process. These details depend on the capabilities of the print spooler and how it is configured.

There is a good reason for all this spooling and queuing. Because print jobs are placed in the print queue only after they are completely spooled, a slow process cannot hold up the print job from any other process. A program that writes one line to the print spooler every five minutes for six hours has no effect on the other print jobs until the text is completely spooled and ready to be moved on to the input queue of the printer.

The problem with printing

Once upon a time there were two distinct versions of UNIX — the System V version and the BSD version. Over time the capabilities of each one were merged into the other to create the somewhat standard set of operations that today is called UNIX. This merging was quite successful in every area of UNIX except one: printing. The two systems had developed very different approaches to printing, and that difference is still with us today. Some other areas of the two versions of UNIX could not be merged, but including the capabilities of both versions solved that problem. However, when you connect a printer to a UNIX computer, you can't use two spoolers with two distinct sets of configuration settings.

The biggest problem comes when sharing printers in a network. The two systems don't communicate with one another.

One of the most time-consuming and potentially confusing areas in UNIX is the configuration and management of printers. Not only do two distinct versions of printer handling exist, but it also seems that every flavor of UNIX adds its own twists and variations. Many UNIX systems use the printer daemon named lpd and store the printer definitions in a file named /etc/printcap. Others use the printer daemon named lpsched to implement something called a printer service.

All printing systems have one thing in common: they use the prefix lp (line printer) on the names of the print utilities. The term *line printer* was coined during the period when the best printers were capable of printing an entire line of text at once. Printing has advanced a great deal, but the name remains.

Using lp and lpr

10 Min. To Go

The two basic print configurations are the reason for the existence of two commands. The lp command usually sends files to be printed by the daemon named lpd, and the lpr command is associated with the lpsched daemon.

For example, if you have a text file named index.html that you want to send to the printer, enter the following command:

```
$ lp index.html
```

If that doesn't work, try the following:

```
$ lpr index.html
```

The lp command originated with System V, and the lpr command originated with BSD. Some systems have one command, some have the other, and some have both. They both do basically the same job of sending text to the print spooler, but some differences in the options are available.

The flags for the two print commands are listed in Table 25-2. There are more options than the ones listed in the table, but the flags that aren't included deal with special situations, such as passing the text through filters before printing and printing data that is not in a standard text format. In some of the options, you will see a reference to a *banner page* (sometimes called a *burst page*) that is printed before the rest of the text. This page is useful when several people are sharing a printer, and you need to identify and separate the output.

Table 25-2   *Printer Command Line Options*

Option	Description
Options for the lp Command	
-c	Copy the file before printing. If you are printing from a file instead of a pipe, and you are printing to a local printer, the spooler will default to using your copy of the file instead of spooling its own copy. The file must not be deleted until the print job is complete.
-d *destination*	The output is to go to the *destination* printer instead of the default. The *destination* can also be a class of printers and the spooler will choose the first one available in the class. For information on printer classes, see the lpadmin man page.
-m	Send mail to the user when the print job is complete.
-n *number*	Print the number of copies specified. The default is to print one copy.
-o nobanner	Do not print a banner page.
-o nofilebreak	If multiple files are listed on the command line, print them all without any sort of break between them.
-q *priority*	Set the print priority from 0 to 39, with 0 being the highest priority. Higher priority jobs print first.
-t *title*	Include the title on the banner page.
-w	Send a message to the terminal when the print job is complete. If the user has logged off, mail will be sent instead.
Options for the lpr Command	
-P *printer*	Send the output to the named printer. If this option is missing, one named in the PRINTER environment variable is used; otherwise, there is a default printer configured into the system.
-r	Delete the source text file as soon as it has been spooled to the printer.

Option	Description
-s	Do not copy the file before printing. If you are printing from a file instead of a pipe, and you are printing to a local printer, the spooler will use your copy of the file instead of spooling its own copy. The file must not be deleted until the print job is complete.
-i *number*	Number of columns to indent on the left. The default is 8.
-h	Do not print a banner page.
-#*number*	The number of copies to print.

Formatting print jobs with pr

The pr utility has nothing to do with the actual printing process, but it can be used to format your output before you send it to the printer. You can pass your text through pr to have a heading with the date and page number added at the top of each page. By using some command line options, you can further refine the format.

The following cat command lists the unformatted text stored in a file named pr.text:

```
$ cat pr.text
The pr program formats text files for printing.
It has a lot of formatting abilities, including the
default of adding a header to each page. It can
organize lists into columns. Pages size can
be inserted using embedded form feeds. It can
even be used to number the lines, display non-
printable characters and merge several text
files into one.
```

The following command demonstrates the result of using pr to format the pr.text file:

```
$ pr -w 56 -n -h "The pr Program" pr.text

2002-02-20 07:36          The pr Program          Page    1

    1 The pr program formats text files for printing.
    2 It has a lot of formatting abilities, including the
    3 default of adding a header to each page. It can
    4 organize lists into columns. Pages size can
    5 be inserted using embedded form feeds. It can
    6 even be used to number the lines, display non-
    7 printable characters and merge several text
    8 files into one.
```

In this example, the -w option is used to specify the page width as 56 characters. The -n option adds line numbers. The -h option changes the title in the heading from the default of the file name to the string specified on the command line.

One very convenient feature of pr is its ability to reformat a single column into multiple columns. The following example uses the file NameList, which contains a sorted list of 38 names as the input file, and organizes the list into seven columns:

```
$ pr -7 -t NameList
apmd       halt         keytable  netfs    portmap    rstatd    smb
arpwatch   httpd        killall   network  random     rusersd   syslog
atd        identd       kudzu     nfs      rawdevice  rwhod     xfs
crond      ipchains     ldap      nfslock  rhnsd      sendmail  xinetd
functions  irda         linuxconf pcmcia   routed     single    ypbind
gpm        kdcrotate    lpd
```

The -7 option on the command line determines the number of output columns, and the -t option omits the headings and footers, leaving just the reformatted text. The number of items in each column is adjusted so that they are as even as possible. The default is to organize the words into vertical columns as shown above, but they can be organized horizontally with the -a option, as in the following example:

```
$ pr -a -7 -t NameList
apmd      arpwatch   atd        crond     functions  gpm       halt
httpd     identd     ipchains   irda      kdcrotate  keytable  killall
kudzu     ldap       linuxconf  lpd       netfs      network   nfs
nfslock   pcmcia     portmap    random    rawdevice  rhnsd     routed
rstatd    rusersd    rwhod      sendmail  single     smb       syslog
xfs       xinetd     ypbind
```

Done!

REVIEW

This session introduces you to a few friendly daemons. There are many more daemons, but the ones described here should give you a feeling for what they are and how they work.

- An Internet services daemon can be configured to dynamically provide services over an internet connection.
- A collection of NFS daemons can be configured to share disks among a collection of networked computers.
- The cron daemon can manage scheduling any number of background tasks.
- Printer daemons spool in print jobs and then queue them out to printers.
- The pr utility can format your printed output.

Session 26 takes a look at the basis of the UNIX Graphical User Interface (GUI). The X Window System is used on most UNIX systems and provides a windowing and mouse pointer interface.

Quiz Yourself

1. What is the advantage of using inetd, the Internet services daemon? (See "The Internet Services Daemon.")

2. What is the function of the daemon named nfsd? (See "The Network File System Daemon.")

3. What is the name of the utility that can be used to make commands execute repeatedly at scheduled times? (See "The Scheduling Daemon.")

4. What is the name of the utility that can be used to have commands executed once at a specified time in the future? (See "The Scheduling Daemon.")

5. Why do the two distinct commands named lp and lpr exist, since they perform the same basic function? (See "The problem with printing.")

The X Window System

Session Checklist

✔ The X connection

✔ An X application

✔ Widgets

**30 Min.
To Go**

This session provides a conceptual overview of the architecture of the X Window System. This system was carefully designed to run in the environment in which UNIX most often finds itself — a network. The application that displays windows and responds to the mouse is separated by a communications link from the program that manages the actual display. X was designed to handle graphics for multiple terminals connected to one computer as well as workstations that have multiple screens associated with the same mouse and keyboard. It is a simple matter to have overlapping windows on a display while the programs behind the windows are running on several different computers.

The X Connection

A file named /etc/services contains a table listing all of the internet protocols. The following samples are just a few of the hundreds of entries in the file:

```
ftp      21/udp   # File Transfer Protocol
smtp     25/udp   # Simple Mail Transfer Protocol
http     80/udp   # WorldWideWeb HTTP
xdmcp    177/udp  # X Display Manager
```

You are probably familiar with the first three entries shown here, but the fourth may be new to you. The entry named xdmcp (X Display Manager Control Protocol, usually called the X protocol) is used by X applications to communicate with a program called an X server (also known as a display manager), as shown in Figure 26-1. In very simple terms, the application uses the protocol to send messages to the server, and the server responds by displaying windows and graphics sent to it — the server then uses the same protocol to transmit mouse and keyboard messages back to the application.

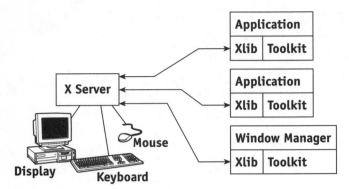

Figure 26-1   *X applications and an X server*

The software that handles the details of communication for an application is in a library named Xlib. Xlib also contains the fundamentals required for windowing, but most applications add to these capabilities by using a toolkit, which contains pre-defined buttons, lists, dialogs, and other such items. With a standard Xlib underlying everything, any X application can be run by any X server — for example, a Gnome application will always run on KDE, and vice versa.

One of the applications shown in Figure 26-1 is a window manager. It is a special application that partners with the X server to perform such tasks as adding decorative frames to the windows and managing the size and location of all the windows. The window manager may also display windows of its own, such as desktop icons and system menus.

Because all X servers use the same protocol, any X server can work with any window manager, and any X application can be run using that combination. Of course, some combinations work better than others.

Addressing the server

Because X is based on an internet protocol, an application and its X server are not necessarily on the same computer. When an application starts running, the first thing it does is make a connection with the server. Because the server can be anywhere on the Internet and more than one display can be attached to a computer, the address of the server includes both the computer name and the ID number of the display. For example, the main display on the computer gryph.belugalake.com would be named like this:

```
gryph.belugalake.com:0
```

An *X terminal* is a physical device that has its own display, keyboard, and mouse. Several X terminals can be attached to the same computer, and they will have the ID numbers 1, 2, 3, and so on. There are also special terminals (such as CAD workstations) that have more than one screen, each of which can be addressed by adding a digit to the right of a decimal point in the ID. For example, if display 2 has three screens, they would be addressed as 2.0, 2.1, and 2.2.

Normally, X applications are run on computers within a local network, and most computers have only one screen, so the most common form of a display name looks like this:

```
gryph:0
```

Even more common is the short form of an address for the main (or only) screen of the local computer:

```
:0
```

When an X application starts running, the first thing it needs is the address of an X server, and the first place it looks for one is on the command line. For example, if you want to run the xeyes application on the main display of a computer named alice, and alice is on your local network, you could enter the command this way:

```
xeyes -display alice:0.0
```

If you don't specify a display on the command line, the application looks for the address in the DISPLAY environment variable. The following command demonstrates the setting of DISPLAY, so it addresses your local screen:

```
$ DISPLAY=:0
$ export DISPLAY
```

If you have the DISPLAY environment variable set, if you are running an X server, and if your current PATH setting includes the directory /usr/bin/X11, you can enter the command xeyes to get the display in Figure 26-2. This is a very old application that has been distributed with X since the beginning. It is only a couple of ovals and a couple of dots, but it takes on a life of its own as it watches your mouse move around the screen.

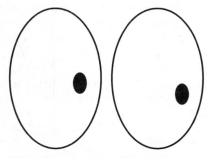

Figure 26-2   *The eyes follow the mouse*

The X messages

A great deal of effort was spent designing the messages that pass between an application and a server to keep the traffic to a minimum. It is not always necessary to transmit an entire window — the only graphic information transmitted by Xlib to the X server are the changes that need to be made. I have run remote applications over a dial-up link to have them display a local window and, while this display isn't snappy, it works surprisingly well.

An X application has one main window, and it may create and destroy other windows while it is running. All of this is done by sending requests to the X sever and responding to the events that come back. There are four kinds of messages:

- **One-way request** — When an application sends a request to have the display changed or updated in some way, it does not wait for an immediate response. As a result, Xlib can gather up several of these requests and send them all at once, making communications more efficient. Most application messages are one-way requests.

- **Round-trip request** — An application sends this kind of message to the server intending to get a response. The message is a query requesting information, such as the size of a window. Unlike one-way requests, these messages cannot be delayed by being batched together because the application is waiting for a response.

- **Event** — An event is sent from the server to the application carrying information, such as the fact that a mouse has been moved or a keyboard key has been pressed.

- **Error event** — An error event is sent from the server to notify applications whenever something goes wrong. These messages are issued if a one-way request was found to be invalid, as in an attempt to draw on a window that doesn't exist.

The messages sent by an application are called requests instead of commands because they may not be obeyed. Although the X server is generally willing to try anything requested of it, the window manager may impose some constraints.

**20 Min.
To Go**

The window manager

The window manager is nothing more than an application that enters into a special partnership with the X server to control the display. The X server can do its job without a window manager, but once the window manager has notified the server of its existence, the server stops obeying requests that come from applications. The X server obeys any request it receives from the window manager, but requests from anywhere else are routed to the window manager for approval. The window manager may approve a request by sending it back to the server, but it may also discard the request and replace it with a request of its own.

The window manager is the reason messages from applications are referred to as requests. Different window managers do things in different ways. For example, you could be using a window manager that tiles the windows instead of allowing them to overlap. If that is the case, an application will not be able to move or resize its window however it pleases. Also, a request by an application to put its window at the top of the stack (the one that is visibly on top of the others) could be suppressed because another application could be displaying an "Are you sure?" message, which has taken priority over everything.

The events arriving from the server are passed back through the window manager to be processed before they are passed on to the application. One of the common jobs of the window manager is to place frames around the windows of an application. These frames normally display a title bar at the top that can be used to move the window to a new location. Usually, buttons are also displayed at the top that can maximize, minimize, and close the window; one button displays a menu that allows the user to send commands directly to the window manager. As far as the X server is concerned, the combination of the frame and its contents is all one window, so the events must be sent to the window manager for decisions to be made about what to do with each event.

An X Application

The following C program is an X application that runs and displays the window shown in Figure 26-3. The appearance of the window shows that it was run in an environment where the Gnome window manager supplied the window decorations. The code of this program has been intentionally simplified (there is no error checking, for example) to easily demonstrate the sort of things an application must do to display a window. The program's inner workings are very simple — each time you click the mouse, an X marks the spot, and if you press any key on the keyboard, the program closes the window and quits.

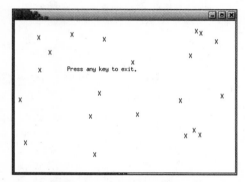

Figure 26-3   *The hellox window after a few mouse clicks*

```
 1 #include <X11/Xlib.h>
 2 #include <X11/Xutil.h>
 3
 4 Display *display;
 5 Window window;
 6 int screen;
 7 XEvent event;
 8 XSizeHints hint;
 9 GC gc;
10 unsigned long foreground;
11 unsigned long background;
12 char msg[] = "Press any key to exit.";
13
14 int running = 1;
15
16 int main(int argc,char *argv[]) {
17     display = XOpenDisplay("");
18     screen = DefaultScreen(display);
19
20     background = WhitePixel(display,screen);
21     foreground = BlackPixel(display,screen);
22
23     window = XCreateSimpleWindow(display,
24         DefaultRootWindow(display),
25         100,200,400,300,
```

```
26              8,foreground,background);
27
28      gc = XCreateGC(display,window,0,0);
29      XSetBackground(display,gc,background);
30      XSetForeground(display,gc,foreground);
31
32      XSelectInput(display,window,
33          ButtonPressMask | KeyPressMask | ExposureMask);
34
35      XMapRaised(display,window);
36
37      while(running) {
38          XNextEvent(display,&event);
39          switch(event.type) {
40          case Expose:
41              XDrawImageString(display,window,gc,
42                  100,100,
43                  msg,strlen(msg));
44              break;
45          case ButtonPress:
46              XDrawImageString(display,window,gc,
47                  event.xbutton.x,event.xbutton.y,
48                  "X",1);
49              break;
50          case KeyPress:
51              running = 0;
52              break;
53          }
54      }
55
56      XFreeGC(display,gc);
57      XDestroyWindow(display,window);
58      XCloseDisplay(display);
59      return(0);
60  }
```

C has a free-form syntax that does not include the numbering shown in this example. The numbers were added so that each line could be referred to in the following list that describes how the program works:

- **Lines 1 and 2** are include statements that bring in the header files containing definitions of all the functions and data structures that are used in the program.

- **Lines 4 through 14** declare the variables that are used in the program. Some of these, such as int and long, are standard C data types, but most are data types defined in the header files.

- **Line 17** calls XOpenDisplay() to make a connection with the X server. No server name is supplied on the call to the function, so the name of the server is taken from the DISPLAY environment variable. The return value is a pointer to a Display struc-ture that contains everything your application could possibly need to know about the display. It contains the connection to X server, locations for queueing output requests and input events, special information about formatting graphics, and much more.

- **Line 18** retrieves specific screen information stored with the Display data. The screen information includes specific details about the physical screen, including its height, width, colors, and information about the root (desktop) window.

- **Lines 20 and 21** use the information about the display and the screen to extract the color values for black and white. This program uses a white background and draws black figures in the foreground.

- **Line 23** is a call to XCreateSimpleWindow() that sends a message to the X server requesting that a window be constructed. The values 100 and 200 are hints about the placement of the upper-left corner of the window, and the values 400 and 300 are hints about the width and height of the new window. This information is formatted into a message and is sent as a request to the X server. If the request is granted and a window is to be constructed, the server considers the hints about location and size. Even if the request is granted, the hints may be ignored.

- **Line 28** creates something known as a GC (Graphics Context). This item contains all the information necessary to issue drawing requests for windows on a specific display. The GC structure contains the background and foreground color information to be used when rendering graphics — if you use several colors, you will need to either create several GCs or change the colors in the ones you have. In this example, the GC background color is set to white and its foreground is set to black.

- **Lines 32 and 33** specify which events are to be sent from the server to this application. To keep traffic to an absolute minimum, the server will not send you any events that you don't specifically request. In this example, a request is made to receive events whenever a mouse button or a keyboard key is pressed, and whenever the window is exposed.

- **Line 35** makes a call to XMapRaised() that sends two requests to the server. Not only does it request that the window be displayed, it also requests that the window be displayed on top of any windows already being displayed.

  If all has gone well with hellox through line 35, the window is displayed on the screen. All you need to do now is wait for an event to arrive from the server, and then decide what to do with it. The events are inserted into an input queue as they arrive at the application. This is necessary because events often arrive faster than your application can handle them.

- **Line 37** is the top of a loop that executes until running is not zero. The first thing that happens in the loop is a call to XNextEvent(), which retrieves the next event from the input queue. The XNextEvent() function is a *blocking call*, which means the function will not return to the program until it has retrieved an event from the queue. All of those windows you have open right on your computer are blocked on their event queue waiting for input from you. This software architecture is known as *event-driven* because nothing happens until an event arrives.

- **Line 39** is a switch statement that branches according to the type of event that has arrived.

- **Line 40** is executed for every Expose event retrieved from the queue. An Expose event is sent to an application when the window is first displayed, and every time after that when the window either has its size changed or is uncovered from being obscured by another window. Some X servers record the content of obscured windows so they can be redisplayed without bothering the application, but it is not required

**10 Min.
To Go**

for them to do so. It is the responsibility of each application to redraw its own windows when requested to do so. In the `hellox` example, if you click on the window a few times and have some X characters showing, they will vanish if you cover the window with another window and restore it. They won't come back because they are not redrawn on the arrival of an `Expose` event. On the other hand, the message string persists because it is redrawn on the arrival of every `Expose` event.

- **Line 45** is executed for every press of any mouse button. The `ButtonPress` event contains information specifying which button has been pressed and the position of the mouse pointer at the time, but this application ignores the button and simply uses the location to paint the letter X on the window.

- **Line 50** is executed whenever the user presses a key on the keyboard. The contents of the `KeyPress` event can be used to determine which key was pressed, but this application just terminates by setting `running` to zero, which causes the loop to fall through the bottom.

- **Lines 56 through 58** do some necessary cleanup. If the process were simply to halt, all this cleanup would take place automatically, but in that case the X server would assume that the program had crashed and issue an error message. It's best to say goodbye before you leave.

To compile this program, you must have the following files on your computer:

```
/usr/lib/libX11.a
/usr/include/X11/Xlib.h
/usr/include/X11/Xutil.h
```

You may find that `libX11.a` is in a different directory, along with the rest of the X11 installation, but all you need to do is create a symbolic link in the right place as follows:

```
$ ln -s /usr/lib/libX11.a /usr/X11R6/lib/libX11.a
```

You can then use the following command to compile the program:

```
$ cc hellox.c -lX11 -o hellox
```

The `-l` (ell) flag on the `cc` command is just a form of shorthand. It instructs the compiler to create the full library name by sticking `lib` on the front of it and `.a` on the back.

Widgets

Looking back at Figure 26-1, you will notice that a toolkit is attached to every application. Programs can be written without a toolkit by using only the functions available in `Xlib`, but it is much easier to use a toolkit. A toolkit contains *widgets* — things like toggle buttons, push buttons, scroll bars, text labels, and so on. Each widget is its own little window that is dedicated to one special purpose.

Glance back at line 23 of the `hellox.c` listing and notice that the call to `XCreate SimpleWindow()` passes, as the second argument, something called `DefaultRootWindow (display)`. This is the ID of the root window (or desktop window, if you prefer) that covers the entire screen. Every window, except the root, must have another window as its parent, and the parent of the `hellox` window is the root. Any window can have child windows, and a child window is attached to its parent and will move every time its parent is moved. If the main window of `hellox` had some small child windows, they would have shown up in front of their parent and moved with it. It is this parent/child relationship that attaches widgets to windows to create dialogs that provide things like text entry widgets and OK buttons. A widget is a small special-purpose window that has its own main loop to respond to the mouse and keyboard.

Some of the more complicated widgets consist of several child widgets of their own. If you see a menu bar across the top of a main window, the entire bar is a widget that is a child of the main window. Each button on the menu bar is a widget, and if you select one with the mouse, a menu appears, displaying a column of button widgets for you to make your choice.

Quite a few widget toolkits have been developed over the years, starting with the Athena widget set that was distributed as part of the original X Window System. The Motif widget set was the first to appear with the beveled edges that everyone now prefers. The KDE and Gnome widget sets are the latest and most popular, but if history does repeat itself, there are more and better widget sets in our future.

Done!

REVIEW

This session introduces you to the inner workings of the X Window System.

- The connection between an application and its window display is through an internet protocol, so windows can be displayed for remote applications.
- A window manager is like any other application, except it becomes a partner with the X server in controlling the display of all windows.
- The messages sent from an application to the display are subject to review and modification by the window manager.
- An X application is event-driven, which means it waits for a message from the X server before it does anything.
- Most applications are written using a toolkit that contains a set of widgets that handle all the details of creating a display.

The following session discusses the archiving of UNIX files. A surprising array of utilities can be used to combine a number of files into a single file, compress files, and uncompress them again.

QUIZ YOURSELF

1. What is an X server? (See "The X Connection.")
2. What is the addressing scheme used by an X server to differentiate among different display screens? (See "Addressing the server.")
3. What kind of messages are passed between the X server and an X application? (See "The X messages.")
4. What technique does the window manager use to make sure commands from an application don't break any display rules? (See "The window manager.")
5. What is meant by the term *event-driven*? (See "An X Application.")

PART

V

Sunday Morning

1. Write an awk program that displays the line number followed by the line itself for each line with more than five fields.

2. Write an awk program that displays the sum of the values in the third field of all input lines.

3. Write an awk program that counts the number of blank lines in a file and prints the total.

4. Write a Perl program that displays the number of arguments on the command line and then displays the first argument.

5. Write a Perl script that populates an array with four values and then displays all four values.

6. Write a Perl script that passes a number to a subroutine and have the subroutine display half the value of the number.

7. Write a Perl script that loops with a counter value from 90 to 95 and prints the value inside each loop.

8. Write a C program that prints the number of arguments on the command line.

9. The make utility reads a script to determine the relationships for compiling and linking programs. What are the two default script names it looks for?

10. If you find a file named core in a directory somewhere, what does that mean?

11. What is the command that can be used to compare two text files and report the differences? And what command can you use to compare three text files?

12. What command can you enter to display the calendar for the month of February of 1988?

13. If you suspect your system is being bogged down by a runaway process, how can you use the top utility to rescue the situation?

14. What procedure can you follow to have a set of commands executed repeatedly at specific times?

15. How is it possible to instruct the at command to execute more than one command at a specified time?

16. If you need to send a simple text file to the print spooler, what command should you use?

17. What can you do to add simple headings at the top of each page of the printed version of a text file?

18. If you are on a computer with only one terminal, and you are running X with a local server, how can you set the environment to start X applications from the command line?

19. Why are messages that are sent from an X application to an X server referred to as requests, and why do the messages contain hints?

20. What is a widget?

PART

VI

Sunday Afternoon

Session 27
Archiving and Compressing Files

Session 28
Security

Session 29
Network Security and the Apache Server

Session 30
When UNIX Boots

Archiving and Compressing Files

Session Checklist

✔ Introduction to archiving

✔ Packing and unpacking

✔ Compressing and uncompressing

✔ Gzipping and gunzipping

✔ Bzipping and bunzipping

✔ Zipping and unzipping

✔ Using cp

✔ Using tar

✔ Special-purpose archivers

**30 Min.
To Go**

Several different ways are available to compress files and to combine them into single files for archiving. This includes the traditional tar and dd utilities to combine multiple files and directories, as well as several data compression utilities. The file combiners and file compressors can (and often are) used in tandem to create compressed archives.

Introduction to Archiving

Files can be copied in three basic ways. The first method is to simply duplicate the files, along with the entire directory structure, in another location. The second technique is to make a copy of each file in a compressed form so that the copies take up less space. The third method is to create a new file that combines all of the files into one. Some archivers can be used to both combine and compress files at once.

There is more than one reason to make copies of your files. Probably the most important one is the safety backups that you create at regular intervals. (You do make safety backup copies of your files at regular intervals, don't you?) Another common use of archiving is to put a collection of files and directories into a single package as a convenient form for transmitting the files from one location to another. If you have a directory full of files that you seldom use, it is convenient to archive the files so they take up less space, although this is not as important as it was when disk space was at a premium.

UNIX provides several different ways to archive files, as shown in Table 27-1. The process is a two-way street — if you archive files, you must also be able to extract them from the archive. For some utilities, the same command is used for both actions. Some of the utilities attach special suffixes to the file names so that they can be easily recognized and so you know which unarchiver to use.

Table 27-1 *Standard Naming Conventions for Archiving*

Archive	Unarchive	Archive Suffix
pack	unpack, pcat	.z
compress	uncompress, zcat	.Z
gzip	gunzip, zcat	.gz
bzip2	bunzip2, bzcat	.bz2
zip	unzip	.zip
tar	tar	.tar

Packing and Unpacking

The pack utility is one of the older archivers, and it isn't used much any more because of its restrictions on the length of file names.

The following command removes the file named index.html and replaces it with a compressed version named index.html.z:

```
$ pack index.html
```

To reverse the action, you can use the unpack command to remove index.html.z and replace it with index.html:

```
$ unpack index.html.z
```

Another way to extract a file after it has been packed is to use the pcat command, which creates a new unpacked file and leaves the packed file intact:

```
$ pcat index.html.z >index.html
```

The pack utility was designed to be used inside a single directory containing only regular files. It is showing its age — file names are limited to 12 characters because it cannot produce file names of more than 14 characters, and it does not work on directories. It uses Huffman encoding for compression, which means that it works best on files that contain repeated byte values, such as text files.

Compressing and Uncompressing

The compress and uncompress utilities were written to be improved versions of pack and unpack.

The following command removes the file named index.html and replaces it with a compressed version named index.html.Z:

```
$ compress index.html
```

To reverse the action, you can use the following uncompress command to remove index.html.Z and replace it with index.html:

```
$ uncompress index.html.Z
```

Another way to extract a file after it has been compressed is to use the zcat command, which creates a new uncompressed file and leaves the compressed file intact:

```
$ zcat index.html.Z >index.html
```

Much like pack and unpack, the compress utility was designed to be used inside a single directory containing only regular files. It doesn't impose a limitation on the length of file names, and its rate of compression is much better than pack's because it uses a more advanced form of compression known as *Lempel-Ziv encoding*. However, it still has limitations because it replaces its input file with a compressed file and it cannot be used to compress directories.

Gzipping and Gunzipping

The gzip and gunzip utilities work very much like compress and uncompress in that they both use Lempel-Ziv compression and replace the file being compressed. The gunzip utility can retrieve files that have been archived by compress, but uncompress may not be able to retrieve a file compressed using gzip. Also, gunzip can retrieve files compressed by pack. The gunzip utility has no difficulty in recognizing files created by other compression algorithms because it ignores the suffix on the file name and uses the file's magic number to identify its contents.

See the discussion of the file **utility in Session 3 for a description of magic numbers.**

The following command removes the file named index.html and replaces it with a compressed version named index.html.gz:

```
$ gzip index.html
```

To reverse the action, you can use the following gunzip command to remove
index.html.gz and replace it with index.html:

```
$ gunzip index.html.gz
```

As with compress, another way to extract a file after it has been gzipped is to use the
zcat command, which creates a new uncompressed file and leaves the compressed file
intact:

```
$ zcat index.html.gz >index.html
```

The gzip utility can also be used to compress several files into the same archive by
naming them all on the command line:

```
$ gzip -c file1 file2 >archive.gz
```

Bzipping and Bunzipping

The utilities bzip2 and bunzip2 work very much like gzip and gunzip. The primary difference between bzip2 and gzip is that bzip2 uses Burrows-Wheeler compression algorithm,
which is a special form of Huffman encoding.

The following command removes the file named index.html and replaces it with a
compressed version named index.html.bz2:

```
$ bzip2 index.html
```

To reverse the action, you can use the following bunzip2 command to remove
index.html.bz2 and replace it with index.html:

```
$ bunzip2 index.html.bz2
```

Another way to extract a file after it has been archived is to use the bzcat command,
which creates a new uncompressed file and leaves the compressed file intact:

```
$ bzcat index.html.bz2 >index.html
```

Files are compressed in blocks, and the blocks are then combined to create a single compressed archive file. The block sizes vary from 100K to 900K and can be specified by using
the option flags -1 (one) through -9. The default is 900K. The only advantage of reducing
the block size is in the rare circumstance that you are using a computer with a small
amount of memory.

**20 Min.
To Go**

Zipping and Unzipping

The zip and unzip utilities are very popular because the zipped files are portable and can
be used to transfer files from one operating system to another. In addition to UNIX, the
same compressed file format can be used by VMS, Mac, DOS/Windows, and several other systems. The program originated as a DOS utility named pkzip that was written by Phil Katz.
The original pkzip was very fast and easy to use, so it wasn't long before versions of it were

written for other operating systems. With so many versions, some strange file formatting incompatibility crept in around Version 2, but if you use Version 5.4 or later of unzip, you will be able to retrieve an archive created by any version of zip.

By default, zip compresses a set of regular files in the current directory, but it is possible to command zip to compress an entire tree full of files and directories. Also, the files being archived are left intact unless you specifically request that they be deleted. To compress a file, you must specify the name of the archive file on the command line.

The following command stores the file named index.html in an archive file named index.zip:

```
$ zip index.zip index.html
```

You can list as many files as you like on the command line and they all will be compressed and stored in the same archive file, which is usually called a *zip file*.

You can use the following command to restore the index.html file to its original state:

```
$ unzip index.zip
```

Many options are available with zip and unzip, and to get a quick list of them, simply enter zip or unzip on the command line with no arguments. You can request that an existing zip file be updated by having files added to it or by replacing existing files with newer versions. It is also possible to encrypt the files with a password, trade off compression size for compression speed, and even convert between UNIX and DOS text formats. The -r option can be used to archive one or more entire directory trees, as in the following example:

```
$ zip -r tree.zip gjhazy alroid mrocan
```

In this example, it doesn't matter whether the named entities are files or directories; they all will be included in the zip file, along with all of their subdirectories and files. When they are restored by unzip, the entire directory tree will be restored with all the files in the right directories.

As far as I know, zip is the only utility that uses -@ as an option flag. Using this option instructs zip to accept the list of file names from standard input. For example, the following command creates an archive containing only the C source and header files from the current directory tree (they are the files with .c and .h suffixes):

```
$ find . -name "*.[ch]" -print | zip chsrc.zip -@
```

The zip utility uses a compression method know as *deflation*, but it will also store files without compression if it saves space, which is the case on very small files and files that have already been compressed.

Using cp

In certain situations, space isn't really a consideration. If you don't need to back up a lot of data and you have plenty of space to do it in, you may want to simplify things by copying the files as they are. For example, if you are working in a directory named /home/devel/frmlproject and you want to make a safety backup before you start changing things, you can use the following script to create a backup named for the current hour:

```
HOUR=`date +%H`
SAFETY=/home/backups/frmlproject/$HOUR
cp -rf /home/devel/frmlproject $SAFETY
```

The %H format on the date command is the number of the hour. The -r option tells the cp command to copy all files and directories, and the -f option tells cp to go ahead and overwrite any files that already exist.

If you want to automatically make a copy of everything once an hour as you work, you can name the script frmlsave in your home directory and add this line to your crontab settings:

```
10 * * * * frmlproject
```

At ten minutes after each hour, a new copy of everything will be saved in a directory named for the hour. Of course, when you are finished working on the files, you need to remember to shut it all down by restoring your original crontab settings and deleting the backup files.

Using tar

The tar (tape archive) utility is the one most commonly used for creating safety backups and for transmitting large collections of UNIX files from one place to another. It will combine an entire tree filled with files and other directories into a single file, which can then be compressed to save space. Although the word *tape* is part of tar's name, and tar was originally written to read and write tape data, it is mostly used to create archives on disk. The file produced by tar is known as a *tar file*, which can be identified by a magic number but usually bears a .tar suffix. To save space, especially for data transmission, you will see other suffixes appended onto it, so you will see names with compound suffixes, such as .tar.gz, .tar.z, and .tar.Z.

The tar utility has an amazing array of options. One option must be used to specify which operation is to be performed, and other options can be added as modifiers. Table 27-2 lists the option flags that are used to select the basic function to be performed — one of these flags, and only one, must be included whenever you run tar.

Table 27-2 *The Five Functions of tar*

Option	Description
-c	Create. The rest of the information on the command line is used as the information necessary to create a new tar file and store files in it.
-r	Replace. The names of the files on the command line are appended to the end of the tar file.
-t	Table. The names of the files in the tar file are listed in a format similar to that of ls. If any names are present on the command line, the listing is limited to just those files.

Option	Description
-u	Update. The named files are appended to the end of the file if they are not already included, or if the version to be included is newer than the one already in the tar file.
-x	Extract. The named files and directories are copied from the tar file and written to disk. Items in the tar file that were stored with relative path names are written to disk using those relative names, but beginning with the current directory. If no files are specified, the entire tar file is extracted. If the archive contains more than one file with the same name, the latest one will overwrite the earlier ones.

As you look through the basic tar functions listed in Table 27-2, you can see how these functions apply to a tape archive. The version of tar that you have on your system will most likely have some additional operations, such as deleting files from the middle of an archive or comparing two tar files and listing all of the items that differ.

If you don't specify a tar file name, the input or output will be the default tape devices. Check the man page on your system for the default, but it is usually a tape drive device node with a name like /dev/mt/0m, /dev/mt0, or /dev/rmt0. The -f option is used to specify a tar file. For example, the following command will list all of the files found in the tar file named scrunch.tar:

```
$ tar -tf scrunch.tar
Terminal
accels/
accels/Terminal
accels/session-properties
accels/gcalc
gcalc
gmenu
```

This list includes the names of all the files and the relative path to each one. The -v (verbose) option can be used to provide you with more information about each file. The listing looks very much like the listing produced by the -1 (ell) option on 1s, as you can see from the following example:

```
$ tar -tvf scrunch.tar
-rw-r--r-- arthur/users     815 2001-12-26 06:37:44 Terminal
drwx------ arthur/users       0 2001-12-14 05:00:41 accels/
-rw-r--r-- arthur/users    1057 2001-12-04 14:55:18 accels/Terminal
-rw-r--r-- arthur/users     330 2000-04-25 18:46:50 accels/session-
properties
-rw-r--r-- arthur/users     368 2001-09-05 11:59:22 accels/gcalc
-rw-r--r-- arthur/users      35 2001-09-05 11:58:36 gcalc
-rw-r--r-- arthur/users      53 2001-05-19 08:15:14 gmenu
```

**10 Min.
To Go**

The same basic command line format that lists the members of a tar file can be used to create a tar file. The following command creates a tar file containing all the files and directories of the current directory, and the -v option causes each one to be listed as it is added to the archive:

```
$ tar -cvf scrunch.tar *
```

The following command extracts the files from the tar file and restores the entire directory tree that contains them:

```
$ tar -xvf scrunch.tar
```

After you create a tar file, it contains all of the files concatenated one behind the other without compression. To store it as an archive, it can be compressed using any of the compression utilities described earlier. The following example produces a file named scrunch.tar.gz:

```
$ gzip scrunch.tar
```

With a normal mixture of text and binary files, you should get a size reduction on the order of 60 to 70 percent. The actual percentage will vary depending on the file types and the overall size of the tar file.

Some of the newer versions of tar include file compression, so the creation of a compressed tar file is just a matter of setting the appropriate flag on the command line. The -z option applies gzip if used with the -c option or gunzip if used with the -x option. The following single command creates a compressed tar file of the files and directories in the current directory:

```
$ tar -cvzf scrunch.tar.gz *
```

The following command applies gunzip and the -x option of tar to extract all the files:

```
$ tar -xvzf scrunch.tar.gz
```

Special-Purpose Archivers

Some archivers are rarely used. They are intended for special purposes and are only needed in rare circumstances where you find yourself in the presence of a strange archive format or when you have a disk or tape problem that must be solved.

Using dd

The dd command copies data from one location to another and may make some conversions during the process. The default for this command is to use standard input and standard output, but you can name the input and output locations on the command line. This utility operates at a low level and can be used to make a sector-by-sector mirror image of an entire disk drive, or write an entire file system to tape.

Many of the services performed by dd are no longer (or very seldom) needed. It can read and write both ASCII and EBCDIC encoded characters, and convert between the two if necessary (EBCDIC is a family of IBM character sets used by mainframes). At the lowest level, dd can read raw data from a disk drive and modify its organization for storage on another disk drive with a different hardware configuration.

The dd command ignores the file system and deals directly with the devices. For example, if you have two identical disk drives and you want to duplicate everything on the drive named /dev/hd/1 to another disk drive named /dev/hd/4, specify the input and output devices, as in the following command:

```
$ dd if=/dev/hd/1 of=/dev/hd/4
```

The following command can be used to restore an entire disk drive named /dev/hda3 from a magnetic tape named /dev/mt0:

```
$ dd if=/dev/mt0 of=/dev/hda3
```

The following command uses zip to compress a file system and write the compressed archive directly to a tape drive:

```
$ zip -r - /usr/workdir | dd of=/dev/mt0 obs=32k
```

Using the - option on zip causes it to write its archive to standard output. The obs option on dd specifies the block size of the output device.

Bad blocks of data will sometimes appear on a tape, making the tape unreadable by the regular software. The dd command is not as particular about errors, and if any portions of the tape can be read, they can be read by dd. The following example reads the entire contents of a tape — bad blocks and all — and stores it in a file named workfile:

```
$ dd if=/dev/mt0 >workfile
```

Some options can be used to persuade dd to skip over bad blocks and other errors in an attempt to get the data from the tape into a disk file so you can work with it. You may have to specifically set the input block size and certain other options, but dd is your best first choice when you are trying to recover data from a bad tape or disk drive.

Using ar

You won't be dealing with the ar (archive) utility much unless you are involved with creating and maintaining libraries of compiled modules. The ar command is capable of creating and modifying a simple archive file that contains a collection of files. Archives of this type are searched by the linker to resolve references made by programs to external executable code. You can use it from the command line, but it is more common to use the cc command and let it use ar to read from and write to the libraries.

Using cpio

The cpio (copy in out) utility can be used to create archives and extract files from them. It can even be used to make modifications to the archived files in certain predefined ways. The archives created by cpio can contain header files with CRC (cyclic redundancy check) values used to verify the validity of the archived files. In a fashion similar to dd, you can use cpio to read and write directly to raw device nodes, which means it is capable of communicating with block devices such as disk and tape drives. Many capabilities are included as part of cpio for doing such things as swapping bytes and otherwise reformatting data to be transferred to and from alien systems (including older versions of itself).

Basically, cpio accepts a list of file names as standard input and then copies the files into a single output stream, as follows:

```
$ ls | cpio -oc >cpiofile
```

The -o flag specifies that the output is a cpio archive file and the -c flag ensures that the format of the output is portable to other systems. The files can be restored from the archive by using the -i flag, which specifies that the input is an cpio archive file, as follows:

```
$ cat cpiofile | cpio -i
```

Done!

REVIEW

In this session, you learn several ways to store files into archives and then retrieve them.

- The oldest and simplest UNIX compression utilities are named pack and compress.
- The gzip and bzip2 compression utilities are similar to one another in both name and operation.
- The most common compression utility is zip because the compressed file format is portable to several different systems, and zip creates an archive as well as compresses the files.
- The tar utility creates an uncompressed archive and can be used in conjunction with a compression utility to create a compressed archive.

The following session takes a look at computer security. In this day of global networks, every system administrator must be concerned with security.

QUIZ YOURSELF

1. From looking at the name of an archive file, what can you tell about the utility that was used to create it? (See "Introduction to Archiving.")
2. What is the limit on the size of file names for pack? (See "Packing and Unpacking.")
3. Some of the utilities use something besides the file name to determine the file type of a compressed archive. What is it? (See "Gzipping and Gunzipping.")
4. What was the original purpose of tar? (See "Using tar.")
5. If you don't specify the name of a tar file by using the -f option, what does tar default to using? (See "Using tar.")

Security

Session Checklist

✔ Introduction to UNIX security

✔ Types of attacks

✔ Security checklist

**30 Min.
To Go**

This session contains a checklist of UNIX security fundamentals. Given the amount of security practices available, and the fact that new security holes are being discovered every day, the list is not exhaustive (in fact, each version of UNIX has its own list). This session also includes a general discussion of the measures you can take to secure your system.

Maintaining the security of one's computer is difficult because it is an unnatural act. Every programmer in the world is working very hard to make computer systems easy for people to use, and security procedures are implemented for the express purpose of keeping people from using them.

Introduction to UNIX Security

Many things about UNIX can help you keep your system secure. There is a very secure password system that assigns user and group identities that you can use to control access to individual files and directories. Every UNIX vendor is aware of security and provides alerts and software updates that you can use to keep your system secure. And the Internet is filled with information and advice.

Many things about UNIX are not designed with security in mind. The system was originally designed as a collaborative software development system to have its facilities shared among a group of programmers. Many versions of UNIX default to almost no security whatsoever, which leaves a newly installed system wide open to attack. Over the years, features such as remote logins, networking file systems, and e-mail have provided new openings for attack. And the popularity of the Internet now provides access to anyone.

All security measures fall into one of four categories:

- **Account security** — The quickest and simplest way for a cracker to enter a system is by using an existing login name and password. Entry often occurs through old accounts that were used by someone no longer working at the company, or accounts with passwords that are too simple and easy to guess.

- **Network security** — If your computer is connected to a network, someone on a remote computer could abuse the privileges you award to that computer. Depending on which UNIX system you are using, either the .rhosts file or the hosts.equiv file is used to grant permissions to remote computers. If the permissions are too broad and the remote system is cracked, so is yours.

- **File system security** — File security is your last level of defense against a cracker. If someone breaks into your system, but does not have root access, your files and directories can still be protected by the access permissions. But don't trust the file settings alone — use the directory permissions setting as well. For example, if write permission is granted to a directory, then any file in that directory can be deleted no matter what its permissions settings.

- **Physical security** — This type of security has to do with locked doors, natural disasters, and trusted employees. Information stored on a system can be destroyed by physically destroying or removing a disk drive. Information can be stolen by someone pilfering a disk drive or a backup tape. And there is the possibility of a fire.

The number one thing you want to guard is the root password. The root password gives the bearer the capability of doing absolutely anything to your system. Every person breaking in to a system would like nothing better than to get a copy of the root password. A cracker with root access for a few minutes can make your system almost permanently wide open.

The number one problem is people using lousy passwords. One experiment showed that when three passwords were guessed (the login name, the login name backward, and then the login name both frontward and backward as one word), up to 30 percent of the accounts on a system could be entered. A woman's name followed by a single digit is a very common password. When these passwords — in addition to a list of about 2,000 common first names — were tried, it was shown that almost 50 percent of the passwords could be cracked.

Session 19 contains some suggestions for selecting secure passwords. You can also use simple unrelated words with some punctuation to create passwords like flame?grab, glib;racket, and spot*shuttle. These passwords are relatively easy to remember, but will never be guessed by someone going through a list or a dictionary.

UNIX provides a simple but effective little trick to help prevent password cracking. If you enter a completely unknown user name, you get a prompt for a password just as if it were a valid name. Thus, if someone tries to crack the system, they won't be able to experiment to find a valid user name and then start working on the password. Also, if you get either the user name or the password wrong, a slight pause occurs before you get the message that your login failed. This pause, which lasts approximately two to three seconds, prevents a cracker from making a connection online from another computer and then trying millions of names and passwords to get in. Even a few hundred tries will become a long process when you have a pause between each try.

One very careless thing to do is to put a password in a script so that you can quickly log in to another system or switch to superuser mode to execute a privileged command. It is very easy to allow a script like this to be readable, which makes the password available to any user that logs in. This is just one of the reasons you want to change the root password from time to time. Changing the root password causes scripts that contain passwords to quit working, and running the script exposes the security hole.

Check your system's documentation for password protection procedures. Most systems enable you to specify the minimum length for passwords and make it possible to set a maximum password age. When a password expires, the user is required to establish a new password. However, some users become attached to their favorite password and will go to a great deal of trouble to avoid changing it — some will change their password as required and then change it back again.

Types of Attacks

Computers are attacked in different ways and for different reasons. Some crackers are attempting to steal information, while others want to disable all or part of the system. Some crackers intend to use your computer as a platform for sending spam or to perform some other deed that requires that they not be traced. One popular sport today is to break in to deface a Web site. Keep in mind that most break-ins are done simply for the sport of it.

Trojan horses

The utility named /usr/bin/passwd is used by root, and by everyone else, to update the passwords stored in the /etc/passwd and /etc/shadow files. With the root password (in the possession of a cracker for just a few minutes), the regular passwd utility can be replaced by another program that does exactly the same thing as the original but also mails the new user name and password to an address that can be accessed by the cracker. Without your knowledge, a person that has broken into your system is constantly being updated with all password changes.

A program that replaces another for the sake of grabbing passwords, or performing other types of mischief, is known as a *Trojan horse program*. The term *Trojan horse* refers to something you see, trust, and willingly give information to, just like the Trojans in the Greek legend. The passwd utility isn't the only program that can be used this way. A program named /bin/login prompts for user names and passwords when you log into the system — it could just as well be replaced with a Trojan horse to capture every user name and password that logs in. The utility named /bin/su requires a user name and password before it allows you to log in as a different user.

Trojan horses can take almost any form. For example, a cracker could slip a program named ls into a directory and have it executed by any user in that directory that has a dot (current directory) included as one of the directories in the PATH environment variable. The dot is used as a convenience to execute programs in the current directory, but there should never be a dot in the path used by root. Not including a dot in the path is not a problem because a dot can be used on the command line to execute a program in the current directory, as in the following example:

```
$ ./setconfig
```

It can be argued that the root user should have no path set and should be required to enter the full path name of all commands, like this:

```
$ /bin/ls
```

Worms

A *worm* is a program that moves from one computer to another and continuously replicates itself until the computers are completely filled and the system is consumed trying to make more copies. Worms have been around for a long time. In the mid-1970s, a program named *rabbit* moved via tape from one mainframe computer to another by infesting data sets (file systems) with copies of itself. It was slow to spread, so it was relatively easy to eliminate by a program named *fox* that did nothing but track down and kill rabbits. The fox had to stay active for some time because many rabbits were stored on tape and they would come to life when the tape was mounted.

The most famous worm is known as the *Internet worm*, which began spreading in November of 1988. Using the high-speed connections of the Internet, it spread rapidly to hundreds of computers. Many people knew that something like this was possible, but it still caught most system administrators by surprise. The Internet worm stole passwords, which could be used to enter other systems, but no other information was stolen and no files were destroyed. However, this worm was tremendously destructive in terms of the effort and cost required to remove it from the network. Many computers disconnected from the Internet until the mess could be cleaned up.

Denial of service

A *denial of service* attack is achieved by sending a great number of Internet messages to a computer. So many messages come in so fast that the computer becomes overwhelmed attempting to process them. There is no way to tell the valid messages from the vicious ones until they are processed, so they are processed very slowly or not at all.

A denial of service can be achieved in several ways. Normally, a cracker first enters several systems and installs software that will issue thousands of requests per second to the target of the attack. All of these systems are then instructed to begin sending messages at the same time. These requests take the form of an Internet packet that requires the target computer to examine the packet and respond in some way. The attack can go on for quite a while because it can only be stopped by shutting off the origins of the messages.

Buffer overflow

Any program that can be accessed from the Internet is a potential vulnerability. Some programs have built-in facilities that make it possible for a cracker to *shell out* from inside the program. This means that it is possible to invoke a shell from inside the program, which, in effect, logs the cracker into the computer with the permissions set to those that were being used by the program.

Even if a program has no built-in facility to shell out, crackers can use *buffer overflow* to achieve the same thing. This sort of vulnerability exists when careless programming has left a hole that allows too much data to be input into a storage location. The programmer expected the arrival of a block of data of a fixed (or maximum) size, so the code is written to copy the entire incoming block of data into a specific location in memory (this location is referred to as the *buffer*). If the block of incoming data is too large, it fills not only the buffer but also the space beyond it (this is the *overflow*). A cracker can cobble up the format and content of the incoming data so that the incoming block is huge and overwrites as much of the program as needed to make the program act differently. If the different action is to provide the cracker with a logged-in shell, then the deed has been done. Many programs that connect to the Internet run with root permissions, so the cracker would have access to a root shell.

This is a very simplified description of buffer overflow cracking. The cracker must do a lot of work to figure out exactly what to use as the overflow data, but after an overflow condition has been discovered, the rest is just a matter of time and effort.

It is not necessary that a buffer overflow provide a login shell. Any number of things can be done once an outsider has the ability to send code to a computer and have it executed.

Security Checklist

The following list contains many of the specific things that you can do to secure your system. If you are responsible for securing systems, you should develop your own checklist (it will be much longer than this one). You will need to go back through the list from time to time (following the installation of new or updated software, for example) to make sure your system stays secure. This list is incomplete because the security situation is constantly changing and you will need to add information that is pertinent to your flavor of UNIX and the software you have installed on it.

As you read through this list, you will notice one basic theme: If you aren't using it, don't leave it running.

Passwords

Check all the passwords. The best way to do this is to try to crack your own system. There is more than one utility designed for this purpose, and a quick search on the Internet will turn up a few. You can also find some of these utilities on the CD-ROM that accompanies this book. Try more than one of them to see which one works best for you. Keep a watch for updated versions of the ones you decide to use.

Make certain that every user of your system knows the correct procedure for creating valid passwords. Depending on their level of computer experience, you could either use a broadcast e-mail message to make suggestions — or you may find it more useful to write a detailed explanation. After all, if your first line of defense fails, all other security measures mean nothing.

Updates and patches

Verify that all security patches and updates have been installed. Patches and updates are provided by every responsible UNIX vendor. You should get on the security mailing list for your UNIX system as well as check the Web site regularly. When a new patch becomes available (usually in the form of a new executable program), you should install it right away. When a new vulnerability is discovered, there will often be a flurry of attacks attempting to get into systems before the door is shut. Unless there is a very fundamental security problem, installing the update will have little or no impact on users — you may have to restart a daemon or two, but that's usually all there is to it.

Before you install the update, validate the digital signature to be certain that you have downloaded the correct version of the file. It is possible that the file was corrupted at the source, or some kind of intervention could have occurred during the download.

The installation of a fix may cause some configuration settings to revert to their default, so you need to verify the overall system security immediately after you install it. Yes, this is a lot of work, but much of the process can be automated by scripts once you get accustomed to it.

Firewalls and services

You need to be behind a firewall. If your local network is not connected to the Internet through a firewall, then you should consider setting one up. It's not that expensive, and it allows you to concentrate much of your network security into a single computer. If the firewall is the only computer exposed directly to the network, you can have complete control over the passwords required for outside access, and you can simply not include software with possible vulnerabilities.

There is nothing particularly magical about a firewall. It is a computer, like any other, that maintains a connection between your local network and the outside Internet. All of the computers on the local network send and receive Internet messages through the firewall. There is no limit to the number of ways a firewall can be configured. It can act as a simple watchdog as messages go by, or it can change the names and addresses of the computers on the local network to mask the actual configuration of the network.

Another important job of the firewall is to act as an Internet filter by removing incoming messages that could be harmful. For example, a computer on your local network may have become vulnerable because some daemon was accidentally started running. Filtering messages from the Internet will prevent external access to the new vulnerability. There is no need to allow packets into your local network that try to access services that you don't provide. The following list contains some services that you are probably not interested in making available outside of your local network:

biff	netstat	shell	telnet
bootp	NeWS	snmp	tftp
echo	NFS	sunrpc	uucp
exec	openwin	supdup	who
link	printer	syslog	X11
login	route	systat	xdmcp

The filtering is done by port numbers, which can be found in the file `/etc/services`. Setting up the filters can be tricky, so check the documentation of your firewall system. Pay particular attention to the ones listed in the file as udp services because these are prime targets for denial-of-service attacks.

Some services do not keep daemons running at all times. You may recall the `inetd` registry discussed in Session 25. Some daemons may also be registered with a program named `portmap`, which listens for incoming Internet packets and starts a daemon when a message for it arrives. The following command displays a complete list of the daemons and port numbers registered with `portmap`:

```
$ rpcinfo -p
```

To prevent outside access to the portmapper, port 111 should be filtered at the firewall. Check the configuration file /etc/inetd.conf to make sure that the permissions on the file are set to 600. Also set the file permissions on /etc/services to 644 to prevent it from being modified. Remove the REXD service from /etc/inetd.conf.

There is a set of BSD commands that provides remote access. They are known as the "r" commands (rlogin, rsh, and so on). If you are using them inside your local network, you will want to filter ports 512, 513, and 514 at the firewall to prohibit access from outside the network. Check the home directories for all users and examine (or delete) $HOME/.rhosts files that grant permissions for remote logins. There should never be an .rhosts file in the home directory of root. Users are able to create .rhosts files to allow remote access to their own login unless a firewall filters the ports.

NFS

10 Min. To Go

NFS (Network File System) allows files to be shared by remote systems over an internet connection, so it is advisable to filter the NFS port 2049 at the firewall to prevent file systems from being accessible outside of your local network.

Make certain that either /etc/exports or /etc/dfs/dfstab (whichever file your system uses) contains only the file systems you wish to share. When you are configuring an NFS system, it is very tempting to share too much and wind up exposing too much to the network. Make sure you export only the file systems that actually need to be exported — the export tree can begin with any directory. Also, no files should be exported to the local computer, either by IP address or by the name localhost.

Mail

Verify that you are using the latest version of sendmail available for your system. There have been numerous security problems with sendmail in the past, but the latest versions seem to be quite secure. Make sure that your version of sendmail does not have the wizard password enabled.

A program named smrsh, which is sometimes included with sendmail, is a restricted version of the shell. It allows you to name the specific set of commands that can be executed by sendmail. You should install and configure smrsh to limit sendmail to only the set of commands you actually need. There is seldom a need to allow incoming mail to delete files.

Certain sendmail configuration settings will make things more secure. A facility known as progmailer can be used to send mail to programs, and it should be disabled if you are not using it. Disable the sendmail wizard password by changing any line beginning with OW in the /etc/sendmail.cf configuration file so it is followed only by a single asterisk. To help detect attempts to exploit sendmail vulnerabilities, set the log level to a minimum of 9.

If you are using majordomo to manage a mailing list membership, make certain that the version number is greater than 1.91.

FTP

If you are supplying FTP (File Transfer Protocol) services, then you are running the ftpd daemon. If you are not using FTP, don't run the daemon, but if you are running it, make sure you have the latest version so you will have all the updates. Because the ftpd daemon is open to the Internet and has the ability to read and write files on the local file system, it may have some security problems. This is especially true if you are providing an anonymous FTP service because there is no specific password required to log in.

If your system is running anonymous FTP but you want to disable it, look in /etc/ passwd to determine the ftp home directory, and then remove the files from the home directory. You should also delete the ftp login entry from /etc/passwd.

Not all FTP software is configurable, but if yours is, carefully look through all of the default settings to make certain you are allowing only what you intend to allow. Limit the users to downloading files, uploading files, and changing directories. Disable delete, overwrite, rename, chmod, umask, and other options that can be used by anonymous users to make modifications to the local disk.

In the file /etc/ftpusers, list all the users that are to be prohibited from logging in as users of the FTP daemon. The list should include root, bin, uucp, ingres, daemon, news, nobody, and guest. Look in the /etc/passwd file and include any other account names that are supplied as part of the default system configuration.

You will find a directory named bin in the home directory of the anonymous ftp login. Make certain there are no executables in this directory that should not be executed by an anonymous user — in particular, no script interpreters such as a shell or Perl. The programs in the bin directory can be executed from a remote location by using the FTP command SITE EXEC (which should be disabled unless you need it). It may be necessary to keep certain commands, such as uncompress or unzip, in the bin directory, but you should consider the capabilities of each program before you put it there. Some versions of tar, for example, allow for the execution of arbitrary commands and can be used to modify the files on your system, which could wind up enabling unauthorized entry.

The owner of the ftp home directory should be root, not ftp. And the permissions of the home directory should be set to 555. If the anonymous user is given write permission to the bin directory, it would be a simple matter to use FTP to store a program there and then use SITE EXEC to run it.

An FTP login from a remote location that requests a list of the files in a directory is given the permission and ownership information on the files. The ownership names are determined by looking in the etc/passwd file in the FTP home directory. This file should not be a copy of the system's /etc/passwd file. In fact, it is best if it contains fictional user names instead of real ones. You should create it from scratch just for this purpose, and set its permissions to 444. A file named etc/group is also used to provide group names, and the same rules apply — that is, the etc/group must be owned by root, contain fictional groups, and have its permissions set to 444.

Additional considerations

You can use chmod to set file permissions in such a way that a shell script, while executing, will switch the group and user ID to that of the owner of the script file. For example, if it is owned by root, the script will run with root permissions. This is known as setting the *effective user ID* of a process and can be quite insecure because the script, or another script it executes, can be modified and made to do anything. The ability to set the effective user ID on scripts is falling out of favor, and some UNIX systems will no longer honor the flags by changing permissions.

Keep a close eye on trusted remote systems. If you routinely allow open access to your network by one or more remote systems, your entire local network can be compromised by your lack of control over the security of the remote system. In this situation, you must regard the remote computer as possibly hostile and limit its access.

The list goes on. If you are put in the position of being responsible for security, gather all the information you can. Contact the vendor of your version of UNIX — they can be very helpful because they have a vested interest in making their systems secure. Search the Internet for tips and for software that can help you check your system. Get a good book on UNIX security and settle down to an evening's reading of fascinating adventures in system configuration. With things going the way they are, there is no such thing as overkill when it comes to security.

And please make your backups. Get a regular plan going and stick with it. From time to time, select a backup volume and make certain it is valid — right after a system crash is not the time to discover that the tape drive is busted. And rotate a copy of your backups to another building at least once a month. Insurance will compensate you for destroyed computers, but data replacement is very hard to come by.

Done!

REVIEW

This session is an introduction to the steps you can take to secure your system.

- The single most important item for system security is the root password. It should be crafted so it is not easily cracked.
- A computer can be broken into in several ways, but all of these ways require a weakness or some kind of cooperation on the part of the computer being invaded.
- It is important to stay informed of possible security problems and update your system with the current, and hopefully more secure, versions of utilities.
- If at all possible, protect your local computer systems with a firewall.

A Web server is a major source of security problems, because the HTTP protocol is capable of reading and writing files on your system and can also be made to execute programs. The next session discusses the operation of a Web site using the Apache Web server.

QUIZ YOURSELF

1. What are the four major categories of security concerns? (See "Introduction to UNIX Security.")
2. How can a simple command such as ls be turned into a Trojan horse? (See "Trojan horses.")
3. What is the first thing to check when analyzing a system's security? (See "Security Checklist.")
4. What is the most common mistake when specifying file systems to be shared? (See "NFS.")
5. What makes FTP such a security concern? (See "FTP.")

Network Security and the Apache Server

Session Checklist

✔ Internet configuration files

✔ Internet configuration utilities

✔ The Apache server

**30 Min.
To Go**

This session discusses some of the primary utilities and configuration files used for UNIX networking. Additionally, a section on the Apache Web server briefly describes its installation and some general Web site security precautions.

Internet Configuration Files

Every Internet message contains three fundamental numbers that are required to route it to its destination:

- **IP address** — The IP address is a 32-bit number that the Internet uses to move the message from its source computer to its destination computer. This address is normally formatted for display, with each of its four byte values as base 10 numbers separated by periods, as in the address 64.70.141.88.

- **Protocol number** — The protocol number indicates the fundamental format of the message. There are many protocols, but most messages are sent as either Transmission Control Protocol (TCP) or User Datagram Protocol (UDP).

- **Port number** — The port number, in conjunction with the protocol number, specifies which application (often a daemon) is to receive the message. For example, port number 80 indicates that the message should be forwarded to the Web server.

The /etc/protocols file

An Internet message comes as a packet that is wrapped, like a sandwich, between a header and footer laid out in a very specific format. This format, known as a *protocol*, has a number that identifies it to the world of the Internet. To be able to recognize this format and unwrap the message, the computer must be able to recognize the number. The numbers that identify the wrapper formats are stored in a file named /etc/protocols.

The /etc/protocols file should never be modified because the numbers are standard throughout the Internet. The Internet will continue to work only as long as every computer agrees on these numbers.

If you take a look at the contents of the /etc/protocols file on your computer, you may be surprised by the number of protocols stored in it. Computers that are linked by an Internet are constantly using some of these protocols to gossip with one another to share address and routing information. If a new computer is added to the network, or an old computer dies, the information gets around very quickly.

There are dozens of special-purpose protocols. If you look in the /etc/protocols file, you will probably recognize TCP (number 6) and UDP (number 17), which are the protocols used most frequently to transmit data. The fundamental difference between TCP and UDP is that TCP is used to send a message when an answer is expected (for example, a request being made to a Web server that it respond with an HTML page), and UDP is designed to send messages that do not require an answer (as in the case of an e-mail message that arrives and is simply stored locally).

The /etc/services file

An Internet message is like an onion. Inside the outer TCP or UDP wrapper is another protocol wrapper that encases the actual message. The inner protocol is also identified by a number, known as the *service number*, and is defined in a file named /etc/services. The service number is also called the *port number*, which is the number used inside a computer to direct the message to its final destination.

Port numbers 0 through 1024 are standard values assigned by Internet Assigned Numbers Authority (IANA). These numbers are referred to as the *well known* port numbers and are used to make it easy to address specific services on a remote computer. For example, the HyperText Transfer Protocol (HTTP) of the World Wide Web is always on port number 80 and Simple Mail Transfer Protocol (SMTP) is always on port 25. The File Transfer Protocol (FTP) uses two port numbers — port number 21, which is used for requests and validation, and port number 20, which is used to transfer files.

The following are some example entries in the /etc/services file:

```
ftp-data    20/tcp
ftp-data    20/udp
ftp         21/tcp
ftp         21/udp
smtp        25/tcp    mail
smtp        25/udp    mail
domain      53/tcp    nameserver  # name-domain server
domain      53/udp    nameserver
http        80/tcp    www www-http
http        80/udp    www www-http
```

```
kerberos     88/tcp     kerberos5 krb5
kerberos     88/udp     kerberos5 krb5
snmp         161/tcp    # Simple Net Mgmt Proto
snmp         161/udp    # Simple Net Mgmt Proto
ldap         389/tcp
ldap         389/udp
https        443/tcp
https        443/udp
exec         512/tcp
biff         512/udp    comsat
login        513/tcp
router       520/udp    route routed     # RIP
uucp         540/tcp    uucpd        # uucp daemon
nfs          2049/tcp   nfsd
nfs          2049/udp   nfsd
```

Each line starts with the name of the protocol. The port numbers are assigned for a specific outer protocol (these examples are all either tcp or udp). On the right, you can see an optional list of alias names for service. Anything following the hash (#) character is a comment and is ignored.

Most of the port assignments are made using the same number for both TCP and UDP even if the particular service doesn't use both. For example, HTTPS is assigned port 443 for both, but it actually uses only TCP for its communications. Some port numbers are shared. For example, if a UDP message arrives for port 512, it is the Biff protocol (which is used to announce the arrival of mail). However, if a TCP message arrives for port 512, it is the EXEC (execute) protocol (which is used for remote program execution). The port numbers range from 0 to 65535, with 0 through 2048 reserved as the well known ports. Port numbers above 49,000 can be dynamically allocated and used by running processes.

You need to modify the /etc/services file only if you are going to be adding or changing a port number. For example, if you want to experiment with a second Web server on a machine that already has one, you could configure the second server for, say, port number 3000 by inserting the following line in the /etc/services file:

```
http        3000/tcp   #experimental web server
```

You can then address the experimental server from your Web browser with a URL format such as the following:

```
http://www.logwoos.net:3000/index.html
```

The /etc/hosts file

The hosts file contains static address information for computers on your local network, along with any other computers that you want to include. Whenever you refer to a computer by its name, the command you are using must have some way to translate that name into an IP address before a message can be sent. This same kind of translation is done on the Internet by sending a query to a *name server*, which performs this translation. Your Internet service provider (ISP) should provide you with the address of one or more name servers that you can use. If you use a dial-up connection, the address of a name server is normally returned to your computer as part of the initial connection sequence, but in some cases you must configure the address of the name server into the routing table described in the next section.

If you have a local network, you will need to provide each member of your network with the address of all the other members. If there are many computers on your local network, it is easiest to use one of them as a name server by configuring a daemon to respond to address requests and then configuring the other computers to send address queries to your local name server.

In a small network, you may want to simply store all the addresses on all the computers by including them in the /etc/hosts file. The following is an example of the contents of such a file:

```
127.0.0.1       localhost    localhost.localdomain
192.168.0.1     arlin        arlin.localdomain
192.168.0.3     rimshot      rimshot.localdomain
192.168.0.2     alice        alice.localdomain
209.61.177.22   ed2go        www.ed2go.com
```

The same list of addresses is required by every computer on the network, and a computer's own address can be included in the file, so the file can be duplicated everywhere on the network by simply copying it from one computer to another. Each line in the file contains an IP address, followed by a list of alias names for the computer. In this example, each computer can be located by its simple name, or by its domain name.

The first line of the file is always named localhost and always has the address 127.0.0.1. This special *loopback address* is used by programs on the local computer to address its own services. Any message sent to the address 127.0.0.1 will never leave the computer — it will turn around and be treated like any other incoming message.

The address space with the first three numbers 192.168.0 is a collection of special addresses. Addresses of this form are limited to the local network and are never sent out to the Internet at large. If all the computers on your LAN have addresses in this form, they cannot directly send or receive messages from outside the network. However, this does not prevent them from communicating through a firewall or being able to establish a dial-up link. A dial-up connection provides its own outside address, and a firewall translates between the internal and external addresses.

The last line in the example hosts file is that of a computer outside the local network. Outside addresses can be included for computers that are contacted often to prevent a remote address lookup every time. The disadvantage is that if the IP address of the remote host changes, contact with it will be lost until the address is corrected in the file.

**20 Min.
To Go**

The /etc/hosts.allow and /etc/hosts.deny files

When an Internet packet arrives, the contents of the hosts.allow file are scanned, and if a specific permission is found for the requested action, access is granted and no further checking is made. If the scan of the hosts.allow file did not specifically grant permission, the hosts.deny file is scanned, and if access is not specifically denied, it is granted. It is common to have one or both of the files empty.

The same syntax is used in both files. Each line specifies a service followed by a colon, which separates it from a list of hosts being granted or denied that particular service. The keyword ALL can be used to specify all services or all hosts. The following example closes a system — every service is denied to every host:

```
$ cat /etc/hosts.deny
ALL: ALL
```

The following example of hosts.allow begins by granting all permissions to every host in the local domain and every host in the domain named belugalake.com. All permissions are also granted to the computer with the IP address 209.61.177.22. Finally, HTTP Web service (specified by naming the daemon to receive the message) is granted to every host except the ones in the domain .hogwarts.net:

```
$ cat /etc/hosts.allow
ALL: LOCAL, .belugalake.com
ALL: 209.61.177.22
httpd: ALL EXCEPT .hogwarts.net
```

The following hosts.deny file will deny all access to the Web server. However, if this hosts.deny file is used along with the previous hosts.allow file, Web server access will have been granted to every host except .hogwarts.net. As a result, no other hosts will cause a look into the hosts.deny file. The second line of the file denies secure shell access to all but two specific hosts on the local network:

```
$ cat /etc/hosts.deny
httpd: ALL
sshd: ALL EXCEPT 192.168.0.2, 192.168.0.3
```

Internet Configuration Utilities

This section describes a set of fundamental UNIX utilities designed to configure and monitor networking. These utilities exist on all UNIX systems, but the capabilities and options for each will vary. Therefore, if you don't find what you want here, check the man page on your system. Networking is such an important part of most UNIX operating systems that most systems include, in addition to the standard utilities, a set of utilities written specifically for that system.

The ifconfig utility

It is likely that your computer is connected to a local network. The connection is usually made with an Ethernet card, but you could use a wireless connection, or even fiber optics. Local area network hardware has its own addressing scheme that has nothing to do with IP addresses. Every Ethernet card is shipped with its own unique address hard-wired into it. An Ethernet address is six bytes long and is usually represented as a series of six hexadecimal digits separated by colons, as follows:

```
08:00:07:a9:b2:2f
```

This number is very different from the IP address that is assigned to the computer and used for internet communications, so the IP address must somehow be translated to the

Ethernet address to get the message from one computer to another over the local connection. The mapping information between IP address and external address is managed by ifconfig. The program is normally only run at boot time to set up the addresses, but you can use it any time to take a peek at the address translations and the status of each connection, as follows:

```
$ ifconfig
eth0      Link encap:Ethernet  HWaddr 00:60:08:34:93:12
          inet addr:192.168.0.1  Bcast:192.168.0.255  Mask:255.255.255.0
          UP BROADCAST RUNNING MULTICAST  MTU:1500  Metric:1
          RX packets:2881343 errors:0 dropped:0 overruns:0 frame:0
          TX packets:6458365 errors:0 dropped:0 overruns:0 carrier:2
          collisions:885530 txqueuelen:100
          Interrupt:10 Base address:0x6900

lo        Link encap:Local Loopback
          inet addr:127.0.0.1  Mask:255.0.0.0
          UP LOOPBACK RUNNING  MTU:16436  Metric:1
          RX packets:2200 errors:0 dropped:0 overruns:0 frame:0
          TX packets:2200 errors:0 dropped:0 overruns:0 carrier:0
          collisions:0 txqueuelen:0

ppp0      Link encap:Point-to-Point Protocol
          inet addr:209.112.169.209  P-t-P:209.112.201.6
Mask:255.255.255.255
          UP POINTOPOINT RUNNING NOARP MULTICAST  MTU:1500  Metric:1
          RX packets:27614 errors:6 dropped:0 overruns:0 frame:0
          TX packets:27886 errors:2 dropped:0 overruns:0 carrier:0
          collisions:0 txqueuelen:3
```

This listing shows three active network connections. The first connection, named eth0, is an Ethernet connection made through a card with an address of 00:60:08:34:93:12. You can see that there has been a large number of packets transmitted and received (TX and RX) with no errors. There have been a large number of collisions, but that is to be expected because it is characteristic of an Ethernet — packets use collision to decide which one goes next.

The connection named lo is the local loopback connection that simply translates anything addressed to 127.0.0.1 to the IP address of the local host.

The connection named ppp0 is a dial-up link using Point-to-Point Protocol (PPP). It bears the IP address assigned to it by the Internet service provider (ISP). This connection shows that quite a few packets have been transmitted and received, and that few errors have been made. The number of errors shown is not out of the ordinary for a dial-up connection, but as you can see, no packets were dropped because of the automatic error correction in TCP/IP.

The arp utility

The arp (Address Resolution Protocol) utility can be used to display the address information of the computers on your local network. The following command was used on a system that was connected by an Ethernet card to two other computers. The information on the other machines includes both the IP address and the Ethernet address:

```
$ arp
Address                 HWtype  HWaddress            Flags Mask      Iface
alice.localhost         ether   52:54:00:E8:E3:22    C               eth0
rimshot.localhost       ether   00:50:4E:03:BD:6D    C               eth0
```

The contents of this table are used when sending messages to map destination IP addresses to Ethernet addresses.

The route utility

The route utility is used to specify where each message is to be sent. The routing is determined by a table that can be viewed by entering the route command with no arguments, as follows:

```
$ route
Kernel IP routing table
Destination     Gateway         Genmask         Flags Metric Ref    Use Iface
pm6.hom.alaska. *               255.255.255.255 UH    0      0        0 ppp0
192.168.0.0     *               255.255.255.0   U     0      0        0 eth0
127.0.0.0       *               255.0.0.0       U     0      0        0 lo
default         pm6.hom.alaska. 0.0.0.0         UG    0      0        0 ppp0
```

The destinations are listed in the first column and are addressed according to the masks in the third column. The second entry in the list causes all packets sent to any address in the form 192.160.0.x to be routed to eth0 because a genmask value of 0 causes it to accept any address value for that byte position. The next line uses the same technique to route any address beginning with 127 to lo. The first line directs all messages addressed to pm6.hom.alaska to be sent through the ppp0 link, and the last line specifies that the default (messages that haven't been specifically sent somewhere else) be sent to the gateway computer named pm6.hom.alaska, which is accessible through ppp0.

This routing table is dynamic. If you were to hang up from the PPP connection, the lines that direct messages to ppp0 would both be removed from the list and the computer would only be able to communicate over the local Ethernet and the loopback.

The route utility has command line options that make it possible for you to modify the table, but you should carefully read the man page on your system before you try to configure any routing. The process can be a bit confusing until you get the hang of it.

The netstat utility

The netstat (network status) utility can be used to display information about current network connections, routing tables, interface statistics, and more. You can display some of the same information with ifconfig and route, but netstat can display it in different formats with different levels of detail. The netstat utility can provide information that ifconfig and route cannot.

If you enter the netstat command with no options, you get a long list of all the current network connections and information about what they are doing. The -r option displays the routing table in the same format displayed by route, but there are options to modify the format. For example, if you specify the -n option, all the addresses listed are numeric instead of being listed by name. If you specify the -i option, the same information is displayed as when you use ifconfig, but you can use other options with the -i option to display more or different information. Most of the display options have a -v flag, for verbose, which causes extra information to be displayed.

The netstat command can be used quite effectively to explore your Internet configuration and help you analyze how it is being used.

The Apache Server

10 Min.
To Go

You can find a version of the Apache Web server for every UNIX operating system, and for many systems that are nothing like UNIX. Apache runs on several versions of Windows, NetWare, and even the old HP3000 operating system MPE. It has proven to be amazingly stable and has every feature that you might need for your Web site.

An Apache installation has four directory trees. You can install the directories wherever you like, but the following list contains some of the common locations:

- **Source** — The source code of Apache is stored in a directory named apache-1.3. You can put this directory in such places as $HOME/apache-1.3 or /usr/local/src/apache-1.3. You will only need this directory if you are not going to install a binary version but intend to compile Apache from source code instead.

- **Server root** — This directory contains the Apache software. Because the software is a collection of shared libraries, the directory is often named something like /usr/lib/apache or /usr/local/lib/apache.

- **Document root** — This directory contains all of the Web pages and CGI scripts that define the content of the Web site. This directory often uses the name /var/www, with subdirectories named /var/www/html to contain HTML files and /var/www/gci-bin to contain CGI scripts. The file named /var/www/html/index.html is the home page of the Web site.

- **Documentation** — The Apache system documentation is quite complete and, as you might suspect, is in HTML format. The documentation can be installed anywhere.

If your installation procedure does not provide the location of these directories, or if you are working on a machine that already has Apache installed, you can always find the directories with the following command:

```
$ find / -name "*apache*" -print 2>/dev/null
```

Installation

Because Apache is the most popular Web server in the world, your version of UNIX most likely comes with its own copy. If so, it should already be compiled and ready to install. There is probably an installation procedure in your system's documentation. If, on the other hand, you don't have a copy, or if you would like to get a later version, you can download Apache from the Internet and install it. To get your copy, go to the following Web site:

```
http://www.apache.org/dist
```

This page supplies links to other sites you can use to download a version for your operating system. You can download and install a binary version ready to install and run, or you can download the source code and compile your own. The name of a file tells you what it contains. The name always includes the Apache version number. It also includes the name of an operating system and whether it is a precompiled version ready to install and run. If no operating system is included with the name, it is a source code version and will have to be compiled.

If you download a binary version of Apache into the /tmp directory, it can be easily installed with the following set of commands:

```
$ cd /tmp
$ gunzip apache_1.3.22-systemname.tar.gz
$ tar xvf apache_1.3.22-systemname.tar
$ cd apache_1.3.22
$ ./install-bindist.sh /usr/local/lib/apache
```

The source is not installed (although you can find it in /tmp/apache_1.3.22). The last line of the command uses /usr/local/lib/apache as the Apache root directory, and stores the documentation in /usr/local/lib/apache/htdocs. Once you have located the documentation and opened it with your Web browser, everything you need to know is at your fingertips.

Security

When you set up a Web server you must, by definition, open the computer to a certain level of access to the outside world. For the most part, a Web server is secure because most incoming traffic is limited to simple page requests. But there are some possible holes and some precautions you should take to prevent attacks. First make sure that you always run the latest version of the Web server so that all security patches are in place.

The Web server should be run as a user with limited accessibility. Create a user in the /etc/passwd file that is in a group of its own and run it from there. That way, if a cracker finds some way through the Web browser, the damage will be limited to the files and directories that can be accessed by that user. At the very least, make certain that the server and none of its processes are run as root. The default installation usually sets this up with an entry in /etc/passwd like the following:

```
apache:x:48:48:Apache:/var/www:/bin/false
```

The portion of this entry that would normally specify the shell program instead specifies the /bin/false program, making it impossible for someone to log in as apache and get shell access.

Spend a little time looking at the configuration options and turn off anything you won't be using. In particular, do not allow CGI scripts to be run if they are not necessary because they are the most common method of entering a system. If you do run CGI scripts, they should be carefully written. A CGI script reads the information included with the incoming URL, and a poorly written script could be manipulated into doing things that the author did not intend. It is best to provide CGI as statically linked executable binaries instead of interpreted scripts, because it is more difficult to corrupt a binary. As part of your regular security rounds, check the programs stored in the CGI directory to make sure nothing has been added or modified.

Done!

REVIEW

This session provides you with a peek at the network configuration and introduces you to some Internet utilities.

- The /etc/protocols and /etc/services files contain the numeric values used to tag messages for identification.
- The /etc/hosts file contains a list of IP addresses — normally the ones on the local network.
- The /etc/hosts.allow and /etc/hosts.deny files control access to the network services of the local computer.
- The ifconfig utility displays the current network status.
- The arp utility displays the local area network addresses.
- The route utility displays the routing information to direct outgoing messages.
- The netstat utility displays information on the current status of the network.
- The Apache Web server can be freely downloaded and installed, and then used to operate a Web site.

The following session pulls together much of the information from previous sessions in the form of an explanation of the procedure UNIX follows to boot itself and start all the processes it is configured to run.

QUIZ YOURSELF

1. What three numbers are required to fully address an Internet packet to its destination? (See "Internet Configuration Files.")

2. What is the difference between the protocol numbers defined in /etc/protocols and those defined in /etc/services? (See "Internet Configuration Files.")

3. What is the difference between an IP address and an Ethernet address? (See "The ifconfig utility.")

4. What is the purpose of the entries in the hosts.allow and hosts.deny files? (See "The /etc/hosts.allow and /etc/hosts.deny files.")

5. What makes CGI scripts a point of vulnerability in your system? (See "Security.")

When UNIX Boots

Session Checklist

✔ In the beginning

✔ The UNIX kernel

✔ System initialization

✔ Running fsck

✔ Mounting devices

✔ The rc scripts

✔ Getty

✔ Shutdown

**30 Min.
To Go**

This session describes the process UNIX follows when it first starts running. The process of booting a computer is the sequence of events that occur from the time the computer is turned on until a prompt appears for a user to log in. Understanding the process required for UNIX to boot itself will take you a long way along the road of understanding UNIX as a whole.

The period of time between reboots of a UNIX system is normally measured in months, and often in years. As long as there is no hardware problem, power failure, or upgrade to a different or later version of the operating system, there is no need to boot the system. Installation of new software is only a matter of loading it into the machine and starting it running. System-level configuration changes are made by modifying a configuration file and then instructing the appropriate daemon to check the configuration settings.

In the Beginning

When a computer is first powered on, a small program executes to initialize the system. This program is stored in read-only memory (ROM), programmable read-only memory (PROM), non-volatile random access memory (NVRAM), or some other type of storage that is not erased when the power is shut off. This program is sometimes called the firmware, boot ROM, or the ROM BIOS (Basic Input/Output System).

The first task performed by the firmware is normally a memory test. This is followed by probes for fundamental devices such as the console terminal and disk drives. It is important that the firmware locate a disk drive (or some other data source) to use as the boot device. The firmware will determine the order in which the search is made. It may start by looking at the SCSI devices for a CD-ROM drive, then look around for a SCSI disk drive, and then move on to other kinds of drives. The search continues until it finds a disk drive that appears to hold a boot program. You can configure some computers to look for a network link to locate the boot program — this is known as a *diskless workstation*.

When a qualifying disk is located, the program found at that location is read into memory and control is turned over to it. This program may be the UNIX kernel, but it may just as well be an intermediate program in the boot sequence of one or two more steps.

If the computer is set up so it can be booted under more than one operating system, the program loaded from the boot sector of the disk is one that allows you to make a choice. It prompts you for input and starts running a timer. If the timer expires before you enter the name of the system you would like (or if you press Return), the default operating system is booted. This program then loads the program found at the location of the chosen operating system and turns control over to it.

Most UNIX systems use a two-stage boot sequence. The first program loaded is not the kernel itself, but instead is a small boot program that has only one job: Load the kernel into memory and turn control over to it.

The UNIX Kernel

The name and location of the kernel varies from one system to another. Some are in the root directory, while others are in a special subdirectory. With some systems, the name varies from one release to the next. Some of the more common names and locations are listed in Table 30-1.

Table 30-1   *Names and Locations of UNIX Kernels*

UNIX System	Kernel Path Names
AIX	/unix
BSD	/bsd
FreeBSD	/kernel
HP-UX	/hpux for version 9, /stand/vmunix for version 10 and later
IRIX	/unix

UNIX System	Kernel Path Names
Linux	Usually /boot/vmlinuz or /boot/bootlx
NetBSD	/netbsd
SCO	/unix
Solaris	The name can vary with each platform and version. It can be /kernel/genunix, /kernel/unix, /platform/version/kernel/unix, or /platform/version/kernel/sparcv9/unix.
SunOS	/vmunix
Tru64	/vmunix
Ultrix	/vmunix

At the very beginning, the kernel has a number of tasks to perform to get things set up. A check is made to see how much memory is available. The kernel then probes for devices attached to the computer. It locates the root and swap partitions on disk and then locates the /dev directory so it will be able to communicate with devices.

You may have noticed a conflict here. The device nodes in the /dev directory are used to access disk drives, but the /dev directory itself resides on one of the drives. To be able to do this, the kernel cheats a bit by having the locations of the fundamental devices configured into itself. This configuration is something that happens as UNIX is being installed. This preconfigured kernel is also the reason why rearranging disk drives and partitions entails a bit more than just changing the file names and locations — the kernel must be reconfigured so that it can find the things it needs at the start.

Once the kernel has gathered up all of this fundamental information, it builds some tables in memory that will be used to contain information on running processes, memory allocation, file accesses, interprocess communications, and so on. As soon as the kernel is ready to manage things, it starts a few processes to handle some special tasks.

Different kernels use different sets of program to perform system tasks, but the tasks themselves are fairly common across all systems. Some kernels choose to perform the tasks themselves instead of starting other processes to do them, but all kernels spawn some tasks. You can see these tasks on your system by entering the following command:

```
$ ps aux | more
```

The kernel tasks are the ones that show up with PID numbers of 0, 1, 2, going up as high as 7 or 8.

The scheduler task

The scheduler, sometimes called the swapper, keeps track of the process priorities, when and how long each process has been running, and decides which process is to run next and how much time it is to have. Several algorithms can be used to handle this job, but the basic procedure is to let a process run for its full time slice unless it starts doing some input or output — at which time the I/O request is put through and the next process on the list begins execution.

The paging task

The paging process manages the space allocated to each process loaded into memory. If a process is idle for a time and some other running process needs some space, the idle process has all or part of itself stored in the swap space on disk while the active process uses the memory. When the idle process needs to start running again, it is pulled from disk back into memory (not necessarily into the same location) and started running again.

It is this paging that allows UNIX to run many daemon processes with almost no overhead. A daemon sitting and waiting for input remains swapped out to disk until some input arrives to cause it to be loaded back into memory. Until such input arrives, the daemon is not taking up system time or memory.

The init task

The init task always has PID number 1, and it is the parent (grandparent, great-grandparent, and so on) of every process in the system except the kernel.

Among the responsibilities of init is the job of starting all other programs that are run on the system. Whenever a command is entered to start a program running, that command is passed on to the init process, which actually starts the new process running.

System Initialization

The init process begins by reading the file /etc/inittab and using the information it finds to start other processes. The following is an example of an /etc/inittab file used on Red Hat Linux version 6.2:

```
#
# inittab       This file describes how the INIT process should set up
#               the system in a certain run-level.
#
# Author:       Miquel van Smoorenburg, <miquels@drinkel.nl.mugnet.org>
#               Modified for RHS Linux by Marc Ewing and Donnie Barnes
#

# Default runlevel. The runlevels used by RHS are:
#   0 - halt (Do NOT set initdefault to this)
#   1 - Single user mode
#   2 - Multiuser, without NFS (The same as 3, if you do not have networking)
#   3 - Full multiuser mode
#   4 - unused
#   5 - X11
#   6 - reboot (Do NOT set initdefault to this)
#
id:3:initdefault:

# System initialization.
si::sysinit:/etc/rc.d/rc.sysinit

l0:0:wait:/etc/rc.d/rc 0
l1:1:wait:/etc/rc.d/rc 1
l2:2:wait:/etc/rc.d/rc 2
l3:3:wait:/etc/rc.d/rc 3
```

```
l4:4:wait:/etc/rc.d/rc 4
l5:5:wait:/etc/rc.d/rc 5
l6:6:wait:/etc/rc.d/rc 6

# Things to run in every runlevel.
ud::once:/sbin/update

# Trap CTRL-ALT-DELETE
ca::ctrlaltdel:/sbin/shutdown -t3 -r now

# When our UPS tells us power has failed, assume we have a few minutes
# of power left.  Schedule a shutdown for 2 minutes from now.
# This does, of course, assume you have powerd installed and your
# UPS connected and working correctly.
pf::powerfail:/sbin/shutdown -f -h +2 "Power Failure; System Shutting Down"

# If power was restored before the shutdown kicked in, cancel it.
pr:12345:powerokwait:/sbin/shutdown -c "Power Restored; Shutdown Cancelled"


# Run gettys in standard runlevels
1:2345:respawn:/sbin/mingetty tty1
2:2345:respawn:/sbin/mingetty tty2
3:2345:respawn:/sbin/mingetty tty3
4:2345:respawn:/sbin/mingetty tty4
5:2345:respawn:/sbin/mingetty tty5
6:2345:respawn:/sbin/mingetty tty6

# Run xdm in runlevel 5
# xdm is now a separate service
x:5:respawn:/etc/X11/prefdm -nodaemon
```

**20 Min.
To Go**

In the /etc/inittab file, all of the lines beginning with a hash (#) character are comments. Toward the top of the file, the comments list short descriptions of run levels numbered 0 through 6. The init process uses one of these run levels to initialize the system:

- **Run level 0** halts the system immediately and does not reboot.
- **Run level 1** is a single user mode that allows only one login. This mode is used only in special circumstances, usually for the superuser to log in and to recover files or configure fundamental system settings.
- **Run level 2** is the same as level 3, except NFS file sharing is disabled.
- **Run level 3** is used whenever a UNIX computer is to be run normally with standard text-based terminals.
- **Run level 4** is unused.
- **Run level 5** is also a fully functional level, but the interface is through the X Window System instead of command line terminals.
- **Run level 6** halts the system immediately and reboots.

In the /etc/inittab file, each command line consists of a series of fields, separated by colons, in the following format:

```
id:runlevels:action:process
```

The id field is a unique identifier of the line. The runlevels field is made up of one or more characters identifying the run level, or levels, for which this command line is to be applied. The action field is the instruction keyword that specifies what is to be done. The process field is the name of the program to which the action is to be applied.

The first command in the file specifies the default run level:

```
id:5:initdefault:
```

This example sets the default run level to 5, but the default can be overridden by passing a different number to the init process. When UNIX boots, the default run level is always used, but it is possible to change the run level after UNIX has been booted. Doing so is rather drastic because the process of switching run levels involves killing all logins and many other running processes (exempt from this are the kernel and the fundamental process it runs as assistants). Initiating a level switch is simply a matter of instructing the init process to execute the commands in /etc/inittab. For example, if you are currently running the system at run level 3 and doing everything from the command line, you can switch to a windowing environment by switching to the root user and executing the telinit command, as follows:

```
$ su -
Password:
% telinit 5
```

This command results in your session (and all other sessions) being immediately logged out because the shell processes are halted. The init process will then read the /etc/inittab file and start all the processes that are supposed to be started for the new run level.

In the example inittab file listed earlier, note the following line:

```
si::sysinit:/etc/rc.d/rc.sysinit
```

This action, named sysinit, executes the named script for every run level, but only during an initial boot. Using telinit to change the run levels will not execute rc.sysinit. The rc.sysinit file is usually a very long shell script that performs some fundamental system-wide initializations. It begins by turning on system logging. It sets some of the fundamental environment variables, such as the default PATH and the HOSTNAME. Some systems use this script to display a banner on the terminals stating that the system is coming up. It is even possible for this script to prompt the user for some option or other, but these prompts should always time out and use a default so the boot process can continue unattended.

 Many of the startup scripts have the letters rc in their names because early versions of UNIX were configured by a single script named /etc/rc. The letters stand for "run command."

Some of the jobs performed by rc.sysinit are the setting of the UNIX system clock according to the hardware clock, setting the font according to the internationalization settings, checking the disk drives for errors, and if the drives are okay, mounting the disk drives as part of the file system accessible from applications.

One very useful cleanup job performed by rc.sysinit is to remove leftover work files from the /tmp directory. Many processes store work files in this directory, and if they are still present during the boot process they should be deleted. There was a time when the directory was simply cleaned out every time the system rebooted, but a more modern approach checks the date stamp on the files and compares it against the current date to determine which ones to delete. Thus, if you are using a utility that is using /tmp for its work files when the plug is pulled on the system, the file will still be present after the reboot, allowing you to recover your data.

The script /etc/rc.d/rc is executed with the ID of the run level passed to it. In the /etc/inittab file, it is executed by a wait action, which causes init to pause and wait while the script is being executed.

Certain other system level actions are specified in /etc/inittab, such as trapping Ctrl+Alt+Del so it can't be used to bring down the system. The powerfail and powerokwait actions are used to specify the steps to be taken if the uninterruptible power supply (UPS) reports a power failure. The final line in /etc/inittab uses the rspawn action to start the processes that prompt for logins. Starting a process with respawn causes it to automatically restart whenever you log out by shutting down your shell program. The last line of the file starts the X login prompt, but only if the run level is 5.

Running fsck

The rc.sysinit script runs fsck (file system check) to check the integrity of each file system, but only if it has a reason to do so. If the last time the system went down was the result of a crash — meaning that the disk drives were not cleanly closed and unmounted — the boot process detects that fact and instructs fsck to scan the file system. The fsck scan will also run if a sufficient amount of time has passed since the last time the disk was scanned.

The errors fsck normally finds are fragments that are not properly connected by i-nodes to the free space. This happens when memory resident portions of the file system don't get written to disk before the system shuts down. The program fsck can safely repair this kind of error, so it goes ahead and fixes it and the boot process continues.

If an error is found that requires some kind of decision to be made, the boot process halts and you are instructed to run fsck manually to repair the disk. If the error is found on some drive other than the boot drive, the boot process will continue when you respond to the prompt, but that drive will not be mounted. You are able to log in as the superuser and run fsck. If, on the other hand, an error of this kind is found on the boot drive, you will need to reboot using some other means (a floppy or a CD), then log in as root and use fsck to repair the problem.

Take a few minutes to read the man page of fsck for your system so you will know how to use it if the time ever comes that you need it. If you can't get to your disk drive, it's too late to read the man page.

Mounting Devices

Disk drives that fsck reports as being okay are mounted to become part of the file system. This is done by entering the following simple command:

```
$ mount -a
```

The mount utility reads the list of disks and directories in the file /etc/fstab to find out how to mount each device as a directory. The following is an example of an fstab file:

```
/dev/hda5                /               ext2    defaults           1 1
/dev/hda1                /boot           ext2    defaults           1 2
/dev/cdrom               /mnt/cdrom      iso9660 noauto,owner,ro    0 0
/dev/fd0                 /mnt/floppy     ext2    noauto,owner       0 0
/dev/hdb1                /home           ext2    defaults           1 2
/SWAP                    swap            swap    defaults           0 0
alice:/home              /mnt/alice      nfs     rw                 0 0
alice:/var/cache/packages /var/cache/packages nfs rw              0 0
```

The first column holds the name of the device node of the device to be mounted. The one named /SWAP is the swap space and is part of the operating system configuration. The last two entries in the first column are the names of directories on a remote computer. The computer name must be included in the /etc/hosts file, and all the appropriate NFS permissions must be in place before it will actually mount.

The second column holds the name of an empty local directory that is to be used as the mount point for the device. The /mnt directory is commonly used as the mount point of removable devices such as floppies and CD-ROMs.

The third column is the file type of the device being mounted. The ext2 file type is the name of one version of the Linux file system. The iso9660 file system is the standard used by CD-ROMs. The swap type is internal to the system. The nfs type is the NFS file systems.

The fourth column is the set of permissions and other characteristics of the mounted file system. The two NFS mounts are assigned both read and write permissions, so the remote disk can be accessed as if it were a local disk controlled by the permissions settings of each file and directory. The floppy disk and CD-ROM drives are both declared as noauto (which means neither will automatically mount when a new disk is inserted) and owner (the owner of the mounted file system is set to be the same as the owner of the device node). The CD-ROM is also tagged as ro (read only).

Adding a new device is simply a matter of physically attaching it to the computer, rebooting the system, adding the appropriate line to this file, and entering the mount command with the -a option.

The rc Scripts

**10 Min.
To Go**

The part of the boot procedure you will find yourself working with most often is the scripts in the directory /etc/rc.d. The main script, named /etc/rc.d/rc, is executed with a single argument specifying the run level. It executes all of the scripts necessary for that run level.

The directory named /etc/rc.d/init.d contains a collection of scripts, each of which follows the same basic format and each of which can be used to start and stop a daemon. For example, a script named crond can be used to both start and stop the cron daemon; a script named nfsd can be used to start and stop the NFS daemon; the httpd script can be used to start and stop the Web server daemon; and so on. Exactly which scripts need to be executed depends on the run level because the different run levels require different combinations of daemons.

Inside the /etc/rc.d directory is a set of directories that are named rc0.d through rc6.d — one directory for each run level. Inside each of these directories, you will find symbolic links to each of the scripts in init.d. All of these link names start with either K or S and two digits, like this:

```
$ ls /etc/rc.d/rc3.d
K03rhnsd@       K65identd@      S13portmap@     S45pcmcia@      S85gpm@
K20rstatd@      K73ypbind@      S16apmd@        S56rawdevices   S86nfslock@
K20rusersd@     K96irda@        S17keytable@    S56xinetd@      S90crond@
K20rwhod@       S05kudzu@       S20nfsd@        S60lpd@         S90xfs@
K45arpwatch@    S08ipchains@    S20random@      S80httpd@       S99linuxconf@
K55routed@      S10network@     S25netfs@       S80sendmail@    S99local@
K61ldap@        S12syslog@      S40atd@         S83smb@
```

The scripts are executed in the order they are listed in the directory, so by adjusting these prefixes, you can specify the order in which the scripts are executed, and whether the daemon is to be started or stopped. Each script beginning with K (kill) is run with the stop option, and any script starting with S (start) is run with the start option. The two-digit numbers simply determine the order of the stops and starts.

If a daemon is not running, running the script to stop it will have no effect, and if it is already running, trying to start it will have no effect. Using the telinit command to switch from one run level to the next will stop all of the daemons that should not be running at the new level, and will start the ones that should be running.

Getty

Several lines in the rc.sysinit script look like this:

```
1:2345:respawn:/sbin/mingetty tty1
```

A getty (short for "Get TTY," and pronounced GET-ee) is a process that monitors a port connected to a terminal to ensure that a program is controlling the port. If no program is running, it starts one named login that prompts for a login name and password. If the login process gets a valid user name and password, the login process replaces itself with a shell program using the information from /etc/passwd to determine which shell to use and what the user ID and group ID are to be.

As long as the shell continues to be in charge of the terminal, nothing else happens with the getty. However, if the shell process dies (which is what happens when you log out) the getty process is respawned, starts the login process again, and the prompt on the terminal looks like the following:

```
login:
```

Shutdown

If you recall the run levels defined in /etc/inittab, you will remember that two levels are used to shut the system down. The following command shuts the system down and has it reboot immediately:

```
$ telinit 6
```

The following command brings the system down immediately, and will not reboot:

```
$ telinit 0
```

The best way to bring the system down is to use the shutdown command, which does some tidying up and then switches to the appropriate run level. The shutdown utility is especially useful if you are bringing down a multiuser system, because you can specify a time in the future when the system is to come down, and shutdown will notify the users that a system halt is imminent. The -r option causes an immediate reboot (run level 6), and the -h option shuts the system down with no reboot (run level 0). The following command brings the system down at the specified time:

```
$ shutdown -h 15:50:00
```

The exact wording will vary from one system to the next, but the sequence of messages displayed to each user looks something like this:

```
Broadcast from root Wed Mar 13 15:43:20 2002...
The system is going down for system halt in 7 minutes.
    . . .
Broadcast from root Wed Mar 13 15:49:20 2002...
The system is going down for system halt in 1 minute.
    . . .
Broadcast from root Wed Mar 13 15:50:20 2002...
The system is going down for system halt NOW!
```

Done!

REVIEW

This session introduces you to the fundamentals of booting a UNIX system:

- **Step 1:** The firmware loads a boot program from disk.
- **Step 2:** The boot program loads the UNIX kernel.
- **Step 3:** The kernel verifies the hardware and starts its helper processes.
- **Step 4:** The disk drives are checked and mounted.
- **Step 5:** The daemon processes are started.
- **Step 6:** The users are prompted to log in.

You should now have a reasonable grasp of the structure and operation of the UNIX operating system. From now on, as you discover more commands and learn more about the bits and pieces of UNIX, you will understand how they fit into the overall context of the structure of UNIX. The knowledge you have gained here can be applied to any version of UNIX that you encounter.

QUIZ YOURSELF

1. How can disk drives be accessed before UNIX has actually checked and mounted the drives? (See "In the Beginning.")

2. What primary task does `init` perform after UNIX is up and running? (See "The init task.")

3. What is a run level? (See "System Initialization.")

4. How are daemons started and stopped? (See "The rc Scripts.")

5. Why should you use `shutdown` instead of `telinit` to halt the system? (See "Shutdown.")

PART

VI

Sunday Afternoon

1. What command can you enter to use `gzip` to compress a file named `glimmer.html`, and what is the name of the compressed version of the file?

2. What command can you use to create a file named `saveall.zip` that contains all of the files and directories in the current directory?

3. What command can you enter to create a tar file named `hinkl.tar` that contains all the files in a subdirectory named `hinkel`?

4. What command can you enter to generate a listing of the files and directories stored in a tar file named `hinkl.tar` and have the listing include the file permissions information?

5. What can you deduce about the files named `ezra.tar.Z`, `lemual.tar.z`, and `otho.tar.gz`?

6. What is a firewall?

7. What does it mean to have a firewall filter data packets?

8. Why are the words `applebutter` and `sasquatch` not good for use as passwords?

9. Why is the FTP server such a security concern?

10. What does the following command do?

    ```
    $ rpcinfo -p
    ```

11. Many port numbers are defined in the `/etc/services` file. The first 1024 of them are reserved for what purpose?

12. Under what circumstances would you want to list the name and IP address of a computer in the `/etc/hosts` file?

13. What sort of address translation is necessary to transmit a message from one application to another over an Ethernet link?

14. The route utility displays a routing table. What is the purpose of this table?

15. What are the two fundamental methods of installing an Apache server?

16. What do you know about a task if its PID number is 1?

17. In the file named /etc/inittab, what is the significance of the following line?

```
id:5:initdefault:
```

18. What is the purpose of the program named fsck?

19. What is a getty?

20. What do the letters rc stand for?

APPENDIX A

Answers to Part Reviews

This appendix contains the answers to the review questions that appear at the end of each part in the book. Think of these reviews as mini-tests designed to help you prepare for the final exam — the Skills Assessment Test on the CD.

Friday Evening Review Answers

1. UNIX originated at AT&T's Bell Labs. The company was unable to sell the early versions of UNIX because it was a regulated monopoly, and the government prohibited the sale as a possible monopolistic practice.

2. The fundamental duties of the UNIX kernel are starting processes, running processes, halting processes, allocating dynamic memory, and responding to system calls made from the running processes.

3. A process running on UNIX cannot interfere with the kernel of the operating system or with any other running process, because the kernel prohibits a process from addressing memory outside of the specific block of memory allocated to that process.

4. A shell is the program that prompts a user for commands and then obeys the commands by starting other programs running or by making system calls to the kernel. A few commands are built into the shell.

5. Telnet is an Internet protocol that allows a user on one computer to log in to another computer. Telnet uses a piece of software to make the connection and then emulates a terminal. On the host computer, a shell is run that sends characters to, and receives keystrokes from, the remote computer.

6. There is no standard appearance or standard form for a graphic window login dialog box. It must provide a way for users to enter their user name and password, but other than that, the dialog box can consist of just about anything.

7. For the shell to be able to locate a program entered from the command line the directory containing the program must be included in the list of directories

contained in the PATH environment variable. The PATH variable can be modified to include any set of directories.

8. A hidden file is one that has a name beginning with a period. The term *hidden file* refers to the fact that the ls command normally does not display the name. To have its name listed, the -a option can be specified on ls.

9. The echo command is a simple utility that copies the command line text to standard output.

10. The who command displays the user name of anyone who is currently logged in, the date the login was initiated, and the port the user's terminal is using.

11. The bin directories all contain executable programs.

12. The pair of dots (. .) refers to the parent directory of the current directory. Therefore, if you use two dots to refer to your home directory, the current directory is an immediate subdirectory of your home directory.

13. File permissions can be set for the owner of a file, the other members of the owner's group, and for everyone else.

14. If the find command is supplied with an asterisk in the file name, the name must be entered in such a way that the shell will not process them. The asterisk must be escaped by a backslash, or the entire file name must be enclosed in quotes.

15. The file command uses the contents of a file named magic that contains locations of special values that determine the meaning of the data.

16. The ps command outputs a list of the currently executing processes. The list includes the status of each process and additional information about each one.

17. A PID is a process ID number that uniquely identifies a single process. A PPID is the PID of a parent process.

18. Any command can be run as a background process by adding an ampersand (&) at the end of the command line.

19. If process 5211 refuses to halt by being sent the default SIGTERM signal, you should be able to kill with the SIGKILL signal, as follows:

```
$ kill -9 5211
```

20. A process that has died for any reason will become a zombie unless it can report its exit status to its parent process. If the parent process isn't listening, the zombie will persist.

Saturday Morning Review Answers

1. The vi editor is a modal editor because it is always operating in one of three modes: the edit mode enables the entering of text, the navigation mode enables cursor positioning in the text, and command line mode enables the entry of editing commands.

2. The yank buffer of the vi editor is temporary storage that holds any characters deleted or copied from the text. The p command can be used to read the yank buffer and insert the characters into the document text.

3. In the vi editor, the character u will immediately undo the previous edit. Traditionally, only one level of undo is available, but some modern vi editors can undo a number of commands.

4. Any key description beginning with C- indicates that the Control key should be held down. The sequence C-x C-c means that you should hold down the Ctrl key while typing the letter x and then the letter c.

5. In emacs, the Meta key is something like the Ctrl key, in that you hold it down while striking another key to modify the meaning of the other key. Not all keyboards have a Meta key, and on some keyboards it is labeled Edit or Alt.

6. Nothing must be done to activate the mouse for the emacs editor. If it is available, the emacs editor will respond to it.

7. In the emacs editor, the indicator of the current text position is called the point. The point is subtly different from a cursor because a cursor indicates a specific character position while the point indicates the space between the characters immediately to the left of the indicated character.

8. To define an environment variable in the Bourne Shell named LASTDIR that contains the string /home/max/prev, you enter the following command:

```
$ LASTDIR=/home/max/prev
```

9. The following command produces a count of the number of files in the current directory:

```
$ ls | wc -w
```

The ls command produces a list of the file names, which is piped to the input of the wc command. The wc command with the -w option outputs only a count of the number of words it receives as input.

10. To list the names of all files in the current directory that begin with J and contain va, enter the following command:

```
$ ls J*va*
```

11. Sourcing a script is having a shell program read and execute it as if the commands in the script were entered directly from the keyboard. That is, no child shell is started to run the commands in the script. For example, to source a script named daysets, you would use the dot command like this:

```
$ . daysets
```

Some shells use the keyword source instead of the dot, in which case the command looks like the following:

```
$ source daysets
```

12. An environment variable is a name that contains a string value. One way to remove its definition is to simply define it as not containing a string, and the shell will drop it. For example, the removal of a variable named MYVAR could be done like this:

```
$ MYVAR=
```

In the C Shell, you use the set command to do the same thing:

```
$ set MYVAR=
```

Another option is to use the built-in unset command as follows:

```
$ unset MYVAR
```

13. The following command stores the string from the date utility into an environ-
    ment variable named TSTAMP:

    ```
    $ TSTAMP=`date`
    ```

    Note that the quotes around date are the grave accent marks (back tics).

14. The Bourne Shell and the Korn Shell both read the /etc/profile script and then
    the ~/.profile script whenever the user logs in.

15. The following command line defines an alias named lhome that lists the files in
    your home directory.

    ```
    $ alias lhome 'ls ~/*'
    ```

16. The following command line defines a function named lhome that lists the files in
    your home directory:

    ```
    $ function lhome {
    >    ls ~/*
    >}
    ```

17. In the Korn Shell and the Bourne-Again Shell, you can use the following command
    to set the editing mode so that it uses editing commands from the emacs editor:

    ```
    $ set -o emacs
    ```

    Or the editing mode can be set so that it uses editing commands from the vi editor
    with the following command:

    ```
    $ set -o vi
    ```

18. The simplest command that lists the occurrences of the word color in a collection
    of HTML files is:

    ```
    $ grep color *.html
    ```

    However, if you want only the file names — rather than each line on which the
    word occurs — you can use the following command:

    ```
    $ grep -l color *.html
    ```

19. The following command searches through the file HamNum and displays every line
    containing a word that begins with a J followed by one or more digits:

    ```
    $ grep 'J[0-9]' HamNum
    ```

20. The following command searches through the file HamNum and displays every line
    ending with nto and every line ending with nxo:

    ```
    $ grep 'n[tx]o$' HamNum
    ```

Saturday Afternoon Review Answers

1. To change the permissions on a file limwid in order to provide yourself with the
   permissions necessary to read, write, and execute the file, but only permit anyone
   else to execute the file, enter the following command:

   ```
   $ chmod 711 limwd
   ```

   The octal digit 7 provides read, write, and execute permissions to the file's owner.
   The octal digit 1 specifies execute-only permissions for the group and for all
   others. The bits match the following permissions flags:

```
-rwx--x--x
-111001001
```

2. A umask value of 033 means that a newly created file is prevented from being assigned execution and write permissions for the file's group members or any other users. The umask bit patterns match permissions flags as follows:

```
-rwxrwxrwx
-000011011
```

3. A hard link is a directory entry that contains a name of a file and the address of the actual data on the local disk drive. A symbolic link is a directory entry that contains a name for the file and the address of a special file type that contains the details for accessing the actual file data, which may be on a different disk drive.

4. Entering the mount command with no arguments lists all of the currently mounted file sytems.

5. A dumb terminal is a physical device made up of a keyboard and a screen for displaying characters. A pseudo terminal is a window opened in the X environment that acts like a dumb terminal by displaying characters and accepting input from the keyboard.

6. A character device is anything that can handle one byte at a time, such as a keyboard or a display screen. A block device is anything that can handle an entire block of data at once, such as a disk drive or a CD-ROM drive. Some devices can do both, such as a tape drive.

7. The file system is mounted, not the disk drive. Mounting a disk assigns an existing directory name to the disk so that you can start using commands such as cd to change directories and ls to list files. Without a file system, none of this would work.

8. The more utility enables you to view a file by moving forward through it one line, or one page, at a time. The less utility does the same, but it also allows you to move backward.

9. The UNIX clock is accurate to only one second (although it is possible for programs to track subsecond durations). The utility that sets the clock is named date and can only be done with root permissions.

10. The ASCII character set assigns a unique number to each character. Placing characters in order by this number means placing them in lexicographic order. The order is somewhat alphabetic, but there are some oddities (such as all uppercase letters preceding lowercase letters).

11. Both man and xman display the documentation stored in the man pages. The man utility is invoked from the command line, which allows you to scroll through the text on the screen. The xman utility is a graphical interface that displays the documentation in a window and allows you to use a scroll bar to move through it.

12. Setting the MANPATH environment variable to a list of directory names instructs the man utility to ignore any other default or configured list of directories and use only the MANPATH list. The directories are listed in the same format as those in the PATH variable. That is, you can name as many directories as you want, separated by colons. For example:

```
MANPATH=/usr/share/man:/usr/local/man:/var/cache/man
export MANPATH
```

13. Documents of the same name do appear in more than one section, so you may need to specify the section in which you want to search. The following example limits the search for the term clock to Section 3:

```
$ man 3 clock
```

14. Outgoing e-mail messages can be piped into either mail or elm, and they are sent without further action required on the part of the sender. The pine program cannot do this because pine always displays a formatted screen and prompts the user for more information.

15. The at-sign in an e-mail address is used to separate the user name from the name of the user's host computer. If no at-sign is present, the entire address is assumed to be the name of a user on the local machine.

16. To use mail to send a message to more than one recipient, you can name all the recipients on the command line, or you can define them as aliases in either the /etc/aliases file or the $HOME/.mailrc file.

17. The write command can be used to send a message to a single user and, possibly, to establish two-way communications with that user. The wall command sends a message to every person currently logged in.

18. The following script duplicates all of the HTML files in the current directory into a subdirectory named pageback:

```
#!/bin/sh
# pback - copy all *.html files to pageback
mkdir pageback 2>/dev/null
cp *.html pageback
```

19. The following script uses formatted output of the date command to display the name of the current day of the week:

```
#!/bin/sh
# today -- print the day of the week
date +%A
```

20. The following shell script uses the output from ls to store the names of all the files of the current directory into a variable named FNAME, and then uses echo to display them:

```
#!/bin/sh
# allfiles - store file names in FNAMES
FNAMES=`ls`
echo $FNAMES
```

Saturday Evening Review Answers

1. The following script displays the first two strings on the command line, or displays only one if the strings are identical:

```
#!/bin/sh
# showunlike -- display both strings only if the two are
#       not identical.
if [ "$1" != "$2" ]; then
```

```
        echo $1 $2
else
        echo $1
fi
exit 0
```

2. The following script uses name suffixes to detect Web pages and Java applets:

```
#!/bin/sh
# detect -- Check to see if the name is either that of
#    an HTML Web page or a Java applet.
case $1 in
*class)
        echo $1 is an applet.
        ;;
*htm | *html)
        echo $1 is a Web page.
        ;;
*)
        echo $1 is an unknown type.
        ;;
esac
exit 0
```

3. The following script copies a file to the /tmp directory only if the file is executable:

```
#!/bin/sh
# copyx -- If the named file is executable copy it
#    to the /tmp directory.
if [ -x $1 ];
then
        cp $1 /tmp/$1
fi
exit 0
```

4. The first line of a well-written script contains the full path name of the shell (or other program) that is to run the script. The path name should be preceded by the #! character pair. The last line should be an exit command.

5. The following script prints Eureka! if the environment variable MUGGLES contains the name of a directory:

```
#!/bin/sh
if [ -d $MUGGLES ]
then
        echo Eureka!
fi
exit 0
```

6. A shell script that displays all the parameters from the command line can be written many ways, but the following script is probably the simplest:

```
#!/bin/sh
for PARM
do
```

```
        echo $PARM
done
exit 0
```

7. The following shell script is one way to display all of the file names in the /tmp directory:

```
#!/bin/sh
TLIST=`ls /tmp/*`
for FNAME in $TLIST
do
    echo $FNAME
done
exit 0
```

8. The following shell script displays each word in the environment variable MYLIST on a line of its own:

```
#!/bin/sh
# mylist - Display each word stored in MYLIST
for MYWORD in $MYLIST
do
    echo $MYWORD
done
exit 0
```

To have the MYLIST environment variable available to the script, it must be both defined and exported as follows:

```
MYLIST="glimmer weave river mugwump"
export MYLIST
```

9. The following shell script changes the permissions on all files in the current directory that end with scpt so they are executable by everyone:

```
#!/bin/sh
# setex - Make all files ending with scpt executable.
FILELIST=`ls *scpt`
for SFILE in $FILELIST
do
    chmod a+x $SFILE
done
exit 0
```

10. The sleep command causes the current shell (whether executed from a script or from the command line) to pause for the specified number of seconds.

11. The name of the home directory for a user is stored in the file named /etc/passwd.

12. The /etc/passwd file must be readable by anyone so utility programs are able to read it to identify and locate other users.

13. A user ID is unique to that one user — it is a synonym for the user name. A group ID can be assigned to any number of users, and is used to allow a specific group of users file accesses that are unique to them.

14. A shadow file is a file that contains user login passwords and can only be read by processes with root permissions, which makes it more difficult to crack.

15. The word DoorKnob is in the dictionary, so it is subject to a dictionary attack. Even with the capital letters mixed in (a good way to make a password more secure), it is still vulnerable to a dictionary attack.

16. The following command translates every letter Z into a Q, and every letter J into a P:

    ```
    $ tr 'ZJ' 'QP'
    ```

17. The following command deletes the fourth line from a file named infour and writes the results to a file named outfour:

    ```
    $ sed '4d' <infour >outfour
    ```

18. The following sed script changes every occurrence of the word rain to the word snow, but does not change the words train or raindrop:

    ```
    $ sed 's/[^a-z]rain[^a-z]/snow/g' <infile >outfile
    ```

19. The following shell script replaces all occurrences of the word Internet with the word internet for all files in the current directory. The output files are assigned the same names as the input files, but they are stored in a subdirectory named lowcase.

    ```
    #!/bin/sh
    rm -rf lowcase
    mkdir lowcase
    FLIST=`ls`
    for FNAME in $FLIST
    do
        sed s/Internet/internet/g <$FNAME >lowcase/$FNAME
    done
    exit 0
    ```

20. The following sed command deletes everything from the beginning of the input file through the first line that contains the word dragon:

    ```
    $ sed '1,/dragon/d' <infile >outfile
    ```

Sunday Morning Review Answers

1. The following awk program displays the line number, followed by the line itself, for any line with more than five fields:

   ```
   $NF > 5 { print NR, $0 }
   ```

2. The following awk program displays the sum of all the values in the third field of all input lines:

   ```
   { total = total + $3 }
   END { print total }
   ```

3. The following awk program counts the number of blank lines in a file and prints the total:

   ```
   NF == 0 { total = total + 1 }
   END {print total }
   ```

4. The following Perl program displays the number of arguments on the command line and then displays the first argument:

```
#!/usr/bin/perl
$count=$#ARGV + 1;
print "$count\n";
print "$ARGV[0]\n";
```

It is necessary to add 1 to the value extracted from @ARGV because the value returned is the maximum index, and indexes begin with zero.

5. The following Perl script populates an array with four values and then displays all four values:

```
#!/usr/bin/perl
@value=("hammer","cannon","cone","sunset");
print "$value[0]\n";
print "$value[1]\n";
print "$value[2]\n";
print "$value[3]\n";
```

The display of the array members could also be done in a loop.

6. The following Perl script passes the number 10 to a subroutine, and the subroutine displays half its value:

```
#!/usr/bin/perl
&divvy(10);

sub divvy {
    $half = @_[0] / 2;
    print "$half\n";
}
```

7. The following Perl script loops, counting from 90 to 95, and prints the value inside each loop:

```
#!/usr/bin/perl
for $value (90 .. 95) {
    print "$value\n";
}
```

This is only one of the many valid solutions to the problem.

8. The following C program prints the number of arguments on the command line:

```
#include <stdio.h>

int main(int argc,char *argv[])
{
    printf("%d\n",argc);
    return(0);
}
```

9. As the default, the make utility looks for a script named either makefile or Makefile.

10. A file named core being found in a directory indicates that a program, running with that directory as its current default, crashed. The core file contains an image of the program as it appeared in memory at the moment of the crash.

11. The diff utility compares two text files and reports the differences between them. The diff3 utility compares three text files.

12. The following command displays the calendar for the month of February 1988:

```
$ cal 2 1988
```

13. If your system has a runaway process, you can use the top utility to discover the PID number of the process, and then use the k (kill) option to halt the process.

14. To have a set of commands executed repeatedly at specific times, each command must be edited into one line of a text file. This line must be preceded by the time at which it will start running. The time is specified numerically by minute, hour, day of the month, month of the year, and day of the week. Any of these numeric fields that contain an asterisk will be assumed to be "any." With command line stored in a file, the crontab command is used to actually schedule the commands. For example, if the file containing the commands is named mycrontab, you can use the following command to schedule the tasks:

```
$ crontab mycrontab
```

15. You can use the at command to schedule multiple commands for execution at the same time in one of two ways. You can enter each command individually, as in the following example:

```
$ at 9:00pm
at> cp -rf /home/fred/workdir /home/fred/backup/workdir
at> EOF
$ at 9:00pm
at> cp -rf /home/fred/hmph/src /home/fred/backup/hmphsrc
at> EOF
```

Because the above two commands are scheduled at the same time by two separate commands, they will execute simultaneously. An alternative approach is to enter both of the commands into the same at command, like this:

```
$ at 9:00pm
at> cp -rf /home/fred/workdir /home/fred/backup/workdir
at> cp -rf /home/fred/hmph/src /home/fred/backup/hmphsrc
at> EOF
```

Because these two commands are entered in sequence, they execute sequentially, with the second command coming immediately after the first.

16. You can use one of two commands to spool text to a printer, and your system may have one or both of them. If the file you want to print is named claymore.text, you can use the lp command to send it to the print spooler:

```
$ lp claymore.text
```

Or you can use the lpr command:

```
$ lpr claymore.text
```

17. To add simple headings at the top of each page of the printed version of a text file, you can run the text through the pr utility before sending it to the spooler. For example, if the file you want to print is named glom.text, you can format it by using a temporary file, as in the following example:

```
$ pr glom.text >/tmp/glomout
$ lp /tmp/glomout
```

You could skip the temporary file and use only one command line, like this:

```
$ pr glom.text | lp
```

18. To be able to start X applications from the command line, you can specify the address of the X server on the command. For example, to run the xcalc program, type:

```
$ xcalc -display :0
```

Alternatively, you can set the DISPLAY environment variable so that no command line option is necessary:

```
$ DISPLAY=:0
$ export DISPLAY
```

19. A message sent to an X server is a request instead of a command because it may be refused by the window manager. For example, if the application wants to move its window to the top of the screen, this request could be refused or modified because it may violate the rules laid down by the window manager controlling the display. Even if a request is granted, the specifics of the request could be modified, so these specifics are called hints.

20. A widget is a special-purpose X window. Examples of widgets are buttons, scroll bars, selection lists, and menu buttons. Some widgets are compound, consisting of several other widgets, such as menus and small dialogs.

Sunday Afternoon Review Answers

1. To use gzip to compress a file named glimmer.html, enter the following command:

```
$ gzip glimmer.html
```

The compressed file will be named glimmer.html.gz.

2. The following command creates a file named saveall.zip that contains all of the files and directories in the current directory:

```
$ zip -r saveall.zip *
```

3. The following command creates a tar file named hinkl.tar that contains all the files in a subdirectory named hinkel:

```
$ tar -cf hinkl.tar hinkel
```

4. The following command generates a listing of the files and directories stored in a tar file named hinkl.tar that also provides file permissions information:

```
$ tar -xvf hinkl.tar
```

5. The files named ezra.tar.Z, lemual.tar.z, and otho.tar.gz are files that have been generated by the tar utility and then compressed. The file ezra.tar.Z has been compressed using the compress utility. The file named lemual.tar.z has been compressed by pack. The file named otho.tar.gz has been compressed by gzip.

6. A firewall is a computer that maintains the Internet connection for a local network and can manage the type and content of traffic passing through it. This makes the firewall a central point for controlling security.

7. A firewall can prevent the arrival of certain types of Internet packets by discarding them. This is called *filtering*. The firewall should filter services that you do not use so they can't be security problems for your internal network.

8. `applebutter` and `sasquatch` are not good passwords because they are both found in the dictionary, and can thus be cracked quickly.

9. An FTP server is a primary security concern because it is connected to the Internet, it allows files to be copied from and written to the local system, it can be used remotely to change directories and list content, it requires no specific password for anonymous logins, and it can even use its EXEC command to remotely execute programs. Care must be taken to limit the ways in which it can do these things.

10. The following command lists the daemons that are automatically started by a message arriving for the daemon:

    ```
    $ rpcinfo -p
    ```

    The process that starts the daemons is named `portmap`. In fact, `portmap` will start the daemon of any process registered with it.

11. The first 1024 port numbers in the `/etc/services` file are reserved for services that are standard across the Internet. They are called the well-known port numbers.

12. If you have computers on a local area network, and there is no name server for the network, you must list the name and IP address of each computer in the `/etc/hosts` files so the computers can locate one another by name.

13. Two address translations must take place. First, the name of the target computer is translated into an IP address, and then the IP address is translated to an Ethernet address.

14. The routing table is used to determine the immediate external or internal destination of an Internet packet. The destination selected by the routing table may be the final target of the message, or it may be an intermediate router that passes it on.

15. An Apache Web server can be installed in the binary form of an executable set of programs ready to run on your operating system, or it can be downloaded as source code and compiled into an executable binary.

16. The task with the PID number of 1 is named `init`, which is responsible for configuring the system at startup and causing the correct daemon processes to start running. It is also the ancestor of all processes in the system.

17. In the file named `/etc/inittab`, the following line specifies that the default run level is 5 — the run level used when the system is booted.

    ```
    id:5:initdefault:
    ```

18. The program named `fsck` (file system check) checks the integrity of a file system. It also has the ability to describe errors and correct them. It is often run at boot time and can also be run from the command line.

19. A `getty` is a program that monitors a port that has a terminal connected and starts the program that prompts for a user login.

20. The letters `rc` stand for "run command." An `rc` script is one that is run to configure the system in some way. The `rc` scripts are normally stored in a directory named `rc.d`.

APPENDIX

What's on the CD-ROM?

This appendix discusses the contents of the CD that accompanies this book. For the latest and greatest information, please refer to the ReadMe file located at the root of the CD. Here is what you will find:

- System requirements
- Using the CD with UNIX
- What's on the CD
- Troubleshooting

System Requirements

Any UNIX system with sufficient free disk space should be able to install and run any of the utilities on the disk drive. The amount of space required ranges from less than 10K to over 30MB. Your computer must also have access to a CD-ROM drive.

To be portable across the different versions of UNIX, the utilities included on the CD are provided in their source code form. Each one includes installation instructions. They are mostly written in C, with a couple of instances of C++, so you will only need the standard compiler and software development environment provided with your system.

If you run into difficulty compiling any of the programs, you may need to install the GNU C compiler and libraries. An installable binary version of the compiler is available at the following Web site:

```
http://gcc.gnu.org
```

If you can't find an installable form of gcc available for your computer, you have the option of downloading the source and compiling it with your regular C compiler. Compiling all of gcc is a lengthy process, so you should set aside a block of time for it.

Make sure that your computer meets the minimum system requirements listed in this appendix. If your computer doesn't match up to most of these requirements, you may have a problem using the contents of the CD.

Using the CD with UNIX

To install the items on the CD to your hard drive, follow these steps:

1. Insert the CD into your computer's CD-ROM drive.

2. Use the ls command on the mount point to verify that the CD has been properly mounted. The mount point on most systems is /mnt/cdrom or something similar, but it can be almost anywhere. If you cannot locate the mount point of the CD, you can find it in the configuration file /etc/fstab. If you are not familiar with the format of the file /etc/fstab, refer to Session 30.

3. If the CD-ROM is not mounted on the mount point, but you see an entry for it in /etc/fstab, enter the following command as the superuser:

   ```
   $ mount -a
   ```

4. If there is no entry for the CD-ROM drive in /etc/fstab, you will need to mount it manually. Enter the following command as superuser:

   ```
   $ mount /dev/cdrom /mnt/cdrom
   ```

   This command mounts the CD-ROM device as the /mnt/cdrom directory. If your device has a different name, exchange /dev/cdrom for the correct device name. You can use any directory name you prefer, but the directory must already exist. See Session 30 for more information.

5. Browse the CD and follow the individual installation instructions for the products listed below.

6. You can unmount the CD by entering the following command:

   ```
   $ eject
   ```

7. If the eject command does not exist, or if it fails, you can unmount the CD by entering the following command as superuser:

   ```
   $ umount /mnt/cdrom
   ```

   Notice the odd spelling of the command. It is umount, not unmount.

What's on the CD

The following sections provide a summary of the software and other materials you'll find on the CD. Everything is supplied in source code form and is licensed in such a way (under the GNU or other open source code license) that you can freely use it for any purpose, with certain expository requirements for commercial use. If you are going to use some of the code for commercial purposes, make certain that you read and comply with its license.

Author-created material

All author-created material from the book, including code listings and samples, are on the CD in the directory named `Author`. The examples are organized by the session number from which they come and consist of the listings of the source code and scripts used as examples in the text.

Security utilities

- `nmap` — The `nmap` (network mapper) utility can be used to explore your local network for possible security problems. It is used successfully for single hosts and for large networks. It explores all ports to determine which ones are open and what software is controlling each one. It analyzes firewalls, message routers, and message filtering. It runs successfully on most UNIX operating systems. It has a number of options that allow you to start out with relatively simple scans and progress into more advanced analysis as you become more familiar with its workings. A version is available for both command line and GUI interface.

- `tcpdump` — The `tcpdump` utility is included with most UNIX distributions. It is a *sniffer* that monitors the networks and displays information found in the headers of Internet packets. Check your man page, but on most systems `tcpdump` must be run as root or as a nonprivileged user after the superuser has enabled the TCP/IP promiscuous mode (which allows anyone to read all packets).

- `snort` — The `snort` utility can be run in one of three modes. It can be run as a packet *sniffer* that reads and displays a continuous stream of all the internet packets entering the system. It can be run as a packet logger that logs all of the incoming and outgoing internet packets to a disk file. It can also be run as a network intrusion detector that will analyze network traffic to detect matches against a user-defined set of rules. It can be configured to take a variety of actions when a match is found.

- `nessus` — The `nessus` utility is a remote security scanner that audits an entire network to locate possible vulnerabilities. It does so by trying to exploit every possible vulnerability on every port. It operates from a scripting language that you can use to customize the tests, and a set of security checks is available online that is updated daily.

- SAINT — The SAINT (Security Administrator's Integrated Network Tool) is an updated and improved version of a utility named SATAN. It is designed to assess the security and vulnerability of a computer network. It gathers information on individual services such as ftp, NFS, finger, and so on, and will locate any incorrect configuration settings that would allow an attacker into the system. The output from SAINT is in HTML format for viewing with a Web browser. Not only can it be used to find security problems, but it also acquires and reports a great deal of information about the organization of the network. SAINT works very well as an exploration tool to analyze the local network, as well as check the security of any adjacent and trusted networks.

- `tripwire` — Tripwire is a tool that checks to see what has changed on your system. Key attributes that should not change are monitored. These attributes include binary signatures, size, and so on. The tripwire open source version on the CD-ROM is only for Linux.

General utilities

- Apache — The Apache server is a free open source Web server that runs on several platforms. It became the most popular Web server on the Internet in 1996 and retains its number one position today. Almost 60 percent of all Web servers are Apache. It has proven to be extremely stable and secure.

- bash — The bash (Bourne-Again Shell) is the default shell of Linux and can be compiled to run on any UNIX system. It is completely compatible with the original Bourne Shell, but also includes many added features.

- bzip2, unzip, and gunzip — These three utilities are used to extract archived files. They are distributed with most UNIX systems today, but are included as source code on the CD in case your system lacks one of them. They are described in detail in Session 27.

- elm — The elm utility is a screen-oriented e-mail client that was written as a replacement for the original (and rather Spartan) UNIX e-mail client named mail. While elm retains the batch processing capabilities of mail, it adds a more robust screen-oriented user interface. A description of elm is in Session 15.

- emacs — The emacs utility began as a text editor, but it has evolved into much more. It can communicate over the Internet and can be used as an e-mail client. It is highly configurable. It is the editor of choice for many programmers, because it comes as source and is portable to every platform. More information on emacs can be found in Session 6.

- findutils — The findutils collection is a group of utilities that you can use to locate files on a disk drive. The find utility is the standard UNIX utility for locating files. The locate utility scans through files containing file names. The xargs utility builds and executes commands read from standard input, usually piped from the find utility.

- gawk — The gawk program is the GNU implementation of the awk programming language. The awk language is an interpretive string processing language that handles all the details of input and output, enabling you to write short scripts to perform complex functions. The awk language is the subject of Session 21.

- grep — Every version of UNIX includes its own grep (get regular expression), but the one on the CD is GNU grep, which has a much richer set of regular expressions available than can be found elsewhere. The grep utility is described in detail in Session 10.

- mtools — The set of mtools utilities can be used to access DOS disks without mounting them first. They are particularly useful for reading and writing to DOS floppies. Included among the commands are mdir, mren, mzip, mmove, mformat, and mdeltree.

- MySQL — The MySQL database server is the most popular open source database system. It is easy to customize, and very fast. Great care was taken to reuse the code internally, which reduces its size, increases its stability, and increases its speed. It can be run under strict transaction control or in a transactionless mode.

- OpenSSH — OpenSSH is a free version of the standard SSH protocols for establishing secure network connections. It encrypts all network traffic, including passwords, to eliminate eavesdropping and connection taps. The ssh utility is intended as a replacement for rlogin and telnet, and sftp is a secure replacement of ftp.

- Perl — A complete Perl language interpreter is included on the CD. Perl is a scripting language that has become very popular on Internet servers for the generation of Web pages but can also be used for general-purpose programming where string manipulation is a large part of the required processing. Session 22 covers Perl programming.

- pine — The pine utility is a reader and writer of e-mail and the Internet newsgroups. The pine program is screen-oriented and is originally configured with very few options, but you can change the configuration as you become more familiar with it. Session 15 provides a description of pine.

- Python — Python is an interpreted, interactive, object-oriented programming language. While it can be used as a standalone language with a windowing interface, it is most popular as a scripting language built into an application, allowing users to stream commands to that application.

- RegExplorer — The RegExplorer program is an interactive utility that you can use to experiment with regular expressions. You can create regular expressions and then enter string patterns to test for matching and mismatching.

- texinfo — The texinfo program implements the official documentation format of the GNU project and produces both printed output and online output. Online viewing uses the same keyboard commands as emacs.

- vim — The vim text editor is a version of vi (the original UNIX text editor) that adds many new features, including multilevel undo. It has macro editing capability and regular expression search and replacement. Session 5 describes the vi editor.

GNU software is governed by its own license, which is included inside the directory of the GNU product. See the GNU license for more details.

Troubleshooting

If you have difficulty installing or using any of the materials on the companion CD, please refer to the ReadMe file located at the root of the CD-ROM for the latest product information at the time of publication.

If you still have trouble with the CD, please call the Hungry Minds Customer Care phone number: 1-800-762-2974. Outside the United States, call 1-317-572-3994. You can also contact Hungry Minds Customer Service by e-mail, at techsupdum@wiley.com. Hungry Minds will provide technical support only for installation and other general quality control items; for technical support on the applications themselves, consult the program's vendor or author.

INDEX

Symbols & Numbers

& (ampersand), 39
* (asterisk), 78
? (backward search), 57, 59
(beginning of comment), 248
{ } (braces), 75
$1 command line argument, 177
$2 command line argument, 177
$3 command line argument, 177
$ (cursor movement), 55, 59
^ (cursor movement), 55
$ (default prompt), 15
. (dot command), 26, 59
.. (dotdot command), 27
! (exclamation point), 55, 59
- file type, 28
/ (forward search), 57, 59
| (OR operator), 195
[ ] (regular expression operator), 109
* (regular expression operator), 109
+ (regular expression operator), 109
~ (tilde), 27, 54

A

%a formatting character, 150
%A formatting character, 150
A command, 60, 279
a command, 60
a flag, 91
a function (sed editing function), 227
absolute address, 26
access denied message, 29
access time (timestamp), 123
account security category, 316
addresses, absolute and relative, 26
AIX (UNIX system), 336
algorithm (rot13 algorithm), 222
alias command, 99–100
ALLPARAMS environment variable, 205
American National Standards Institute (ANSI), 258
ampersand (&), 39
Apache Web server
    document root, 332
    installation, 332–333
    security measures, 333
    server root, 332
    source code, 332
applications
    defined, 9
    Display Manager Control Protocol, 294
    terminal emulator, 134
ar utility, 313
archiving. See files, archiving, and compressing
arguments. See command line arguments
arp configuration utility, 330–331
Ash Shell (ash), 103
assemblers, 6
asterisk (*), 78
at command, 286
attacks (security attacks)
    buffer overflow, 318–319
    denial of service attack, 318
    trojan horses, 317
    worm program, 318
-aux options (ps command), 108
awk command, 237–239
awk programs
    -F option, 245
    one line programs, 244
    storing in files, 239–240

B

%b *formatting character, 150*
%B *formatting character, 150*
b *(block special) file type, 28*
-b filename *expression, 193*
b *function (*sed *editing function), 227*
back tics, 183
backslash character (\), 30
backups, security measures, 323
backward search (?), 57, 59
basename *command, 207*
bash *command, 102–103, 177, 366*
Basic Input/Output System (BIOS), 336
BEGIN *pattern, 242*
beginning of comment (#), 248
Berkeley System Distribution (BSD), 97
/bin *directory, 24*
/bin/sh *directory, 212*
block node, 132
blocking call, 299
BLUEMAX *environment variable, 90*
/boot *directory, 24–25*
booting process
    file system check, 341
    getty process, 343
    init task process, 338
    kernel path names, 336–337
    mounting devices, 341–342
    overview, 335
    paging process, 338
    rc scripts, 342–343
    scheduler task process, 337
    shutdown command, 343–344
    system initialization, 338–341
Bourne Shell
    command line expansion, 78–79
    command line prompt, 73–74
    command line prompt, redirection operators,
        list of, 81
    environment variables, defining, 75–76
    environment variables, standard set of, 76–77
    /etc/profile directory, 74–75
    Korn Shell versus, 100
Bourne-Again Shell
    compatibility with other shells, 103
    history of, 102–103
braces ({ }), 75
brute force, 216
BSD. See Berkeley System Distribution
buffer overflow, 318–319
bunzip *utility, 308*
ButtonPress *event, 300*
bzip *utility, 308, 366*

C

%c *formatting character, 150*
C -p *command, 101*
c *(character special) file type, 28*
c$ *command, 60*
c^ *command, 60*
-c filename *expression, 193*
-c *flag (*grep *utility flag), 113*
c *function (*sed *editing function), 227*
-c *option (print command line option), 288*
-c *option (*tar *utility), 310*
C program, writing and compiling
    command line arguments, example of, 259–260
    core files, dumping, 267–268
    dosform() function example, 265
    Hello world example, 257–258
    hexadecimal dumping program example, 260–263
    makefile command example, 266–267
    multiple source file example, 263–264
    source files, compiling separate, 265–266
    unixform() function example, 264–265
C Shell
    alias command, 99–100
    default prompt, 96
    defining environment variables in, 97–98
    history command, 96–99
    startup and shutdown, 97
C Shell command, 86, 176
cal *utility, 280*
calendar, 277
*calendar feature (*emacs *editor), 64*
case sensitivity
    logging in procedures, 14
    searches, 58
    vi command, 55
case *statement, 194–195*
cat *command, 25, 146, 275*
cc *command, 265–266*
CD
    author-created material, 365
    installing items on, 364
    security utilities, 365
    troubleshooting, 367
cd *command, 24*
CD-ROM drives, 138
CDPATH *variable, 76*
CGI. See Common Gateway Interface
cgi.bin *default directory, 249*
char *data type, 259*
character nodes, 132
*character sets feature (*emacs *editor), 64*
characters
    deleting, 57
    deleting all occurrences of, 222
    overwriting, 57

chgrp *command, 126*
chmod *command, 120, 322*
chown *command, 126*
chsh *command, 96*
cksum *utility, 90*
clocks, setting
   date command, 149–150
   near time system, 149
   overview, 148–149
   real time system, 149
   time command, 151–152
cmp *command, 271–272*
command line arguments
   backup utility example, 178
   C program example, 259–260
   displaying, 177
command line options
   print jobs, 288–289
   processing, 208–209
command line prompt, 73–74, 81
commands. See also utilities
   alias, 99–100
   awk, 237–239
   basename, 207
   bash, 102–103, 177, 366
   c$, 60
   c^, 60
   C -p, 101
   cat, 2,5, 146, 275
   cc, 265–266
   cd, 24
   chgrp, 126
   chmod, 120, 322
   chown, 126
   chsh, 96
   cmp, 271–272
   cp, 124–125
   csh, 86
   cw, 57, 60
   d$, 60
   date, 20, 149–150
   dd, 60, 312–313
   df, 133
   diff, 148, 272–276
   du, 26
   dw, 57, 60
   echo, 18–19
   elm, 168–170, 366
   emacs, 69–70
   entering multiple on one line, 90
   env, 17
   ex, 54
   exit, 21, 181
   exit code for, 189
   find, 82, 98–99
   findutils, 366

finger, 172
foreach, 254
G, 60
gawk, 366
getopts, 208
grep, 366
groupadd, 218
hash, 90
head, 145
history, 98–99
homehide, 101
hsave, 182
if, 191–192
kill, 42, 180
less, 144–145
ln, 128
lon, 176
lp, 287
ls, 16, 27, 74
mail, 166–167
makefile, 266–267
makefsys, 136
man, 20, 155–156
memorizing, 90
mkdir, 125–126, 178
more, 143–144
mount, 341–342
mtools, 366
mv, 123–124
n, 60
newfs, 136
nice, 39–40
nohup, 157
0, 60
od, 146
outfile, 223
pine, 170–171, 367
ping, 203
pr, 289–290
print, 240
printf, 241
ps, 35
pwd, 15
read, 204
readonly, 90–91
rm, 125
rmdir, 126
rsh, 103
save, 182
sdiff, 276
set, 91, 97
shift, 181, 209
showrunnum, 251
shutdown, 343–344
sleep, 203

Continued

commands (continued)
  sort, 147–148
  ssh, 103
  statls, 190
  storing in files, 225–226
  su, 88
  sysinit, 340
  tail, 145
  tar, 310–312
  test, 192–194
  time, 151–152
  touch, 122
  tr, 221
  tty, 132
  u, 60
  ulimit, 92
  umask, 122
  umount, 136
  unalias, 100
  uniq, 148
  unset, 89
  w, 60
  wall, 173
  wc, 148
  whatis, 160
  which, 32
  who, 19–20, 176
  wksh, 103
  write, 173
  x, 57, 60
  xman, 161–162
  y$, 60
  yw, 60
  yy, 60
  zcat, 308
  ZZ, 60
Common Gateway Interface (CGI), 247
comparing files
  text files, three, 273–274
  text files, two, 272–273
  two, 271–272
completion code, 180
compress **utility, 307**
compression. See files, archiving and compressing
configuration utilities
  arp utility, 330–331
  ifconfig utility, 329–330
  netstat utility, 331–332
  route utility, 331
configuring disk drives, 136
connections, types of, 11
console connection, 11
core files, dumping, 267–268
cp **command, 124–125**
cpio **utility, 313–314**
cracking passwords, 216–217

CRC. See cyclic redundancy check
creating device nodes, 135
cron **daemon**
  cron files, 285
  cron jobs, 285
  fields, list of, 284
csh **command, 86**
.cshrc **file, 97**
Ctrl+B (start of text), 21
Ctrl+C (end of text), 21
Ctrl+D
  end of file character, 21, 173
  end of message, 166
cursor movement ($), 55, 59
cw **command, 57, 60**
cyclic redundancy check (CRC), 90, 313

D

%d **formatting character, 150**
%D **formatting character, 150**
d$ **command, 60**
d **(directory) file type, 28**
-d filename **expression, 193**
D **function (**sed **editing function), 227**
d **function (**sed **editing function), 227**
-d **option (print command line option), 288**
daemons
  cron, 284–286
  defined, 9, 281
  inetd, 282–283
  nfsd, 282–283
  printer, 286
date **command, 20, 149–150**
dcount.function **file, 102**
dd **command, 60, 312–313**
default prompt ($), 15
deflation, 309
deleting
  characters, 57
  files, 125
  text, 56
demopage.cgi **file example, 248**
denial of service attack, 318
dependencies, 267
/dev **directory, 24–25, 134**
/dev/null **directory, 81, 178**
/dev/ptsy1 **directory, 134**
/dev/ptys0 **directory, 134**
device drivers
  communication of, 131
  defined, 9
device nodes
  block nodes, 132
  character nodes, 132
  creating, 135

defined, 132
error output text, 135
files versus, 132
hard disk drive, 133
overview, 131
pseudo terminal, 134
special types of, 134–135
terminal, 132
df *command, 133*
diagnostics (man page section heading), 159
diff *command, 148, 272–276*
directories
  addressing, 25
  /bin, 24
  /bin/sh, 212
  /boot, 25
  cgi.bin default directory, 249
  creating, 125
  /dev, 24–25, 134
  /dev/null, 81, 178
  /dev/ptsy1, 134
  /dev/ptys0, 134
  /etc, 25
  /etc/csh.login, 97
  /etc/dfs/dfstab, 321
  /etc, 24–25
  /etc/fstab, 136, 364
  /etc/group, 213–214
  /etc/hosts, 327–328, 342
  /etc/hosts.allow, 328–329
  /etc/hosts.deny, 328–329
  /etc/inetc.conf, 321
  /etc/inetc.config, 281
  /etc/inittab, 338–339
  /etc/passwd, 107, 203, 211–213
  /etc/profile, 74, 100
  /etc/protocols, 326
  /etc/rc.d/init.d, 342
  /etc/rc.d/rc, 342
  /etc/rd.d, 342
  /etc/services, 107, 320, 326–327
  /etc/shadow, 214–215
  /etc/shells, 104
  /home, 25
  /lib, 25
  list of, 24–25
  /mnt, 25
  removing, 126
  /root/work/lfiles, 127–128
  /tmp, 25
  /usr, 24
  /usr/bin, 24
  /usr/bin/passwd, 317
  /usr/bin/perl, 248
  /usr/bin/X11, 295
  /usr/bin/X11/xman, 161

  /usr/contrib/man, 155
  /usr/lib, 24
  /usr/local/lib/apache, 333
  /usr/local/man, 155
  /usr/sbin, 24
  /usr/share/man, 155
  /usr/X11R6/man, 155
  /var, 24–25
  /var/spool/cron, 284
  /var/www, 332
disk drives, installation steps, 135–136
diskless workstation, 336
disks, accessing
  local, 282
  remote, 283
DISPLAY *environment variable, 17*
docompare*() subroutine, 253*
document root (Apache Web server), 332
DOS/Windows formatted text files, 263
dosform*() function, 264*
dosform.o *file, 267*
dot command (.), 26, 59
dotdot command (..), 27
du *command, 26*
dumb terminal, 11
dumped core, 267
dumping files, 146–147, 267–268
duplicating files, 124–125
dw *command, 57, 60*
dynamic allocation, 10

E

%e *formatting character, 150*
e b *command (*sdiff *command), 277*
e *command (*sdiff *command), 277*
e *flag, 91*
-E *flag (*grep *utility flag), 113*
e-mail
  e-mail client, 165
  elm command, sending message using, 168–170
  logins, displaying, 172–173
  mail command, sending messages using, 166–168
  permissions, granting and denying, 170–171
  pine command, sending messages using, 170–171
  receiving and responding to, 173
  wall command, sending message using, 173
e r *command (*sdiff *command), 277*
*echo area (*emacs *editor), 66–67*
echo *command, 18–19*
*editing functions (*sed *editing functions), 227–228*
EDITOR *environment variable, 168*
effective user ID, setting, 322
egrep *utility, 112*
elisp program, 63
elm *command, 168–170, 366*

emacs **commands, 69–70, 366**

emacs **editor**
  appearance of, 65
  calendar feature, 64
  character set feature, 64
  custom features, 65
  echo area, 66–67
  exiting, 66
  Internet feature, 64
  keys and commands, 67–68
  mode line, 67
  overview, 63
  portability of, 65
  programming feature, 64
  screen description and term definitions, 66–67
  text searches, 68–69
  tutorial feature, 64
  word processing feature, 64

encomma **script, 203**

encrypted passwords, 212

END **pattern, 242**

env **command, 17, 80**

environment variables
  ALLPARAMS, 205
  BLUEMAX, 90
  defined, 17
  defining in C Shell, 97–98
  defining your own, 75–76
  DISPLAY, 17
  EDITOR, 168
  examples of, 17
  HNAME, 183
  HOME, 17, 182
  HOSTNAME, 17
  JAVA HOME, 17
  MAIL, 17
  NUM, 206
  NUMSET, 183
  ONSET, 183
  OPLETTER, 208
  OPTARG, 209
  OPTIND, 209
  PATH, 17
  PREFIX, 182
  removing definitions of, 89
  SHELL, 17
  within shell, exporting, 86–87
  shell scripts and, 182
  UPPERLIMIT, 86
  USAGE, 209
  USER, 17
  WINDOWID, 17
  ZILIST, 206

escape characters, 109

/etc/csh.login **directory, 97**

/etc/dfs/dfstab **directory, 321**

/etc **directory, 24–25**

/etc/fstab **directory, 136, 364**

/etc/group **directory, 213–214**

/etc/hosts **directory, 327–328, 342**

/etc/hosts.allow **directory, 328–329**

/etc/hosts.deny **directory, 328–329**

/etc/inetc.conf **directory, 321**

/etc/inetc.config **directory, 281**

/etc/inittab **directory, 338–339**

/etc/passwd **directory, 107, 203, 211–213**

/etc/profile **directory, 74, 100**

/etc/protocols **directory, 326**

/etc/rc.d/init.d **directory, 342**

/etc/rc.d/rc **directory, 342**

/etc/rd.d **directory, 342**

/etc/services **directory, 107, 320, 326–327**

/etc/shadow **directory, 214–215**

/etc/shells **directory, 104**

ex **command, 54**

exclamation point (!), 55, 59

exec() **system call, 44**

exit code
  defined, 180
  successful and failed command, 189

exit **command, 21, 181**

Expose **event, 299**

expressions, examples of, 78–79

F

-f filename **expression, 193**

f **flag, 91**

-F **flag (**grep **utility flag), 113**

false statements, testing for, 189–193

fgetc() **function, 262**

fgrep **utility, 112**

File Transfer Protocol (FTP)
  disabling, 322
  security measures, 321–322

file **utility, 31–32**

files. See also files, archiving and compressing
  comparing, 272–274
  creating new, 53–54
  deleting, 125
  device nodes versus, 132
  dumping, 146–147
  duplicating, 124–125
  internal system structure, 138–141
  linking, 126–129
  merging differences between, 274–276
  name of, changing, 123–124
  permissions, setting, 119–120
  permissions, setting initial, 121–122
  permissions, setting read and write only, 125
  permissions, transferring ownership of, 126
  soft limit settings, 92

storing awk programs in, 239–240
storing commands in, 225–226
timestamps, adjusting, 123
files, archiving and compressing. See also files
ar utility, 313
backups, creating, 309–310
bunzip utility, 308
bzip utility, 308
compress utility, 307
cpio utility, 313–314
dd command, 312–313
gunzip utility, 307–308
gzip utility, 307–308
overview, 305
pack utility, 306–307
reasons for, 306
shadow files, 214
standard naming conventions for, 306
tar utility, 310–312
uncompress utility, 307
unpack utility, 306–307
unzip utility, 308–309
zip utility, 308–309
find **command, 82, 98–99**
find **utility, 29–30**
findutils **command, 366**
finger **command, 172**
firewalls, 320–321
flags
a flag, 91
-c flag (grep utility flag), 113
e flag, 91
-E flag (grep utility flag), 113
f flag, 91
-F flag (grep utility flag), 113
grep command, 113–114
-H flag (grep utility flag), 114
-h flag (grep utility flag), 114
-I flag (grep utility flag), 113
-L flag (grep utility flag), 114
-l flag (grep utility flag), 114
n flag, 91
-s (grep utility flag), 114
shell flags, 91
t flag, 91
u flag, 91
v flag, 91
-v (grep utility flag), 114
x flag, 91
floppy drives, 138
formatting characters, list of, 150–151
fopen() **function, 262**
foreach **command, 254**
forward search (/), 57, 59
fork() **system call, 43–44**
FreeBSD (UNIX system), 336

FTP. See File Transfer Protocol functions
dosform(), 264
fgetc() function, 262
fopen() function, 262
main() function, 257
printf() function, 262
rand() function, 245
sed editing functions, list of, 277–278
SimpleWindow function, 300
sprintf() function, 262
strcat() function, 262
unixform(), 264
XMapRaised() function, 299
XNextEvent() function, 299

G

G **command, 60**
-g filename **expression, 193**
G **function (**sed **editing function), 227**
g **function (**sed **editing function), 227**
gawk **command, 366**
getopts **command, 208**
getty **process, 343**
glolist.html **file, 124**
gnu.html **file, 107**
Google Web site, 163
graphic login procedure, 14–15
Graphical User Interface (GUI), 38
grave accent marks, 183
grep **utility**
advanced techniques, 108
defined, 106
egrep utility, 112
fgrep utility, 112
files, searching multiple using, 107
flags, list of, 113–114
piping output into, 108
groupadd **command, 218**
gunzip **utility, 307–308, 366**
gzip **utility, 307–308**

H

%h **formatting character, 150**
%H **formatting character, 150**
h **command (**top **utility), 279**
-h filename **expression, 193**
-H **flag (**grep **utility flag), 114**
-h **flag (**grep **utility flag), 114**
H **function (**sed **editing function), 227**
h **function (**sed **editing function), 227**
h **key (cursor movement), 52, 60**
-h **option (print command line option), 289**

hard disk drive. See disk drives, installation steps
hard links, 128
hash command, 90
head command, 145
helloworld.c file example, 258
hexidecimal dumping program example, 260–263
hidden files, 16
history command, 98–99
HNAME environment variable, 183
hold space, 224
/home directory, 15, 24–25
HOME environment variable, 17, 182
HOME variable, function of, 76
homehide command, 101
HOSTNAME environment variable, 17
hosts.allow file, 328–329
hosts.deny file, 329
HP-UX (UNIX system), 336
hsave command, 182
.html suffix, 226
Huffman encoding, 308
Hungry Minds Customer Care, 367
HyperText Transfer Protocol (HTTP), 326

I

%I formatting character, 150
i command, 60
i function (sed editing function), 227
-I flag (grep utility flag), 113
-i option (print command line option), 289
IANA. See Internet Assigned Numbers Authority
IDE. See Integrated Drive Electronics
if command, 191–192
ifconfig utility, 329–330
index.html file, 145, 272
index.html/gz file, 307
index.html.z file, 306
index.zip file, 309
inetd daemon, 282–283
inetd registry, 320
inFile variable, 264
info utility, 163
init process, 8, 338
i-nodes
    diagram of, 140
    organization of, 139–140
input, standard input, 79
installing
    Apache Web server, 332–333
    CD items, 364
    disk drives, 135–136
Integrated Drive Electronics (IDE), 132
Internet
    arp configuration utility, 330–331
    e-mail and, 165–166

/etc/hosts file, 327–328
/etc/hosts.allow file, 328–329
/etc/hosts.deny file, 328–329
/etc/protocols file, 326
/etc/services file, 326–327
ifconfig utility, 329–330
Internet Services daemon, 282–283
Internet worm, 318
IP address, 325
loopback address, 328
netstat configuration utility, 331–332
port number, 325
protocol number, 325
route configuration utility, 331
Internet Assigned Numbers Authority (IANA), 326
Internet Service Provider (ISP), 327
interrupts, 131
IP address, 325
IRIX (UNIX system), 336
isprint() function, 262

J

%j formatting character, 150
j key (cursor movement), 52, 60
JAVA HOME environment variable, 17
.jpeg file, 108

K

k command (top utility), 279
-k filename expression, 193
k key (cursor movement), 53, 60
kernel
    defined, 9
    dynamic allocation, 10
    function of, 10–11
    system call, 9
KeyPress event, 300
kill command, 42, 180
Korn Shell
    Bourne Shell versus, 100
    command history, 100–102
    function definitions, 101–102

L

l command (sdiff command), 276
l function (sed editing function), 228
-L (grep utility flag), 114
-l (grep utility flag), 114
l key (cursor movement), 53, 60
-l option, 36
l (symbolic link) file type, 28
LANG variable, function of, 76

Lempel-Ziv encoding, 307
length*() function, 245*
less *command, 144–145*
/lib *directory, 24–25*
line operations, 55–56
line printers, 287
linking
   files, 126–129
   hard links, 128
   symbolic links, 128
Linux (UNIX system), 337
listargs.c *file, 259*
ln *command, 128*
localhost *file, 328*
logging out, 21
logging procedures
   case sensitivity, 14
   command line login procedure, 14
   command line prompt, 15–16
   graphic login procedure, 14–15
.login *file, 97*
logname *utility, 93*
LOGNAME *variable, 76*
lon *command, 176*
loopback address, 328
loops
   Perl programming language and, 254–255
   ping command, 203
   read command, 204
   until keyword, 204–205
   while loop, 201–203
lp *command, 287*
ls *command, 16, 27, 74*

M

%m *formatting character, 151*
%M *formatting character, 151*
M *command (*top *utility), 279*
-m *option (*print *command line option), 288*
mail *command*
   reading messages using, 166
   sending messages using, 166
   sending text files using, 167
AIL *environment variable, 17*
MAIL *variable, 76*
.mailrc *file, 167*
main() *function, 257*
major number, 131
makefile *command, 266–267*
makefsys *command, 136*
man *command, 20, 155–156*
man pages
   coding example, 157–159
   defined, 155
   displayed in xman window example, 162

   section heading, list of, 159
   section names, list of, 156
   viewing description of, 160
merging file differences, 274–276
messages. See e-mail
minimum system requirements, 363–364
minor number, 131
mkdir *command, 125–126, 178*
/mnt *directory, 24–25, 342*
model editor. See vi *editor*
modification time (timestamp), 123
month of year, viewing current, 277
more *command, 143–144*
mount *command, 136, 341–342*
mtools *command, 366*
mv *command, 123–124*

N

%n *formatting character, 151*
n *command, 60*
N *command (*top *utility), 279*
n *flag, 91*
N *function (*sed *editing function), 228*
n *function (*sed *editing function), 228*
-n *(*grep *utility flag), 114*
-n *option, 203*
-n *option (print command line option), 288*
-n string *expression, 193*
nessus *utility, 365*
NetBSD (UNIX system), 337
netstat *configuration utility, 331–332*
Network File System (NFS)
   local disk, accessing, 282
   remote disk, accessing, 283
   security measures, 321
newfs *command, 136*
newindex.html *file, 272*
NFS. See Network File System
nfsd *daemon, 282–283*
nice *command, 39–40*
nmap *utility, 365*
nohup *command, 157*
non-volatile random access memory (NVRAM), 336
NUM *environment variable, 206*
numeric operators, list of, 251
NUMSET *environment variable, 183*

O

O *command, 60*
-o *option (print command line option), 288*
object files, 263
octal form, file permissions, 120–121
od *command, 146*

one liners, 229
ONSET *environment variable, 183*
onxyz *file, 123*
operators
    numeric, list of, 251
    regular expressions, list of, 109
    string, list of, 251
OPLETTER *environment variable, 208*
OPTARG *environment variable, 209*
OPTIND *environment variable, 209*
OR operator (|), 195
orphan process, 43
outfile *command, 223*
output
    env command, 80
    redirecting, 79
    standard output, 79
    viewing, 79
outString *character array, 262*
ownership (file ownership), 126

P

%p formatting character, 151
p *command, 60*
P *command (*top *utility), 279*
-p filename *expression, 193*
P *function (*sed *editing function), 228*
p *function (*sed *editing function), 228*
-P *option (print command line option), 288*
p *(pipe) file type, 28*
pack *utility, 306–307*
parent process ID (PPID), 38
partitioning, 135
passwords
    cracking, 216–217
    cracking, protection against, 316
    encrypted, 212
    /etc/group directory, 213–214
    /etc/passwd directory, 211–213
    /etc/shadow directory, 214–215
    security measures, 14, 216, 319
    selecting good, 217
    setting, 216
patches and updates, verifying installation of,
        319–320
PATH *environment variable, 17*
PATH *program, 17*
PATH *variable, 77*
pattern space, 224
Perl programming language
    # (beginning of comment) character, 248
    character string program example, 252
    conditional execution, 251–253
    docompare() subroutine, example of, 253
    Hello, World program example, 248
        introduction to, 247–248
        looping and, 254–255
        popularity of, 247–248
        subroutines, 250–251
        variables, storing string values in, 249
        Web page program example, 248–249
permissions
    access denied message, 29
    converting settings, 121
    e-mail, granting and denying, 170–171
    editing, 120
    octal form of, 120–121
    setting, 119–120
    setting, initial, 121–122
    setting, read and write only, 125
    string example, 29
    transferring ownership of, 126
    turning on/off, 120
physical security category, 316
PID. See Process ID
Pike, Rob, 7
pine *command, 170–171, 367*
ping *command, 203*
pipe, redirecting output from, 80
Point-to-Point Protocol (PPP), 160
port number, 326
portmap *program, 320*
ports
    defined, 131
    pseudo ports, 19
post mortem, 31
PPID. See parent process ID
pr *command, 289–290*
PREFIX *environment variable, 182*
print *command, 240*
print jobs
    command line options, list of, 288–289
    formatting, using pr utility, 289–290
    line printer, 287
    lp command, program example, 287
    problems with, 287
    process of, 286
print spooler, 286
printer daemon, 286
printf() *function, 262*
printf *statement, 241*
Process ID (PID), 37
processes
    address column, 38
    background, starting, 39
    CMD command column, 37
    init, 8
    isolation of, 8–9
    killing, 42
    listing running, 35–38
    nice heading, 38

orphan process, 43
PID (process ID) column, 37
PPID (parent process ID), 38
prioritizing, 8
prioritizing, with nice command, 39–40
priority heading, 38
signaling, 40–42
size column, 38
starting, 8
teletype column, 38
TIME column, 38
types of, 9
UID (User ID) column, 37
viewing, using top utility, 278
wait channel column, 38
zombie process, 43
.profile *file, 74*
programmable read-only memory (PROM), 336
protection, password protection, 316–317
pr.text *file, 289*
ps *command*
   aux options, 108
   -e option, 35–36
   -l option, 36
PS1 *variable, 77*
PS2 *variable, 77*
pseudo ports, 19
pseudo terminal device nodes, 134
pwd *command, 15*
PWD *variable, 77*

Q

q *command (*sdiff *command), 277*
q *command (*top *utility), 279*
q *function (*sed *editing function), 228*
-q *option (print command line option), 288*
question mark (?), 57
quoting, 82

R

%r *formatting character, 151*
%R *formatting character, 151*
r *command (*sdiff *command), 276*
r *command (*top *utility), 279*
-r filename *expression, 193*
r *function (*sed *editing function), 228*
-r *option (print command line option), 288*
-r *option (*tar *utility), 310*
rand() *function, 245*
rc *scripts, 342–343*
rc.sysinit *file, 340*
readonly *command, 90–91*
read-only memory (ROM), 336

redirection operators, 81
reform.o *file, 267*
regdirtest *script, 192*
RegExplorer program, 367
regexpr1 *expression, 195*
regular expressions
   defined, 105
   examples of, 106, 110–112
   grep utility, 106–108
   operators, list of, 109
   pattern matches, testing for, 194–196
relative address, 26
remote procedure call (RPC), 283
*Remote Shell (*rsh*), 103*
remote systems, security measures, 323
return value (man page section heading), 159
reverse quotes, 183
Ritchie, Dennis, 6–7
rm -f *command, 125*
rm -r *command, 125*
rm *command, 125*
rmdir *command, 126*
ROM. See read-only memory
root directory, 23
root login, 23
root window, 23
/root/work/lfiles *directory, 127–128*
rot13 *algorithm, 222*
route *configuration utility, 331*
rsh *command, 103*
runlevels *field, 340*

S

%S *formatting character, 151*
s *command (*sdiff *command), 276*
s *command (*top *utility), 279*
-s filename *expression, 193*
s *function (*sed *editing function), 228*
-s (grep *utility flag), 114*
-s *option (print command line option), 289*
safety *subdirectory, 178*
SAINT *utility, 365*
save *command, 182*
scheduler task process (booting process), 337
SCO (UNIX system), 337
scripts
   adjusting environment using, 197–198
   C Shell, 176
   command line arguments, 177–181
   completion code, 180
   crazy directory example, 178–179
   defined, 175
   exit code, successful and failed command, 189

Continued

scripts (continued)
sort, 147–148
kill command and, 180
logins, displaying, 176
Perl language script, 177
predefined variables, list of, 179
regtest script, 191
showvars command example, 180
summit, 242–243
using multiple, 179–181
SCSI. See Small Computer System Interfaces
sdiff *command, 276–277*
search engines, 163
searching text, 57–58
*Secure Shell (*ssh*), 103*
security
account security category, 316
Apache Web server, 333
backups, 323
buffer overflow, 318–319
denial of service attack, 318
effective user ID, setting, 322
file system security category, 316
File Transfer Protocol services, 321–322
firewalls, 320–321
introduction to, 315
nessus utility, 365
network security category, 316, 321
nmap utility, 365
passwords, cracking, 217, 316
passwords, entering, 14
passwords, securing, 319
passwords, setting, 216
patches and updates, verifying installation of, 319–320
physical security category, 316
remote systems, 323
SAINT utility, 365
sendmail, verifying latest version of, 321
snort utility, 365
tcpdump utility, 365
tripwire, 365
Trojan horse attacks, 317
worm program, 318
sed *editor function*
editing functions, list of, 227–228
one liners, 229
overview, 223
sending messages
using elm command, 168–170
using mail command, 166–168
using pine command, 170–171
using wall command, 173
sendmail, security measures, 321
server root (Apache Web server), 332
service number, 326

set *command, 91, 97*
set-group-ID bit, 194
set-user-ID bit, 194
shadow files, 214
SHELL *environment variable, 17*
shell scripts
adjusting environment using, 197–198
C Shell, 176
command line arguments, 177–181
crazy directory example, 178–179
defined, 175
environment variables and, 182–183
kill command and, 180
logins, displaying, 176
Perl language script, 177
predefined variables, list of, 179
regtest script, 191
showvars command example, 180
using multiple, 179–181
shells
C Shell program, 86
completion code, 180
defined, 10
. (dot command), 89
environment variables in, exporting, 86–87
flags, list of, 91
login, creating new, 88
selecting best, 95–96
starting different, 85–86
starting to execute commands from file, 87–88
switching between different, 96
switching between different, using chsh command, 104
unset command, 90
shift *command, 181, 209*
SHLVL *variable, 86*
showrunnum *command, 251*
showzi *script, 206*
shutdown *command, 343–344*
SIGABRT *signal, 41*
SIGALRM *signal, 41*
SIGBUS *signal, 41*
SIGCHLD *signal, 41*
SIGEMT *signal, 41*
SIGFPE *signal, 41*
SIGHUP *signal, 40*
SIGILL *signal, 41*
SIGINT *signal, 40*
SIGKILL *signal, 41*
signals (process signals), 40–42
SIGPIPE *signal, 41*
SIGPWR *signal, 41*
SIGQUIT *signal, 40*
SIGSEGV *signal, 41*
SIGSYS *signal, 41*
SIGTERM *signal, 41*

SIGTRAP *signal, 41*
SIGUSR1 *signal, 41*
SIGUSR2 *signal, 41*
Simple Mail Transfer Protocol (SMTP), 326
SimpleWindow*() function, 300*
slash character (/), 57
sleep *command, 203*
Small Computer System Interfaces (SCSI), 132
snort *utility, 365*
Solaris (UNIX system), 337
sort *command, 147–148*
sorted.text *file, 147*
sorting text files, 147–148
source code (Apache Web server), 332
source files
    compiling separate, 265–266
    program example, 263–264
special files. See device nodes
spooler. See print spooler
sprintf() *function, 262*
ssh *command, 103*
standard error, 79, 81
standard input, 79
standard output, 79
starting
    processes, 8
    processes, background, 39
    shell, different type of, 85–86
startup, C Shell, 97
statls *command, 190*
status code
    defined, 180
    interpreting, 190
stderr *file, 264*
stdin *file, 264*
stdio.h *file, 259*
stdout *file, 264*
sticky bit, 194
storing
    awk programs in files, 239–240
    commands in files, 225–226
strcat() *function, 262*
string operators, list of, 251
strings, replacing with other, 223
su *command, 88*
subroutines
    defined, 250
    output program, example of, 251
    uses for, 250
summit *script, 242–243*
SunOS (UNIX system), 337
superblock, 140
sychronization, 140–141
symbolic links, 128
synopsis (man page section heading), 159
sysinit *command, 340*

system call, 9
system initialization, 338–341
system requirements, 363–364

T

%t *formatting character, 151*
%T *formatting character, 151*
T *command (*top *utility), 279*
-t number *expression, 193*
t *flag, 91*
-t *option (print command line option), 288*
-t *option (*tar *utility), 310*
tail *command, 145*
tar *command, 310–312*
TC Shell, 96
TCP. See Transmission Control Protocol
tcpdump *utility, 365*
tee *utility, 80*
Telnet client program, 11
Teoma Web site, 163
TERM *variable, 77*
terminal device nodes, 132
terminal emulator
    connections and, 11
    defined, 134
test *command, 192–194*
testing
    false statements, 189–193
    true statements, 189–193
texinfo *program, 367*
text
    editing, 55–57
    removing extra spaces in, 222
    searching through, 57–58
text files
    comparisons between, 272–274
    removing lines in, 148
    selecting, 148
    sorting, 147–148
    viewing, 143–147
tic marks, 183
tilde (~), 27, 54
time *command, 151–152*
timestamps, 123
TMPDIR *variable, 168*
top *utility*
    interactive commands for, 279
    screen display of, 278
touch *command, 122*
tr *command, 221*
Transmission Control Protocol (TCP), 325
tripwire, 365
Trojan horse attacks, 317
Tru64 (UNIX system), 337

true statements, testing for, 189–193
tty *command, 132*
*tutorial feature (*emacs *editor), 64*

U

%U formatting character, 151
u *command, 60, 279*
-u filename *expression, 193*
u *flag, 91*
-u *option (*tar *utility), 311*
UDP. See User Datagram Protocol
UID. See User ID
ulimit *command, 92*
Ultrix (UNIX system), 337
umask *command, 122*
umount *command, 136*
unalias *command, 100*
uncompress *utility, 307*
uniq *command, 148*
Universal Serial Bus (USB), 137
UNIX
   connecting to, 11
   development of, 7
   history of, 5–6
   structure of, 6–8
   UNIX philosophy, 6
unixform() *function, 264*
unixform.o *file, 267*
unpack *utility, 306–307*
unset *command, 89*
unsorted.text *file, 147*
until *keyword, 204–205*
unzip *utility, 308–309, 366*
updates and patches, verifying installation of,
     319–320
UPPERLIMIT *environment variable, 86*
USAGE *environment variable, 209*
USB. See Universal Serial Bus
User Datagram Protocol (UDP), 325
USER *environment variable, 17*
user/home/pagers *file, 124*
User ID (UID), 37
/usr *directory, 24*
/usr/bin *directory, 24*
/usr/bin/passwd *directory, 317*
/usr/bin/perl *directory, 248*
/usr/bin/X11 *directory, 295*
/usr/bin/X11/xman *directory, 161*
/usr/contrib/man *directory, 155*
/usr/lib *directory, 24*
/usr/local/lib/apache *directory, 333*
/usr/local/man *directory, 155*
/usr/sbin *directory, 24*
/usr/share/man *directory, 155*
usr/X11R6/man *directory, 155*

utilities. See also commands
   ar, 313
   arp, 330–331
   bunzip, 308
   bzip, 308
   cal, 280
   cksum, 90
   compress, 307
   cpio, 313–314
   egrep, 112
   fgrep, 112
   file, 31–32
   find, 29–30
   grep, 112–114
   gunzip, 307–308
   gzip, 307–308
   ifconfig, 329–330
   info, 163
   logname, 93
   nessus, 365
   netstat, 331–332
   nmap, 365
   pack, 306–307
   route, 331
   SAINT, 365
   snort, 365
   tee, 80
   top, 278–279
   uncompress, 307
   unpack, 306–307
   unzip, 308–309
   zip, 308–309

V

v *command (*sdiff *command), 276*
v *flag, 91*
-v *(*grep *utility flag), 114*
/var *directory, 24–25*
/var/spool/cron *directory, 284*
/var/www *directory, 332*
vi *commands, 59–60*
vi *editor*
   case sensitivity, 55
   cursor movements, 52
   development of, 52
   options, setting, 58–59
   overview, 51
vi *navigation mode, 101*
vim *text editor, 367*

W

%w formatting character, 151
%W formatting character, 151
w *command, 60*

-w filename *expression, 193*
w *function (*sed *editing function), 228*
-w *option (print command line option), 288*
wc -l *command, 87*
wc *command, 148*
wcc.html *file, 107*
Web page program, example code using Perl,
     248–249
well known port, 326
whatis *command, 160*
which *command, 32*
while *loop, 201–203*
who *command, 19–20, 176*
widgets, 300–301
window manager, 296
WINDOWID *environment variable, 17*
Windowing Korn Shell (wksh**), 103**
Wisenut Web site, 163
wksh *command, 103*
word operations, 56–57
word processing feature (emacs *editor), 64*
worm program, 318
write *command, 173*

%x *formatting character, 151*
%X *formatting character, 151*
x *command, 57, 60*
x *flag, 91*
x *function (*sed *editing function), 228*
-x *option (*tar *utility), 311*
-x filename *expression, 193*
xdmcp *protocol (X Display Manager Control Protocol)*
     application and server diagram, 294
     DISPLAY environment variable, example of, 295

event message, 296
mouse click program, example of, 297–300
one-way request message, 296
round-trip request message, 296
window manager, 296
X terminal, 294
Xlib library, 294
X terminal connection, 11
XCreateSimpleWindow() *function, 299*
Xlib *library, 294*
xman *command, 161–162*
XMapRaised() *function, 299*
XNextEvent() *function, 299*
XopenDisplay() *function, 298*

%Y *formatting character, 151*
y$ *command, 60*
y *function (*sed *editing function), 228*
yank buffer, 56
yw *command, 60*
yy *command, 60*

%Z *formatting character, 151*
-z string *expression, 193*
zcat *command, 308*
ZILIST *environment variable, 206*
zip *utility, 308–309*
zombie process, 43
ZSH Shell (zsh**), 103**
ZZ *command, 60*

Hungry Minds, Inc.
End-User License Agreement

8. **General.** This Agreement constitutes the entire understanding of the parties and revokes and supersedes all prior agreements, oral or written, between them and may not be modified or amended except in a writing signed by both parties hereto that specifically refers to this Agreement. This Agreement shall take precedence over any other documents that may be in conflict herewith. If any one or more provisions contained in this Agreement are held by any court or tribunal to be invalid, illegal, or otherwise unenforceable, each and every other provision shall remain in full force and effect.